THE
HISTORY OF
ADVERTISING

40
MAJOR BOOKS
IN FACSIMILE

Edited by
HENRY ASSAEL
C. SAMUEL CRAIG
New York University

A
GARLAND
SERIES

REPETITION EFFECTS

OVER THE YEARS:

An Anthology of Classic Articles

EDITED BY
C. SAMUEL CRAIG
BRIAN STERNTHAL

GARLAND PUBLISHING, INC.
NEW YORK & LONDON
1986

For a complete list of the titles in this series
see the final pages of this volume.

Introduction copyright © 1985 by C. Samuel Craig, and
Brian Sternthal.

Library of Congress Cataloging-in-Publication Data

Main entry under title:
Repetition effects over the years.
   (The History of advertising)
   1. Advertising—Effective frequency—Addresses,
essays, lectures.   I. Craig, C. Samuel.   II. Sternthal,
Brian.   III. Series.
HF5827.R43   1985   659.1'11   84-46069
ISBN 0-8240-6763-0 (alk. paper)

Design by Donna Montalbano

The volumes in this series are printed on
acid-free, 250-year-life paper.

Printed in the United States of America

Contents

Introduction

"The Curve of Forgetting," Charles H. Bean (*Archives of Psychology*, Vol. 3, No. 21, 1912)

"The Factors Affecting a Permanent Impression Developed Through Repetition," Edward K. Strong (*Journal of Experimental Psychology*, Vol. 1, No. 4, 1916)

"The Relative Memory Values of Duplication and Variation in Advertising," Henry F. Adams (*The Journal of Philosophy, Psychology and Scientific Methods*, March 16, 1916)

"The Conditions of Retention," C. W. Luh (*Psychological Monographs*, 1923)

"Memory Span: A Review of the Literature," Albert B. Blankenship (*Psychological Bulletin*, January, 1938)

"The Remembering and Forgetting of Advertising," Hubert A. Zielske (*Journal of Marketing*, January, 1959)

"Why Continued Advertising is Necessary: A New Explanation," Paul M. Carrick, Jr. (*Journal of Marketing*, April, 1959)

"Frequency Effects Over Time," Richard H. Ostheimer (*Journal of Advertising Research*, February, 1970)

"On Advertising Wear Out," Valentine Appel (*Journal of Advertising Research*, February, 1971)

"Frequency Effects Revisited," Michael L. Ray, Alan G. Sawyer, and Edward C. Strong (*Journal of Advertising Research*, February, 1971)

"Why Three Exposures May Be Enough," Herbert E. Krugman (*Journal of Advertising Research*, December, 1972)

"How Many Advertising Exposures Per Day?" Steuart Henderson Britt, Stephen C. Adams, and Allan S. Miller (*Journal of Advertising Research*, December, 1972)

"Television Commercial Wearout," Allan Greenberg and Charles Suttoni (*Journal of Advertising Research*, October, 1973)

"Repetitive Advertising and the Consumer," Andrew S. C. Ehrenberg (*Journal of Advertising Research*, April, 1974)

"Repetition in Media Models: A Laboratory Technique," Michael L. Ray and Alan G. Sawyer (*Journal of Marketing Research*, February, 1971)

"Advertising Wearout: An Experimental Analysis," C. Samuel Craig, Brian Sternthal, and Clark Leavitt (*Journal of Marketing Research*, November, 1976)

"Television Commercial Wearout: An Information Processing View," Bobby J. Calder and Brian Sternthal (*Journal of Marketing Research*, May, 1980)

Introduction

Repetition Effects over the Years

Repetition and its effect on individuals' responses to advertising has been an issue of enduring interest. This interest stems from the fact that the effects of repetition offer a basis for the design of media strategy and a general understanding of how individuals respond to advertising. The articles included in this anthology were selected to portray the historical development of inquiry pertaining to repetition effects during this century. Collectively they offer insight into the bases for the current view about how repetition affects advertising strategy and the appropriateness of various repetition strategies in enhancing a communication's impact.

Much of the work on repetition effects conducted early in this century was motivated by Ebbinghaus's seminal research on forgetting. Along these lines, inquiry focused on documenting that memory for advertising involved the same process as memory for other stimuli and that repetition of advertising messages enhanced their learning. Bean (1912) provides an historical perspective on repetition. Specifically, he addresses the issues related to the rate of forgetting, the shape of the curve over time, and the nature of the relationships. He begins with Ebbinghaus and also includes much of his own research. Strong (1916) presents the results of a number of experiments he conducted dealing directly with print advertising. This is one of the first studies dealing directly with advertising materials. Adams (1916) presents similar work, also examining print advertising stimuli. In Luh (1923), "The Conditions of Retention," we have an extensive review of the repetition literature. He presents considerable research evidence dealing with the curve of retention under a variety of different conditions. Another comprehensive review is provided by Blankenship (1938) as he examines the literature related to memory span.

Documentation of the fact that repetition facilitated the learning of advertising messages and the attendant observation that people were exposed to many ads stimulated inquiry about the conditions that qualified repetition effects. One such factor is the interval between message repetitions, which was based on memory principles derived from psychological investigations dealing with massed versus spaced stimulus presentations. This work indicated that varying the repetition interval affected the impact of an advertising message. The first serious attempts to look at repetition in the marketing literature involved Zielske (1959) and Carrick (1959). Zielske, in particular, has become a classic in the literature and examines repetition effects under different schedules. Carrick makes a case for the necessity of continuity in advertising schedules.

From the early 70's on, most of the literature on frequency effects appeared in either the *Journal of Advertising Research* or the *Journal of Marketing Research*. Ostheimer (1970) looked at frequency effects over time. Appel (1971) began to study the problem of wear-out, or situations where the number of repeat exposures decreased the overall effectiveness of the advertising. Ray, Sawyer, and Strong (1971) took a more detailed look at factors affecting repetition of advertisements. Krugman (1972) began to advance the notion that a limited number of exposures may be sufficient. He was less concerned about overlearning and more concerned with the number of ad repetitions required to get over some threshold. Britt, Adams, and Miller (1972) began to look at the question of how many ads people are actually exposed to. Greenberg and Suttoni (1973) considered the problem of wear-out that was examined earlier by Appel. Ehrenberg (1974) looked at general effects of repetition. Ray and Sawyer (1971) examined the problem of calibrating repetitions so that the information can be incorporated into media models. Finally, Craig, Sternthal, and Leavitt (1976) examined the phenomenon of wear-out for print ads, and Calder and Sternthal (1980) extended this to television.

While this collection does not represent all the articles on repetition, it provides a good sampling of the research and provides an indication of the historical evolution. Many of the earlier works, from the teens and 20's, are difficult to locate. More importantly, they contain some fundamental findings that have been ignored in subsequent research. Even though most of the early research was dealing with printed material, much of what has been found is still valid today with more complex stimuli.

It is hoped that this collection, along with the rich bibliographies contained in each article, will provide the researcher with a valuable resource that will help contribute to an understanding of repetition effects as they relate to advertising and stimulate additional research.

C. Samuel Craig
Brian Sternthal

Acknowledgements

The following articles, reprinted from the Journal of Advertising Research, are copyright by the Advertising Research Foundation:

"Frequency Effects Over Time," © 1970,

"On Advertising Wear Out," © 1971,

"Frequency Effects Revisited," © 1971,

"Why Three Exposures May Be Enough," © 1972,

"How Many Advertising Exposures Per Day," © 1972,

"Television Commercial Wearout," © 1973,

"Repetitive Advertising and the Consumer," © 1974.

The American Marketing Association has granted permission to reprint the following articles from the Journal of Marketing and Journal of Marketing Research:

"The Remembering and Forgetting of Advertising," © 1959,

"Why Continued Advertising is Necessary: A New Explanation," © 1959,

"Repetition in Media Models: A Laboratory Technique," © 1971,

"Advertising Wearout: An Experimental Analysis," © 1976,

"Television Commercial Wearout: An Information Processing View," © 1980.

THE CURVE OF FORGETTING

CHAPTER I

HISTORICAL SURVEY

THE problems that present themselves in connection with the topic of forgetting are (1) the rate at which forgetting progresses, (2) the form of the curve showing the relation of forgetting to the lapse of time, and (3) whether there are any constant relations between either the rate of forgetting or the shape of this curve, on the one hand, and, on the other, the kinds of subject matter or the kinds of reagents, or the amount or manner of the practise or learning.

The first application of modern scientific methods in the study of memory and of forgetting was the work of Ebbinghaus, which he published in 1885.[1] Ebbinghaus assumed that when experience has weakened in its susceptibility to recall the remaining association strength can be measured best by the number of repetitions that it saves in relearning. Another person served him as subject in preliminary experiments; but in the principal experiments Ebbinghaus acted both as experimenter and subject. As he admits, his results are, therefore, of much less value especially for general psychology. The material learned in the experiments in forgetting consisted of 163 series, each containing 13 nonsense syllables. Every syllable contained a consonant, a vowel and then another consonant. Ebbinghaus took especial pains to avoid any succession of letters or of syllables that might suggest devices in learning. He read a series and then recalled as many syllables as possible until he reproduced the whole series once without an error. Whenever a series could not be promptly recalled in its entirety he read the remainder from the paper. The rate was kept constant at 150 syllables per minute by means of a metronome. Seven of the series were memorized one day and one was relearned at each of seven intervals of various lengths. The data of the shorter periods were the average results of from 12 to 16 series, and those of the larger intervals of from 22 to 26 series.

The results of this investigation of Ebbinghaus I present in the form of a table of arrays and a table of central tendencies and meas-

[1] "Über das Gedächtniss," Leipzig, 1885.

1

TABLE I

RESULTS OF EBBINGHAUS

The Arrays of the Per Cents. Retained

Per Cent.	20 Minutes	1 Hour	9 Hours	1 Day	2 Days	9 Days	31 Days
60	5						
55	5						
50	1	4					
45	0	5	1	3	1		
40	1	3	1	2	3	1	1
35		3	6	9	1	3	2
30		1	2	4	7	6	7
25			2	3	4	3	6
20				2	3	7	8
15				2	4	3	9
10				1	2	0	6
5					1	2	6
0–5						1	
Average Deviations	4.3	5.1	4.3	7.2	9.0	10.4	7.9
Probable Errors ..	2.1	4.2	0.8	3.7	7.6	7.9	7.0
Averages	58.2	44.2	35.2	33.7	27.8	25.4	21.1
Modes	55–60	45	35	35–	30–	20–30	15

ures of variability. It can be seen that the portions of the work that were necessary to be performed again were approximately, after 20 minutes 1/3, after 1 hour 1/2, after 9 hours 2/3 —, after 24 hours 2/3 +, after 6 days 3/4, and after 31 days 4/5. His statement of his conclusions from these results is, "The ratio of what is retained to what is forgotten varies inversely as the logarithm of the time."

Besides being the first experimental research in this group of phenomena, this was the first very extended laboratory investigation of the mental processes that are not closely paralleled by definite, commensurate, physical stimuli. In addition to this, all who have carried on experimental investigations in memory, and most especially in forgetting, will agree that the task as it was performed by Ebbinghaus required closeness of application and patient persistence that was nothing less than heroic. However, the fact that his work has more than one claim to a place among pioneer achievements is sufficient excuse for several imperfections in his methods.

There is good reason for believing that his work might have been more valuable for general psychology had he, with equal diligence, experimented upon several other persons. This most usual criticism of his method is atoned for in a measure by the fact that one could scarcely have been as severely exacting in his methodological requirements in that case as Ebbinghaus was with himself. Besides, learning depends so largely upon attention that any one to whom the problem was not of primary interest could not be so constant in conditions for reaction as the one to whom the research was all-important. The aim of Ebbinghaus was merely to break the ground, thus to disclose only the predominant, and therefore the most common, factors in learning and in forgetting. Of course, there was a greater possibility of mistaking some individual factors for general phenomena than there would have been in case of a number of subjects. There is indeed no assurance that the regularity in this curve was in no degree due to his knowledge of the problem and of the results to be obtained. Therefore, although there were some advantages in experimenting upon himself, there is ample reason for believing that there is considerable justness in the criticism. The subject matter that Ebbinghaus supposed to be as simple as any that could be found was probably not so simple in possibilities for association or so single in forms of imagery as material that has been chosen by several other investigators more recently.

In reading the syllables from a paper he did not avoid the possibility of dwelling longer upon the syllables difficult to remember than upon others, and of unwittingly glancing back in review of refractory association links. This objection is stronger nevertheless in connection with his experiments for the analysis of memorizing than with reference to studies of forgetting, because more time spent upon the less associable members of the series equalizes among all members the degrees of permanence. This quality is indeed the primary disideratum in units of measure. However, it is more satisfactory to first make the members as equal as possible, and then thoroughly to control the manner and the time of their exposure. Although, according to the results of Ebbinghaus more than one third of the forgetting of nonsense syllabes takes place during the first twenty minutes, more than one half in one hour, nearly two thirds in nine hours, and more than two thirds within twenty-four hours, only one third of his data constitutes the evidence for these four out of the seven intervals. The slow loss between nine hours and one day in comparison with that preceding and following this interval is one of the doubtful results that might have been determined with a greater degree of certainty and with small sacrifice, if the experiments had been better distributed.

We are able to improve upon the methods of Ebbinghaus, not because of the lack of value of his research; but owing to the fact that his studies have supplied a general method of investigation, and thus aroused an interest in this group of phenomena that has resulted in a fruitful series of researches, and a better understanding of the problems and difficulties to be met in this field of investigation.

While the first part of the investigation that is reported later in

TABLE II

RADOSSAWLJEWITSCH'S RESULTS

	Adults		Children	
	Without Meaning Per Cent. of	With Meaning Per Cent. of	Without Meaning Per Cent. of	With Meaning Per Cent. of,
Time	Forgetting	Forgetting	Forgetting	Forgetting
After 5 minutes	2.5	0.0	8.8	3.4
After 20 minutes ...	11.4	4.4	14.6	10.97
After 1 hour	29.3	19.1	22.7	23.05
After 8 hours	52.6	42.1	37.0	38.75
After 1 day	31.1	20.3	28.3	21.01
After 2 days	39.1	33.2	31.9	29.0
After 3 days	——	43.5	—	—
After 4 days	——	45.5	—	—
After 5 days	——	43.5	—	—
After 6 days	50.7	57.6	42.4	42.0
After 7 days	——	50.0	—	—
After 14 days	59.0	70.0	46.1	49.4
After 21 days	62.2	52.4	49.5	47.3
After 30 days	79.8	76.1	66.2	75.7
After 60 days	——	——	94.3	85.4
After 120 days	97.2	——	—	—

this thesis was in progress (1903–04) P. R. Radossawljewitsch was also studying forgetting. By having twenty-seven subjects, both adults and children, he avoided the individual character of the work of Ebbinghaus. He employed nonsense syllables similar to those of Ebbinghaus; but presented the syllables after the manner of Müller and Schumann, so that the manner of reading them was better controlled. The syllables were fixed on a cylinder that rotated so as to expose one syllable at a time through an opening in a screen. He used also subject matter with meaning. Each series consisted of two stanzas of Schiller's translation of "The Siege of Troy," which the reagents read throughout repeatedly until they could reproduce them twice without an error. Radossawljewitsch believed as did Müller and Pilzecker, that two repetitions gave much greater assurance of association strength than the single correct repetition of Ebbinghaus. Each of these two kinds of subject matter was relearned after various intervals, and the numbers of repetitions in learning and relearning were the measures of gain and loss. As shown by Table II. and the curves (Fig. 3), Radossawljewitsch's results indicate that we forget rapidly at first, then rather abruptly slower, and that the later rate gradually decreases. His curve of forgetting rises slower in the beginning and faster in the later portion than that of Ebbinghaus (see Fig. 3). In the cases of adults and children, with meaningless subject matter and with material with meaning, the association strength at the end of one day was greater than at the end of eight hours or at the end of two days. In the results of Ebbinghaus there was a decrease in the rate of forgetting at about the same point. Radossawljewitsch also found a period of relatively slow forgetting between six days and twenty-one days. These later periods of retarded forgetting have no corresponding periods in Ebbinghaus's results.

Radossawljewitsch verified the results of Ebbinghaus in that long series of nonsense syllables are not forgotten as rapidly as short series. The reasons assigned for this fact are the greater amount of practise that longer series require and the enlistment of better attention by the consciousness of the relative largeness of the task.

Both adults and children were found by Radossawljewitsch to forget material without meaning more rapidly than material with meaning, especially during the first two days. His adult observers forgot $\frac{1}{3}$ of the material with meaning in 2 days and of the subject matter without meaning in about 1 day. They lost $\frac{1}{2}$ of the matter with meaning in 7 days, and of that without meaning in 6 days. Within 30 days they forgot $\frac{3}{4}$ of the poetry and $\frac{4}{5}$ of the nonsense syllables. The children lost association strength somewhat faster than the adults; but their curves for the same kinds of subject matter were quite similar.

The forgetting of connected ideas was studied by E. N. Henderson.[2] Among his subjects were school children of grades five, six and seven, high school pupils, university summer school students, college students, and graduate students. He selected as subject matter five very dissimilar passages of thoroughly coherent discourse, such as students of various degrees of development might be expected to learn and later to reproduce in class. His experiments were performed in school rooms. As much of one selection as possible was learned in three minutes, and immediately written. Two days later and four weeks later they again wrote as much of the selection as they could. The measures used were the topics, sub-topics, details and words that were memorized and that were later reproduced. He endeavored to find by means of these results the amounts forgotten within different lengths of time, the relation of age and training to the amount learned and to the amount retained, the relation of the rate of learning to the rate of forgetting, and of intelligence to forgetting. He compared also the ability to retain details with

[2] "Das Behalten und Vergessen bei Kindern und Erwachsenen nach experimentellen Untersuchungen," Leipzig, 1907.

[3] "The Study of Memory for Connected Trains of Thought," *Psy. Rev.* Monograph Suppl., Vol. V., No. 6.

TABLE III

HENDERSON'S RESULTS

		Ideas			Words	
	Gains	Per Cent. Lost in 2 Days	Per Cent. Lost in 28 Days	Gains	Per Cent. Lost in 2 Days	Per Cent. Lost in 28 Days
Summer students ...	23.1	8.8	13.6	44.2	23.3	32.3
Public school pupils	35.3	4.7	13.2	54.6	10.4	23.5
High school students	38.8	11.5	30.5	48.9	16.7	35.9
College students	39.4	25.5	31.5	53.3	39.0	47.4
Graduate students ..	43.1	23.2	36.5	58.2	32.3	49.7
Average	35.9	14.7	25.1	51.8	24.3	37.8

the permanence of larger topics. As shown by Table III. the rise in his curve of forgetting of ideas is eight times as rapid per day during the first two days as it is per day during the first month as a whole. The forgetting curve for words is nine times as fast in its rise per day during the first two days as it is per day during the first month as a whole. In both ideas and words there is a small irregular increase in the retentive ability from the younger, less mature to the older, more mature observers. Henderson believed this to be due to the greater ability on the part of the older subjects to read and to understand the subject matter rather than to any fundamental difference in memory.

Those who learn most rapidly retain a large percentage of either ideas or words; but the correlation of the two tendencies is not very high.

Two teachers made a list of their pupils in the order of their abilities, and this ranking was compared with the ranking of the same pupils in these experiments. It was found that there was almost no correspondence between these rankings among the pupils of the grammar grades. But in the higher grades there was a close relation. The most advanced reagents were superior to the less mature in grasping and in retaining general meaning. This is probably partly due to the exclusion of inferior minds from the higher classes.

The more mature students lost a larger percentage of words than of ideas. This difference was much greater with the younger, less mature subjects.

From the data of his investigation of memory for paired associates, E. L. Thorndike finds it possible to derive a few important conclusions concerning forgetting. His observers were twenty-two college seniors and graduate students. Each unit of the memory task was the ability to write the English equivalent for a given German word. One hundred or more pairs of associates of this kind were practised one hour. A new list was used each day on which practise occurred until twelve hundred pairs had been repeated.

Then the same lists were practised again. Tests were inserted from time to time. All but two subjects learned more than 90 per cent. of all the words in from 2 to 5 entire rounds. After the twenty-two subjects had practised on the average 38 hours they remembered an average of 1,030 words at the end of 3 days, and 620 words after 42 days. Tests made upon seventeen of these persons on closing the last study period and at intervals after practise show that they forgot approximately .05 within 1 hour, .10 during 3 days and from .40 to .50 by the end of 40 days.[4]

W. F. Book devotes a small portion of his most thorough-going study of learning to the investigation of the permanence of impressions.[5] He uses data from only one subject. The apparatus was a typewriter to which was attached Duprez markers which recorded (*a*) the number of letters, (*b*) the number of words printed, (*c*) the number of shiftings of the carriage, and (*d*) the number of times that is necessary for the observer to look at the keyboard. In order to discover any irregularities in the effort put forth while writing, the pulse record was taken by means of tambours adjusted to the temples of the observer. The subject practised a half hour per day 174 consecutive days with the keys of the typewriter visible. After an interval of five months he practised 60 days with the keys hidden by a screen. During the second period, his copy was a short sentence which he practised 120 times per day until he could write it 100 times per minute. The number of strokes made on the last ten days of this practise were compared with the number of strokes made in a similar manner during a ten days test, five months later, and with the number of strokes during another test, 17 months after the end of the 60 days practise. The average number of strokes per day during the last ten days practise were 1,508. The average of the first test was 1,443 and that of the second test 1,611. If these are the numbers that should be compared, there was a loss during the five months between the practise and the test, but a gain instead of a loss, as one might expect, during the twelve months between the first and second tests. Book accounts for this gain by means of the same theory that he offers in explanation of the plateaus in the curve of learning. He believes that during the 60 days of practise, in addition to the fixing of the right reactions, tendencies to many wrong reactions must have accumulated, and that these tendencies have been eliminated before the second test.

However, by careful inspection of this table it becomes evident

[4] *Pscychological Review*, XV., pp. 132–135 (1908).

[5] ''The Psychology of Skill,'' Univ. of Montana Pub. in Psychology, Vol. I. (1908), Bul. 53, Psy. Series No. I., pp. 75–79.

that there is a gradual gain during each group of ten days, especially during the second test. Judging also from my experience with the typewriter, there is in each of these tests ample room for gain through practise. During the first test the total number of strokes was 14,424 and during the second test 16,081. This makes a grand total of 30,505 strokes after the completion of regular practise. That the gain is due to practise is even more probable in the light of the fact that the tests serve as reviews of so much practise, of the 174 days of general practise with the keyboard visible and of the 60 days of practise on the same subject matter that was repeated in the tests. Moreover, the repetitions in the tests are quite advantageously distributed for progress in learning. Further evidence for this view is found in his curve of regular practise (p. 80). The curve rises at the diminishing rate characteristic of curves of practise, finally rising between 50 days and 60 days a few more than 100 strokes. If practise had proceeded 20 days longer there is every indication that it would have gone above the point (1,611 strokes) reached by the end of the two tests. The difference between the last day's work in the regular practise (1,698 strokes), and the first day's work in the first test (1,365 strokes), indicates a loss through forgetting of 333 strokes in 5 months. Likewise the difference between the numbers of strokes of the last day in the first test (1,472 strokes) and the first day of the second test (1,390 strokes) gives a loss of 82 strokes in 12 months. There would seem also to be a loss in both these cases if, instead of using one day's work as the basis of comparison, we use the average data of three days. The first difference would be 151 strokes, the second 83 strokes. The ratio of the loss in the earlier period with the loss in the later period according to these measures agrees with most studies of forgetting.

Therefore the apparent gain that Book finds in these results can not be shown to exist except when we compare groups of ten days each. These evidences throw considerable doubt upon the need of any explanation other than that of learning, forgetting and re-learning.

The problem of Ebert and Meumann[6] was to discover whether subject matter that is readily learned is forgotten more rapidly or more slowly than that which requires greater labor in memorizing. Each of five subjects memorized by the method of right associates a series of 12 and one of 16 nonsense syllables, and by the method of learning a series of successive members throughout, another series of 12 and also one of 16 nonsense syllables. Two observers learned in

[6]"Uber einige Grundfragen der Psychologie der Ubungsphanomene im Bereiche des Gedächtnisses," *Archiv für die Gesamte Psy.*, 1904, 4, 193.

addition two stanzas each of "The Siege of Troy." The material without meaning that had been learned was relearned by one observer after an interval of 75 days, by a second after 85 days, by a third after 91 days, by a fourth after 146 days, and by a fifth after 156 days. The matter with meaning was relearned by one subject after 146 days and by the other after 156 days. I have condensed Ebert and Meumann's results for meaningless subject matter into Table IV. The most evident facts about these results is that by the use of one of these methods more of the easier series was forgotten, and by the other method more of the harder series was forgotten. Therefore the method of right associates seems to be better adapted to the sixteen syllable series than to the twelve syllable series. With the other method the reverse appears to be true. It may be noted also that there is better correlation between the length of the interval of delayed recall and the amount forgotten. This is doubtless due to the fact that, not only the series, but also the observers were not the same for any two intervals. The subject matter with meaning learned by the consecutive method was more easily learned than nonsense syllables. As in the case of subject matter without meaning, no forgetting occurred, and the observer with the shorter of the two periods was 25 per cent. more able to relearn a stanza at the end of the interval of delay than at the termination of practise.

TABLE IV

EBERT AND MEUMANN'S RESULTS

| | Method of Right Associates | | | | | | Method of Consecutive Members | | | | | |
| | 12 Syllables | | | 16 Syllables | | | 12 Syllables | | | 16 Syllables | | |
Intervals	Learning	Relearn	Per Cent. Loss	Learn	Relearn	Per Cent. Loss	Learn	Relearn	Per Cent. Loss	Learn	Relearn	Per Cent. Loss
75 days	8.0	5.0	37.5	8.0	6.5	18.8	6.0	6.0	0.	8.0	7.0	12.5
85 days	4.0	3.5	12.5	7.0	7.0	0.	7.0	7.0	0.	10.0	7.0	30.0
91 days	12.5	7.5	40.0	7.5	7.5	0.	11.0	10.0	9.1	18.0	12.0	33.3
146 days	1.5	2.0	—33.3	4.0	4.0	0.	4.0	4.0	0.	5.0	4.0	20.0
156 days	8.0	7.5	6.3	5.5	5.5	0.	5.0	5.0	0.	5.0	6.0	—20.0
Gross Av.	6.8	5.1		6.5	6.1		6.6	6.5		9.2	7.2	
Per cent. Av.		12.6				3.8			1.8			15.2

An experimental study of the curve of forgetting was made also with pathological subjects by Ziehen.[7] He used this type of observers because one is justified by the principles of psychopathology in expecting that the ability of most patients to recall what they have

[7] "Das Gedächtnis," Berlin, 1908.

learned when they are at successive stages of disease should correspond to the ability of normal persons to recall at different stages of
forgetting. He says, "Investigations have shown that loss of memory
images is quite slow for a considerably extended time (ziemlich
beträchtlichen Zeit), and then there is exceedingly rapid loss."
This "critical point" of the curve has a position dependent upon
the disposition of the learner, the kind of incentive, and other factors.

He states that it has been experimentally demonstrated by others
and by himself that, from this critical point on, the recent is forgotten more rapidly than the more remote by most of those having
memory defects. The few exceptions are in special types of insanity.
Ziehen's explanation for this phenomenon is that we recall nothing
unless its reproduction is necessitated by some experience that pre-
cedes it; and as the old experience has become consciously and sub-
consciously, or cortically, more connected during the intervening
time than has been possible for the recent experience, this new experience is more difficult to recall until it has had time to thus become a more intimate part of the individual.

Moreover Ziehen finds that forgetting is not all passive, but that
holes are torn in the memory image, and also older images are modified by the play of newer associations in normal individuals similar
to the way in which they are distorted in pathological amnesia.

In none of the other investigations that I have been able to find
does the curve of forgetting have the form described by Ziehen. The
nearest approach to it is the curve found by Radossawljewitsch,
which rises slowly during the first five minutes, and then much more
rapidly. I believe that the solution of problems in arithmetic, which
he used as one form of subject matter, usually depends largely upon
a fundamental principle and a group of related, subordinate principles. When the fundamental principle finally passes below the
threshold of recall, the dependent principles would thereby lose
suddenly a large part of their association strength. But this explanation could scarcely be applied to his other subject matter, six,
eight and nine place numbers. Ziehen's description of his method
and results is not complete enough to permit much use to be made
of his conclusions.

Several more recent investigations of kindred problems have led
to conclusions concerning forgetting. The following declaration is
made by A. Renda:[3] "Forgetting is not merely an accidental characteristic of mental function, but is the result of an active process of
dissociation. It is a means by which consciousness gets rid of re-

[3] "L'oblio saggio sull' attivita selettiva della coscienza," Torino, Bocca.
1910, p. 229.

dundant material.'' Pieron[9] says that forgetting is like auto-catalysis in chemistry in that it is a change that ensues in a memory image by reason of the presence of transforming agencies in the image itself. These views have evidences, but no counter-evidences in the results of the other investigations previously quoted.

The results of Ebbinghaus and Radossawljewitsch resemble each other in that the rate of forgetting is more rapid at first than later; but they disagree in the amount of difference between the early and the late portions, in the degree of abruptness in the change, and in the other irregularities in the curve. Ziehen's curve seems to be radically different from all the others. Several of the investigators have found data for too few intervals to furnish much assistance in harmonizing these curves until there is additional investigation in the same field.

[9] ''L'evolution de la memoir,'' Paris, 1910.

CHAPTER II

The Problem and the Method

INVESTIGATION has revealed the fact that two kinds of results arise from the insertion of intervals into an act of learning. If recall is delayed, the association links become weaker. If practise is interspersed with periods of relative inactivity, the repetitions have greater value. The most advantageous degree of the distribution of practise through the interjection of periods of rest has been theoretically but not experimentally determined. Nor is the cause of this phenomenon much more than a question under discussion. Even the practise curve has been determined only as to its general form, and there is disagreement concerning its details. Moreover in the case of forgetting, as has been shown by the previous chapter, not only the details, but also the general trend of the curve is in dispute.

The results of investigation make it probable that we forget faster immediately after practise than later. The earlier part of Radossawljewitsch's curve rises more slowly and the latter part more rapidly, however, than that of Ebbinghaus, and has several stages of slow forgetting that are not present in the curve of Ebbinghaus. Explanations of these differences have been either theoretically proposed or are merely foreshadowed by the results.

This thesis is an endeavor to study the same field with several kinds of subject matter and various methods. The fundamental problem is whether all forgetting is governed by the same general law. The secondary aim is to discover, if possible, why the results of various investigations do not more fully agree.

The first group of experiments reported in this thesis was performed in 1903 in the University of Chicago, and was discontinued after five months because of the demands of a new position. In the mean time Radossawljewitsch began his investigation of practically the same problem. His work was published in 1904. The second group of experiments of this thesis was performed with entire classes in the Indiana State Normal School in Terre Haute, and by reason of its nature, it covered a long period (1904–09). The last three groups were performed under the direction of the department of psychology at Columbia University during 1909 and 1910.

Previous researches have shown incidentally that learning and forgetting take unlike forms and progress at varying rates with the

12

slightest differences in subject matter and in types of learners, with relatively trivial deviations in method, with changes in health or in time of day, as well as with an increase or a decrease in the periods between practise and recall. However, both phenomena have shown constant relations between controlled conditions and consistent results. Therefore, the choice of subject matter and of methods has been with this end primarily in view. It should be possible to isolate a factor of this nature for study without departing from the conditions of learning in daily life including those of school. Facts are no less scientific when practical. The derivation of principles from that source paves the way for their most convincing verification through successful application.

As simple subject matter without meaning can be learned easiest and most rapidly by the so-called "trial and success method" and complex subject matter with meaning by more rational methods, there is likely to be some difference in the manner in which they are forgotten. The content to be learned will, then, be simple and complex material similar to that of practical life.

As far as possible such subject matter was chosen as would appeal to but one sense department, and would not be a stronger stimulus to persons of one age, sex or race than to those of another age, sex, or race. In the first group of experiments the subject matter was a series consisting of one muscular movement repeated many times. In the second group a number of sensations constituted the series. The subject matter in the third group was complex. Each member of the series of stimuli was responded to by a corresponding member of a series of movements.

The methods were also made to correspond as far as possible with those which are most serviceable in daily life. All conditions were kept constant except the intervals between practise and recall. The short periods that were necessary for the making of records and to readjust apparatus were timed carefully so as not to allow any differences in the association strength or in the values of new repetitions owing to variations in the distribution. Sufficient control was exercised to make the results comparable; nevertheless, the limitations were so few that after the experiments were well begun, the reagents were unconscious of restraint. The stimuli were presented to the most used sense, vision, and were responded to by movements. Series were practised as a whole, as in everyday life rather than piecemeal as is too often done in school. The observers were all adults with no very individual tendencies. The details of method in the individual experiments will be discussed in their particular chapters.

CHAPTER III

THE FORGETTING OF A RELATIVELY SIMPLE MOTOR ACT

THE experimental work in this chapter .was performed in the University of Chicago during 1903–04. Although the data can be of little value in the determination of the curve of forgetting they throw some light on the conditions of learning. The earliest plan was to begin the study of forgetting by using a series consisting of the repetition of one act in which the motor element is highly dominant. Throwing was chosen as being a distinctly human acquisition that is probably not based on an innate tendency as such, and that is typical of common forms of manual skill.

It soon became evident that it is more difficult to secure accurate scores in throwing than it is in other kinds of target practise. In an effort to obtain reliable scores, the target was made to undergo several transformations. The final and most successful target consisted of hollow cylinders made of wire mosquito netting of diameters corresponding to the diameters of the circles used in the targets of most of these experiments. These cylinders were closed at one end, and strengthened with a ring of stiff wire at the open end. They were placed within each other in the order of size, and supported so that the curved wall of one was equidistant from the corresponding walls of the others. The open end of this compound cylinder was placed toward the thrower so that one and three fourths inch wooden balls, when thrown, would pass into one or another of the cylinders according to the accuracy of the throws. When a projectile struck the edge of a cylinder, it fell into the next larger one, because each cylinder was shorter than the next larger, and adjusted so that its open end was five inches further from the thrower than that of the next larger cylinder. The entire target was mounted so that a projectile rolled toward the closed end of the cylinder into which it had been thrown and into a trough-like crease or groove in the lower side of the cylinder where it took its place in line with others that scored equally with it. Along each crease was read directly the score made by lodging any specific number of projectiles in that division of the target during a series of one hundred throws. After having read the scores, a small metal plate, that covered an opening opposite the rear of each groove, was swung to one side to allow the balls to roll out of the target in preparation for another series.

14

It was readily ascertained by preliminary experiments that, when other conditions were constant, series thrown by the right hand, by the left hand, in the under-hand, in the over-hand, and in the direct modes did not improve at parallel rates with equivalent amounts of practise, nor did they decline equally during the same interval. Successive series with one hand and with one kind of throwing movement were adopted as the most nearly comparable.

One reagent was a university professor, and ten other observers including the writer were graduate students in psychology. Each reagent was free to throw in a manner of his own choice except that he was required to continue throwing in the same manner throughout a group of experiments. The throws were made to coincide with the strokes of a metronome bell. Further preliminary experiments were performed to find the rate of throwing that yielded the greatest progress. Five persons were found to have individual rates at which throws could most advantageously succeed each other. These rates were always as rapid as projectiles could readily be picked up and thrown. Later each of two reagents performed one thousand throws with each of the following intervals. There are too few subjects in

TABLE V
The Value of Intervals during Practise

	30.0 Sec.	60.0 Sec.	120.0 Sec.	180.0 Sec.
Per cents. gained	49.2	24.9	6.3	6.7
Per cents. gained	57.8	14.3	23.2	10.0
Average gained	53.5	19.6	14.8	8.4

this preliminary test, to serve as conclusive evidence that with this kind of material, the shorter the interval the more rapid is the progress in learning; but these evidences indicate a likelihood that Bergström's principle, "the acquisition and retention of associable words varies approximately as the interval between the members of a series," may apply only to complex subject matter with meaning. In relatively meaningless matter, for example in throwing, the formation of a series out of the mere repetition of an act, the progress seems to vary approximately inversely as the number of repetitions within a given time. The only limits to this in throwing were that the speed should not exclude the accurate picking up of projectiles and the aiming and proper swinging of the arm in throwing, and the avoidance of fatigue. This would not warrant the division of subject matter into two distinct classes to be learned in two very different ways; but it would mean that the intervals between members of series and between entire series should depend upon the degree of complexity of the series. Ebbinghaus states that the more repetitions of nonsense syllables he could crowd into a given time, the quicker he could learn them. Lottie Steffens found that with her subjects rapid learning was not necessarily conditioned by many repetitions within a short time. Moreover it has been shown that with simple subject matter the trial and success method, as it is called, produces quicker, surer results, whereas it has been repeatedly demonstrated that subject matter with meaning is learned more economically by thinking one's way through at first. Because of the results gained in these tests, the throwing was done as rapidly and as persistently throughout each period as the picking up of projectiles and the avoidance of fatigue would permit. Other preliminary tests made it evident that a target to be thrown at by inexperienced men and women at a distance of six meters, should be about a meter in diameter. It also became evident that the projectiles should, if possible, be adapted to the size of the thrower's hand; but that an average size would be about one and three fourth inches in diameter. Slight inequalities in the weights of projectiles used resulted in relatively great deviations in scores. The general effect of practise made the point at which the practise of each series began a variable quantity. The influence of this defect was reduced somewhat by finding what per cent. of the gain was lost through delay.

In the principal experiment of this group such meager gains were made in throwing one hundred times that the loss due to delayed recall could not be measured with any degree of certainty. Persistent throwing several hours per day during a series of days yielded more commensurate gains; but the decrease in association strength was proportionately slow. In order to find whether the small scores were due to a defect in the method or to the inability of the psycho-physical organism to habituate itself rapidly to this kind of reaction, the apparatus was so modified as to record the force as well as the direction of each throw. Back of each corner of a square wooden target of one meter side was fixed a large tambour with its three inch rubber membrane on the side towards the wall, against which the target was suspended by ropes. A screw was driven into the wall in such a way that its head, which was two inches in diameter, rested against the middle portion of the membrane. The air chambers of these tambours were connected by means of tubes with one tube which led to a Marey tambour. When a projectile hit the target, the momentum with which it struck was recorded on a revolving kymograph drum by the pen of the Marey tambour. The throws were at first very unequal in force, but they rapidly and regularly became equal as practise proceeded, and with an equal degree of regularity they became unequal in intensity with longer and longer intervals of forgetting (Fig. 1). Therefore much more progress was being made in learning to throw than was evident in terms of control of the direction of the throwing movements. As the increase or the decrease in the amount of energy expended is more immediate and more simple than the guidance of movement, its mastery is probably more easily acquired in games and in work.

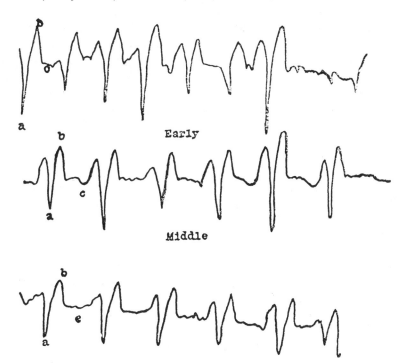

FIG. 1. Pantographic copies of records of the force of throws. Points *a* were made by the hitting of the target. The record of the greatest recoil and of the lesser recoils are indicated by *b* and *c* respectively. The "early" curves were made near the beginning of a seris of 100 throws and the "final" curves were near the end of that series.

The complexity of the control of movement in three-dimensional space was evident in the fact that the spots that recorded the "hits" were arranged in the form of an ellipse with its long axis parallel with the motion of the arm. This axis shortened much faster than the other axis as skill increased, and was relatively short with persons who were accustomed to throwing in the manner used. Skill in throwing is therefore largely ability to release a projectile at the proper moment. All of the reagents reported that they found themselves strenuously endeavoring, while throwing, to avoid "wild" throws, that is, "hits" beyond their usual limits, and also were conscious of trying to strike the bull's-eye. Sometimes one of these purposes and sometimes the other was uppermost in mind. Total scores showed later that near the boundary of each reagent's field, was a ring-like area in which the "hits" were more numerous than in closely neighboring portions. In the region of the bull's-eye there was a somewhat similar sudden increase in the number of "hits." "Wild" throwing was usually due to the momentary straying of the attention or to loss of confidence owing to previous "wild" throws. After about fifty throws of a practise series, the score almost always decreased, and the "wild" throws increased unless the bull's-eye was varied in color or in some other quality to overcome this inconstancy of attention. The necessity of this renewal of the stimulus was probably due to the monotony of a series that was merely the repetition of one sensori-motor act.

The larger the number of muscles involved in a psycho-physical act, the greater is the number and variety of possible reactions, and therefore the slower is the progress. The rate of learning is more rapid in the use of the preferred hand than in the use of the other hand.

In so far as the results of this group of experiments have value, they indicate that the conditions of progress in the study of forgetting are: a series consisting of varied members preferably with meaning, rather than a series composed of repetitions of one short interval between simple reactions and of longer intervals the more complex the reactions; attention kept at its highest intensity, if necessary, by means of devices; as small a group of muscles as possible, muscles previously coordinated in other acts but not in the one that is being practised.

CHAPTER IV

THE FORGETTING OF SENSATIONS WITH RELATIVELY LITTLE MEANING

AFTER having spent several months in the almost fruitless efforts to modify the methods and apparatus of the experiment described in the previous chapter. I endeavored to retrieve the loss by performing a group of experiments during spare moments while teaching. This work is a study (1) of how meaningless, relatively simple subject matter decreases in association strength, (2) of the manner in which students often forget what they learn in class, and (3) of how students recall under class-room conditions.

The experiments were performed with entire classes of students in the Indiana State Normal School. These students had largely attained the degree of physical and mental maturity of college sophomores. Nearly one third of them were men, and more than two thirds were women.

The subject matter was a consecutive series of nine consonants that had been found by experiment to be about equally difficult to remember. Vowels were omitted in order to avoid the possibility of combining members of a series into syllables. Consonants were chosen rather than numerals; because consonants furnish an opportunity for recall not only by reproduction but also by identification; whereas the selection of nine digits from among the few would not be a fair test of recall. Most persons are habituated in the use of numbers, and even of letters in calculation, and are familiar with the employment of letters as initials and symbols without definite reference to what they symbolize; but, as a rule, they do not use words and syllables in that manner. Therefore, letters have not such a strong tendency as words or syllables to suggest meaning. For these reasons a series consisting of letters was chosen as a type of meaningless content. These letters were presented successively, and each series was repeated as a whole. Each consonant in the series was presented one second with no perceptible interval between the presentations. The letters were one and one half inches in height, and were arranged at intervals of three inches in a vertical column on a sliding screen. In front of the letters was a stationary screen with an opening through which one of the letters at a time could be seen. On the back of the sliding screen opposite each letter a small roller was fixed with its axis perpendicular to the surface of the screen.

These rollers were placed alternatingly on two parallel lines which were drawn vertically along the middle of the sliding screen. Behind this screen a pendulum was suspended at its middle point. This pendulum carried a bob at each end. Attached to the front of the pendulum rod was a metal half ring with a radius of about two inches. Its concave side was upward and its center coincident with the point of support of the pendulum. It was so placed that one of the rollers resting upon it supported the sliding screen. When owing to the swinging of the pendulum, this roller passed through an opening at the middle of the half ring, it allowed the screen to fall until the next roller was caught by the half ring. One second later it, in turn, fell through the opening. It is evident that while a roller rested on the half ring, one of the letters was being exposed through the slit. The half ring was padded at places where the rollers first struck, in order to diminish the noise resulting from the impact. Three additional rollers permitted the swings of the pendulum to become regular before the exposures began. As one series was used for all intervals of delayed recall each group of students served for only one interval. Preliminary experiments indicated that this plan would be better than that of using different series and of having each class serve for several intervals. Besides, as the Indiana State Normal School is not an institution of research, I preferred not to use much time for an experiment after it ceased to be a profitable exercise for the students. However the whole quantity of results shows that it would have been better to have experimented with several series with the same subjects.

It was not a totally new experience for the students in these classes to take part in psychological experiments; but there was enough unusualness about it to increase the tendency to vocalize the letters. They were therefore urged to abstain from moving the vocal organs. This reduced the action to about its normal degree. It was made clear that if any one failed to do honest work, he would gain nothing, and that the science of psychology would probably lose. Even those did faithful work who were known by their teachers to need watching in examinations. The mode of procedure was as follows: Each reagent was given a slip of paper bearing a number. After the presentation of the entire series the reagents of one group were allowed two minutes during which to write the letters that could be remembered, and as far as possible to place them in the order in which they had been presented. They then folded the papers in each case so as to conceal during the remainder of the experiment, the letters which they had just written. In this manner, the presentation of the same series, the writing, and the folding were performed six times; but any reagent who was moderately sure before any presentation that he had correctly written the series withdrew from the experiment by occupying himself with some other interest or duty. When all had finished, they recorded their physical condition as good, medium, or poor. The papers were then collected.

After a period of from one to twenty-eight days, each subject was supplied with paper on which he placed the number that he had found on the paper given him when the experiment was begun. This made it possible for me to compare his two papers. He then reproduced and recorded the letters and their order in so far as he was able. To this he added the information that was necessary in determining the value of his results. One item was the condition of his health. Another was whether any part of the series had been recalled during the interval, and whether he had been able to crowd it out by turning his thoughts to more interesting matter. He stated also whether he had associated the letters with initials or words and whether he had used rhythm or had vocalized.

Another group of subjects were allowed one and a half minutes to select the letters of the series from among the eighteen consonants of the alphabet and a half minute in which to arrange in the original order the nine consonants of the series, which were shown them in mixed order. Thus were obtained data for the comparison of the methods of selection, reproduction and reconstruction.

The tables do not include the results (a) of students who were present for only one part of an experiment, (b) of the few who did not understand how the experiments were to be performed, (c) of the subjects who recalled more than one letter of the series during the interval of forgetting, (d) of the reagents who associated some of the letters with initials or other subject matter, (e) of one observer who was not strictly honest in her work, and of several who were accidentally aided in reproduction, (f) of reagents whose health conditions were not normal or whose sight was too defective to produce reliable results. After these had been dropped, the results of 756 subjects constituted the Table VI., and of 348 constituted Table VII. The subject matter that could not be recalled after intervals of one to twenty-eight days is shown in terms of reproduction in Table VI., and in terms of recognition and reconstruction in Table VII. In both tables each gross measure is the average of the number of errors after the interval of delay opposite which the measure stands. The per cent. of the given subject matter that was forgotten is in a companion column. As there were nine letters in each series, nine omissions were possible. Therefore each omission was valued at $\frac{1}{9}$ of 100 per cent. It was expected that insertions would occur only when opportunities for insertion were made through omissions; but inspection and calculation show that there is no correlation between the omissions and the insertions. Hence each letter inserted was also valued at $\frac{1}{9}$ of 100 per cent. There is no general agreement concerning the methods of evaluating errors of order. Every plan is based upon a theory of the manner in which

TABLE VI

THE METHOD OF REPRODUCTION

Intervals	Omissions		Insertions		Errors of Order		Totals		Av. Per Cent. Per Day	Observers
	Gross	Per Cent. of 9 Errors	Gross	Per Cent. of 9 Errors	Gross	Per Cent. of 9 Errors	Gross	Per Cent. of 27 Errors		
1 day	1.1	12.2	0.5	5.6	1.4	15.6	3.0	11.1	11.1	41
4 days	1.1	12.2	0.6	6.7	2.4	26.7	4.1	15.2	3.8	114
7 days	1.6	17.8	0.6	6.7	3.1	34.4	5.3	19.6	2.3	140
14 days	2.6	28.9	0.9	10.0	2.3	25.6	5.8	21.5	1.5	298
21 days	2.2	24.4	0.9	10.0	2.6	28.9	5.7	21.1	1.0	123
28 days	2.0	22.2	1.3	14.4	2.4	26.7	5.7	21.1	0.8	40

members are associated in a series. In the case of the series of letters whenever one member was one removed from its given place in the series there were on an average as many evidences of weakness in the association links as when one member was from two to eight removes from its proper locality. Therefore in this group of experi-

TABLE VII

THE METHODS OF SELECTION AND RECONSTRUCTION

Intervals	Selection Omissions		Insertions		Reconstruction Errors of Order		Totals		Observers
	Gross	Per Cent. of 9 Errors	Gross	Per Cent. of 9 Errors	Gross	Per Cent. of 9 Errors	Gross	Per Cent. of 27 Errors	
1 day	0.7	7.8	0.4	4.4	1.9	21.1	3.0	11.1	21
4 days	0.9	10.0	0.4	4.4	2.9	32.2	4.2	15.5	100
7 days	1.3	14.4	0.4	4.4	3.7	41.1	5.4	20.0	40
14 days	1.8	20.0	0.6	6.7	2.8	31.1	5.2	19.3	55
21 days	1.6	17.8	0.7	7.7	3.1	34.4	5.4	20.0	92
28 days	1.9	21.1	1.3	14.4	2.9	32.2	6.1	22.6	40

ments one letter out of place was counted one error of order regardless of the number of letters between it and its proper locality.

Table VI. contains the data obtained by the method of reproduction. Table VII. consists of results of the methods of selection and of reconstruction. Table VII. was produced in one group of ex-

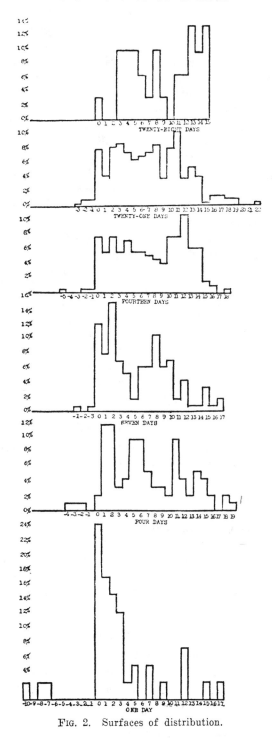

Fig. 2. Surfaces of distribution.

periments and is therefore not given as two separate tables. In both Tables VI. and VII. the total per cent. of errors is not, like the total gross errors, the sum of the errors in the three preceding columns; but it is the per cent. of the total twenty-seven errors that are possible in each experiment.

The errors of Table VI. increase rapidly during the first fourteen days. During the remainder of the twenty-eight days no additional errors are evident in the results. According to the method of reproduction, therefore, ⅓ of the gain is lost by the end of the first day, and ⅔ within 14 days. By the method of selection also the errors are found to increase rapidly for 14 days with few additional errors thereafter; but the errors of the insertion of letters increase rather gradually to the end of the period studied. Seven days is the limit of rapid forgetting according to the method of reconstruction. The loss of association strength after seven days is rather slow. The increase in errors of insertion is greater than in errors of omission, and in errors of order.

The surfaces of distribution (Fig. 2) were constructed from the errors in the method of reproduction and therefore correspond to Table VI. As the numbers of cases reported in connection with the six intervals are quite unequal, each surface is made on the basis of percentage of error. There would be no cases, of course, with less than zero errors, were it not that for unaccountable reasons, a few individuals made more errors at the close of practise than during the test. A large percentage of individuals made no errors when the interval was one day; and this percentage decreased with the lengthening of the interval, as shown by the mode that was at zero when the intervals were shortest, and that arose to the larger measures as the intervals lengthened. But there seems to be another mode that fluctuates somewhat within the range 8 to 12 errors, and has a tendency towards larger measures as the intervals lengthen. This indicates that the subjects who participated in these experiments may have belonged to two distinct groups. Most of the members of one group made from zero to 4 errors, and those of the other group from 8 to 12 errors when the delays are from 1 to 28 days. If under some circumstances the cause of one of these modes, and under other circumstances the cause of the other is dominant, considerable differences in the curve of forgetting, such as show themselves between the results of different investigators, might easily arise. Therefore I endeavored to find two or more causes of loss in association strength. The most profitable ones are two or more groups of reagents who do not react alike under a given set of conditions. The mode of reaction must necessarily be one that increases the number of errors of one of the types of observers and either leaves the errors of the other type unchanged, or decreases them, or increases them at a different rate. Even though all reagents had been instructed to practise no more after they were moderately sure that they had written all the letters in their correct order once, only 24 per cent. of them ceased at the stage of practise desired; whereas 39 per cent. exceeded this limit, on the average, by a little more than $1\frac{1}{2}$ repetitions, and the remaining 37 per cent. believed that they had reproduced the letters in their proper order before they had done so. The data of these three groups were made into separate tables and into corresponding surfaces of distribution with the hope of thus separating the two or more types that are responsible for the existence of more than one mode. But the general form of surfaces representing the segregated groups bore the bi-modal character of the composite surfaces.

Guided by numerous clues of the above type, a group of experiments was performed in order to discover the cause of this bi-modality. The observers were Normal School students, distributed by influences that had nothing to do with their individual abilities into three sections of a class in psychology. The method of experimentation was similar in many respects to that of the other group described in this chapter. Each paper was made to indicate whether the reagent was a man or a woman, white or colored, and in good, medium, or poor physical condition on each day of the experiments. The studies being pursued, and an accurate estimate of the average number of hours and fractions of hours per week spent in study were also reported. The interval was seven days in all experiments in this group. The reagents in section A were allowed to have the impression that the experiment was complete at the end of practise. Sections B and C were told that they would be required to reproduce the series later, and that they should therefore avoid discussing the experiment and should have a more interesting subject matter ready to absorb the attention whenever the series entered the mind. Section C was instructed to avoid the use of devices in learning. Section B was directed to use rhythm with three members of a series to the measure. No mention of devices was made to section A until practise had been completed. After practise and after recall, subjects of all sections recorded their introspections regarding the use of rhythm, association, and other aids.

Tables VIII. and IX. make possible a general comparison of sections A, B, and C. The expectation of the final test did not decrease the number of errors made by the members of section C, as they made a larger number of mistakes than the observers in section A, none of whom knew that this test was to be given. The difference between the results of these two sections may have been due, however, to the other differences in the method of conducting the experiment, the permission and prohibition of devices. There is evident a secondary mode in the neighborhood of 4 in the total distributions, and also in all partial distributions of sections *A*, *B*, and *C*, that deviate sufficiently from the primary mode near zero and one. The cause of the bimodality that we are studying in this group of experiments is not evident therefore, in any factor that is shown in Tables VIII. or IX.

TABLE VIII
CENTRAL TENDENCIES AND DEVIATIONS

	Omission			Insertion			Order			Totals		
	A	*B*	*C*	*A*	*B*	*C*	*A*	*B*	*C*	*A*	*B*	*C*
Averages	0.91	0.4	1.08	0.25	0.2	0.3	1.75	0.8	1.65	2.92	1.4	3.04
Medians	0.79	0.32	0.63	0.38	0.42	0.26	0.13	0.17	1.0	3.3	0.62	0.83
Modes	0	0	0–1	0	0	0	1.0	0	0	1.0?	0?	0–1?
Av. Dev.	0.94	0.59	0.81	0.44	0.35	0.42	2.02	0.96	1.49	1.79	1.65	2.4
Probable Errors										1.04	0.9	1.92

Both groups of experiments described in this chapter were performed during a prosperous industrial period. As is usual under such circumstances, fewer of the most capable young men were attracted to the schools in which preparation is made for the ill-paid vocation of the teacher. Consequently, in general, the women in the Indiana State Normal School were doing school work of a somewhat higher grade than was being done by the men. Men and women were, therefore, two groups that might forget at different rates. As

TABLE IX
THE SEXES AND FORGETTING

	Men		Women	
	No.	Errors	No.	Errors
Group *A*	3	6	29	93
Group *B*	2	7	13	14
Group *C*	2	7	21	63
	7	20	63	170
		Av. = 2.86		Av. = 2.89
				Dif. = 0.03

the larger number of errors would be expected to appear in the results of the students whose class grades were the lower, and as about one student among three was a man, it seemed probable that the men's errors constituted the secondary mode. However, as shown in Table IX., the women made nearly the same per cent. of errors as the men. Therefore the two modes are not due to the difference in sex.

There were not enough colored reagents to have as great an influence as was shown by the surfaces of distribution.

Sixty-nine per cent. of group *A* and 38 per cent. of group *C* used rhythm. Table X. shows that these observers retained 16.12 per cent. more of what they had learned than was retained by members of the same groups who did not use rhythm. Group *B*, all of whom used rhythm as directed, made 57.23 per cent. fewer errors than those who were able to avoid rhythm in group *C*. However, if these facts account in any measure for the bimodality that is found in the results of this chapter they can not be the sole cause; for the distribution of group *B*, in which all rhythmized, contains as much evidence of bimodality as that of groups *A* and C (Table VIII.). Rhythm reduced omissions about ⅔ in number, insertions ⅓ and errors of order ½. Therefore it prevents omissions especially and aids much in retaining the order of a series. It is possible that this would throw the errors into two groups.

TABLE X

THE USE OF RHYTHM

	Rhythm				No Rhythm			
	Omissions	Insertions	Order	Totals	Omissions	Insertions	Ordor	Totals
Group *A* ...	1.07	0.25	1.6	3.0	1.00	0.83	2.33	4.2
Group *B* ...	0.33	0.1	0.9	1.33				
Group *C* ...	0.93	0.33	1.93	3.13	1.33	0.22	1.56	3.11
A and *C* ...	2.00	0.58	3.53	6.13	2.33	1.05	3.89	7.31
Average	1.00	0.29	1.77	3.07	1.17	0.53	1.94	3.66
				Differences = .17	.24	.17	.59	

Gain through rhythm .... 16.12 per cent.

In order to find whether the two modes could be due to differences in sensory type, an effort was m/.de to determine in a general way whether the subjects were predominantly visual or auditory. Twenty numbers of three digits each were alternately either pronounced or exposed to their view. The period of presentation, which extended from the end of a pronunciation to the beginning of the next pronunciation or from the end of an exposure to the beginning of the next exposure were equalized by the means of a metronome. The observers were instructed to keep the sound of each spoken number in mind throughout its period and to look at each visible number during its entire period. Each period was four seconds in length. After the presentation of the whole series, all the numbers that could be remembered were written in one column. The number of members of the visual and of the auditory presentations that were written correctly determined the type. Only those whom the results designated as pronouncedly of the one type or of the other were included in Table XI. An inspection of the table will show that there is no relation between visualizers and audiles that indicates that either type learns much faster than the other. But when both avoid rhythm (sec. *C*) the visualizers forget 150 per cent. more than do the audiles. When both use rhythm (sec. *B*), the auditory type loses 350 per cent. more than the visualizers. These

TABLE XI

SENSORY TYPE

	No.	Auditory Errors	Av. Errors	No.	Visual Errors	Av. Errors
Group *A*	4	17	4.2	23	71	3.1
Group *B*	4	7	1.8	5	2	.4
Group *C*	6	12	2.0	7	36	5.1

reactions unite in the verdict that both are influenced by rhythm but that audiles depend more upon rhythm than do visualizers. This is in agreement with those theories of rhythm which assign a larger place to hearing than to sight as a means of acquisition of the rhythmic tendencies of consciousness. Table XII. shows the rela-

TABLE XII

RATE OF LEARNING

	Rapid No.	Errors	Av. Errors	Medium No.	Errors	Av. Errors	Slow No.	Errors	Av. Errors
Group *A*	20	58	2.6	7	24	3.4	5	17	3.4
Group *B*	7	3	0.4	4	2	0.5	4	16	4.0
Group *C*	9	27	3.0	7	23	3.3	6	19	3.2
	36	88		18	49		15	52	
		Average ..	2.44		Average ..	2.72		Average ..	3.47
		A.D.	1.7		A.D.	2.3		A.D.	2.0
		P.E.	.04		P.E.	1.7		P.E.	1.7

tions that were found between the rate of learning and the rate of forgetting. In collating this table, individuals were classed as slow, medium or fast on the basis of the repetitions that were necessary in learning a series. This classification corresponded quite closely with the time spent in the preparation of lessons and with my knowledge of the kind of work done by each student for other teachers as well as for myself.

The table shows that the rapidity of learning and the rapidity of forgetting were in inverse ratio with each other. The slow learners forgot 42.3 per cent. more during the seven days than the rapid learners. The average deviations and probable errors of the losses in association strength were much smaller in the case of the rapid learners than in case of the slow learners. Hence rapid learners are more alike in their manner of forgetting than are slow learners. This is no doubt due to the greater regularity and smaller number of wrong reactions which are the essentials of speed. All gained through the use of rhythm except the slow learners. However, two modes are evident in nearly all of these distributions.

By means of rhythmical repetition (sec. *B*), the rapid learners decrease their errors due to forgetting 87 per cent.; the medium learners also diminish their errors nearly 85 per cent.; but the slow learners lose 25 per cent. more. These variations do not make a gradual transition from large through medium to slight change in rate of forgetting; but we can state with some degree of assurance that rhythm aids rapid learners, and hinders slow ones.

There were differences in the rates of forgetting, however, between rhythmizers and non-rhythmizers, between audiles and visualizers, and between rapid and slow learners. Moreover, when visualizers and rapid learners used rhythm, there were decided diminutions in their errors; but when they avoided rhythm, they increased their errors; and when audiles used rhythm, there was also a slight falling off of errors; but when slow learners used rhythm, the errors were increased about $\frac{1}{3}$. According to these results the two groups of observers could be either rhythmizers and non-rhythmizers, or audiles and visualizers, or slow learners and rapid learners, were it not that in each case a secondary mode is apparent in the neighborhood of 4 errors. This appearance of a secondary mode whenever distributions extended from zero to 4, together with the appearance of a similar bimodality in the distribution of Ebbinghaus for 2 days, 6 days, and 31 days (see Table I.), and also my failure in grouping the measures so as to find the cause in too few measures, are indications of a difference in results that is worthy of further investigation.

CHAPTER V

FORGETTING OF SENSORI-MOTOR EXPERIENCES

IN previous groups of experiments the investigations have been made with simple subject matter. In one case, the series consisted of a single motor reaction repeated a number of times. In another case, the members of the series were varied. Throwing was chosen for the earliest investigation as representative of a usual type of simple manual skill. The aim of a second study was to find the rate, and the manner in which simple sensory subject matter that has no meaning to the learner establishes and loses association strength. In the experiments discussed in the present chapter, the reaction to be acquired is highly complex. An effort was made to combine in it as many as possible of the conditions essential to the delineation of the curve of forgetting and to the comparison of the methods of securing data to that end.

In order to learn and to forget in a thoroughly typical way, I endeavored to choose one of the common tasks of learning in which the reaction was clearly sensori-motor, with the intellectual element present and dominant in the early stages of learning but subordinate later. This kind of material seemed desirable because investigations have shown that in order to exemplify the most usual procedure in learning, the early stages should demand much more than the mere sensory and motor reactions. The later stages should progress most rapidly when thought is most actively supplying devices to abbreviate the acts, and to rectify errors. At last, the presence of a stimulus should result in motor response more readily without the intervention of thought than when thought is present. As most learning passes through these stages, numerous examples were at hand; but typewriting was believed to fulfill the requirements best owing to the fact that there are necessarily not only pairs of associates consisting of members of a copy as stimuli to be related to members of a keyboard, but also a consecutive series, each member of which is a pair of associates because the letters are combined as words and sentences and the position of each key becomes known through its direction and distance from every other key as used in a series. Owing to these complexities the learning of typewriting requires much intelligent guidance. It is typical of the most practical accomplishments of the pupil in school, such as penmanship, reading aloud, drawing, and the fundamental processes in numbers. The operation of a typewriter was therefore chosen as the subject matter of this group of experiments.

The typewriter was a Remington, No. 6, with the writing invisible. A screen was so placed as to conceal the keyboard from the reagent and thus to insure his confining himself to the so-called "touch method." On the screen at about reading distance from the reagent was placed a copy of the series to be learned. A paper in the machine preserved the evidences of the keys which had been struck. The subject sat in an office chair which could be adjusted to his most convenient height. A stop watch was used by the experimenter to measure the time required in writing the series. Whenever *B*, the writer, served as subject, it was necessary for him to perform the duties of experimenter also. The watch was then operated by means of the following device: A small wooden base was clamped near the edge of the top of the typewriter desk. Two metal brackets mounted on this base supported a seven inch wooden lever in such a way that it could be rotated about its middle point. Between one arm of the lever and the base, the watch was held on edge, with its stem in a small round depression in the lever, and the edge opposite the stem was fitted into an oblong depression in the base. A downward pull upon this arm of the lever started or stopped the second hand, or returned it to zero. This pull was made by the pressure of the foot upon a pedal. One end of this pedal was hinged to a foot stool, and the other end transmitted the downward motion to the arm of the lever by means of an ordinary bird-cage chain and spring. The spring was employed to lengthen the "life" of the stop-watch. When the pressure was released, the lever was restored to a horizontal position by the combined action of the spring in the stem of the watch and a small coil spring that drew the other arm of the lever towards the base.

Six reagents served in this group of experiments. All were graduate students in psychology except one. This one, *V*, was the only woman in the group. She was a junior in college, and had completed an introductory course in psychology. *B*'s purpose in serving as a reagent was primarily to gain first-hand critical knowledge of the methods. If *B*'s reactions had been perceptibly affected by knowledge of the experiment or by any anxiety when the method disclosed its weaknesses, his data would not have been included in the results. The absence of any indication of such influences signifies that the keeping of the observers in ignorance of their time records was a needless precaution. The writer, *B*, was one of the five who were beginning typewriting. *C* was the only subject who knew the arrangement of the keys on the keyboard before beginning the experiments. He had begun the third stage on a similar keyboard, the Oliver, but was quite out of practise. The others were prompted at first by a diagram of the keyboard, which was placed on the screen below the copy. After having located the desired letter on the diagram, there remained the difficulty of striking its key. As it was usually quicker and easier to recall the motor action associated with a letter than to find it, the diagram was used only when necessary.

During the first stage, each series consisted of seven letters of one bank of keys used in mixed order three times. These twenty-one letters were presented in typewritten form, and were separated by spaces into groups of three letters each. This grouping of the letters made the series easier to read. When the reagents became able to locate the keys readily they practised until groups of letters began to become units of reaction and then were initiated into experiments in the second stage. During this second stage of practise the subject matter of the series was a phrase of five words. These phrases were so selected as to present as equal degrees of difficulty as possible. At the beginning of each experimental period a record was made of the reagent's condition for work, and of what he had been doing before the experiment. Then owing to the fact that the mind requires time to adjust itself to an occupation, a rather difficult series was written three times as a warming-up exercise. Following this the series that was practised during the previous period, was tested by three repetitions. Finally the subject practised a new series thirty times. The manner of repeating each of these series was as follows: When the experimenter gave the signal, "Ready," the reagent placed his hands in any position of preparedness on the keyboard that he chose. He refrained from lowering his eyes to the copy, until the experimenter started the watch and at the same time signaled, "Begin." The reagent wrote the series once, and immediately after striking the last key said "Now"; whereupon the experimenter stopped the watch. A rest of thirty seconds then intervened during which the experimenter recorded the time, his observations, and the introspections of the reagent. The rest after every tenth repetition was lengthened to one minute to give an opportunity for the recording of more detailed introspections. On the completion of thirty repetitions, the experimenter induced the retrospection of the process as a whole by means of questions. An interval was allowed to elapse before the series practised was tested and a new series learned. The lengths of these intervals were 4, 7, 14, 21, 28 and 35 days. One hundred and twenty-four experiments were performed in this group. However not all results could be included in the tables owing to unusual conditions. Besides, reagent E left school before the experiments in Tables XVI. and XVII, were completed. As is usual in studies of forgetting, the curve is found in terms of the amount of gain that eventually has been lost through delay. The average time required in writing the series the first three times, minus the time consumed in writing it the last three times during practise, served as the measure of the gain. In like manner, the loss was found by subtracting the average of the three repetitions at the close of practise from the average of the test three given after the interval. Therefore the amount that was forgotten was equal to the loss divided by the gain.

TABLE XIII
First Stage in Typewriting
Seconds Gained through Practise and Lost through Forgetting

Reagents	M		P		E		B		V	
	Gains	Losses	Gains	Losses	Gains	Losses	Gains	Losses	Gains	Losses
1 day	27.3	3.9	26.3	3.1	18.3	.5	29.6	9.7	39.9	8.7
4 days ...	23.5	6.4	19.0	6.1	24.2	3.5	32.4	18.1	23.1	7.3
7 days ...	8.8	2.4	8.7	4.5	19.8	10.2	27.4	16.2	24.0	13.6
14 days ...	9.5	4.3	27.0	10.9	36.4	24.2	17.2	11.0	61.9	38.3
21 days ...	11.8	7.7	33.0	18.8	18.4	16.7	16.7	12.3	26.6	18.9
28 days ...	7.2	4.5	8.6	5.5	5.9	5.3	39.3	27.7	6.0	4.8
35 days ...	5.7	4.9			21.7	15.3	40.4	39.8		

TABLE XIV
First Stage in Typewriting
Per Cent. Forgotten

Reagents	M	P	E	B	V	Average
1 day	14.3	11.8	2.7	32.8	21.8	16.7
4 days	27.2	32.1	14.5	55.9	31.6	32.3
7 days	27.3	51.7	51.5	59.1	56.7	49.3
14 days	45.1	40.4	66.2	63.9	61.8	55.5
21 days	65.2	56.9	90.7	73.7	71.1	71.5
28 days	62.5	63.9	89.8	70.5	80.0	73.3
35 days	85.9		70.5	98.5		84.9

The results of practise on the typewriter previous to the stage in which words begin to act as wholes are the subject matter of Tables XIII., XIV., and XV. These tables show that the amount forgotten was, during the first day more than $\frac{1}{5}$, by the end of 4 days nearly $\frac{1}{3}$, during 7 days $\frac{1}{2}$, and during the entire period, 35 days, more than $\frac{3}{4}$. However, there was little loss after the 21st day; for $\frac{1}{2}$ of it took place within the first 5 days. Nearly $\frac{1}{2}$ of the loss of the first week had taken place by the close of the first day. As observer

TABLE XV

C's Results

	Gain	Loss	Per Cent. Forgotten
1 day	13.0	2.3	17.7
4 days	16.6	4.1	25.3
7 days	13.1	3.8	29.0
14 days	86.3	38.7	44.8
21 days	12.0	6.3	52.5
28 days	11.5	5.8	50.4
35 days	24.3	13.6	55.9

C had reached the expert stage in typewriting at a previous time; but was out of practise when he began to serve in these experiments, and as the other observers were all beginners, his results were collated in Table XV. His losses were, during the first day less than $\frac{1}{5}$, during the first 4 days $\frac{1}{4}$, during the first 21 days $\frac{1}{2}$, and during the 35 days, $\frac{3}{5}$. It is evident that only $\frac{1}{10}$ was forgotten during the last two weeks of the period that was studied. *C* wrote as slowly as the others during the early experiments and made as large gains but smaller losses. His general progress, therefore, was much more rapid than that of the beginners until he approached the fastest speed that he had ever attained. Both his gross gains and losses then became small; but the per cent. of his losses throughout the period averaged about $\frac{3}{4}$ of that of the beginners. The results of the writer, *B*, were allowed to be a part of Tables XIII. and XIV. because they showed no advantages or disadvantages arising from his more intimate knowledge of the purpose and plan of the experiments and of his own time record and errors.

TABLE XVI

Second Stage in Typewriting

Seconds Gained through Practise and Lost through Forgetting

Reagents	M		P		B		V	
	Gains	Losses	Gains	Losses	Gains	Losses	Gains	Losses
7 days	19.8	7.9	27.8	5.8	14.9	5.6	16.5	3.8
14 days	9.1	6.2	19.1	11.2	17.2	7.6	7.7	5.9
21 days	11.8	9.9			14.1	10.3	26.6	18.9
28 days					19.6	18.7		

TABLE XVII

Second Stage in Typewriting

Reagents	Per Cent. Forgotten				
	M	P	B	V	Averages
7 days	39.9	20.9	37.2	23.6	30.4
14 days	68.1	58.6	44.2	76.6	61.9
21 days	83.9		73.0	71.1	76.0
28 days			94.5		94.5

TABLE XVIII

SECOND STAGE. C'S RESULTS

	Gains	Losses	Per Cent. Forgotten
7 days	19	— 4	—21.1
14 days	11.5	6	52.2
21 days	50.5	12	23.7
28 days	92	—20	—21.7

Tables XVI., XVII., and XVIII. are composed of the results obtained after it had become no longer necessary to think separately of each letter and its corresponding key; and when words began to serve as units in this period the progress in learning was slower than in the previous period, and the rate of forgetting was even slower. The amount lost was, during the first 7 days almost $\frac{1}{3}$, during the first 14 days $\frac{2}{3}$, and during the first 21 days more than $\frac{3}{4}$. Nearly all that had been learned was forgotten by the end of 28 days. As shown in Table XVIII., by the time the beginners were in this stage of typewriting, C was no longer making definite losses within intervals as short as those which we have been studying.

TABLE XIX

SECOND STAGE. FEW REPETITIONS IN PRACTISE

Intervals	Gross Gain	Gross Loss	Per Cent. Forgotten
5 minutes	141	25	18.4
20 minutes	140	48	35.3
60 minutes	141	77	54.6

In Table XIX. are presented the results of experiments like those in Tables XVI. to XVIII. except that the sentences were practised twenty times instead of thirty. B was the only subject. Four sentences were tested after five minutes and showed a loss of one fifth of what had been gained. Four were allowed an interval of twenty minutes with a loss of one third. Finally four sentences were tested sixty minutes after the end of practise, and resulted in the forgetting of two thirds of what had been learned. Therefore Table XIX. shows greater losses during the first 20 minutes and almost as great losses during 60 minutes as took place according to Table XVII. in the first 7 days and the first 14 days. It is clear then that if subject matter of this kind is well memorized the losses are much slower than when the association links are not so thoroughly established; but that the last part of the curve rises more slowly with twenty repetitions than with thirty repetitions.

The time of writing a series was often decreased at the expense of accuracy. On the other hand, in the effort to avoid all inaccuracies the subjects purposely diminished the speed in parts of the series where mistakes could be avoided without especial care. In these cases the least suggestion of carefulness, such as was brought about by the discovery of an error in previous work, resulted in slower time on the next trial. In other words, when attention was focused on accuracy, the time was lengthened and rendered much more variable than when exactness was subordinated to speed. It seems expedient, for these reasons, for the reagents to exert themselves chiefly for rapidity, and at the same time, to endeavor to give accuracy as close a second place in consciousness as possible. In practise every error of order was accompanied, on an average, by 7 errors of omission and 9 errors of insertion. Practise reduced these omissions 49 per cent., the insertions 73 per cent., and the mistakes of order 50 per cent. during the first stage of practise. The average amount of this reduction of errors that reappeared owing to delays in recall was in the cases of omissions 26.3 per cent., of insertions 2 per cent., and of errors of order 88 per cent. It is evident that although the insertions were more numerous than the two other types of error, their number was reduced more rapidly by practise and was much more slowly increased by subsequent delay. Practise had almost equal effect upon omissions and cases of wrong order; but forgetting increased errors of order more than three times as fast as errors of omission. Hence, errors of order, although much less frequent than the other two types were the most difficult to get rid of by means of practise. This statement is also supported by the fact that *C*, who was in the third stage of typewriting, made relatively more mistakes of order than were made by other subjects.

The method which has been employed in the preceding experiments can be called a method of reproduction, as contrasted with the saving or relearning method of Ebbinghaus. As it has been employed in this chapter, the method of reproduction consists in first determining the gain in a certain associative performance due to a specified amount of practise, and then determining the loss of proficiency that results from a given interval of no practise. The loss divided by the preceding gain shows what proportion of the gain due to practise has been lost in a period of no practise, and therefore may properly be regarded as a measure of the amount forgotten. The results of this method are in general agreement with the familiar results of the saving method, but seem to be subject to more variation. It was now desired to institute a direct comparison between the two methods, with a view to ascertaining which gave the more regular and reliable results.

With this in view, an experiment was conducted in which both the method of reproduction, as above described, and the method of relearning, were employed together. The performance studied was, as before, typewriting; and, as before, the experiment began with a specified amount of practise, which was followed by an interval of no practise. After this interval, still as before, a test was conducted to determine how much of the gain through practise had been lost in the interval; but now this test was followed by a new period of practise, continued until the former high point of practise was again reached. The time required to relearn the performance and regain the former proficiency could be compared with the time required to reach this proficiency in the first period of practise.

The subject matter of each experiment consisted of a couplet from Longfellow's "Evangeline." As great care as possible was exercised in the selection of couplets that were equally easy to write on the typewriter. The subjects were two normal school students. Both were men whose age and degree of maturity was about the same as that of college juniors. As previous experiments have not given evidence in favor of keeping the observer ignorant of his errors and his time, and as the group of experiments was necessarily too brief for much to be accomplished in the touch method of typewriting, the writing and the keys were allowed to be visible, and the observer started and stopped the watch and reported the time. Nevertheless, all this work was done under close supervision. Before practise and before the final test, the alphabet was written twice as a warming-up exercise. The couplet was practised thirty minutes.

TABLE XX

METHOD OF REPRODUCTION

Seven Days Interval

Experiment		First	Last	1st Test	Gain	Per Cent. Gain	Loss	Per Cent. Loss		
H	III.	3.08	2.8	4.67	1.00	32.5	2.59	259.00		
	IV.	3.00	1.75	3.00	1.25	41.7	1.25	100.00	H's Av. .	140.0
	V.	3.92	2.00	3.17	1.92	38.40	1.17	60.9	G's Av. .	63.4
G	I.	16.00	7.00	13.50	9.00	56.2	6.50	72.2	Total Av.	101.7
	V.	2.91	1.87	2.83	1.05	36.1	0.96	91.4	A.D.	51.6
	VI.	13.50	6.00	8.00	7.50	55.6	2.00	26.7	P.E.	17.3

An interval of one half minute followed each repetition as a rest, and as an opportunity to record the time and to report introspections. Each series was relearned to its former degree of proficiency either seven days or fourteen days after it had been first learned. The time required to write the couplet the first time and the last time in practise and also the first time in the relearning of it were used as the means of determining the gain and the loss, by the method of reproduction. These results are found in Tables XX. and XXI.

TABLE XXI

METHOD OF REPRODUCTION

Fourteen Days Interval

Experiment		First	Last	1st Test	Gain	Per Cent. Gain	Loss	Per Cent. Loss		
H	I.	20.00	8.00	10.08	12.00	60.0	2.08	17.3	Total Av.	31.4
G	IV.	4.00	2.00	2.91	2.00	50.0	0.91	45.5	A.D.	14.1
									P.E.	8.5

The number of repetitions in learning and in relearning were the data of the relearning method, and were used in constructing Tables XXII. and XXIII.

TABLE XXII

METHOD OF RELEARNING

Seven Days Interval

Experiment		Repetitions in Learning	Repetitions in Relearning	Per Cent. Necessary in Relearning		
H	III.	13	4	30.8		
	IV.	13	5	38.5	H's Av. ..	39.8
	V.	4	2	50.0	G's Av. ..	44.8
G	I.	4	2	50.0	Total Av.	42.3
	V.	9	4	44.4	A.D.	5.8
	VI.	5	2	40.0	P.E.	2.0

TABLE XXIII

METHOD OF RELEARNING

Fourteen Days Interval

Experiment		Repetitions in Learning	Repetitions in Relearning	Per Cent Necessary in Relearning		
H	I.	3	2	66.7	Av.	66.7
G	IV.	6	4	66.7	A.D.	0

The tables show that according to the method of relearning the losses of the two reagents are almost equal. The average deviations and probable errors in Tables XXII. and XXIII. are such as would indicate relative freedom from erroneous measures. The average losses of both reagents are according to the method of reproduction greater in 7 days than in 14 days. Besides, *H*'s average per cent. in the 7 days according to the table of reproduction is 2.3 times *G*'s average; but according to the table of relearning the two averages are almost equal. In the reproduction table for 14 days, *G*'s average per cent. is nearly three times that of *H*. But in the corresponding table of relearning the per cents lost are exactly equal. In Tables XX. and XXI. the average deviations are about half as large as their respective averages and the probable error in Table XX. is ¼ as great as its average. On the other hand in Table XXII. the average is more than seven times as large as the average deviation and more than ten times as large as the probable error, and in Table XXIII. the average deviation is zero. There is no doubt, therefore, of the superiority of the results in the tables of measurements by re-learning to the tables of measurements by reproduction. However, differences between reproduction and relearning are not much greater in these tables than might be expected, in view of the fact that only one measure, instead of the average of three measures, as elsewhere in the chapter, was the basis of the calculations of gain and of loss in reproduction. The method of reproduction is subject to large chance errors in the single measurement.

The results of this chapter may be summarized as follows: The curve of forgetting has been determined for the complex associative performance of typewriting a specified list of letters or of words. This curve has been found to have the same general character as that familiar from the work of Ebbinghaus on much simpler perform-ances; the similarity consists in a more rapid rate of forgetting soon after cessation of the learning than later. But the actual rate of for-getting has been found to depend very largely on the amount of learning preceding the period of forgetting. When the amount of learning is small, the forgetting is at first rapid, but when the amount of learning is greater the forgetting starts at a much slower pace than is shown in the Ebbinghaus curve. In the latter case, the rate of forgetting is not excessively rapid at first, and, though it de-creases, it decreases more slowly than in the usual curve.

CHAPTER VI

Discussion of Results and General Conclusions

It will be remembered that this investigation is (1) a further study of the curve of forgetting as to its form and as to the rate of loss in association strength after practise has ceased, and (2) a search for reasons for the dissimilarities in the curves already found.

The curves that have been obtained by others in the more extensive investigations of forgetting are shown in dotted lines in Fig. 3. The curve of Ebbinghaus for nonsense syllables rises with great rapidity during the first day, undergoes a marked decline in rate during the following five days, and ascends slowly during the remaining 25 days. Radossawljewitsch's curve for the same kind of material makes its rapid ascent within the first two days. The change to slower rates of loss is somewhat more gradual than that of Ebbinghaus; but the latter portion of the curve shows a more rapid rate of forgetting than was found by Ebbinghaus. My curves for meaningless subject matter indicate that association strength decreases remarkably during the first day. Almost all of the loss that is shown by the curve which was determined by the method of selection had taken place by the end of the first week. The curve found by the method of reproduction rises very little after the second week. Radossawljewitsch's curve for the forgetting of matter with meaning does not differ greatly from his curve for meaningless subject matter except that it is much more irregular and therefore more difficult to interpret. His curve for material with meaning is slower than his other curve until the end of the third day, and indeed it indicates less decline in the ability to learn after an interval of a month. My curves for typewriting show a great loss of association strength during the first week and a gradual falling off in the amounts forgotten during the remainder of the month. This diminution in the amount forgotten is not so evident in the curve of the second stage as in that of the first stage of typewriting. Observer C, who had once attained considerable ability in typewriting but was out of practise when he began to serve as subject, produced a curve that rises rather rapidly during the first day, at a gradually decreasing rate to twenty-one days, and slowly thereafter. In his second stage his curve, if it were delineated, would be so irregular that it would give no evidence either of gain or of loss. It is evi-

40

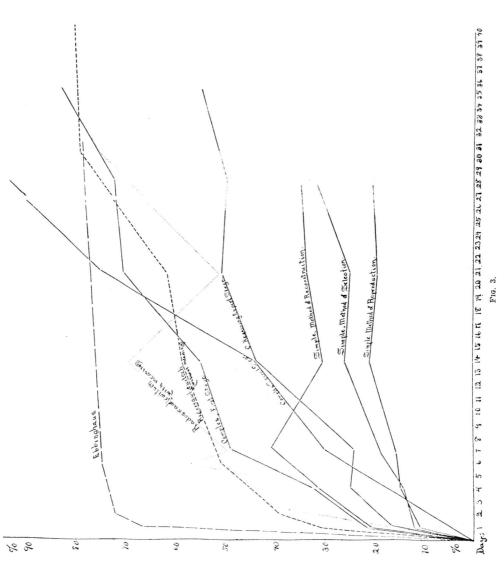

Fig. 3.

dent that to a considerable extent the form of the curve of forgetting resembles that of the curve of learning. However, the forgetting curve for nonsense syllables has a more abrupt change from its rapid rise than is found in memory curves. This short turn in the curve is probably due to the primary dependence of the memory of meaningless subject matter upon the innate retentiveness of the brain centers that are immediately involved; and, owing to the poverty of meaning, it is dependent only in a secondary way upon the few indefinite interactions that can be set up with other centers. These are such trivial relations that they rapidly decline, and after a remarkably short period, the slowly fading impressions of the other sort are all that remain.

The curve of forgetting may be studied (1) as to its general form; and (2) as to the absolute rate of forgetting. Suppose the general form of the curve to be constant, and to have the roughly "logarithmic" character signalized by Ebbinghaus—a form indicating that the rate of forgetting is most rapid at first and becomes slower and slower—and suppose further that the absolute rate of forgetting varies with conditions. Then it is clear that a rapid absolute rate of forgetting would make the rise of the curve very steep at first, and would lead to an apparently abrupt transition from this rapid forgetting to the slower forgetting that ensues. On the other hand, a slow absolute rate of forgetting would cause the initial rise of the curve to be less steep and the transition from this to the ensuing portion of the curve less abrupt. But such changes leave the general character of the curve unchanged; they affect only a certain "parameter" of the curve, and could be obliterated, in the graphic representation of the facts, by simply altering the horizontal scale of the graph, making this scale proportional to the absolute rate of forgetting. Reducing the horizontal scale would change a slowly rising curve, with a gradual transition from the initial to the later phase, into a rapidly rising curve with an abrupt transition from the initial to the later phase.

Inspection of the various curves in Fig. 3 shows that the differences between them are approximately of the sort just described. They differ in the absolute rate of forgetting, but not in the general character of the curve. All belong approximately to the logarithmic type. The results of the present study have not brought to light any curve of forgetting of a definitely different type. Such divergences as have appeared are probably to be considered as accidental variations. Much the same can be said of the divergences from the logarithmic type of curve which are emphasized by Radossawljewitsch[9]

[9] *Op. cit.*

in particular the apparent recovery between 8 and 24 hours. He found that less was forgotten in 24 hours than in 8 hours—or, at least, that the saving in relearning was greater after 24 than after 8 hours. This may reasonably be attributed to the fact that the 8-hour interval brought the relearning into an unfavorable time of the day, while the 24-hour interval allowed sleep to intervene and brought the time of relearning back to the original hour of the day, with all conditions, external and internal, most nearly identical with those of the first learning.

In brief, a survey of previous results as well as of the results of the present study gives no warrant for altering the general character of the Ebbinghaus curve of forgetting, nor for introducing any other general type of curve alongside of that.

But as regards the absolute rate of forgetting, the literature of the question, as well as the experiments herein reported, gives abundant evidence that this is a variable quantity. The rate of forgetting depends on the following factors:

1. It depends on the degree to which the material has been learned before the commencement of the period of forgetting. This was already indicated in the original experiments of Ebbinghaus, since he found that any study of the material beyond the point necessary for one correct reproduction made it easier to relearn the material later, or, in other words, diminish the degree of forgetting after a given interval. The rate of forgetting was slower when "over-learning" had occurred than when the study had been barely sufficient to reach the standard of one correct recitation. It is probable that the slow rate of forgetting found by Radossawljewitsch was the result of his requiring such an amount of study as would make possible *two* correct recitations in succession, instead of only one; for this author found that the amount of study needed for two correct recitations was often considerably more than that required for one correct recitation. It is likely that others of the discrepant results in the literature, in regard to the rate of forgetting, depend on this matter of overlearning.

In one of the experiments of Chapter V., a direct comparison is instituted between the rates of forgetting when preceded by different amounts of learning. When the subject of this experiment practised a list of words on the typewriter 30 times, he forgot, after 7 days 37.2 per cent., after 14 days 44.2 per cent., after 21 days 73.0 per cent., after 28 days 94.5 per cent. But when the initial learning was limited to 20 repetitions, he forgot 18.4 per cent. in 5 minutes, 35.3 per cent. in 20 minutes, and 54.6 per cent. in 60 minutes. The curves of forgetting in the two cases have the same general form, but the absolute rate of forgetting is much more rapid after the smaller amount of practise.

A method developed in this same chapter, though not employed specifically for the problem now under discussion, seems specially adapted to its study, in that it permits of a measure of the amount of "overlearning" in terms of proficiency acquired instead of simply in terms of the number of repetitions. The proficiency being measured by the speed of performance, the subject practises a given performance till he reaches a certain degree of proficiency, and then, after an interval of forgetting, practises again, or relearns, till he reaches the same degree of proficiency as before. In different experiments, the degree of proficiency to be attained can be varied, and the curve of forgetting thus traced from different starting points. Though the test has not been made with exactly this method, the probability is, from the results at hand by a slightly different method, that the curves of forgetting would have the same general form from whatever level of proficiency they start, but that the rate of forgetting would become slower and slower as the initial level of proficiency was raised. Book,[10] it will be recalled, after attaining a considerable degree of proficiency in the use of the typewriter, interrupted practise for a year, and then found but a few minutes fresh practise needed to reach his former level. The saving method of computation here indicates a forgetting of less than 1 per cent. in a year.

2. The rate of forgetting probably depends on the distribution or concentration of the process of learning. This is indicated by results of Ebbinghaus, Jost and others. When the practise leading to a certain degree of proficiency has been distributed over several days, the rate of forgetting is slower than when the practise has been concentrated in time, though the proficiency reached be the same in the two cases.

3. The rate of forgetting varies with the performance or material learned. It is slower for meaningful than for nonsense material. Aside from meaning in the intellectual sense, it is probable that other differences in the kind of performance affect the rate of forgetting. Thus skill in throwing at a target (Chapter III. above), though slowly acquired, was slowly forgotten—almost too slowly to furnish the basis for a study of the curve of forgetting. Again, in the typewriting experiments (Chapter V.), though the number of repetitions constituting the first learning of a performance was not greater than is often necessary in learning a list of nonsense syl-

[10] "The Psychology of Skill," p. 76.

lables, yet the rate of forgetting of the typewriting act was notice-
ably slow. Such performances as typewriting or throwing at a
target differ from the recitation of lists of nonsense syllables in pos-
sessing a sort of motor meaning or significance. They do not appear,
introspectively, as meaningless performances, but seem to accomplish something, and it is possible that this practical meaning is like
meaning of the more intellectual sort in favoring the retention of
what has been learned.

4. The rate of forgetting varies according to the method by
which it is measured. Different rates are to be expected according
as retention is measured by power of reproduction or by time of relearning. The results in Chapter V. would indicate, though not very
reliably, that the rate of forgetting is more rapid when measured in
terms of reproduction than in terms of relearning. Reproduction
seems certainly the more direct test of the present strength of old
associations, and relearning measures, rather the effect of fresh
study upon the old associations; but the method of reproduction is
the more subject to accidental error.

The method of reproduction gives different results according as
time or accuracy is the criterion; and if accuracy is the criterion,
the rate of forgetting comes out differently according to the kind of
errors that are counted. If omissions are counted, forgetting appears to occur more rapidly than when insertions are counted. Insertions, the easiest errors to eliminate through practise, are the
slowest to reappear during the intermission of practise. Errors of
order are rather difficult to eliminate, and quickly reappear after
intermission of practise. It is clear that these divergences of result,
according to the unit of measurement, are not simply indications of
unreliability in the methods, but are evidences that any statement
of the rate of forgetting, without specification of the kind of loss,
have little if any meaning. Measurements in terms of time have
usually been treated as if free from such limitations; but this is not
justified unless there is constancy in all these other respects.

Further, the rate of forgetting comes out differently according
to the manner of recall adopted in the test for power of reproduction (Chapter IV.). This is by reason of the fact that one form of
recall makes use of one kind of elements of the past experience, and
another form of recall another kind of elements. When the method
of reconstruction is employed, the subject can neglect all phases of
the past experience except the original order of the members of the
series. The method of selection or recognition tests only the ability to
recognize the former experiences when they are again presented.
The reproduction of the whole series in proper order would seem to

make the greatest demands upon the associations and to be the most complete method. But the curve of forgetting can properly be measured by any of these methods, and the curve, or at least the rate of forgetting, differs with the method. Order is forgotten with great rapidity at first and much less rapidly later. The ability to recognize is lost rather gradually. The ability to reproduce is lost rather rapidly at first, and the transition to the period of slow forgetting is sometimes gradual and sometimes abrupt.

5. The rate of forgetting shows individual differences in retentiveness. The present study has not revealed any sex difference in this respect. It appears, from the work of earlier investigators, that the rate of forgetting depends on age. Probably, the other factors concerned in forgetting being equal, young children forget more rapidly than adults.

THE FACTORS AFFECTING A PERMANENT IMPRESSION DEVELOPED THROUGH REPETITION

BY EDWARD K. STRONG, JR.

George Peabody College for Teachers

One of the most interesting psychological problems now confronting us is that concerned with the distribution of intervals of time between working periods. It is now recognized in certain industries that a man can do more work with less, fatigue by working in spurts and then resting than by working at a slower but steady pace. Neither the psychologist nor the physiologist has had much to do with these industrial adaptations. But both knew enough in an academic way to have made some valuable prophecies in days gone by. Today both should strive for a clearer and better understanding of the principles underlying these problems, as through such knowledge should come many valuable contributions to industry, as well as to education.

The application to education looms much more important when we substitute the term 'presentation of stimuli' for 'working-period.' The whole problem of one-hour versus five-hour courses comes then under this heading. Likewise the problem of how long classes should be held is included here. And then again the manner of presentation of a subject is involved: Should a topic be taken up and finished and then another similarly treated, or should they be unfolded little by little over a considerable lapse of time. Many other such topics will occur to the reader, all of which hinge on this general subject of how stimulations can be best distributed so as to bring about the greatest permanent effect.

There are at least two general methods of approach to this field of investigation. We may first take up and study one factor, such as the interval between stimulations, and vary it alone while keeping all the other factors constant. This method undoubtedly gives us the most detailed information as to the value of the particular factor under study, but it often leads us to manufacture total situations far from what we should meet in every day life. And then when we have in this way discovered how each factor operates, this method will in all probability require further experimentation to discover how two or more factors will behave when united together. Over against this method is the second one where combinations of various factors as we find them in life are studied. Here we may discover just how the several factors may operate together but we may not be able to discover the laws of behavior of each one separately.

The writer believes both these lines of attack are needed. For that reason the experiment reported in the *Psychological Review* of March, 1914,[1] in which advertisements were shown at intervals of one month, has been repeated. In the new experiments different intervals of time between successive presentations have been employed. A number of interesting relations have been found through a comparison of the various details of the experiments. The writer believes that many more such relations are still to be discovered, possibly from the data now on hand, but more likely after more such experiments have been run.

THE EXPERIMENT

The same set of advertisements was used here as in the experiment reported in the *Psychological Review* of March, 1914. (For a detailed description of the set see that article.) The 288 advertisements were so arranged in four groups (dummy magazines) that we had some firms advertising once, some twice, and some four times. And moreover, we had the firms divided so that an equal number used respectively quarter-page advertisements, half-page advertisements, and one-page advertisements.

[1] E. K. Strong, Jr., 'The Effect of Size of Advertisements and Frequency of their Presentation,' *Psychol. Rev.*, 21, March, 1914.

Comparisons can consequently be made between any of the following propositions:

Firms using full pages and advertising 4 times
"   "   "   "   2   "
"   "   "   "   1 time
"   "   half pages   "   4 times
"   "   "   "   2   "
"   "   "   "   1 time
"   " quarter pages   "   4 times
"   "   "   "   2   "
"   "   "   "   1 time

In these experiments the sheets, on which all the advertisements were pasted, were given to the persons being tested and they were instructed to look them through at their leisure. It was suggested that they look them through in the same way that they turn the pages of an advertising section of any magazine, looking at what interested them and ignoring the rest. In each case they were timed by a stop-watch.

In what will be referred to as Experiment I. the four dummy magazines were looked through by the subjects at their leisure, *all at the same sitting.* Four weeks later they were tested by the recognition method as to what firms they had seen in the four dummy magazines.

Experiment II. differs from the above in that an interval of *one day* occurred between the perusal of each of the four dummy magazines. The test followed here also four weeks after the first set of advertisements was seen.

Experiment III. differs from Experiment II. in that an interval of *one week* intervened between each set of advertisements instead of one day.

Experiment IV. differs from the above (1) in that the interval of time between the four dummy magazines was *one month*, and (2) in that the *test occurred sixteen weeks* after the first set was seen. This is the experiment reported in the March, 1914, *Psychological Review.*

The number of individuals who served as subjects in these four experiments was as follows:

Experiment I.   6 men and 12 women, or a total of 18
    "   II.   10   "   15   "   "   25
    "   III.   12   "   10   "   "   22
    "   IV.   10   "   11   "   "   21

(As there were 24 firms which advertised once in ¼-page, ½-page, and 1-page space, and 12 firms which advertised twice and 12 firms which advertised four times in each of these sized advertisements, the probable errors are determined on the basis of from 12 × 18 cases (the minimum) to 24 × 25 cases (the maximum). Such a large number of cases gives us very low probable errors, already indicated in the March, 1914, article. It has not seemed worth while to report the probable errors of Experiments I., II., and III. for this reason.)

Results

1. *The Results from Experiments I., II., III., and IV*

Table I. gives us the results from the first three experiments. They are also presented in Plate I., where the data for the three different sized advertisements are averaged together. The results show very clearly that an interval of one week between the successive presentations of a firm's advertisements gives a greater permanent impression at the end of the month than if the advertisements are seen on successive days at the commencement of the month, of if they are seen all at the same sitting.

At least four factors enter into this final determination. First, the length of time between seeing a particular advertisement and the day of the test. Second, the interval of time between the successive exposures, already pointed out. Third, the total number of advertisements seen at one time (42 pages of advertising seen at one time in Experiments II., III., and IV. and 168 pages in Experiment I.). And fourth, the effect of the size of the advertisement. Each of these factors will be discussed presently, but it is well to have them in mind in considering the gross results of these experiments.

In order now to compare the data in Table I., where the

TABLE I

SHOWING THE PER CENT. OF FIRMS REMEMBERED PER READER FOR EACH OF THE
NINE COMBINATIONS OF SPACE AND FREQUENCY

Test made four weeks after first dummy magazine was seen.

1. *When the 4 Dummy Magazines Were Seen One Right After the Other*
(*Experiment I.*)

Frequency	Size of Ads.			Av. 3 Sizes
	¼ Page	½ Page	1 Page	
1 time.................	3.4	5.0	10.1	6.2
2 times.................	4.6	8.2	15.9	9.6
4 times.................	4.8	12.4	16.6	11.3

2. *When the 4 Dummy Magazines Were Seen 1 Day Apart*
(*Experiment II.*)

Frequency	Size of Ads.			Av. 3 Sizes
	¼ Page	½ Page	1 Page	
1 time.................	4.5	8.5	13.2	9.4
2 times.................	8.0	11.6	20.7	13.4
3 times.................	12.5	15.6	20.4	16.2

3. *When the 4 Dummy Magazines Were Seen 1 Week Apart*
(*Experiment III.*)

Frequency	Size of Ads.			Av. 3 Sizes
	¼ Page	½ Page	1 Page	
1 time.................	3.7	9.8	19.9	11.1
2 times.................	9.0	13.7	23.9	15.5
3 times.................	10.5	26.8	29.2	22.2

test followed one month after the first advertisements were
seen, with the data from Experiment IV., where the test
followed four months after the first advertisements were seen,
it is necessary to make allowance for the amount that would
be normally forgotten in the interval between one month and
four months. A separate series of three experiments were run
for that purpose and the results are shown in Table II.

TABLE II

SHOWING THE EFFECT OF TIME UPON REMEMBERING ADVERTISEMENTS

The average firm was remembered immediately after by 50.5 per cent. of the readers.
"   "   "   "   "   one month after by 14.9 per cent. "   "   "
"   "   "   "   "   four months after by 8.6 per cent. "   "   "

Evidently, then, in the interval between one month and four months there has been a decrease in memory from 14.9 per cent. to 8.6 per cent. Expressed in a ratio the relative amounts remembered after one month and four months are 100: 58.

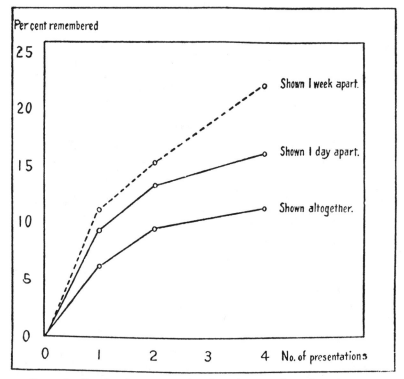

PLATE I. Showing the per cent. of readers who remember a firm when one, two, and four advertisements are shown (1) altogether, (2) at intervals of 1 day, and (3) at intervals of 1 week: the test following 4 weeks after the first set was seen.

When the averages of the data in Table I. have been multiplied by this decimal (0.58) we have the figures as given in the first column of Table III.

This decimal (0.58) is apparently a trifle too high, for when the value of one presentation in Experiment III. as given in Table I. is multiplied by it, we get a value of 6.4. Now, if anything, this value in Experiment III. should be slightly less than that in Experiment IV. (*i. e.*, 6.1 per cent.).

In the former there were 15 concerns whose advertisements appeared only once, say on January 1, 21 other concerns whose advertisements appeared on January 8, 15 more on January 15, and 21 more on January 22. The lengths of time between

TABLE III

SHOWING THE PER CENT. OF FIRMS REMEMBERED PER READER FOR EACH OF THE NINE COMBINATIONS OF SPACE AND FREQUENCY

Test made 16 weeks after first dummy magazine was seen. (Data in Experiments I., II., and III. taken from Table I. and multiplied by the decimals 0.58, 0.47, or an average of the two.)

	Times Ads. Were Seen	Correction Decimals			Ratios
		× 0.58	× 0.47	Av. of Two	
1. When the four dummy magazines were seen one right after the other...	1	3.6	3.0	3.3	1.00
	2	5.6	4.7	5.2	1.58
	4	6.5	5.4	6.0	1.82
2. When the four dummy magazines were seen 1 day apart..	1	5.1	4.6	4.9	1.00
	2	7.8	6.6	7.2	1.47
	4	9.4	7.9	8.7	1.78
3. When the four dummy magazines were seen 1 week apart.	1	6.4	5.4	5.9	1.00
	2	9.0	7.3	8.2	1.39
	4	12.8	10.9	11.9	2.02

No correction decimal, data actually obtained with 16 week interval.

4. When the four dummy magazines were seen 1 month apart	1	6.1	6.1	6.1	1.00
	2	7.3	7.3	7.3	1.20
	4	9.2	9.2	9.2	1.51

seeing the advertisements and the test for these four groups were then, respectively, 16 weeks, 15 weeks, 14 weeks, and 13 weeks. Now in the latter the four groups were shown on January 1, January 29, February 26, and March 26. And the lengths of time between seeing the advertisements and the test for these groups were, respectively, 16 weeks, 12 weeks, 8 weeks, and 4 weeks. No other factor, besides this one of difference in interval of time, enters into the two experiments. Hence the figure in Experiment IV. should be higher than that in Experiment III. for concerns showing one advertisement, because there was a shorter interval of time on the average between the exposure and the test in Experiment IV. than in Experiment III. The average length of time between exposure and test per advertisement in the former was 9.7 weeks, while in the latter it was 14.4 weeks. Interpolating from our data in Table II. we should expect, if we express the percentage remembered in Experiment IV. as 100, that the percentage remembered in Experiment III. would be 88. This would mean that one presentation in Experiment III. should have a value of 5.4 (6.1 × 0.88) instead of 6.4.

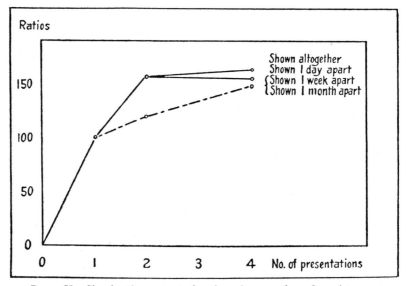

PLATE II. Showing the per cent. of readers who remember a firm when one, two, and four advertisements are shown (1) altogether, (2) at intervals of 1 day, (3) at intervals of 1 week, and (4) at intervals of 1 month: the test following 16 weeks after the first set was seen.

If 5.4 is the correct value then our correction decimal should not be 0.58 but rather 0.47. The latter decimal would give us the figures in the second column of Table III.

An average of the two sets of data thus worked out gives us the third column in Table III. These figures are plotted in Plate II. It is clear from the table and plate that a greater permanent impression is made four months later, when a firm advertises for four successive weeks and then stops, than if it advertises once a month during that period, or on four successive days, or advertises in four different magazines which are seen by a reader at the same time. It is also clear that the latter procedure is the least efficient of the four distributions. But from the data and the plate it is not at all clear whether advertising on four successive days or on four successive months will give the greater returns. The latter distribution is favored by the data here. But the probable errors of our determination are greater than the differences.

The writer was so certain that intervals of one day would be found superior to those of a few minutes, a week, or a month, that he stated at one time that "of all intervals between successive repetitions that of a day's length will give us our maximum results."[1] This conclusion was reached on the basis of the work of Starch, Pyle, Ebbinghaus, etc. But it is clear that, when there is a long interval of time between exposure and the final test, presentations on successive days are not so effective as when they occur at intervals of one week.

2. *The Effect of Different Intervals of Time between Seeing an Advertisement and its Recognition*

Table II. presents what data there are in existence on this particular point. The curve of forgetting for recognition memory (in the case of unconnected words) has already been shown to approximate the curve as given us by Ebbinghaus for recall memory.[2] We would naturally suppose then that the great bulk of the loss in what is remembered immediately after seeing the advertisements and one month later occurs during the first two days. If this is the case the amount forgotten in the interval between two days after the original presentation and the test bears a nearly constant ratio to the interval of time. Various calculations of the writer on this

[1] E. K. Strong, Jr., 'Two Factors which Influence Economical Learning,' *Jour. Philos., Psychol. and Sci. Methods*, XI., Feb. 26, 1914.

[2] E. K. Strong, Jr., 'The Effect of Time-Interval upon Recognition Memory,' *Psychol. Rev.*, XX., Sept., 1913.

basis in different experiments have checked up with directly obtained data, as closely as could be expected.

3. The Effect of Different Intervals of Time between the Successive Presentations of Advertisements when Tested at a Considerable Time Later

If the data in Table III. are expressed in ratios in terms of the value of advertisements seen once, we have the ratios given in column four of that table. These are plotted in

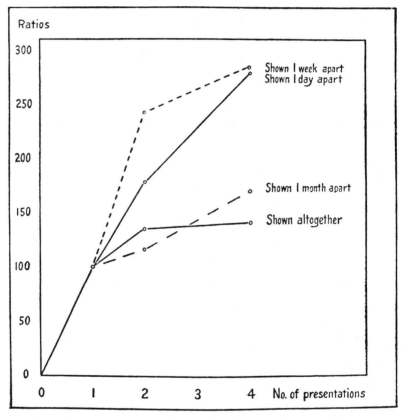

PLATE III. Showing the cumulative effect of two and four repetitions over one with the four methods of distribution. The value of one presentation is in each case called 100 and the other values are expressed in ratios of this value.

Plate III. With one exception, *i. e.*, the effect of four presentations a week apart, the curves show very clearly that the

shorter the interval of time between the successive presentations the greater is the cumulative effect.

But the relation between 'intervals of time' and 'permanent impression' from successive stimulations is not so
simple as would appear from Plate III. In Plates IV., V.,
and VI. are shown the same relations as in Plate III. but here
restricted, respectively, to ⅓-page advertisements, ½-page
advertisements and 1-page advertisements, instead of giving
an average of all three sized advertisements.

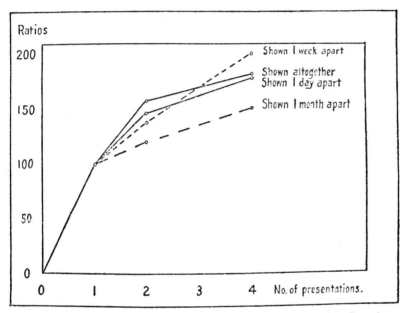

PLATE IV. With ¼-page advertisements. Showing the cumulative effect of two
and four repetitions over one with the four methods of distribution. The value of
one presentation is in each case called 100 and the other values are expressed in ratios
of this value.

The first fact that appears from a study of these plates is
that a relatively greater effect is made by the first presentation of a large advertisement than by a small advertisement,
as compared to the effect made by two or four presentations.
Or possibly, the relation should be expressed as follows:
A second presentation adds relatively more to the permanent
impression when the advertisement is small than when it is
large.

A second fact that appears is that repetition within a few minutes has relatively little effect upon ¼-page advertisements as compared with repetition at longer intervals of time, but that it has much greater effect with ½-page advertisements, and has the greatest effect of all our intervals of

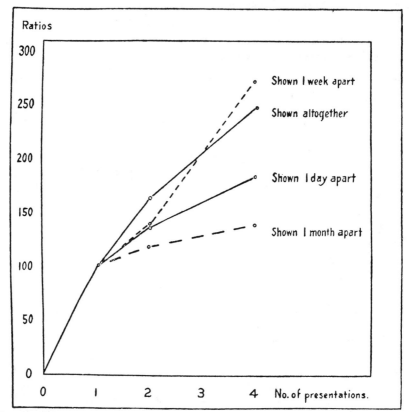

PLATE V. With ½-page advertisements. Showing the cumulative effect of two and four repetitions over one with the four methods of distribution. The value of one presentation is in each case called 100 and the other values are expressed in ratios of this value.

time upon 1-page advertisements. On the other hand, repetition at intervals of one month has (with one exception) the least effect of all the intervals regardless of the size of the advertisements.

Our general conclusion as to the effect of different intervals of time upon the permanent impression, *i. e.*, the shorter the interval of time between the successive presentations the greater is the cumulative effect, holds exactly for 1-page advertisements and nearly so for ½-page advertisements, but not at all for ¼-page advertisements.

The results obtained here support previous work as to the greater impression made by the first stimulation than by any succeeding one. But they do not entirely support Smith's[1] extreme statement that "the first repetition is undoubtedly the best, *i. e.*, more is learned by it than by any other repeti-

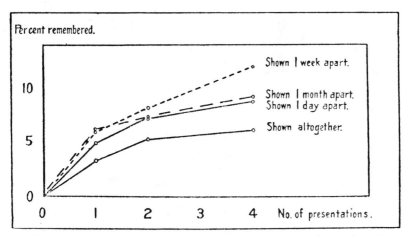

PLATE VI. With 1-page advertisements. Showing the cumulative effect of two and four repetitions over one with the four methods of distribution. The value of one presentation is in each case called 100 and the other values are expressed in ratios of this value.

tion, or, in fact, by all the other repetitions put together." In his experiment, as in these, here, the subjects were not directed to learn but simply to notice what was presented to them. Smith's conclusion is correct as far as our data go with the full-page advertisements, for here three more repetitions have not doubled the effect of the first one. The same holds true in the case of ½-page advertisements when the intervals were either one month or one day apart, and in the case of ¼-page advertisements when the intervals were either

[1] W. G. Smith, 'The Place of Repetition in Memory,' *Psychol. Rev.*, III., 1896, 21–31.

one month or a few minutes apart. But in four cases, the three additional repetitions more than doubled the effect of the first repetition.

4. The Effect of Seeing Varying Totals of Advertisements at One Time

The writer has already shown at some length that as you increase the number of advertisements which are seen at any one time, you decrease the effectiveness of the permanent impression from any one of them.[1] "Increasing the number of advertising pages from 42 to 168 resulted in a decrease in the percentage remembered among the 42 pages from 14.9 per cent. to 7.8 per cent. That means that the situation in which but 42 pages are glanced at allows a 91 per cent. greater impression to be made (from identically the same advertisements) than that which can be made when 168 pages are glanced at."

5. The Effect of Different Sized Advertisements upon the Permanent Impression

If we average the effect of the one, two, and four presentations together, as given in Table I. and the last part of Table II. in the March, 1914, article, we have the following as the value of ¼-page, ½-page, and 1-page advertisements, respectively:

	¼-page	½-page	1-page
When shown all together	4.3	8.5	14.2
When shown 1 day apart	8.3	11.9	18.1
When shown 1 week apart	7.7	16.8	24.3
When shown 1 month apart	4.9	7.0	10.7
Average	6.3	11.1	16.8

If these are expressed in ratios, we have:

	¼-page	½-page	1-page
When shown all together	100	198	330
When shown 1 day apart	100	143	218
When shown 1 week apart	100	218	316
When shown 1 month apart	100	143	218
Average	100	176	267

[1] Op. cit. (see note 2).

These ratios are higher than those previously reported in this particular experiment, which were 100: 141: 215, but are very similar to ratios obtained in other experiments, as given in the March, 1914, article, *i. e.*, 100: 166: 241 as the average of four experiments.

More recently the attention-value of various sized advertisements in the *Saturday Evening Post* has been ascertained.[1] In this case 285 individuals were canvassed and from this

TABLE IV

THE ATTENTION-VALUE OF DIFFERENT SIZED ADVERTISEMENTS IN THE *Saturday Evening Post*

Size of Advertisements	Supposed Value, *i. .e*, Percentage of Size of a 1-Page Ad.	Value as Obtained in this Experiment Expressed in Terms of a 1-Page Ad.	Theoretical Value, *i. e.,* Based on the Square Root Law
2 page..................	200%	149%	141%
1 page..................	100	100	100
½ page.................	50	81	71
2 cols. × 8″............	31	70	56
2 " × 6½............	25	57	50
2 " × 5	21	44	45
2 " × 4	17	41	40
1 " × 7	14	32	37
1 " × 5½............	11	32	34
1 " × 4½............	9	25	31
1 " × 3½............	7	28	27
1 " × 2½............	5	21	23
1 " × 1½............	3	25	18

number 90 were found who had handled that week's edition. Of these 88 were tested by the recognition method as to what advertisements they had seen in the last number of the *Saturday Evening Post*. In Table IV. are given the results as they bear on the value of space. They are expressed in terms of ratios of the attention-value of a full-page. It is clear from this table (based on 113 advertisements) that attention-value does not vary directly with the size of the space, but does vary very closely with the square-root of the size of the space. The figures, indeed, correspond as closely as one could expect.

Generally speaking our previous conclusion is correct,

[1] E. K. Strong, Jr., 'A Study of the *Saturday Evening Post*,' Association of National Advertising Managers' Research Bulletin No. 7, Mar., 1914.

i. e., 'that the attention-value of space increases approximately as the square-root of the increase in area and not directly with the increase in area.' This is exactly so in some cases: in others the increase in attention-value is in excess of the square-root ratio by as much as 25 to 30 per cent.

6. *Relative Strength of these Four Factors*

Undoubtedly the third factor—the effect of varying numbers of advertisements seen at one time—is the most important factor as affecting the total impression. An increase from 42 to 168 pages of advertising results in a decrease of 48 per cent. in the effectiveness of the impression from any one advertisement. The difference as shown in Plate I. between the data of Experiments I. and II. is due to this factor of seeing 42 advertisements at one time versus 168 advertisements at one time. It must be due to this factor, as the difference in the number of days between presentation and testing is too slight to account for any appreciable difference in the amount remembered. Now we have seen in Section 3 that repetition within a few minutes has a greater effect than at longer intervals with 1-page advertisements. If this is actually true, then it would seem that if we had shown the four dummy magazines in Experiment I. at intervals of one hour instead of one right after the other, there would have been a greater permanent impression made with the 1-page advertisements than by any of the other distributions used here. It is, however, possible that the greater cumulative effect from seeing the advertisements within a few minutes is due to the fact that the first impression made in Experiment I. was very slight. This conception is suggested by the fact that all the types of distribution have a greater cumulative effect upon small advertisements than large ones. If this latter conception is true then our above prophecy is not necessarily correct. The matter can only be settled by actual experimentation.

As was shown in the March, 1914, article, the same total amount of space is more effective when used in large amounts than when used in small amounts but more frequently.

Table V. shows this fact very clearly. Here the value of a
¼-page advertisement shown once is called 100. In all but
two of the thirty-two cases the large space seen less often is
more effective than the smaller space seen often.

TABLE V

Showing the Value of the Nine Combinations of ¼-page, ½-page, and 1-page
Space Presented Once, Twice, and Four Times

Each value is stated in terms of the value of a ¼-page advertisement shown once.

Size of Adver-tisement	Number of Presentations	Shown Altogether	Shown One Day Apart	Shown One Week Apart	Shown One Month Apart
¼-page ad.....	1 time	100	100	100	100
¼-page ad.....	2 times	135	178	243	116
½-page ad.....	1 time	147	189	259	155
¼-page ad.....	4 times	141	278	284	171
½-page ad.....	2 times	241	258	370	184
1-page ad.....	1 time	297	293	538	229
½-page ad.....	4 times	365	347	724	216
1-page ad.....	2 times	468	460	646	276
1-page ad.....	4 times	488	452	789	342

Possibly the relationship is something as follows: When
an advertisement is seen it arouses many associations more or
less well established. A large advertisement on the average
arouses many more such associations than a small advertisement. But the increase in number is never in proportion to the
increase in space. All these associations tend to be welded into a
complex giving us the new conception desired by the advertiser. We have then finally as resulting from the impression,
a more or less clearly formed new conception—a sort of higher-
order association formed from the old associations. The
more associations which were aroused the better formed is
the complex. When the second advertisement is seen it
again arouses this complex and adds to it one or more new
associations. But we must judge from our data that the
higher-order association is more readily developed when the
many old associations (with possibly some new ones) are all
aroused at the same time than when some are aroused at one
time and then later aroused again in a different setting. (It

should be remembered here that the repetition consisted in these experiments not of the same original advertisements but of new ones which were more or less similar to the first advertisement displayed.) It is very likely true that in the case of the small advertisement, the total impression from the first advertisement varied much more from that of the second advertisement than when large space was employed. There would be in this case less overlapping of the associations in the repetition of the small advertisements and more emphasis upon new associations (new to the complex) than in the case of the large advertisements.

At first thought it would seem as though the results in Sections 5 and 6 could not be harmonized. First we see that attention-value of large advertisements is never proportional to their size. Hence the argument arises, use small space for effective advertising. Then we see in Section 6 that a full-page advertisement is more effective than four quarter-page advertisements. Now the argument must surely be, use large space for effective advertising. Can both be correct? To the writer it seems than common advertising practice supports both as correct. When the advertisement is expected practically to complete the sale, as in mail-order advertising, we find generally small space is employed. Mail-order houses are the only advertisers who are in a position really to know the effect of their advertising. The fact that they ordinarily use small space seems to demonstrate that small space is more efficient than large space. And such advertisers constantly affirm that this is so. Now, on the other hand, when it is not expected that the first advertisement will sell the goods but that only after many such advertisements have been run will the advertiser reap the effect of the advertising, as in advertising pianos, autos, etc., we find that large space is used almost altogether. It is doubtful if any such advertiser has ever been able really to demonstrate the value of this style of publicity. But certainly at the present time the majority of such campaigns are carried on in this way. We should conclude, then, by saying that in Section 5 is given the relative attention-value of advertisements of varied sizes when there is but one presentation, whereas in Section 6 there is given the relative attention-value of advertisements of various sizes when the factor of repetition is taken into account. In the first case the attention-value is measured after one repetition; in the second case after many repetitions.[1]

CONCLUSION

1. A greater permanent impression is made (*i. e.*, 16 weeks after the first presentation) when a firm advertises for four successive weeks and then stops, than if it advertises once a month during that period, or on four successive days, or advertises in four different magazines which are seen by a reader at the same time. The last form of distribution is the least efficient. The second and third are approximately equal.

2. The permanent impression, after the first two days, apparently dies out gradually and in a direct ratio to the total length of time which has elapsed.

3. It would seem that the greater the initial impression the less will be the added impression from successive repetitions.

4. It would also seem that the greater the initial impression (*i. e.*, one-page advertisements here) the more does repetition within a few minutes affect the total impression as compared with repetition at longer intervals such as a day or longer.

5. As you increase the number of advertisements which are seen at any one time you decrease the effectiveness of the permanent impression from any one of them.

[1] The factors discussed in this paper are, of course, not the only ones that enter into the question as to what size of space will be most effective. Large space may be very ineffective from the advertising standpoint but very effective from the manufacturing standpoint. That is, it may cost more per dollar spent for advertisers to use large space than small space, but it may save far more through producing a larger total of sales, thus cutting down the cost of production. It is probable that economic factors, such as this, now dominate the reasons for selecting one size of advertisement over that of other sizes. But when small differences in the cost of salesmanship will seriously affect the entire business the psychological factors considered in this section are all important. See W. A. Shryer, 'Some Mail Order Weaknesses and their Cure, Advertising and Selling,' May, 1915.

6. The value of space in advertising as affecting permanent impressions increases approximately as the square-root of the increase in area, or sometimes at a somewhat greater rate.

7. The same total amount of space is more effective when used in large amounts less often, than when used in small amounts but more frequently.

VOL. XIII, No. 6.   MARCH 16, 1916

THE JOURNAL OF PHILOSOPHY
PSYCHOLOGY AND SCIENTIFIC METHODS

THE RELATIVE MEMORY VALUES OF DUPLICATION AND VARIATION IN ADVERTISING

THE investigation to be described in this paper is a continuation of one recently published entitled, "The Relative Importance of Size and Frequency in Forming Associations."[1] In that paper, the relative memory values of a full-page advertisement shown once, a half-page shown twice, a quarter-page shown four times, and an eighth-page shown eight times were determined. In all cases where an advertisement appeared more than once, exact duplicates were used.

The question then arose, which has the greater memory value, two or more duplications of the same advertisement, or two or more advertisements of the same commodity, each advertisement differing from the other either in picture, or in wording, or in both? The following experiment was devised to test this point.

Two dummies were prepared, one of which contained advertisements which when repeated were duplicates. The other consisted of different advertisements of the same commodity, but the advertisements were variations, not duplicates. The first dummy, in which duplicates were used, was made up as follows:

> 4 full-page advertisements appeared once.
> 4 full-page advertisements appeared twice.
> 4 full-page advertisements appeared 4 times.
>
> 4 half-page advertisements appeared once.
> 4 half-page advertisements appeared twice.
> 4 half-page advertisements appeared 4 times.
>
> 4 quarter-page advertisements appeared once.
> 4 quarter-page advertisements appeared twice.
> 4 quarter-page advertisements appeared 4 times.

[1] This JOURNAL, Vol. XII., pages 477 ff.

The second dummy was made up in the same way, variations of advertisements of the same commodity being used instead of duplicates. The advertisements were all the size of those contained in the *Saturday Evening Post*. The same subjects, 40 in number, were used in both tests. It is frankly acknowledged that too few subjects were employed, but since the results agree so closely with those of others who have investigated the first part of the problem, it is believed that a publication of our findings is warranted.

Each subject was handed one of the dummies and was told to look it over at his leisure, turning each page of the advertising section. The average time taken by each subject with each dummy was about 10 minutes. After finishing with the dummy, he was instructed to write down all that he could remember about the advertisements which he had seen. One week or more afterwards, he was handed the other dummy and given the same instructions. Half of the subjects started with the dummy containing duplicates; the other half with the dummy containing variations.

RESULTS

The results obtained from the first dummy are presented in the table below. The figures show the total number of credits received by each form of presentation of the material. Since in both dummies certain advertisements were shown but once, the average of the results was used to determine the value of the advertisements shown but once:

	Once	Twice	4 Times
Quarter page..................	16	26	45
Half page....................	32	37	83
Full page....................	47	80	108

If the quarter page shown once is considered the standard of stimulation, the half page shown once and the quarter page twice represent a doubling of the stimulation. Were both repetition and increase in size of equal value, the figures for the half page appearing once and the quarter page appearing twice should be the same, but they are not, indicating rather that size is a more important factor than repetition. This point will shortly be considered more in detail. Similarly, the full page shown once, the half page shown twice, and the quarter page shown four times represent four times the amount of stimulation. The full page shown twice and the half page shown four times are eight times the standard stimulus and the full page shown four times is sixteen times the standard.

If the table given above is reduced to ratios, the quarter page appearing once being taken as the standard, the following table is obtained:

	Once	Twice	4 Times
Quarter page..................	1.00	1.62	2.82
Half page....................	2.00	2.32	5.19
Full page....................	2.94	5.00	6.76

If, from this table, another one is prepared, showing the effect of constantly doubling the amount of stimulation, the following is obtained:

Units of Stimulation				
1	2	4	8	16
1.00	2.00 1.62	2.94 2.32 2.82	5.00 5.19	6.76
Average...........1.00	1.81	2.69	5.10	6.76

These ratios vary approximately as the 1.35 root of the amount of the stimulus.

The differences in memory value between repetition and size have been disregarded in the tables so far. The table given below shows the effect upon memory of increasing size. The quarter page, no matter whether it is presented once, twice, or four times, is considered as the standard, and the half- and full-page values are reduced to ratios of the quarter page.

	Quarter	Half	Full
Once.........................	1.00	2.00	2.94
Twice........................	1.00	1.42	3.08
4 times......................	1.00	1.84	2.40
Average......................	1.00	1.76	2.80

These ratios vary approximately as the 1.3 root of the number of presentations or amount of stimulation. the 1.3 root of 1 being 1, of 2 approximately 1.70, and of 4 about 2.9.

Before trying to establish correlations between these results and those of other investigators, I shall present the rest of my material. When all the data are at hand, definite relations will be easier to establish.

Turning now to a consideration of the effects of frequency of insertion, we regard one presentation of the material as the stanard and reduce the other values to ratios of it. The table showing these ratios follows:

	Once	Twice	4 Times
Quarter page..................	1.00	1.63	2.81
Half page....................	1.00	1.16	2.60
Full page....................	1.00	1.70	2.30
Average.....................	1.00	1.49	2.57

Here we find that the ratios vary approximately as the 1.6 root of the number of presentations.

The conclusion which we are forced to accept by this part of the experiment is that size is of more importance in the formation of associations than repetition. This point will be considered more in detail at a later period.

With the second dummy, which was made up of varied advertisements of the same commodity where repetition was necessary, the following totals were received by each of the different arrangements:

	Once	Twice	4 Times
Quarter page..................	16	46	85
Half page....................	32	86	117
Full page....................	47	108	149

Reducing this table to ratios of one presentation of the quarter page, as was done with the other dummy, we obtain the following:

	Once	Twice	4 Times
Quarter page..................	1.00	2.88	5.31
Half page....................	2.00	5.37	7.31
Full page....................	2.94	6.75	9.31

Another table, showing the effects of repeatedly doubling the amount of stimulation, follows:

Units of Stimulation				
1	2	4	8	16
1.00	2.00	2.94	6.75	9.31
	2.88	5.37	7.31	
		5.31		
Average..........1.00	2.44	4.54	7.03	9.31

These figures do not follow an X^n curve. But they do indicate quite forcibly that variability is a more important consideration than duplication in advertising.

Turning now to the consideration of the effect of size, the following table gives the ratios, considering the quarter page as the standard:

	Quarter	Half	Full
Once	1.00	2.00	2.91
Twice	1.00	1.84	2.35
4 times	1.00	1.38	1.76
Average	1.00	1.74	2.35

These figures agree fairly well with the results obtained from the dummy containing duplicates, giving, however, a slightly lower ratio for the full page. The average of the two is given below:

	Quarter	Half	Full
Duplicates	1.00	1.76	2.80
Variations	1.00	1.74	2.35
Average	1.00	1.75	2.58

A comparison of these results with those of other experiments will now be made. Scott[2] found the following ratios, his results being uncorrected for familiarity:

	Quarter	Half	Full
Recognition	1.00	2.32	3.74
Recall	1.00	2.52	5.53
Average	1.00	2.42	4.64

His general conclusion is that there is a more than proportionate increase in memory value with increase in size of the advertisements.

Starch[3] gives the following figures. Where the ratios representing the memory value are uncorrected for familiarity he obtained the first set of ratios; where correction was made for familiarity, he obtained the second set of values:

Quarter	Half	Ful	Two Pages
1.00	2.43	5.23	6.98
1.00	1.77	3.44	4.41

Starch's results agree with Scott's in that, when uncorrected for familiarity, they show a more than proportionate increase in memory value with increase in the amount of space used. Where familiarity is allowed for, however, the ratios show a less than proportionate increase.

Strong[4] gives the results of several experiments, showing the effect of increasing space. His ratios follow:

[2] Scott, W. D. "The Psychology of Advertising," pages 168–169.
[3] Starch, D. "Advertising," pages 30 and 48.
[4] Strong, E. K. *Psychol. Rev.*, Vol. 21, pages 137 ff.

	Quarter	Half	Full
(*A*)	1.00	1.41	2.15
(*B*)	1.00	1.11	1.13
(*C*)	1.00	2.39	3.65
(*D*)	1.00	1.53	2.34
(*E*)	1.00	1.66	2.41
Average	1.00	1.62	2.34

Strong's results indicate a less than proportionate gain in memmory value with increase in size in all cases but one.

If we take the results of all of these investigations and average the ratios, it may bring out an approximate truth. In averaging the ratios, all of the experiments will be considered to be of equal value, no allowance being made for the greater number of subjects used in certain of the experiments. The ratios are given below:

	Quarter	Half	Full
Scott	1.00	2.32	3.74
Scott	1.00	2.52	5.53
Starch	1.00	2.43	5.23
Starch	1.00	1.77	3.44
Strong	1.00	1.41	2.15
Strong	1.00	1.11	1.13
Strong	1.00	2.39	3.65
Strong	1.00	1.53	2.34
Strong	1.00	1.66	2.41
Adams	1.00	1.76	2.80
Adams	1.00	1.74	2.35
Average	1.00	1.87	3.16

These ratios for the half- and full-page spaces are undoubtedly higher than they should be. For in four of Strong's experiments, in one of Starch's, and in Scott's there is little if any selection of the advertisements used. The general scheme was to use the advertising section of some current magazine as the material in the experiment. The greater familiarity of the half-page and especially of the full-page advertisements undoubtedly raised the ratios for those sizes somewhat above the normal memory value. For in advertising, as elsewhere, there is a natural selection going on, so that the full pages tend to represent those firms which have advertised successfully for some little time. The mere fact of familiarity gives to these advertisements all the value to be derived from repetition, either from duplicated advertisements, or, more probably, from varied advertisements. We shall see below that variation in the form of presentation is a very important principle in relation to memory value.

If we accept Starch's[5] method of allowing for familiarity, we

[5] Starch, D. "Advertising," page 34.

find that the quarter page should be allowed 100 per cent., the half page 73 per cent., the full page 63 per cent., and the two page 62 per cent. of the values actually received. Reducing the half-page and the full-page values by these amounts in the seven experiments mentioned above, we obtain the following ratios.

	Quarter	Half	Full
Scott	1.00	1.69	2.36
Scott	1.00	1.84	3.50
Starch	1.00	1.77	3.44
Strong	1.00	.81	.71
Strong	1.00	1.74	2.39
Strong	1.00	1.13	1.48
Strong	1.00	1.21	1.52
Average	1.00	1.46	2.20

Taking the other series of experiments, in which the advertisements were selected to avoid undue familiarity, though the values were undoubtedly somewhat affected by it, we obtain the following set of ratios:

	Quarter	Half	Full
Strong	1.00	1.41	2.15
Adams	1.00	1.76	2.80
Adams	1.00	1.74	2.35
Average	1.00	1.64	2.43

A word should be said in explanation of the differences which exist between Strong's results and ours. In the first place, our advertisements were possibly slightly more familiar than his. In the second place, the time intervals in the two experiments were different. Strong presented his duplicated advertisements one month apart and tested a month later. In our experiment, the successive presentations of the material occurred within a space of 10 minutes and the test followed immediately after. The effect of this should be to raise our values somewhat,[6] since our averages are made from one, two, and four presentations of the material.

The reason for going into so much detail in connection with the influence of space is because we wish to obtain some definite data which may be used in making a comparison between the experimental results and those obtained in actual advertising business. The business returns were obtained from Shryer's "Analytical Ad-

[6] Strong, E. K. *Psychol. Rev.*, Vol. 21, page 147, footnote.

"From data now being accumulated we find that shorter intervals, as one week, give ratios indicating a greater effect from two or four presentations than shown here."

vertising,''[7] where he shows the number of inquiries received by quarter-page, half-page, full-page, two-page, and three-page advertisements.

His results show the total number of insertions of the advertisements of each size, the total number of inquiries, the advertising cost, and the cash returns. We are interested here primarily in the average number of inquiries per insertion. Obviously, Shryer's results do not indicate the actual memory value of the advertisements, though his displays must have been remembered to a certain extent to have obtained any responses at all. Naturally, also, many persons must have remembered the advertisements who did not write to him. His book, however, is one of the few places that the writer knows of where accurate, practical data may be obtained. His figures indicate the actual efficiency of his advertisements and because of this fact, it will be instructive to include his material here. His results, reduced to ratios of the average number of inquiries per insertion, follow:

	Quarter	Half	Full	2-Page	3-Page
P. 171–5....................	1.00	1.46	2.22	—	—
P. 190....................	1.00	1.60	2.27	1.01	4.17
Average....................	1.00	1.53	2.25	1.01	4.17

The first three of these ratios are quite trustworthy, depending as they do on 109 insertions of quarter-page advertisements, 79 insertions of the half-page, and 91 insertions of the full-page. It is interesting to note that the ratios, if we except the one representing the two-page value, vary approximately as the 1.7 root of the space occupied by the advertisement. It seems probable, everything considered, that the value of space varies somewhere between the 1.35 root and the square root of the space occupied, depending upon the conditions under which the experiment is performed. The most probable value is in the neighborhood of the 1.7 root. This statement holds for both memory value and actual efficiency in pulling replies.

The problem of the frequency in insertion of the advertisement is the next one which needs discussion. A comparatively slight amount of work has been done on this point, so the facts are not so definitely known. A summary of the experiments which have been performed will disclose the available data.

Strong's[8] results show the ratios for one, two, and four presenta-

7 Shryer, W. A. ''Analytical Advertising.'' pages 171–175, 190.

8 Strong, E. K. *Psychol. Rev.*, Vol. 21, page 146.

tions to be 1.00 : 1.25 : 1.62. Our results with duplicated advertisements give these ratios: 1.00 : 1.49 : 2.57. The average of the two is 1.00 : 1.37 : 2.10. It will be seen that these values are somewhat lower than those obtained for increase in size of the advertisements. It seems to be pretty well proved, then, that size is a more important factor from the standpoint of memory than is frequency of insertion where the repeated advertisements are exact duplicates.

A comparison will again be made with the practical results which are obtained by working over the figures given by Shryer.[9] He gives a large number of figures showing the results of consecutive advertising. The number of inquiries received from the first, second, and so on up to the seventh insertion of the advertisement, are given. Since both the number of insertions of the advertisement and the resulting number of inquiries were so irregular, they were all reduced to ratios and the ratios averaged. The records for classified advertisements were not considered, for it is generally admitted that there is a considerable difference in the attitude which persons take towards the two kinds, classified and display, the former appealing primarily to those who are already interested in the proposition. It is rather amusing that if one takes Shryer's results as they stand, they prove the existence of cumulative value, the very thing which they were supposed by him to disprove.

In working out his results, the writer has added together the results of consecutive insertions of the advertisement, thus showing the total number of inquiries pulled by the first insertion alone, by the first two, by the first three, etc. The figures, reduced to ratios, follow:

	Number of Insertions						
	1	2	3	4	5	6	7
Inquiries.........	1.00	2.01	3.03	4.33	5.23	6.58	7.84

These figures are to a certain extent untrustworthy and misleading, for out of the 30 or more tables from which they were derived, fully half contained too few figures to be entirely dependable. The 16 tables which contained 100 inquiries or more for the first insertion were considered apart, for it was thought that the greater the number of inquiries, the less relative effect some slight accidental variation would have. The table made up of these ratios follows:

	Number of Insertions						
	1	2	3	4	5	6	7
Inquiries.........	1.00	2.08	2.78	3.46	4.20	5.64	6.28

[9] Shryer, W. A. "Analytical Advertising," pages 82–114.

These figures show a lack of cumulative value, except in the case of the second insertion, and this lack is enhanced when we consider another argument of Shryer's.[10]   He states that an advertisement which is inserted but once will still pull inquiries during the second, third, and fourth months and backs up his statement by a list of 10 examples.   The relative efficiency of an advertisement which has appeared but once is shown for the first, second, third, and fourth months in the following table of ratios:

1	2	3	4
1.00	1.68	1.83	1.94

Taking Shryer's figures as they stand, uncorrected for the piling up effects of one insertion, we find that they are somewhat higher than those obtained by the experimental method with duplicates, as will be indicated by the following table:

	1	2	4
Experimental..................	1.00	1.37	2.10
Shryer......................	1.00	2.08	3.46

If we try to correct his figures roughly by obtaining the ratio of efficiency of the repeated advertisements to the piling up effects of one insertion alone, we obtain the following ratios:

1	2	4
1.00	1.24	2.21

His figures, with correction, show a very close resemblance to those obtained by the experimental method.

On the average, it appears that increased space is more effective than duplication of advertisements, with both the experimental and the practical results, as will appear from the following table:

Experiment.

	Units of Stimulation		
	1	2	4
Size...........................	1.00	1.64	2.43
Duplication....................	1.00	1.37	2.10
Practical Test.			
Size...........................	1.00	1.53	2.25
Duplication....................	1.00	1.24	2.21

The table is also interesting in that it points out the very close and striking resemblance between the laboratory tests on memory values and the business tests on practical efficiency.

[10] Shryer, W. A.   ''Analytical Advertising,'' pages 114–115.

When we consider the effect of varied advertisements rather than duplicates, we find that repetition is a greater factor than increase in size, as the following table will show:

	Once	Twice	4 Times
Quarter page	1.00	2.88	5.31
Half page	1.00	2.70	3.66
Full page	1.00	2.30	3.17
Average	1.00	2.63	4.05

These ratios are considerably above those obtained for increase in size of the advertisements, which were 1.00 : 1.64 : 2.45.

We are also justified in stating that duplication has a much lower memory value than variation. The following table will make this clear:

	Duplication	Variation
1 appearance	1.00	1.00
2 appearances	1.49	2.63
4 appearances	2.57	4.05

This table shows very strikingly that variation possesses a very much greater memory value than duplication.

There are at least two reasons why this should be the case. In the first place, the degree of attention is undoubtedly an important factor. When we see a duplicated advertisement the second time it is relatively uninteresting, consequently the second impression is not as great as the first. But with the variation, there is always the novelty of a new advertisement so that attention may be at its maximum.

In the second place, where duplicates are used but one type of appeal can be successfully employed. This may be for the reader an uninteresting one, consequently he may neglect the advertisement entirely. Where variations are used, however, it is possible to make as many different types of appeal as there are variations in the series. In addition to producing greater attention, variation is more likely to connect the advertisement with the individual's series of interests, thus tending to give it a greater memory value.

Since Shryer's advertisements have been running consistently in a fairly large number of magazines, it is a very probable supposition that those who answered his advertisements had been influenced both by duplications and variations of the advertisements. If such were the case, and we assume it to be, it would be interesting to compare his ratios with our ratios representing an average of the two tendencies. Such a comparison follows:

	Once	Twice	4 Times
Duplication....................	1.00	1.49	2.60
Variation.....................	1.00	2.63	4.05
Average......................	1.00	2.06	3.33
Shryer's.....................	1.00	2.08	3.46

These figures, which are strikingly similar, show a high degree of correlation between the experimental test of memory and the practical test of efficiency.

SUMMARY.

1. Increasing size gives a higher memory value than increasing the number of repetitions of an advertisement when exact duplicates are used.

2. Variation is about twice as effective as duplication.

3. There is a very close correlation between the memory value of the different forms of presentation of the material and the practical efficiency of the same forms of presentation in pulling inquiries.

HENRY F. ADAMS.

UNIVERSITY OF MICHIGAN.

XXXI *PSYCHOLOGICAL REVIEW PUBLICATIONS* Whole No. 142
1922

sychological Monographs

EDITED BY

JAMES ROWLAND ANGELL, YALE UNIVERSITY.

WARD C. WARREN, PRINCETON UNIVERSITY (*Review*)

JOHN B. WATSON, NEW YORK (*J. of Exp. Psych.*)

SHEPHERD I. FRANZ, GOVT. HOSP. FOR INSANE (*Bulletin*) and

MADISON BENTLEY, UNIVERSITY OF ILLINOIS (*Index*)

TDIES FROM THE PSYCHOLOGICAL LABORA-
TORY OF THE UNIVERSITY OF CHICAGO

The Conditions of Retention

BY

C. W. LUH

Proféssor of Psychology, Southeastern University, Nanking, China

---

PSYCHOLOGICAL REVIEW COMPANY

PRINCETON, N. J.

AGENTS: G. E. STECHERT & CO., LONDON (2 Star Yard, Carey St., W. C.)
PARIS (16 rue de Condé)

CONTENTS

PAGE

   I. Introduction.   I

  II. The Amount of Retention as a Function of the Method of Measurement.   12

 III. Retention as a Function of the Degree of Learning.   43

 IV. The Effect of Extending the Time Limit for Recall upon the Amount of Material Recalled.   55

  V. The Relation between the Amount of Error and Other Factors.   62

 VI. The Duration and the Speed of Recall.   68

 VII. Individual Differences and Correlations.   73

VIII. Conclusion.   85

I. INTRODUCTION

The problem of the present study is to investigate the nature of the curve of retention under certain variable conditions. The conditions that can be independently varied are numerous. Only two series of experiments have been systematically carried out:

(1) Varying the methods of measuring the amount of retention and

(2) Varying the degree of mastery in the original learning.

As established by Ebbinghaus,[1] the curve of retention for nonsense syllables drops very rapidly during the first 20 minutes after learning. More than half of the original material is lost at the end of the first hour. The subsequent fall of the curve becomes less and less abrupt until about 1 day, when the curve runs almost parallel to the abscissa. Similar but far less extensive experiments were performed upon himself with meaningful material, *i. e.,* poetry. From these results Ebbinghaus deduced the following equation of the curve which has remained a classic of forty years' standing:

$$b = \frac{100\ k}{(\log t)^c + k}, \text{ or } \frac{b}{100 - b} = \frac{k}{(\log t)^c}$$

In this formula b = percentage of retention, 100 — b = percentage of forgetting, t = length of the interval in no. of min., and k and c are constants.

With Müller and Schumann,[2] the technique was greatly improved in the construction and the presentation of the syllable series. Their results corroborated those of Ebbinghaus, though the amount of forgetting was less than previously reported.

[1] "Ueber das Gedächtniss: Untersuchungen zur experimentellen Psychologie," Leipzig, 1885. Eng. Tr. by Ruger and Bussenius, Teachers' College, Columbia University, 1913.
[2] "Experimentelle Beiträge zur Untersuchung des Gedächtnisses," *Zeitschr. f. Psychol.,* Vol. VI, 1893.

It was in 1903-04 that Radossawljevitch[3] attempted a more careful determination of the curve on a much more extensive scale. He employed altogether 29 subjects, as against Ebbinghaus' one, who was himself. Availing himself of the improved technique of Müller and Schumann, he further introduced accent and rhythm into the act of learning. On the whole, the curve he described conforms to the Ebbinghaus type. The amounts of forgetting after relatively short intervals were less than either Ebbinghaus or Müller and Schumann discovered.

Finkenbinder,[4] who re-attacked the problems in 1912, first used the *anticipation* method in presentation. By that method the subject was required to anticipate each syllable by pronouncing it aloud within the exposure period of the syllable preceding. Successful anticipation of the whole series constitutes the standard of learning. Altogether eleven different intervals were used, and these were carefully distributed so as to eliminate diurnal variations. He summarized his data as follows: "The curve of forgetting for nonsense syllables in series of twelve, as determined by the lapse of time, is a uniformly progressive curve much as Ebbinghaus found, but under the conditions of our investigation, the progress of forgetting is slower than Ebbinghaus found it to be, but somewhat faster than Radossawljevitch found."[5] Then from his numerical data he found this astonishingly simple equation: Forgetting = 10 (log. of time in No. of min. + 1), and apologized for its simplicity.

In the above quoted investigations, the method for measuring the amount of forgetting was the relearning or "saving" method. Forgetting is expressed as a quotient of the amount of time for relearning and for the original learning. Strong[6] first undertook

[3] "Das Behalten und Vergessen bei Kindern und Erwachsenen," Leipzig. 1907.

[4] "The Curve of Forgetting," *Amer. Jour. Psychol.*, Vol. XXIV, 1913.

[5] *Ibid*, p. 32. Finkenbinder used series of 12 syllables each; Ebbinghaus, 13; Radossawljevitch, 8, 12 and 16. Finkenbinder should have compared his results with that part of R's data which were derived from 12-syllable series only.

[6] "The Effect of Time Interval upon Recognition Memory," *Psych. Rev.*, Vol. XX, 1913, pp. 334 ff .

to extend the investigation with other methods of measuring results. The method used in his experiments was the method of recognition, or selection, and for material he constructed series of common English words of 40 each. Out of each 40, a second series of 20 words was drawn at random, which latter served as the exposure list. The first list of 40 was given the subject for recognition after the lapse of a designated interval of time. From these the subject was required to select the exposure list. The experiments included 14 intervals and 5 subjects, but only 15 measures for each interval. The curve of retention thus determined was similar in shape to that of Ebbinghaus. The two almost agreed as to actual amounts of forgetting until after the lapse of the 4-day interval. Strong, therefore, concluded that "there is no difference in the form of the curve for retention in recall and recognition memory." By this he did not specify whether he implied the logarithmic formula, or only the general shape of the curve as to its initial drop and negative acceleration.

Bean[7] thought that the Ebbinghaus tradition could be substantiated on more extensive grounds. In his experiments two distinct kinds of material were used, (1) series of 9 consonants of the English alphabet, and (2) typewriting. In (1) he used two methods for the measurement of retention. A. The method of written reproduction, in which the subjects were allowed 2 min. to reproduce the series of consonants which had been learned from 1 to 28 days previous to recall. B. The method of selection and reconstruction, in which the subjects spent 90 secs. in selecting the original series of 9 out of the total group of 18 which was being presented, and then took 30 secs. to put the original 9 in the right order. In (2) typewriting, Bean adopted a method similar to that used by Book in his pioneering studies in typewriting.[8] Bean's results may be summarized as follows:

The curve of forgetting may be studied (1) as to its general

---

[7] "The Curve of Forgetting," *Archives of Psychol.*, Vol. XX, No. 3.

[8] "The Psychology of Skill," *Univ. of Montana Publications in Psychology*, Vol. I, 1908, Bull. 53. Psy. Series No. 1.

form; and (2) as to the absolute rate of forgetting. According to him, the curves he presented differ from those of earlier investigators and among themselves, not in general form, but only in absolute initial amount. Supposing the logarithmic type of curve to be general, then an initial high amount of forgetting will lead to apparently abrupt transitions. As to the cause of the variations in the absolute or initial amount, numerous conditions may be mentioned. 1. Degree of learning. 2. Distribution or concentration in the process of learning. 3. Different kinds of material. 4. Different methods by which retention is measured 5. Individual differences. On the whole, he would conclude that all curves of forgetting are logarithmic curves.

As we shall later develop, the methods he used for measuring the amount of retention were mostly crude and inaccurate. He did not give any measurement for the statistical validity of his data. Further, he himself did not attempt to find equations, or rather one general equation, for his own data, and we have to take his conclusions only as pious opinions. Finally, in his experiments, none of the conditions he mentioned was controlled and independently varied.

An even more sweeping generalization than Bean's was offered by Piéron.[9] He developed a formula which was believed to satisfy all the conditions of immediate and permanent memory, retention and forgetting, muscular contraction and the phylogenetic development of retentive phenomena, etc. That formula is $m = \dfrac{k}{t^a (\log t)^c}$, where m = percentage of "saving," t = length of the interval, and k, a and c are constants. Then putting a = o, it takes in Ebbinghaus' curve for human retention. $m = \dfrac{k}{(\log t)^c}$, as a congenial member of the "family."[10] But these deductions were based on no surer foundation than a few observations upon some pond snails.

[9] "L'Évolution de la Mémoire," Paris, 1910, pp. 256-60.
[10] Notice how ingenuity is accentuated by forgetting k in Ebbinghaus' formula. This is permissible when t is very large. But E's formula is significant only when it is small.

All the above writers seem to concur with the Ebbinghaus tradition and to agree on these points.

(1) Retention decreases with time.

(2) Forgetting is more rapid at first.

(3) The curve of retention is generally uniform so that one can state it in terms of a mathematical formula. Radossawljevitch indeed located a sudden deviation at the end of the 8 hr. interval, but that was smoothed out in Finkenbinder's experiments after the elimination of diurnal variations.

(4) There is a question as to whether

A. The curves approximate each other so closely that one can regard them as being chance deviations from some ideal curve, or

B. They belong to a single family with one or more variable parameters which assume different values according to different conditions. Strong inclines toward the former alternative, but Bean explicitly favors the latter.

It is to be noticed that conclusions 1 to 3 are but descriptive summary statements of the facts as observed under their particular experimental conditions, while 4 is a mathematical deduction. By "the Ebbinghaus type of curve," one may simply mean that facts can be so described and graphically represented, without implying that they satisfy any kind of an equation. Neglecting all mathematical complications, may not the phenomena of retention and forgetting be, *under all conditions,* much as Ebbinghaus described them?

In the light of these conclusions, Ballard's[11] results become significant. He experimented on school children with Latin nouns, nonsense poetry, geometric diagrams, nonsense syllables, prose, material for logical memory, but above all with ballad poetry. For the vast majority of his subjects, the material was not completely learned. Written reproduction was required after the lapse of a certain interval. He found that the highest proficiency of retention, as measured by the amount of repro-

[11]"Obliviscence and Reminiscence," *Brit. Jour. Psych. Monograph Supplements,* Vol. I, 1913, No. 2.

duced material, was reached not immediately after learning, but, as a rule, at the end of two days. The graphs in Fig. I are illustrative.[12] Both A and B are curves of retention for children about 12 years of age. The amount remembered immediately after learning is taken as the basis on which the percentage repro-

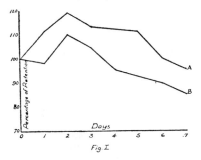

Fig. I

duced later is calculated. Graph A. was based upon "The Wreck of the Hesperus," with 20% of the material remembered in the "primary test." B. was based upon "The Ancient Mariner," with 40% of the material remembered.

These results of Ballard directly contradict every one of the conclusions reached by the previous writers. Yet his data seem to be at least as valid and reliable as those of our earlier investigators in forgetting.

This apparent dilemma suggested to us what was, in a way, anticipated by Bean. When the conditions of learning and recalling are changed, not only will the "absolute" amount of forgetting change, not only will the mathematical formula change, but the phenomenon of negative acceleration may also disappear. The conditions under which Ballard experimented were greatly different from those of other investigators. The following were the most important:

(1) The age of the subjects. Ballard's subjects who manifested these peculiarities were all children. Compared with his own work upon adults, the results indicate that the curve is a

[12] *Ibid,* p. 5.

function of the age of the subjects. Other investigators worked mostly with adults.

(2) The kind of material. Ballard used but little nonsense material and did not work on a separate curve of retention for nonsense syllables. The Ebbinghaus type of curve is a curve for nonsense syllables *par excellence.* Ebbinghaus' and Radossawljevitch's experiments with meaningful material were only supplementary to their principle problem and were haphazardly performed.

(3) The degree of learning. In Ballard's experiments, the material was only partly learned. The degree of learning for the curves quoted above was 20% and 40%. The subjects had to stop at a given time limit. In all previous work, except that of Strong, the material was learned at least to the first errorless recitation.

(4) The method of measuring the amount of retention. Before Ballard, the method that was generally used was the "saving" method. Bean and Strong tried the "selection" method, but not very extensively. Ballard, however, found the written reproduction method to be more suitable for group experiments.

This comparison suggests the question as to *whether the curve of forgetting, or of retention, is a function of these conditions, or more specifically, whether each condition determines a special curve.* The present study is an attempt to answer this question. This can be carried out only by varying the above mentioned conditions independently and systematically. Unfortunately, Ballard's technique has necessitated a program which demands more time than we can at present afford. We have, therefore, limited the scope of the problem by taking up only the third and fourth factors, leaving the first two to a later investigation.

General Description of the Experiments

The experiments were performed in the Psychological Laboratory of the University of Chicago, the first series from May to August, 1919, and the second from October, 1919, to February, 1920.

(1) *Material*

Series of nonsense syllables of 12 each were used. With the English alphabet, a list was made of all possible combinations of two consonants joined by a vowel in the middle, except those which end in y. From this list we eliminated all the English, French, German and Latin words. The revised collection was then submitted separately to four graduate students of the department who checked every syllable which happened to call up immediate meaning associations. All syllables thus marked out by more than one of the observers were further eliminated from the final list.

In the construction of the series, Müller's[13] rules were observed as closely as possible. That is,

(1) All the initial and final consonants of the same series are different.

(2) Since we did not resort to the use of diphthongs, we had five vowels as against Müller's twelve. The terms were arranged so that no two of four consecutive syllables have the same vowel.

(3) No two consecutive syllables have any consonant in common.

(4) No group of consecutive syllables constitutes a polysyllabic word or a phrase.

Thus we have improved upon Müller in at least two respects. (1) He overlooked monosyllabic words, which, perhaps, is not so serious an omission in German as in English. (2) While he allowed a syllable to end with the initial consonant of the preceding syllable, we excluded all such cases.

Since in our investigation we required the subject to spell each syllable letter by letter, instead of pronouncing it as a whole, we are no longer concerned with Gamble's rules[14] which were formulated as safeguards against the inherent defects of English orthography. We also think that spelling the syllable letter by letter tends to minimize its meaning associations.

[13] *Op. cit.*, p. 106.
[14] "A Study in Memorising by the Reconstruction Method," *Psych. Rev.*, *Monograph Supplements*, Vol. X, No. 4, p. 22.

Altogether about 90 series were constructed so that a subject could serve extensively without resorting to learning a single syllable twice.

(2) *Apparatus*

The apparatus was an ordinary rotating drum used in the Chicago laboratory for most of the memory experiments. After the series were typewritten on strips of white manila card, they could be easily fixed to the drum. One syllable was exposed at a time through an aperture in the screen attached to the posts of the drum. It was found more convenient to run the apparatus by hand than by a mechanical device, since the experimenter had to keep his eyes on the aperture in order to be perfectly sure that the subject spelled the syllable completely before the succeeding one was exposed.

In experiments like these, every moderately loud noise may be disturbing. For this reason the experimenter had to keep the time by running a telephone wire from an adjacent room in which a metronome was set at two seconds.

In the later part of the first series of experiments and throughout the second, it was thought worth while for purposes other than that of the present study to keep minute records of every correct or incorrect response. A Remington typewriter No. 6, invisible, served as the apparatus, so that the subject would not be distracted by what was being recorded. Two keys were arbitrarily chosen to mark success and failure. The striking of the key made a noise every two seconds. The effect of this apparently disturbing factor was inappreciable, so far as we can determine from the practice curves of the individuals.

(3) *Method of Presentation*

The subject was seated at a convenient distance in front of the rotating drum. Before the presentation of every new series, the experimenter gave the signal "ready," one second after which the first syllable was exposed. This signal became superfluous after one or two weeks of practice. The.time of exposure for each syllable was 2 secs. No restriction was made as to the method of learning, excepting that the subject was warned not to form artificial meaning associations. Beginning with the second exposure of the series, he was instructed to attempt to anticipate each syllable by spelling it aloud before it was exposed. Usually 6 seconds were allowed between successive presentations of a series, during which the experimenter shifted the drum and made the necessary records. A series was considered learned once the subject successfully anticipated every syllable. All series were learned by successive presentations in a single sitting.

Each subject was required to return at the same time of the day, but could skip two or three days in succession between series. Only one series was learned in a day. Occasionally the learning of a new series followed immediately after the recall of the preceding one. But this never happened in the second series of experiments.

The different intervals and the methods of measurement, as will be described later, were distributed according to a tentative scheme drawn for each subject. Sometimes that schedule had to be slightly changed, but care was always taken to reduce to a minimum the effect of uncontrolled practice.

Each subject was given 4-6 series for preliminary practice. These results were not counted. (Subject C, who learned only 20 series, began to work late in the summer. Only 2 practice series were possible with this subject. His results could have been improved by giving 2 or more additional preliminary series).

(4) *Subjects*

Ten subjects a day were all we could handle. We had two groups of ten each. The first group included one instructor and three graduate students of the department and six Chinese students of the University who had one time or another taken some work in psychology. In the second group, there were six graduate students and one senior of the department, including the experimenter. The other three were Chinese students of the University, two of whom never had any work in psychology. Subject Y, a Chinese student who learned 20 series in the summer, served again as one of the ten. When the experimenter served as subject, the series were given by Mr. T. L. Wang, who had also served in previous experiments. In this case, the series were made according to rules unknown to the experimenter. They were very similar to the ordinary ones.

Apparently the Chinese students had no serious difficulty in learning this type of material. They were able to memorize directly without translating the exposed material into Chinese equivalents. On the whole, they learned the series very much faster than did the Americans.

II. THE AMOUNT OF RETENTION AS A FUNCTION OF THE METHOD OF MEASUREMENT

In the first series of experiments, two methods of recall were used, which together furnished five measurements of the amount of retention.

1. The Anticipation and Relearning Methods. In one half of the series given to each subject, the method of presentation in relearning was identical with that of the original learning.

(A) Thus, the subject was required to anticipate the series at the very first presentation, at the rate of 2 sec. for each syllable. The number of correct syllables was recorded. That number, expressed as a percentage of the whole series, established a measurement of retention in terms of anticipatory recall.

(B) After the first record was taken, the series was exposed as many times as necessary for complete relearning. A measurement of retention was thus furnished by the "Saving Method."

2. The Reproduction, Recognition and Reconstruction Methods. These methods were used with the other half of the series given to each subject.

(C) The subject was first furnished with a recall blank, on which were three columns of figures from 1 to 12, each with a blank space to the right. He was instructed to write down the original series in the right spatial order, beginning with the left hand column, but not necessarily in the same temporal order as the series was learned. At the end of 1 min. the experimenter gave a signal, at which the subject began to write in the middle column, filling out spaces that had been left open during the first minute, or correcting any mistake that he thought had been made. Another signal was given at the end of the second minute. At this, the subject changed to the right hand column. Three more minutes were allowed for further reproduction and correction. The subject could, of course, "give up" at any time, or finish the whole series before the lapse of the first or second

12

minute. A time record was also taken for each series completed within the above 5 min. This constituted a measurement of retention by the Written Reproduction method.

(D) Immediately following upon written reproduction, a group of 24 syllables was given the subject, out of which he was required to select the original 12, no more and no less. At the end of 90 sec. the experimenter quietly took a record of the number of correct and incorrect syllables selected up to that time. A similar record was taken when the subject completed the selection of 12 syllables, correctly or incorrectly, together with a time record. The time limit, 90 sec., was determined from the averages of the preliminary records of all the subjects in the first series of experiments. This process gave a measurement of retention in terms of Recognition.

(E) Finally, the subject was furnished with the original 12 syllables on separate slips of white manila card and was required to reconstruct the order of the series. The actual order of reconstruction was recorded, and also the amount of time spent in the reconstruction process. This we may call the Reconstruction or Rearrangement method of recall.

Intervals of Time

Five intervals of time, *i. e.*, 20 min., 1 hr., 4 hrs., 1 day, and 2 days, were selected with two considerations in view.

(1) To facilitate comparison with earlier reports, it was necessary to fix our program into that of other investigators. Accordingly, intervals which had not been included in the work of one or more of our predecessors do not appear in our plan. We further took into consideration whether the points on the curve to be thus empirically determined would be likely to represent an equation, if there be one. Cf. Table VII.

(2) We also tried to avoid the effect of diurnal variations. Later we found that the 4 hr. interval was too long for our purpose. Any interval longer than 4 hrs. and shorter than 24 would be too much beyond our control.

Methods of Scoring

(1) Anticipation. With this method complete retention is the successful anticipation of every syllable. There are 12 syllables in each series. On the basis of 12 one can easily convert an actual score into percentage terms.

(2) Relearning. The usual "saving method" was used, in which the number of presentations in relearning minus one, divided by the number of presentations in learning minus one, multiplied by 100, gives the percentage of forgetting.

(3) Written Reproduction. First, the reproduced amount is compared with the possible amount. X correct syllables reproduced is scored at $X/12$, which, multiplied by 100, gives a percentage score. A syllable with only 2 letters correct is scored $\frac{1}{2}$, as is also one with the initial and final consonants inverted.

Secondly, we took into consideration the position and sequence of each reproduced syllable. The difficulties for such minute scoring are two. (1) The relative value of the reproduced amount on the one hand and of position and sequence on the other can only be arbitrarily determined. (2) By chance the subject may reproduce a certain number of syllables in the original position or sequence without actually remembering either, and it is well nigh impossible to score this chance factor. In the present study, the total amount of reproduced material will be roughly scored $\frac{1}{2}$, and position and sequence $\frac{1}{4}$ each. It is assumed that material contributes as much value as position and sequence put together, and the latter are again considered to be equal in value. The chance factor is neglected. The records are, therefore, scored too high, but the extent of this effect one can easily approximate when we come to deal with the method of scoring reconstruction. Any such arbitrary process will, of course incur all the criticism that has been heaped upon Lyon[1] by writers like Kjerstad.[2] The latter, however, also neglected the chance factor. Our interpretations will be based mainly upon

[1] "A Rapid and Accurate Method for Scoring Nonsense Syllables and Words," *Amer. Jour. Psychol.*, Vol. XXIV, 1913, pp. 525-31.

[2] "The Form of the Learning Curves for Memory," *Psych. Rev., Monograph Supplements*, Vol. XXVI, 1919, No. 5, pp. 14 ff.

the first method of scoring, which does not take into account position and sequence.

Further, unlike the other methods of scoring, the values for written reproduction are independent of the amount of error made in recalling. The amount of error may also be reduced to percentage scores when compared with the actual or the possible amount of retention, *i. e.*, the amount of error may be computed as a percentage either of the whole series or of the reproduced material only.

(4) Recognition. When a number of syllables originally learned are mixed up with an equal number of new ones and then presented to the subject for recognition, the outstanding fact is that, by pure chance, one will most probably draw half of the original ones. Bean[3] overlooked this difficulty. Consequently, all his values were above 50% even to the end of the 28th day.

To eliminate this chance factor, Strong[4] devised the formula,

$$\text{Retention} = \frac{\text{Correct recognitions}}{\text{Total no. presented}} \times \frac{\text{Correct} - \text{incorrect recognitions}}{\text{Correct} + \text{incorrect recognitions}} \times 100.$$

No doubt, this formula takes into account the extremes of probability. That is, out of X things learned, a recognition of X/2 is scored 0, while a recognition of X is scored 100. Beyond that, the formula is exposed to numerous difficulties and seems to defeat its own purpose. The author pointed out that "it penalizes mistakes a little more than is warranted on a basis of chance." As a matter of fact, it penalizes sometimes too much and sometimes too little. In other words, the scores given on this basis are not always proportional to the probability. That proportionality, it seems to me, ought to be the criterion for the validity of the formula. For instance, $\dfrac{8}{24} \times \dfrac{8-1}{8+1} \times 100 = 25.9\%$.

Similarly, 8 correct ones and 2 incorrect ones would be scored 20.0%, and 8 correct ones and 3 incorrect ones 15.6%. Now

---

[3] *Op. cit.* His reproduction method is not any better. When one is required to write down 9 out of 18 consonants it is most probable that 4 or 5 will be correct, even though one does not realize there are *only* 18 consonants in the English alphabet.

[4] *Op. cit.* p. 355. Cf. *Psych. Rev.*, Vol. XIX, pp. 457 ff.

when 24 members are presented, the respective probabilities for
these three combinations to occur are $\dfrac{945}{52003} : \dfrac{3465}{52003} : \dfrac{9075}{52003}$.
provided that, by pure chance, one is as likely to take 9 as 10 or
11. It is very difficult to see how the chance factor is counter-
balanced by giving scores such as the above.

Again, suppose that of the total group presented, the subject
selects only 1 and that 1 be correct. According to the formula,
this performance would be scored $\dfrac{1}{\text{Total no.}} \times \dfrac{1-0}{1+0} \times 100$.

But if in the total number presented, the number of original ones
is equal to the number of new ones, the subject will be just as
likely to draw a correct one as an incorrect one. Such a performance should be scored 0.

Other defects of the formula, while not inherent and unavoidable, result from assumptions which one makes in applying it.
Thus Strong required his subjects to classify their judgments
according to degrees of certainty. After the first class, i. e.,
the most certain one, is scored by his formula, the second and
third classes cannot be penalized as rigidly, since chance has
been greatly reduced by the exclusion of the correct ones in the
first class.

Further, on the basis of the first class as 1, Strong scored the
second class ¾, and the third class ¼. These values are entirely arbitrary and have nothing to do with the formula. But
this method of scoring, together with the last named oversight,
certainly helped to make his curve of recognition memory something like Ebbinghaus' curve.

In the formulation of our own method of scoring, we first
take it for granted that, if there were no chance factor, each
score should then increase upon the next by a constant amount.

Then we calculated the probability of each kind of combination.
Thus, when the total group of 24 is presented, there are 2704156
possible ways to take 12. These are classified as follows:

No. in which there are 12 correct and 0 incorrect,   1
	11	1	144
	10	2	4356
	9	3	48400
	8	4	245025
	7	5	627264
	6	6	853776
			etc.

Six correct is the highest probability, the combination which is most likely to occur on the basis of pure chance. If we next regard this probability as 100% chance, we have

6 correct and 6 incorrect,	100.00% chance,
7	5	73.47%
8	4	28.70%
9	3	5.67%
10	2	.51%
11	1	.02%
12	0	.00%

Everything below 6 correct may be disregarded. Now divide 100 into 6 equal intervals, from 6 to 12, for scores when the chance factor is not deducted. Deducting from each interval the relative amount of chance, the final scale is

TABLE I

CORRECT	INCORRECT	PRELIMINARY SCORE	CHANCE	FINAL SCORE
6	0	0.00	100.00	0.00
7	5	16.67	73.47	4.42
8	4	33.33	28.70	23.76
9	3	50.00	5.67	47.17
10	2	66.67	.51	66.33
11	1	83.33	.02	83.31
12	0	100.00	.00	100.00

By extending this method, we can score recognition (1) *for any number of things presented,* (2) *for any number selected* (*not necessarily one-half of the number presented*)*, and* (3) *for any number of correct or incorrect things selected.* This may be seen from Table II, which can be extended indefinitely. In scoring, we can make use of this table and save a tremendous amount of time.

One must remember that these values are the most probable values. That is, in the long run, they will measure actual efficiency. Another method, and a more logical one, to score probability is to take, for instance, a performance of X correct choices and 12 — X incorrect ones, and see how probably that performance would happen, supposing the subject actually knows only 1, 2 or any number of the correct things selected. Score the number that the subject is supposed to know in order to make such a performance most probable.

However, this method does not serve our purpose, because it sometimes gives ambiguous results. For example, if a performance is 9 correct to 3 incorrect, we do not know whether the subject should be credited with 8 or 9 which he is supposed to remember. For

Supposing he knows 9, then the probability for him to get

9 correct is...............220/455
10 " " 198/455
11 " " 36/455
12 " " 1/455

Supposing he knows 8, then the probability for him to get

8 correct is...............495/1820
9 " " 880/1820
10 " " 396/1820
11 " " 48/1820
12 " " 1/1820

But the highest probability of the first column is equal to that of the second column.

$$\frac{220}{455} = \frac{880}{1820}$$

Shall the subject be credited 8 or 9?

TABLE II

Table for Scoring Recognition Memory, 24 presented,

12 correct + 12 incorrect

NO. CORRECT	NO. SELECTED											
	1	2	3	4	5	6	7	8	9	10	11	12
1	00.00	00.00	00.00	00.00	00.00	00.00	00.00	00.00	00.00	00.00	00.00	00.00
2		09.03	00.00	00.00	00.00	00.00	00.00	00.00	00.00	00.00	00.00	00.00
3			18.06	06.57	00.00	00.00	00.00	00.00	00.00	00.00	00.00	00.00
4				29.54	12.31	05.42	00.00	00.00	00.00	00.00	00.00	00.00
5					39.40	26.78	10.11	04.82	00.00	00.00	00.00	00.00
6						49.05	34.93	25.03	09.03	04.52	00.00	00.00
7							57.82	48.06	32.40	24.07	08.51	04.17
8								66.52	55.39	47.40	31.21	23.76
9									74.96	66.39	53.91	47.17
10										83.32	73.25	66.33
11											91.67	83.31
12												100.00

(5) Reconstruction. In this method, we encountered the same difficulty of chance success, and so far as we know, no attempt was made to eliminate this factor in previous studies. We first divide our problem into (A) position and (B) sequence. It is evident that, by chance, one may put a part of the series in the original position and sequence.

(A) Take position first. Assuming perfect chance in the rearrangement of n things, the number of ways for X of the n things to be out of the original order is the number of n things taken X at a time, minus the number of permutations of X things in which the X things are *not all* out of the original positions. For 12 things, the probability for any number of them to be out of position as compared with any other number, is

0 positions out,	1
2	66
3	440
4	4455
5	34848
6	244860
7	1468368
8	7342335
9	29369120
10	88107426
11	176214840
12	176214841
	479001600

Taking 17621841 as 100% chance and following the same procedure as in the recognition method, we have the results as given in Table III.

TABLE III

POSITIONS OUT	PRELIMINARY SCORE	CHANCE	FINAL SCORE
12	00.00	100.00	00.00
11	09.09	100.00	00.00
10	18.18	50.00	09.09
9	27.27	16.67	22.72
8	36.36	4.17	34.84
7	45.45	.83	45.07
6	54.55	.14	54.47
5	63.64	.02	63.63
4	72.73	.00	72.73
3	81.82	.00	81.82
2	90.91	.00	90.91
0	100.00	.00	100.00

The principle applied in the development of this scale is not limited to a series of any particular number.

(B) Sequence. Here we failed to formulate a simple mathematical statement of the relative amounts of chance and had to depend upon empirical data. By casting a series of 12 members 1000 times and recording the chance sequences of the members, we obtained the results given in Table IV.

TABLE IV

MEMBERS OUT OF ORIGINAL SEQUENCE

	1	2	3	4	5	6	7	8	9	10	11	
1st 100 trials	0	0	0	0	0	0	1	5	15	42	37	100
2nd	0	0	0	0	0	1	0	4	13	41	41	100
3d	0	0	0	0	0	0	2	5	10	35	48	100
4th	0	0	0	0	0	0	1	4	19	34	42	100
5th	0	0	0	0	0	0	0	4	14	45	37	100
6th	0	0	0	0	0	0	1	5	20	32	42	100
7th	0	0	0	0	0	0	1	3	18	37	41	100
8th	0	0	0	0	1	0	0	4	12	37	46	100
9th	0	0	0	0	0	1	1	3	18	33	44	100
10th	0	0	0	0	0	0	1	3	13	36	47	100
	0	0	0	0	1	2	8	40	152	372	425	1000

Comparing the totals with each of the 10 groups, we concluded that these results were regular enough to be a valid sample. We then followed exactly the same procedure as in the scoring of position and obtained the final scale as given in Table V.

TABLE V

0 out of sequence,	Score 100.00
1	90.91
2	81.82
3	72.73
4	63.64
5	54.42
6	45.24
7	35.68
8	24.70
9	11.68
10	1.13
11	.00

(C) After scoring both position and sequence, the average of the two was taken as a rough measurement of Reconstruction memory. This final process is arbitrary and may be entirely superfluous. It does not furnish any more adequate measurement of reconstruction than position and sequence taken separately, since the resulting values do not lend themselves to a clearer interpretation.

QUANTITATIVE DATA

The results from these five methods of measurement are tabulated in Table VI and graphically represented in Fig. II.

TABLE VI

PERCENTAGE OF RETENTION

	20 min.	1 hr.	4 hrs.	1 day	2 days
Anticipation*	67.8	50.2	39.0	17.8	10.0
Relearning*	75.0	65.9	54.9	52.1	47.7
Written reproduction........	88.1	82.1	60.5	39.2	26.7
Reconstruction	91.5	89.7	75.4	50.9	38.6
Recognition	97.8	94.6	93.3	74.6	71.5

From Table VI and Fig. II, the phenomena of retention may be generally stated as follows:

(1) The amount of retention decreases with time.

(2) On the whole, forgetting is most rapid at first, but there are two notable exceptions. A. The curve for recognition slopes down much more rapidly from 4 hrs. to 1 day than from 1 to 4 hrs. B. In reconstruction, the decrease in the amount of retention is more rapid from 1 hr. to 4 hrs. than from 20 min. to 1 hr.

(3) All the curves are relatively uniform and can be described by mathematical formulae.

*In the latter part of this series of experiments, it was found necessary to counteract the effect of diurnal variations by distributing the 4-hr. series more carefully. Some of these series were given at the regular learning time of the day for each subject; the rest were given either 4 hrs. before or after that time. This procedure was carried out only for anticipation and relearning. Subject K's records were excluded from the above averages for not being so distributed.

Because of a mistake in scoring, subject D's 5 records had to be excluded from the averages for anticipation.

Altogether, the averages for anticipation represent 28 records from 8 subjects; relearning represents 33 records from 9 subjects; the rest include 35 records from 10 subjects.

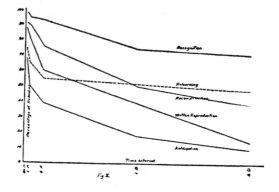

Fig. X

(4) Four of the curves stand invariably in a given order. Recognition gives the highest values. Reconstruction occupies the second position. Written reproduction follows as a close third. Anticipation always has the lowest value.

(5) The relation of the values for relearning varies with the time interval. As may be seen, its order is fourth for the 20-min. interval and second for the 2-day interval.

In general, these conclusions are in harmony with the results of earlier investigations, except those of Ballard. These results are brought together in Table VII and compared with those of the present study.

In relearning, the present results approach most closely to those of Finkenbinder. In no instance is the difference more than 10%. Finkenbinder used practically the same technique as our own, excepting that we required the subject to spell the syllable instead of pronouncing it as a whole.

With the "saving method," an increase in the number of presentations in learning increases the amount of retention, while an increase in the number of presentations in relearning decreases the same. Since the number of presentations in relearning is almost always smaller than that of learning (except in cases of 100% forgetting), every increase of equal or nearly equal magnitude in the number of presentations in both learning and relearning will increase the amount of forgetting, or, in other words, it decreases the amount of retention thus calculated.

TABLE VII

INTERVALS	Relearning					Recognition	
	EBBING.	RADOSSAWLJEVITCH		FINK.	LUH	STRONG	LUH
15 sec.			*			84.6	
5 min.		97.5	95.9			72.7	
15 min.						62.7	97.8
20 min.	58.2	88.6	89.8		75.0		
30 min.				75.0		55.5	94.6
1 hr.	44.2	70.7	75.3	72.8	65.9	57.3	94.6
2 hrs.				69.4		47.2	93.3
4 hrs.				64.4	54.9	50.6	93.3
8 hrs.	35.8	47.4	66.5	65.5		40.6	
12 hrs.				63.8		41.1	
16 hrs.				63.0			
24 hrs.	33.7	68.9	70.2	57.8	52.1	28.8	74.6
36 hrs.				58.8			
2 days	27.8	60.9	72.3	55.6	47.7	22.9	71.5
3 days				52.1			
4 days						19.3	
6 days	25.4	49.3	59.5				
7 days						9.6	
14 days		41.0	51.4				
21 days		37.8	48.6				
30 days	21.1	20.2	27.0				
42 days						6.3	
120 days		2.8	3.3				

*Averages reconstructed from R's principal experiments which included only series of 12 syllables. The column immediately to the left, as quoted by F., represents averages from 8, 12 and 16 syllable series.

Other things being equal, it takes a subject more presentations to spell a series correctly than to pronounce it correctly, both in learning and relearning. This may explain the fact that the relearning values reported in the present study are lower than those of Finkenbinder.

Similarity of technique does result in proportional similarity of quantitative data. It points toward the possibility of establishing norms, though not one norm or one general curve of forgetting, for various conditions of retention. Other numerical differences between the present study and previous reports may be easily accounted for by individual differences and the disparity of methods.

The difference between our recognition values and Strong's is sometimes as high as 50%. There is no cause for wonder, however, since the data were collected under as divergent conditions as imaginable. The material, the degree of learning and the methods of scoring were all different. Our data will have to be distorted a great deal before they can conform to the Ebbinghaus type of curve. Even if we could derive a general equation which satisfies both sets of values, it would be so complex and obscure that scientific interpretation would be better off without it. Here lies the danger of speculation without specifying the conditions and variables which enter into the determination of our values.

MISCELLANEOUS COMPARISONS

1. The Difference between Scoring the Number of Syllables and of Letters in Anticipation.

There are altogether 12 syllables, or 36 letters, in each syllable series. Since a syllable may be only partly anticipated, *i. e.,* when only one or two letters of the syllables are anticipated in the correct position and sequence, it is evident that scoring the number of letters will give higher values than scoring the number of syllables. The increment is, however, very small, as can be seen from Table VIII.

TABLE VIII

			29.min.	1 hr.	2 hrs.	1 day	2 days
Anticipation,	scoring	12 syllables	67.8	50.2	39.0	17.8	10.0
"	"	36 letters	70.2	54.2	41.6	19.7	10.5

That there is a positive difference at each interval in favor of the number of letters indicates the existence of partial retention which is not ready enough for successful anticipation but which is nevertheless effective. One might anticipate this fact from the nature of the case, quite independent of the magnitude and the probable error of the difference. Such partial retention may be due to one of two causes, or to both. (1) One part of a syllable may be forgotten more rapidly than another part. (2) The association link may be so weakened that it cannot be reinstated within the short time limit of 2 sec. We shall later see that extending the time limit for recall increases the score by a far greater amount than does the present process. A time limit is detrimental to partial retention.

It is important to notice that by scoring the number of letters instead of syllables, the shape of the curve is not materially changed. In Fig. III, the curves for the number of syllables and for the number of letters may be compared by direct inspection.

2. The Difference between Scoring the Whole Series With and Without the First Syllable.

This was done on *a priori* grounds. Apparently, there seems to be a difference between the anticipation of the first syllable of the series and of the other eleven. For each of the eleven, anticipation is facilitated by that part of the series which is already exposed. The associative bond is aroused by so many "cues," such as visual, auditory and vocal, which are not available for the first syllable. Such is not the case with written reproduction. For there the subject may begin from any point of the series and run forwards and backwards.

Specifically speaking, the ground for singling out the first syllable of the series is perhaps insecure. Association is effective not only between immediately consecutive syllables, but also in the most criss-cross way imaginable.[5] So even the recall of the first syllable will be helped by the anticipatory re-instatement of the succeeding members. But in general, one may consider the association between two like members of a series as quantitatively different from that between one of these members and another dissimilar factor.

When the first syllable was thus excluded, we obtained the comparative results of Table IX.

TABLE IX

	20 min.	1 hr.	2 hrs.	1 day	2 days
For 12 syllables	67.8	50.2	39.0	17.8	10.0
" 11 "	64.9	46.0	32.0	13.0	8.3

Quite beyond our expectation, the averages for 12 syllables exceed those for 11 at every interval. The first syllable was more

[5] Cf. Ebbinghaus, *Op. cit.,* Ch. IX.

often correctly anticipated than the average of the other 11. Thus the lack of associative "cues" seems to be more than compensated by the favorable effect of primacy, and our *a priori* conclusions become groundless.

3. The Difference between Scoring and Not Scoring Position and Sequence in Written Reproduction.

As already stated, written reproduction was scored (1) as to the gross amount of retention and (2) as to that factor plus position and sequence. In the latter case, the gross amount was scored $\frac{1}{2}$ and position and sequence $\frac{1}{4}$ each. The comparative results are presented in Table X.

TABLE X

	20 min.	1 hr.	4 hrs.	1 day	2 days
With position and sequence	80.3	73.1	50.3	32.5	22.6
Without position and sequence	88.1	82.1	60.5	39.2	26.7

Scoring position and sequence apparently decreases the amount of retention. It is, of course, much more probable for a syllable to be reproduced than to be reproduced in the original position and sequence. On the other hand, it is also remarkable that there are not so many instances in which a syllable is remembered as to its position and sequence but only vaguely in specific content. The above differences would certainly be more prominent if we had taken into account the extent of chance in our method of scoring.

Later we shall see that the decrease in the amount of retention due to scoring position and sequence is not limited to the conditions of this series of experiments. The phenomenon was reproduced in a second series of experiments in which the degree of the original learning was varied. *Still the difference in amount is not such as to change the general shape of the curve.* Compare Fig. III for this series of experiments.

4. The Difference between Scoring Preliminary and Final Records.

In describing the methods of scoring, we mentioned that records were taken of the amount of error in written reproduction, of the amount of material recalled upon the lapse of preliminary time limits in recognition and written reproduction and of the amount of time spent in the whole process of recall in recognition, reconstruction and written reproduction. These results will be presented and compared in another section.

5. *Corroborative Data from the Second Series of Experiments.*

In the second series of experiments, the Reproduction, Recognition, and Reconstruction methods of testing results were used when the material was learned with different degrees of mastery. When the degree of learning was exactly the same as in the first series of experiments, the two series of values corroborated each other to a remarkable extent. The values for both series of experiments are presented in Table XI. A fuller description of the conditions of the second series is to be found at the beginning of Chapter III.

TABLE XI

	20 min.	1 hr.	4 hrs.	1 day	2 days
Written reproduction					
1st series of experiments......	88.1	82.1	60.5	39.2	26.7
2d series of experiments......	90.6	85.8	64.8	45.6	40.2
Average	89.4	84.0	62.6	42.4	33.5
Scoring position and sequence					
1st series of experiments......	80.3	73.1	50.3	32.5	22.6
2d series of experiments......	86.5	81.2	58.0	37.5	33.5
Average	83.4	77.2	54.2	35.0	28.1
Recognition					
1st series of experiments......	97.8	94.6	93.3	74.6	71.5
2d series of experiments......	95.8	95.0	91.6	77.6	78.9
Average	96.8	94.8	92.5	76.1	75.2
Reconstruction					
1st series of experiments......	91.5	89.7	75.4	50.9	38.6
2d series of experiments......	89.3	90.4	74.9	48.6	44.0
Averages	90.4	90.1	75.2	49.7	41.3

For the shorter intervals, the validity of either set of values is self-evident and beyond question. But the difference between the two sets increases with the length of the interval. This fact is to be later considered as a characteristic of individual differences in the ability to recall.

In written reproduction, when position and sequence were scored, the values of the first series were not so closely reproduced in the second series for the short intervals but more closely reproduced for the long intervals. The validity of the long interval values is questionable. As to the short intervals, we have already stated that the method of scoring position and sequence is not very reliable.

Comparison and Interpretation of data

From Fig. II, two general phenomena are easily observable. (1) The curve for relearning does not fall as rapidly as the other curves and it intersects with the reconstruction and written reproduction curves as the length of the interval is increased. Were it possible to fit each series of empirical data to an ideal curve or family of curves, one would still be confronted with the difficulty that relearning does not satisfy quite the same type of equation as the other memory processes. By increasing the number of constants, we might represent all the series of values by a general logarithmic equation which applies to all conditions, but our ignorance of the actual and specific course of forgetting would be as profound as ever. Suppose that the values of all the constants are given or calculated, which is a wild supposition in the light of our present knowledge of memory processes. We could then be sure of only one thing, viz., *Relearning and the other processes do not satisfy the same type of logarithmic equation.*

(2) With the exception of the relearning curve, the other curves are more or less similar. The similarity becomes more prominent at the end of the 4-hr. interval. It may even be said that after the lapse of that interval, the difference between any two memory processes except relearning and probably recognition, measured at any time, is a definite amount which is constant for those two processes. Recognition is in many respects similar to relearning. It favors the longer intervals and partial retention.

This similarity of the curves is reproduced in the second series of experiments, as may be seen in Table XI.

(*1*) *Comparison of the Relearning and the Other Curves.*

One possible reason for the disparity as discussed under (1), one might assume, may be traced back to defects in the methods of measurement, which do not take into enough consideration the amount of partial retention. As we shall later develop, the processes of memory fade away gradually, from complete retention to bare recognition. One may thus be led to expect that the amount of partial and uncertain retention increases in direct proportion to the length of the interval. Could we devise a finer method by which each memory process is measured in its *entirety,* the score for each interval would be increased by the amount of partial retention. But the increment would make very little difference in the shape of the curve for the shorter intervals when the total amount of partial retention is rather small; and in fact, we see that the fall of the relearning curve is similar to the others for the short intervals. In other words, the defects in the methods of measurement could not be so easily detected when the interval is short. For the long intervals, these defects could be remedied only by carefully scoring the amount of partial retention. Since the latter is thought to increase with the time interval, the results thus scored would manifestly be a curve which slopes down much less abruptly and approaches a type like that of relearning.

Now the argument as here presented assumes at least two things. A. A more accurate method of measurement will bring to light the amount of partial retention so much so that the shape of the curve will be changed. B. The amount of partial retention increases with the time interval.

As to B, we suggest that this assumption is not always true and shall try to demonstrate the fact in Ch. IV.

Assumption A seems more plausible only because we cannot develop a method of such magical accuracy. If the methods of measurement were the only faulty factor, then the improvement of technique by way of refining these methods would in proportion make the other curves approach more closely the relearning type of curve. However, within the limits of our investigation, the shape of the curves do not materially change on account of minute variations in the methods of measurement. The following facts indicate that the differences under consideration are more fundamental than merely a matter of technique.

(a) In anticipation, scoring the number of letters as well as syllables increases the value by including partial retention, *but the increments are not such as to make the curve fall less rapidly than does scoring the number of syllables alone* (Fig. III).

(b) In written reproduction, scoring position and sequence in addition to the amount of reproduced material does not change the shape of the curve very appreciably. When position and sequence are not scored, more allowance is made for partial retention, for a syllable which is retained only as to its content and not its relative order is scored as much as one which is completely retained. According to the proposed theory, scoring position and sequence would make the curve fall much more rapidly. This is not a fact.

(c) In recognition and written reproduction, as will be discussed later on, extending the time limit for recall so as to make more room for the reinstatement of partial retention does not change the general shape of the curve, though the increment of the score after the extension of the time limit in recognition does increase with the length of the interval so that the curve slopes toward the abscissa more gradually. (For recognition in the first series of experiments, see Fig. III.)

Thus, scoring partial anticipation, neglecting position and sequence in written reproduction and, finally, extending the time limit for recall all fail to eliminate the apparent difference between the relearning curve and the other curves. The assumptions of the theory cannot be substantiated.

It is doubtful whether the relearning curve can be directly compared with any of the rest. Relearning, being a composite method, may be analyzed into anticipation and subsequent learning. Most probably, the subsequent learning is a function of the amount of anticipation. The more the amount of anticipation, the less the number of presentations necessary for relearning

If any such causal connection be found to be generally valid, then the relearning values can be constructed from the original learning and the amount of anticipation. Only such analysis could bring out any natural relationship that may exist between the

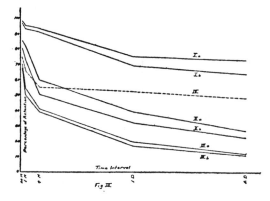

amount of retention and the time necessary for relearning. For the present these two factors cannot but be treated as independent values, particularly for the following reason.

The values for relearning are based upon the time of learning and relearning, the proficiency of retention being measured by a ratio of time; while the values for the other curves are built on an almost totally different criterion. With the latter, the standard of proficiency is not the length of time, but the ability to retain the whole series, and different degrees of retention are measured as steps approaching that standard.

For this reason, the time for relearning cannot be interpreted in terms of the amount of retention, but both must be taken into consideration in order to understand the phenomenon of retention quantitatively. A score made by the "saving method" cannot be converted into another score except as to mean the amount of time saved. As to the measurements for the amount of retained material, the same course of reasoning will lead to the conclusion that these measurements do not indicate anything as to the relative difficulty experienced in mastering the material. For instance, 60% of retention is three times as high as 20% with respect only to the actual amount of material; it explains nothing as to how it was acquired, or how much it is really worth as compared with another amount acquired with the expenditure of a larger or smaller amount of time.

Perhaps a consideration of the shape of the learning curves for memory as involved in the relearning method will bring to mind more distinctly the disparity between the two standards of measurement, namely, time and amount. If in both learning and relearning, the effect of each presentation of the series upon learning were constant, the learning curves would then satisfy equations of the first degree such as hypothetically represented in Fig. IV. Further, if the effect were constant for relearning

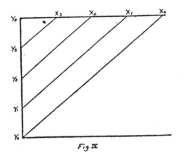

Fig IV

after any time interval and with any amount of actually retained and reproduced material, then the curves would be parallel. In such a case, the amount of retention would be a function of the time necessary for relearning, and *vice versa*. For, referring to Fig. IV, the amounts of retained material after different time intervals are Y_0Y_3, Y_0Y_2, etc. Correspondingly, according to the "saving method," the percentages of retention and forgetting are calculated according to distances on the line parallel to the abscissa which represents the number of presentations necessary for learning or relearning. X_0Y_4 is the number of presentations in learning. X_3Y_4 is the number of presentations necessary for relearning after the lapse of an interval when the amount of retained material as represented on the ordinate, is Y_0Y_3. The percentage of forgetting for that interval is $X_3 Y_4 / X_0 Y_4$. It corresponds to the amount $Y_3 Y_4$. Similarly, $X_2 Y_4 / X_0 Y_4$ corresponds to $Y_2 Y_4$, $X_1 Y_4 / X_0 Y_4$ corresponds to $Y_1 Y_4$, etc. It is clear that since the learning curves are supposed to be parallel, the percentages of forgetting, or of retention, thus calculated from the abscissa would always be proportional to the percentages calculated from the ordinate. *Then the curves of retention based upon the "saving method" and upon the amount of recalled material would be similar, when plotted on the same scale.*

As a matter of fact, the learning curves for memory are not parallel straight lines. Practically all the curves so far determined are negatively accelerative, including especially the recent work of Kjerstad.[6] This is also corroborated by our own results in both learning and relearning. The degree of negative acceleration in the relearning process also varies with the time-interval or the amount of actually retained material. That is, if the curves follow the same law of negative acceleration, they can then be represented as in Fig. V. In the figure, $Y_3 Y_4$, $Y_2 Y_4$, etc. represent respectively the amounts of forgetting after different time intervals, $X_3 Y_4$, $X_2 Y_4$, etc. represent respectively the corresponding number of presentations necessary for relearning for each of the assigned time intervals. From that figure, two facts become self-evident.

a) Not only do X and Y differ in the scale and unit of measurement, but the functional relationship between the two is not so simple as that represented in Fig. IV and not such as could be easily determined. Referring back to Fig. II, this difference in the units of the scales and this complex and unknown functional relationship between them would mean that the absolute height of the retention curve for relearning, as compared with that of the other retention curves, cannot be interpreted by mere inspection. The absolute values of the curves cannot be directly compared.

b) But the more significant fact is that these very characteristics of the learning curves will directly lead to the particular difference between the shape of the relearning curve for retention and of the other retention curves, as seen in Fig. II. In Fig. V, the number of presentations, $X_3 Y_4$, $X_2 Y_4$, etc. increases *at first* more rapidly than the corresponding amounts of forgetting,

[6] *Op. cit.*

Y_3 Y_4, Y_2 Y_3, etc.; but less rapidly when the amount of actually retained material is small, *i. e., when the time interval is increased.* Now if we plot the values on the ordinate against the variable of time in such manner as manifested by the retention curves

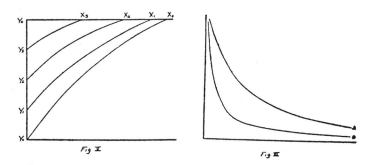

Fig I   Fig II

for the amount of reproduced material (A), and if we further draw a curve (B) for the retention values as determined from the abscissa on the basis of (A), their relationship will be such as given in Fig. VI. The difference between the two is exactly what we observed in Fig. II.

Thus, the difference between the relearning curve for retention and the other retention curves is not due to the phenomenon of retention as such, but to the characteristic of the learning curve. If the latter were invariably a simple logarithmic curve, it would necessarily follow that the *forgetting* curve as determined by the "saving method" would be logarithmic. When this relationship obtains, as claimed by most of our predecessors, it is important to remember that,

a. The curve of forgetting for the saving method is logarithmic only because it involves the ratio of two logarithmic learning curves.

b. Similar phenomena cannot be expected to reappear when the same factors are not involved.

The Unsatisfactoriness of the Relearning Method.

It is now evident that neither time nor amount is a complete measurement for retention, but both are not equally *convenient*.

A. The first unsatisfactoriness of the relearning method is that it achieves much less validity of data for the same expenditure of time as compared with the other methods.

'As a test for validity, we use the mean deviation of the values of all the series which a subject learns or reproduces for each specific interval. This M. D. may be made directly comparable with other M. D.'s by applying Pearson's formula $V = \dfrac{100\,M.\,D.}{Median}$.

The greater the coefficient V, the less is the validity. Five of the subjects learned five series for each of the five intervals in the first series of experiments. Five is a ridiculously small number for such statistical treatment. If, however, all the results point uniformly in one direction, most probably there is an actual difference in the degree of validity of these values. Table XII presents the results for only two intervals, 20 min. and 1 hr. Beyond that, the variability of the relearning method becomes so large as to make such comparison superfluous and meaningless. A ? mark indicates that, of the two intervals and the two particular methods compared, the coefficient of variability is larger for one method at one interval, and for the other at the other. In a similar way, a + sign means larger variability for relearning at both intervals.

TABLE XII

SUBJECT	ANTICIPATION	RECOGNITION	RECONSTRUCTION	W. REP.
D	?	+	+	?
Le	?	+	?	+
Lo	?	+	+	?
R	+	?	?	?
W	?	+	+	+

Of all the paired comparisons, none is distinctly in favor of the relearning method. Its coefficient of variability is higher than that of any other method. That is, for equal expenditure of time and energy, relearning produces less satisfactory results than does any other method.

B. In addition to the above, the relearning method makes impossible certain correlation studies which are easily accessible to the other methods. Questions like the following have to be answered one way or another. (a) What is the relation between the speed of learning and the amount of retention for each interval? (b) For all the series learned by the same subject, what is the relation between the difficulty of learning and the amount of retention, etc.? As to question (a), the problem of the correlation between "immediate" and "permanent" memory has claimed a goodly number of working days. Very little has been written on question (b), but Ebert and Meumann[7] once raised the problem whether subject matter that is readily learned is forgotten more rapidly or more slowly than that which requires greater labor in memorizing. In dealing with these problems, the relearning method was generally used. Relearning, as we already discussed, involves two learning processes. Suppose a number of syllable series to be learned in X, X', X", . . . presentations and relearned in Y, Y', Y", . . . presentations. The amounts of forgetting will be $\dfrac{Y}{X}, \dfrac{Y'}{X'}, \dfrac{Y''}{X''}, \ldots$ Learning and forgetting involve the same factor X, X', X", . . . That fact deprives any correlation study of its real significance. If it is further argued that the percentage of retention is determined by X—Y, X'—Y', X"—Y", ... which are independent values, we suggest that these values can be more reasonably established by some other methods which directly measures the amount of reproduced material.

(2) *Comparison of the Curves which Represent Only the Amount of Reproduced Material.*

We have explained why the relearning and the other curves are different in general form, and now proceed to the problem why these other curves differ in absolute numerical value. But we cannot treat the problem without first proving that the numerical differences are real and not adventitious.

First, we can refer back to the data for each individual subject, which constitute the group averages. From the group curves, recognition has a higher value than reconstruction for each of the five intervals. The same relation holds for reconstruction and written reproduction, and for the latter and antici-

[7] "Ueber einige Grundfragen der Psychologie der Uebungsphenomene im Bereiche des Gedächtnisses," *Archive f. Gesamte Psy.*, Vol. IV, 1904, pp. 193-4.

pation. This particular order of proficiency for the several measurements of retention holds true for the majority of the subjects. Thus, of the 20 individual values, 10 from each series of experiments, which constitute the final recognition score for the 20 m:n. interval, only one is higher than its corresponding value which goes to make the final score for reconstruction for the same interval, etc. Table XIII presents these facts in brief.

TABLE XIII

PERCENTAGE OF INDIVIDUAL CASES WHICH CORRESPOND TO GROUP RESULTS

	20 min.	1 hr.	4 hrs.	1 day	2 days
Anticipation cf. written reproduction*	100	100	87	87	75
Written reproduction cf. reconstruction	60	75	75	70	65
Reconstruction cf. recognition	95	80	95	95	95

* Only 8 values from 8 subjects in the 1st series of experiments. The rest are constituted of 20 values from 20 subjects in both series of experiments.

Secondly, the validity of the numerical differences may be proved by the magnitude of their probable errors, as presented in Table XIV.

TABLE XIV

	20 min.	1 hr.	4 hrs.	1 day	2 days
Difference between					
Antic. and Wr. Rep............	20.3	31.9	21.5	21.4	16.7
P. E. of difference.............	4.5	3.7	5.5	7.0	6.1
Difference between					
Wr. Rep. and Reconstruction...	1.0	6.1	12.6	7.3	7.8
P. E. of difference	1.1	1.7	2.7	4.5	4.3
Difference between					
Recons. and Recognition......	6.4	4.7	17.3	26.4	33.9
P. E. of difference.............	1.5	1.9	2.2	4.3	4.3

The P. E. of the difference between reconstruction and written reproduction can be reduced by increasing the number of subjects. In other words, the values for reconstruction and written reproduction may be slightly changed with the increase in the number of subjects, especially for the 20 min. interval. That there is a positive difference in favor of reconstruction at each of the intervals is unmistakable. The validity of all the other differences is self-evident.

Returning now to the group curves, we further find that, while after the lapse of the 4 hr. interval the course of the curves become more or less parallel, such is not the case for the shorter intervals. There the decreases in value are more abrupt for certain curves than for others. On the whole, the one that begins the lowest at 20 min. falls the most rapidly so that the curves become farther and farther apart as the length of the interval increases. So the Ebbinghaus tradition is substantiated by our data to that extent.

However, the negative acceleration theory of the curve of forgetting does not hold for all of our values. The two notable exceptions, as may be seen from pp. 21-22 are:

1. In recognition, the transition from 1 hr. to 4 hrs. is much less accelerative than that between 4 hrs and 1 day.

2. In written reproduction, the curve approaches a straight line between 20 min. and 4 hrs.

A significant fact is that these exceptions in the first series of experiments were reproduced in the second series. Further, imposing a time limit upon the act of recognition and scoring position and sequence in written reproduction did not in the least ameliorate these peculiarities. Is the curve of forgetting a logarithmic curve, as has been repeatedly maintained? These facts must be taken into consideration and explained.

One must also remember the course of the curves after the lapse of the 4-hr. interval, as described in a preceding paragraph. What is its bearing on a general logarithmic equation?

From the above, we may still conclude that, of two memory processes, the one that commands a higher "initial" amount of forgetting tends to fade away more rapidly than the other. This acceleration approaches a limit at the end of 4 hrs., and does not resume its initial course even to the end of 2 days.

One word as to what is meant by an "initial" amount of forgetting, a term first used by Bean. When retention is measured at the end of 20 min., we see only a cross-section of the stream of forgetting, to use James' old metaphor. From our data we cannot determine whether the grade of the headwaters is steep or level, or where the grade actually begins. In other words, we do not know what the "initial" amount of forgetting is, for each process. The quantitative differences as we measure at the end of 20 min. may doubtless be traced back to differences of the same kind. We assume that, if at 20 min., retention as measured by the anticipation method is less than by the recognition method, this was also true for shorter periods than 20 min., though not in the same ratio and by the same amount. But in fact, forgetting for one process may not begin at the same point as for another.

This is particularly true for written reproduction, recognition and reconstruction. When the method of presentation in the original learning is different from the method of testing, we can no longer compare directly the amount of immediate retention with the values that determine the curves of forgetting. In anticipation and relearning we know that the amount of retention immediately after learning is 100% so that we can trace these curves back to Y_0, i. e., where the length of the interval is 0. But in the other three methods, the forgetting curves begin at 20 min. and we cannot go back any further. It is perhaps unfortunate that we did not vary the methods of the original learning as well as the methods of testing, but then we would have introduced another constant and would have made our data more difficult to interpret.

Very likely, the quantitative differences between any two processes measured at any time may be greatly reduced by transposing the curves so that the points of "initial" forgetting coincide. All this may be empirically determined. Unless such problems are solved, the term "initial" forgetting will remain as meaningless as the "logarithmic" curve of forgetting.

Possible Explanations for the Quantitative Differences.

The conditions are complicated. Perhaps no single explanation is sufficient, but the following are more than likely.

1) The temporal order in which the methods were applied. In one half of the series given to each subject, anticipation was tested before relearning. In the other half, written reproduction was the first test applied. Recognition followed after written reproduction, and reconstruction after recognition. The high

retention values for recognition and reconstruction and the low values for anticipation and written reproduction may partly be due to the presence or absence of a preceding recalling process. For the present, we cannot determine whether that effect actually exists and to what extent. It is probable, however, that the effect of a preceding recalling process may simply reduce the duration of the succeeding recalling process without changing the amount of recall of the latter. In Ch. VI we shall see that the average duration of the written reproduction process was longer than for recognition, and the latter longer than for reconstruction. It is possible, of course, that a preceding recalling process affects both the amount and the duration of a succeeding one.

Apparently, the explanation does not cover all the facts. Reconstruction followed after recognition but gave much the smaller values.

2) The duration of the several processes. The duration of the anticipation process was 24 sec.; that of written reproduction, 5 min.; while recognition and reconstruction did not have time limits. So the order of the numerical values corresponds to the order of the duration of the processes. But as we shall later discuss in full, it took the average subject much less than 5 min. to complete the written reproduction process. The actual duration of recognition was not half as long as written reproduction, and that of reconstruction was still shorter. The actual differences in duration are not proportional to the numerical differences in the retention values. Written reproduction had the longest duration but gave the lowest retention values except anticipation.

3) Differences in the units of measurement. In anticipation and written reproduction, the scores were based upon the amount of reproduced material. The requirement of the recognition method was merely that the different members be re-instated upon the presentation of the original series. In reconstruction, only position and sequence were required. The implication would be that the numerical differences under discussion cannot be taken too seriously.

However, this kind of explanation is, in a way, begging the question. In written reproduction, recognition and reconstruction, we scored *the same records* for different values. Were the scales and units identical, we could not have had more than one value. The required explanation is this: Given different methods of scoring the same records, why do the results differ in such a characteristic way? The proposed explanation only tells us that we should not have used those methods. So we are led to the fourth probable explanation which seems to us to be most reasonable.

4) The conditions of recall. The experimental situations under which the subject was required to recall were vastly different. Our measurements took into consideration, among other things,

a) The retention of the separate parts of a serial act of memory as called for by
   (a) Written reproduction, and
   (b) Recognition.
b) The associative links that connect and combine these parts.
c) The readiness with which they are recalled, as measured by
   (a) The amount of time necessary for recall and
   (b) The amount of material recalled within a given time limit.

These factors are not equally important in all the methods of measurement. *The number of these factors involved and the extent to which they are involved determine the quantitative differences.* Thus, by order of the difficulty of recall, (Figs. II and III), the four methods are ranked:

1. Anticipation.
2. Written reproduction, scoring position and sequence.
2a Written reproduction, not scoring position and sequence.
3. Reconstruction.
4. Recognition, with time limit.
4a Recognition, without time limit.

Analyzing the number of factors involved, they follow:

1. Anticipation. Factors a) and c) are both important. b) is necessary for complete re-instatement, but once a mistake is made, it is automatically corrected by the exposure of the syllable.

2. Written reproduction, scoring position and sequence. Factors a) and b) are equally important. c) is involved only to the extent of being able to reproduce the material within 5 min.

2a Written reproduction, not scoring position and sequence. The conditions are the same as in 2, minus b).

3. Reconstruction. Only b) is involved, being the complementary of 2a.

4. Recognition, with the time limit. a) is only slightly involved, b) not at all and c) only to the extent of being able to select the 12 syllables within 90 sec.

4a Recognition, without time limit. Only a) is partly involved.

From this we conclude that

1. The quantity of recall depends upon the number of restricting factors in the recall situation. The greater number of such factors and the more exactingly they operate, the less the amount of recall.

2. The proportionality between the number of such factors and the amount of recall is an index to the practical validity of our methods of measurement. The scores given by these methods are directly comparable.

It is, therefore, meaningless to say that forgetting in general follows a certain equation. There can be as many curves of forgetting as there are situations and methods of measurement. We know almost nothing as to the "initial" amount of forgetting and very little as to the general shape of any curve. It may be harmless to say that forgetting is a logarithmic function of time, so long as we remember that the significant thing that should influence future investigations is not the logarithm, but the determination of the constants. The latter we cannot deduce from generalizations, but can only measure under variable conditions.

III. RETENTION AS A FUNCTION OF THE
DEGREE OF LEARNING

In the second series of experiments, the condition that was varied was the degree of the original learning. The ten subjects of the second group served throughout these experiments, each learning at least 44 syllable series, besides preliminary practice trials. The series and the degrees of learning were distributed according to the following scheme.

1. Altogether we used four degrees of learning.
   A. 100% learning, with the same conditions as in the first series of experiments.
   B. 150% learning, in which the subject was given one half of the number of presentations in addition to what was required for the first errorless anticipation of a series. Thus, if a series was learned in 10 presentations, 5 more were given. If 9, also 5.
   C. 67% learning. The average number of presentations was calculated for each subject after he had learned 20 series besides the preliminary trials. In 67% learning, he was given two-thirds of that number of presentations. (The average number was previously taken to be the total number minus one, *i.e.*, the number of presentations in which there was actual anticipation. In the present case, the *total* number was used.)
   D. 33% learning. By the same process of computation, one-third of the total number of presentations was given.

2. In 100%, 67% and 33% learning, the intervals used were the same five as in the first series of experiments. Two of these were omitted for 150% learning, but four others were added. So there were seven intervals for 150% learning, viz., 2 hrs., 3 hrs., 4 hrs., 6 hrs., 12 hrs., 1 day and 2 days. The 2-hr. and 3-hr. intervals were arbitrarily chosen after they had been tried out

on several subjects. The object was to select such intervals as would facilitate the comparison of the retention curves for 150% learning with the other curves from the same series of experiments.

Two series were given each subject for each interval and each degree of learning. All the series for 100% and 150% learning except the 2-hr. and 3-hr. ones were completed by each subject before he tried 67% or 33% learning. The average number of presentations for learning these 20 series furnished the required basis of computation for determining 67% and 33% learning. The 2-hr. and 3-hr. intervals for 150% learning were added at the end of the whole series of experiments in order to trace the curves of forgetting further back toward the ordinate. One extra 6-hr. series was given each subject also toward the end of the experiments in order to counteract the effect of diurnal variations.

For each degree of learning, care was taken to distribute the long and short intervals evenly.

Only the written reproduction, recognition and reconstruction methods of measurement were used in recall.

QUANTITATIVE DATA

The results of the experiments are tabulated in Table XV and graphically presented in Figs. VII-IX.

TABLE XV

	20 min.	1 hr.	2 hrs.	3 hrs.	4 hrs.	6 hrs.	12 hrs.	1 d.	2 d.
Wr. Rep.									
150% learning..			88.0	84.4	81.9	65.6	54.4	38.5	30.8
100%	90.6	85.8			64.8			45.6	40.2
67%	85.4	72.5			65.8			41.5	24.8
33%	67.7	54.0			42.7			26.2	13.7
Recognition									
150%			97.5	95.8	93.3	91.6	92.5	83.2	72.8
100%	95.8	95.0			91.6			77.6	78.9
67%	93.2	93.3			84.7			73.7	61.5
33%	73.3	64.4			54.6			45.7	25.5
Reconstruction									
150%			87.5	92.1	90.8	78.9	81.3	43.4	43.9
100%	89.3	90.4			74.9			48.6	44.0
67%	92.0	77.9			65.3			56.6	31.8
33%	75.6	61.9			48.1			26.0	20.0

1. *The Range of Differences.*

As may be seen from Table XV, recognition, as a rule, gives the highest value for each interval and for each degree of learning. Reconstruction generally occupies the second place and written reproduction the last. Now if we take the difference between the highest and the lowest values for each interval and for each degree of learning, we can make a comparative study of the range of the differences. The facts are presented in Table XVI.

TABLE XVI
RANGE OF DIFFERENCES

	20 mm.	8 hrs.	4 hrs.	1 day	2 days
33%	7.9	10.4	11.9	19.5	12.8*
67%	7.8	20.8	19.4	17.1*	36.7
100%	6.5*	9.2*	26.8	28.0	38.7
150%			11.4*	44.7	42.0

In this table the highest value for each interval is underlined and the lowest marked with an asterisk. The tendency is for the highest value, *i. e.,* the greatest range, to occur at the shorter intervals for the lower degrees of learning and at the longer intervals for the higher degrees of learning. The tendency for the occurence of the smallest range is *vice versa.* These facts reflect the characteristic way in which the different retention curves approach the x—axis with the increase in the length of the time interval.

In general, the above range of the differences increases with the time interval, but at different rates for different degrees of learning. Theoretically, a higher degree of the original learning, of course, increases the amount of retention for all the methods of measurement. But it particularly favors the more difficult methods for the shorter intervals so that the range of the differences between the easiest and the most difficult methods is small. As the time interval is lengthened, this advantage rapidly disappears. So the different curves fall gradually apart, and the range of the differences increases accordingly.

With a lower degree of learning, the effect is generally to decrease the amount of retention for all the intervals and all the methods of measurement, but the special advantage is on the side of the easier, not the more difficult, methods. This effect increases the range of the differences for the shorter intervals, or at least keeps it as large as for the higher degrees of learning, which means that the range will be proportionally greater. Another characteristic result of a lower degree of learning is that, while the curves for all the methods of measurement begin rather low, they fall very slowly and keep almost parallel to each other. The range of the differences is thus kept within a small variation. For the higher degrees of learning, the curves fall at such different rates that they grow farther and farther apart.

We have, therefore, at least three types of curves resulting from varying the degree of the original learning and at the same time using three methods of measurement. Type 1 begins high and falls slowly. Type 2 begins high and falls rapidly. Type 3 begins low and falls slowly. In order to establish a general formula for all these types, the numerical differences must be more accurately determined.

2. Increase in the Degree of Learning and Diminished Returns in the Amount of Retention.

In Figs. VII-IX one can easily observe that the difference between the curves for 33% and 67% learning is the greatest, that between the curves for 67% and 100% learning very much less, and that between the curves for 100% and 150% learning the least of all. The curves for 100% and 150% learning often cross each other so that it is sometimes difficult to tell whether an increase of 50% of learning actually resulted in any increase in the amount of retention. In written reproduction they cross for the first time at a point whose abscissa represents an 8-hr. interval. Previous to that point the difference between the curves is distinct. There is a more decided difference between the 100% and 150% curves for recognition and reconstruction. Table XVII presents the difference for all three methods of measurement and for all the intervals. The probable errors of the differ-

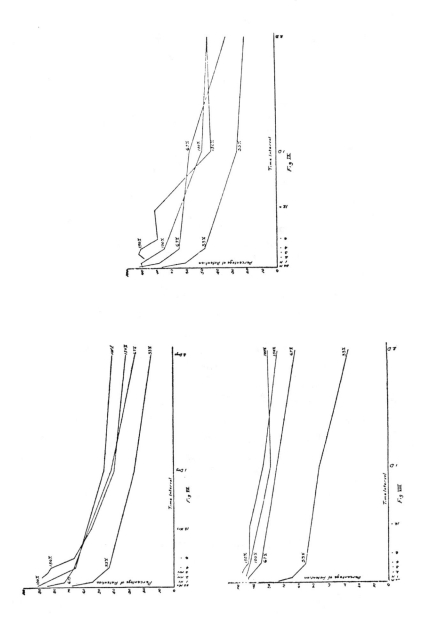

ences are not included. They are very high for the smaller differences. The larger differences are self-evident.

TABLE XVII

	20 min.	1 hr.	4 hrs.	1 day	2 days
Written Reproduction					
Difference 33 and 67%....	17.7	18.5	23.1	15.3	11.1
67 and 100%....	5.2	13.3	—1.0	4.1	15.4
100 and 150%....			17.1	—7.1	—9.4
Recognition					
Difference 33 and 67%....	19.9	28.9	30.1	28.0	36.0
67 and 100%....	2.6	1.7	6.9	3.9	17.4
100 and 150%....			1.7	5.6	—6.1
Reconstruction					
Difference 33 and 67%....	16.4	16.0	17.2	30.6	11.8
67 and 100%....	—2.7	12.5	9.6	—8.0	12.2
100 and 150%....			15.9	—5.2	—0.1

— sign indicates that, of the two values compared, the one for the higher degree of learning is numerically smaller.

At the outset, one might assume that this phenomenon of diminished returns could be due either to (1) practice effect or to (2) difficulties in the original learning.

(1) As the series of experiments occupied more than three months, the proficiency of learning for most of the subjects was somewhat improved. The extent of this improvement we shall develop in another section. After five weeks of practice in 100% and 150% learning, there is no wonder that they could now use the 67% of the average number of presentations to greater advantage. The average number was calculated from the learning of the first 20 series when the practice effect was still increasing. By this factor one might partly explain why the difference between the curves for 100% and 67% learning is so meagre.

But one cannot explain the still smaller difference between the curves for 150% and 100% learning by the same theory. Further, what is true of 67% learning is to a less extent also true of 33% learning. The difference between the latter and all the other curves is the greatest of all. How could the assumed practice effect have influenced 33% learning so differently?

(2) When the degree of learning is reduced to 33%, the

amount of material originally learned is greatly decreased. One cannot be expected to retain what he never learned. So instead of giving the amount of retention for 33% learning as a percentage of the whole syllable series, one might also argue that it should be stated as a percentage of the number of syllables actually learned.

The last statement, however, amounts to saying that instead of 33% or 67% learning, we should have had 100% learning. Doubtless we would then expect the resulting retention curve to coincide with the ordinary retention curve for 100% learning.

In fact, the number of syllables actually reported is a very poor measurement of the degree or the amount of learning. The subject was required to learn the series by anticipation, spelling the syllables aloud. What he did not correctly report after 33% or 67% learning could very often be correctly reproduced even at the end of a comparatively long interval. This phenomenon was particularly manifest for the more efficient learners who required only from 1 to 3 presentations for 33% learning. The effect of the last presentation in the original learning was not brought out by subsequent anticipation. When the total number of presentations was not more than 1 or 2, this last effect became increasingly important. Our records prove that the ability to recall without original correct anticipation occurred with more or less frequency for all the subjects. We may further mention that one of the subjects could not develop the habit of spelling aloud what he learned in the first few presentations.

A far more plausible explanation for this phenomenon of diminished return is that *the effect of the different degrees of learning upon the amount of retention follows the same sequence as does the learning curve for memory.* If negative acceleration is characteristic of the acquisition of immediate memory, as has been repeatedly proved, one may assume that the same phenomenon will reappear in the measurement of permanent memory, which differs from the former only by the introduction of a longer time interval.

From the shape of the learning curves for memory, it has

been concluded that the phenomenon of diminished returns holds (1) for immediate recall and (2) for all degrees of learning up to 100%. We can now state in the light of our data that, within the limits of our experiments, this phenomenon also holds (1) for delayed recall and (2) for more than 100% learning.

However, even on this theory one can hardly explain the negative differences in the amounts of retention between 150% and 100% learning for certain intervals. In Table XV, the value for 150% learning is lower than for 100% learning at the end of 1 and 2 days for written reproduction; at the end of 2 days for recognition; at the end of 1 day for reconstruction. At the end of 2 days for reconstruction the values for the two curves are practically equal. It is impermissible to extend the law of negative acceleration to cover these negative cases. One can hardly conceive of an increase of 50% of learning as resulting in an actual decrease in the amount of retention. In Chs. IV and V we shall find that the characteristic deviations for 150% learning are not limited to these unexpected changes in the amount. There we shall offer a general explanation for all these facts.

With the exception of these peculiarities for 150% learning, the phenomenon of diminished returns seems to be quite as general for delayed recall as for immediate memory. Naturally one would look for a common cause for both phenomena unless there are reasons for the contrary. We further maintain that the similarity between these effects is not a coincidence, but almost a mathematical necessity. Given the effect of diminished returns in the curve for immediate retention, one will have to make some wonderful assumptions for not expecting the same effect to appear in delayed recall. This may be clearly seen in Fig. X. The curves presented therein are hypothetical.

When the phenomenon of diminished returns occurs with immediate memory, a simple way to state this fact is to give the general equation of the curve, $y = a - e^{-x}$. When nothing is learned, the curve passed through the point of the origin. Hence,

(1) $y = 1 - e^{-x}$.

The limit of y will be 1, *i. e.*, the mastery of 100% of material regardless of the degree of over-learning.

Supposing that the phenomenon of diminished returns did not reappear in delayed recall, the curve for the retention values corresponding to various degrees of learning would have to be

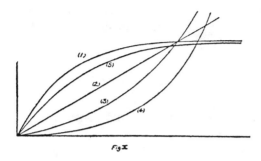

Fig x

either a straight line or one with positive acceleration. For the former, we have the equation y = mx + b. When nothing is learned, nothing is retained. Therefore,

(2) y = mx.

When the value of m is properly chosen, the curves will intersect with each other as in the figure.

If instead of linear regression, there were more or less positive acceleration, we could also generalize the fact by stating the equation.

(3) y = Ax + Bx² + Cx³ + ...

For certain values of the constants the curves (1), (2) and (3) will meet at the same point, which represents that for practical purposes the material is so well mastered that there can be no further forgetting.

Now if we compare the curves between this point of intersection and the point of origin by mere inspection, it becomes clear that for whatever values of the constants, the maximum difference between (1) and either (2) or (3) will not occur in the immediate neighborhood of either of the points, but somewhere in the middle.

Further, curve (1) is fixed. (2) is also fixed when the value of m is determined. Equation (3) is an endless series. x is positive. Assuming all the constants to be positive, then the fewer terms we take, the more abrupt will be the change in curvature, such as curve (4) in the figure.

From this description of the curves one can see that, given the effect of diminished returns in the learning curve for memory, the same effect will not appear in delayed recall only on one of these two conditions.

A. A certain medium degree of learning is the least effective with respect to the amount of retention. This amount will be increased with more learning and also with less learning. Or

B. The degree of learning has no considerable effect upon the amount of retention. It remains very meagre for all degrees of learning until the latter attains a critical value when all of a sudden the amount increases to nearly 100% and forgetting disappears.

Unless and until either one of the conditions is empirically fulfilled, the conclusion still holds true that the phenomenon of diminished returns is general for both immediate and delayed recall. The learning curve and the curve constructed on the basis of the diminishing amounts of retention due to different degrees of learning are related to each other somewhat as (1) and (5). In the latter, the parameter assumes the value a, less than unity.

Ebbinghaus[1] long ago discovered this tendency of diminished returns, though this is not clearly stated in his monograph. Thus he found that the amount of retention after one day was a function of the number of presentations used the previous day. That number was varied from 8 to 64, by intervals of 8. "For each three additional repetitions which I spent on a given day on the study of the series, I saved, in learning this series 24 hours later, on the average, approximately one repetition; and, within the limits stated, it did not matter how many repetitions altogether were spent on the memorization of the series." In Sec. 34, where he treated retention as a function of repeated learning, he concluded, "The effect of the repetitions is at first approximately constant, the saving which results from these repetitions increases accordingly for a while proportional to their number. Gradually,

[1] *Op. cit.,* Ch. VI, Sec. 22-23; Ch. VIII, Sec. 34.

the effect becomes less; and finally, when the series has become so firmly fixed that it can be repeated almost spontaneously after 24 hours, the effect is shown to be decidedly less."

The last conclusion quoted above is self-evident, and clearly corroborates our results. The other statements may be misleading. When the effect of the increase in the degree of learning upon the amount of retention is said to be "constant," or to increase by arithmetical progression, it amounts to saying that, *according to his "saving method," it is negatively accelerative.*

The formula for the "saving method" is $Q = \dfrac{100\,(L—WL)}{L}$, in which Q is the percentage of saving, L the time required for learning, and WL the same for relearning. The formula holds when L is equal to or greater than WL. When such is the case, a constant numerical increment to both the numerator and the denominator such as in his experiment, $\dfrac{(L+3)—(WL—1)}{L+3}$, $\dfrac{(L+6)—(WL—2)}{L+6}$, $\dfrac{(L+9)—(WL—3)}{L+9}$, ... , will make each term increase in value, but its difference from the immediately preceding term decrease in value. The effect is thus negatively accelerative.

When L is smaller than WL, as in incomplete learning, Ebbinghaus used as a basis for computation the hypothetical L that would have been spent had it not been for the previous incomplete learning. The amount of saving was a percentage of that hypothetical L, thus neglecting the amount of time that was actually spent on the previous day. If this amount of time had been taken into consideration, then the effect of the increase in the degree of the original learning upon the amount of retention could be shown to be negatively accelerative throughout his investigation.

3. A Further Word Regarding the General Shape of the Curves.

In the last chapter the difficulties for stating a general equation which would satisfy all the phenomena of forgetting were fully elaborated. The reader is now referred to Figs. VII to IX. A general "logarithmic" equation must make allowance for the crossing and recrossing of the "families" of written reproduction and reconstruction curves. Some of these irregularities may indeed be traced back to inaccuracies in the data and may not reappear in another series of experiments of the same kind, but we maintain that any mathematical statement of the Ebbinghaus tradition will require more experimental background.

Perhaps the most embarrassing group of curves is that for recognition. It would be just as easy to fit the corresponding curves of forgetting to equations of the first degree as to more complicated logarithmic equations. These curves are more or less parallel, more or less approaching linear regression, and as often tending to positive as to negative acceleration. One thing we can definitely state is that, on the whole, they are not logarithmic.

It was pointed out in the last chapter that relearning based on the "saving method" produces a type of curve vastly different from the results of the other methods which measure the amount of reproduced material. Now it becomes further evident that among the latter group, recognition *sometimes* has its unique curves which are as different from those of the other methods as relearning is from all the rest. Under certain circumstances it may happen that each of these curves will take on a logarithmic form. Strong's curve for recognition memory, for instance, is like Ebbinghaus' curve for the "saving method," and the former can certainly be used as illustrative of Bean's generalized statement. We do not maintain that relearning, anticipation, written reproduction, recognition, reconstruction, etc., each has a general curve. We only indicate that the logarithmic assumption and even the phenomenon of negative acceleration may totally disappear upon further investigation.

However, if the problem be put in such a way that we have to choose between Ebbinghaus and Ballard, then the former type of curve is much closer to our own results.

IV. THE EFFECT OF EXTENDING THE TIME LIMIT FOR RECALL UPON THE AMOUNT OF MATERIAL RECALLED

In written reproduction, as described above, a record was taken at the end of the first minute of recall and another at the end of the second minute, when the subject did not finish recalling within these time limits. These preliminary records, together with the other records which were completed within 1 or 2 min., may be taken as indicative of the proficiency of written reproduction memory up to 1 and 2 min. of recall respectively.

In recognition similar preliminary records were taken at the end of 90 sec. without the subject's knowledge. The difference between these 90 sec. records and the complete records has been referred to in Ch. II.

We present in Table XVIII the comparative results for the written reproduction methods for four degrees of the original learning. The values for 100% learning are averages from both series of experiments. When the same written reproduction records were scored for position and sequence, the preliminary values were slightly changed. These values are tabulated in Table XIX to facilitate comparative study. Similar results for the recognition method are presented in Table XX.

1. Comparison of the Written Reproduction Results.

It was indicated in connection with a discussion on anticipation and relearning that partial retention is not as readily recalled as complete retention. Within certain limits, the duration of the recalling process may directly correspond to the strength of the association. However, the tendency for the amount of recall to increase upon extending the time limit very soon becomes ineffective. One conclusion we can draw from Tables XVIII and XIX is that the effect of extending the time limit for recall with the written reproduction method becomes less and less important

55

beyond 1 or 2 min. The extension from 1 to 2 min. increases the scores by a far greater amount than does a further extension from 2 to 5 min. This particular effect is quite independent of minute variations in the method of measurement. Scoring position and sequence does not in the least change the relative importance of the successive extensions of the time limit. The

TABLE XVIII

WRITTEN REPRODUCTION, COMPARISON OF PRELIMINARY AND FINAL RECORDS

	20 min.	1 h.	2 h.	3 h.	4 h.	6 h.	12 h.	1 day	2 days
150% learning									
1 min.			75.9	60.0	57.9	43.0	34.6	26.0	22.9
Difference..			8.2	16.5	13.1	13.7	8.7	5.7	3.1
2 min.			84.1	76.5	71.0	56.7	43.3	31.7	26.0
Difference..			3.9	7.9	10.9	8.9	11.1	6.8	4.8
Complete ...			88.0	84.4	81.9	65.6	54.4	38.5	30.8
Total D....			12.1	24.4	24.0	22.6	19.8	12.5	7.9
100% learning									
1 min.	75.6	69.2			44.3			30.8	26.4
Difference..	10.5	10.8			11.5			7.3	3.8
2 min.	86.1	80.0			55.8			38.1	30.2
Difference..	3.3	4.0			6.8			4.3	3.3
Complete	89.4	84.0			62.6			42.2	33.5
Total D....	13.8	14.8			18.3			11.6	7.1
67% learning									
1 min.	69.8	47.7			42.5			31.7	21.5
Difference..	12.7	14.0			16.2			6.6	2.7
2 min.	82.5	61.7			58.7			38.3	24.2
Difference..	2.9	10.8			7.1			3.1	.6
Complete	85.4	72.5			65.8			41.4	24.8
Total D....	15.6	24.8			23.3			9.7	3.3
33% learning									
1 min.	59.8	43.1			31.2			21.5	12.7
Difference..	6.2	7.1			8.8			4.5	.4
2 min.	66.0	50.2			40.0			26.0	13.1
Difference..	1.7	3.8			2.7			.2	.6
Complete	67.7	54.0			42.7			26.2	13.7
Total D....	7.9	10.9			11.5			4.7	1.0

latter also holds for all degrees of the original learning except for the 12-hr., 1-day and 2-day intervals with 150% learning. In these exceptional cases the second extension of three minutes seems to be more effective than the first extension of one minute. Two of these intervals, 1 day and 2 days, correspond to the points

TABLE XIX

WRITTEN REPRODUCTION, COMPARISON OF PRELIMINARY AND FINAL
RECORDS, SCORING POSITION AND SEQUENCE

	20 min.	1 h.	2 h.	3 h.	4 h.	6 h.	12 h.	1 day	2 days
150% learning									
1 min.			72.4	56.7	53.3	38.2	32.4	22.9	20.0
Difference..			8.5	16.4	11.7	12.5	8.2	4.3	1.8
2 min.			80.9	73.1	65.0	50.7	40.6	27.2	21.8
Difference..			3.8	9.3	10.0	7.9	10.1	5.0	2.4
Complete			84.7	82.4	75.0	58.6	50.7	32.2	24.2
Total D....			12.3	25.7	21.7	20.4	18.3	9.3	4.2
100% learning									
1 min.	71.1	64.4			39.4			26.3	22.9
Difference..	9.4	8.9			9.0			5.7	3.0
2 min.	80.5	73.3			48.4			32.0	25.9
Difference..	2.9	3.9			5.8			3.0	2.2
Complete	83.4	77.2			54.2			35.0	28.1
Total D....	12.3	12.8			14.8			8.7	5.2
67% learning									
1 min.	65.1	42.0			36.4			26.1	17.2
Difference..	12.8	12.5			13.6			5.2	2.5
2 min.	77.9	54.5			50.0			31.3	19.7
Difference..	2.6	9.6			7.4			2.2	.3
Complete	80.5	64.1			57.4			33.5	20.0
Total D...	15.4	22.1			21.0			7.4	2.8
33% learning									
1 min.	53.3	37.7			26.2			17.7	9.5
Difference..	6.1	5.7			6.8			3.6	.2
2 min.	59.4	43.4			33.0			21.3	9.7
Difference..	1.3	4.2			2.2			.2	.8
Complete	60.7	47.6			35.2			21.5	10.5
Total D....	7.4	9.7			9.0			3.8	1.0

where the retention values for the 150% learning curve decrease very rapidly, as noticed in the last chapter. The facts still await an explanation, but we shall have to postpone further discussion to the end of Ch. V.

With increase in the length of the time interval, the same decline in the effect of extending the time limit is also observed. Previous to the lapse of the 4-hr. interval, the increment due to extending the time limit grows larger and larger. It then suddenly decreases with time. This characteristic change of the increment prevails under various conditions. It holds for all degrees of learning. It is not altered by scoring position and se-

TABLE XX

RECOGNITION, COMPARISON OF PRELIMINARY AND FINAL RECORDS

	20 min.	1 h.	2 h.	3 h.	4 h.	6 h.	12 h.	1 day	2 days
150% learning									
90 sec.			96.7	94.1	91.1	91.5	88.7	85.8	72.8
Complete			97.5	95.8	93.3	91.6	92.5	83.2	72.8
Difference..			.8	1.7	2.2	.1	3.8	—2.6	.0
100% learning									
90 sec.	95.7	93.8			91.5			71.2	69.4
Complete	96.8	94.8			92.7			76.1	75.2
Difference..	1.1	1.0			1.2			4.9	5.8
67% learning									
90 sec.	92.9	94.6			85.2			72.6	61.5
Complete	93.2	93.3			84.7			73.7	61.5
Difference..	.3	—1.3			—.5			1.1	.0
33% learning									
90 sec.	75.0	66.0			54.3			44.6	29.4
Complete	73.3	64.4			54.6			45.7	28.5
Difference..	—1.7	—1.6			.3			1.1	—.9

quence, nor is it minimized when the increment is computed as a percentage of the total score.

The strength of retention for the different syllables is, therefore, not equal. Some are more easily recalled than others, and consequently take less time. When the time interval is lengthened, the more difficult and uncertain ones deteriorate first. The amount of this partial retention increases in value for the first few hours after learning. Thereafter, not only does retention as a whole deteriorate with time, but the strength and the amount of partial retention also decrease so that its re-instatement upon the extension of the time limit becomes less and less probable. The assumption as presented in Ch. II which states that the amount of partial retention increases with the time interval for all memory processes is evidently unsound.

We can mention the fact in this connection that from 4 hours to 1 day is a long interval, and that in the latter case, sleep occurs between learning and relearning. Increase in the degree of the original learning seems to arrest this change in the magnitude of the increment, though very ineffectively. Thus, with 150% learning there seems to be a plateau in the effect of extending the time limit for the intervals from 3 to 12 hours inclusive, and then the sudden decrease. This would mean that the growth of the total amount of forgetting is arrested to that extent. In 100%, 67% and 33% learning, the abruptness of that change which occurs at the lapse of the 4-hr. interval to the increment resulting from longer durations of the recalling process is also somewhat proportional to the degree of the original learning.

2. *Comparison of the Recognition Results.*

Coming now to recognition, the effect of extending the time limit beyond 90 sec. is quite different from the results we just discussed. In some respects, the conclusions from these two methods of measurement are contradictory. If we can directly compare the magnitude of the scores, the increment for recognition is very much smaller. But a more significant contrast is that, with 100% learning, the increment for recognition is almost constant in value until the lapse of the 4-hr. interval, and then suddenly increases for the 1-day interval and becomes still higher at the end of 2 days. This contradicts what we have found in written reproduction in every particular. Assuming that partial retention takes more time for recall, as we have done, these characteristics of the recognition process seem to corroborate Strong's[2] conclusion which maintains that in recognition memory the amount of partial recognitions does not decrease in time as rast as the amount of recognition as a whole. One may even conclude that the partial recognitions actually increase with the length of the interval.

With 150% learning there seems to be a general increase of the effect of extending the time limit upon the amount of recognition until the lapse of the 12-hr. interval. At that point the increment disappears. The subjects seemed to have selected all the syllables they could recognize at the end of 90 sec., the rest of the process being chance performance. It is difficult to think of an increase of 50% in the original learning as affecting a decrease in the amount of recognition. A tentative explanation of this fact will be presented at the end of Ch. V.

For 67% and 33% learning, there is no sudden change of

[2] *Op. Cit.*, pp. 352 ff.

the increment as with 150% Extending the time limit for recognition does not result in any appreciable change in the numerical values either way, except that at the end of the 2-day interval for 33% learning, it affects a considerable decrease in the total score. This is to be expected if we remember that finally the amount of partial recognition may itself decrease so that even the presentation of the original material does not avail. Nevertheless, the subject was required to complete the selection of 12 syllables, depending upon chance; hence, there was a decrease in the total score. This final decrease in the amount of partial recognition is also hastened by a less complete degree of learning. Thus, while the numerical value for the 2-day interval with 67% learning is not changed by the extension of the time limit for recall, the corresponding score was decreased by 3.9 with 33% learning.

3. The Gradation of the Memory Processes.

The results from both methods of measurement seem to indicate that written reproduction and recognition memory are quite different, but the difference is still one of degree, not of kind. One process may pass over to the other. Judging from commonsense, recognition memory lasts longer than the ability to reproduce *ad verbatim*. What fails even the vaguest recall may, upon the presentation of the object, flash into distinct recognition. On the other hand, if enough time be allowed, one can as a rule recognize what he can recall. It seems that the memory processes are graded in some such way as the following:

A. Complete retention.

B. Partial retention, which takes time for recall, and may involve errors, as will be seen in another chapter.

C. Still less permanent retention which may completely escape written reproduction, but which, nevertheless, may be reinstated in recognition.

D. Partial recognition memory which can be developed upon extending the time limit for recall.

E. Retention that cannot be measured even by the method of recognition. It approaches complete obliviscence and occurs at the end of a fairly long interval after incomplete learning.

Condition A gives place to B soon after learning, at least with a great part of the retained material. Thereafter B approaches C faster than A does B so that the total amount of B decreases with the lapse of the 4-hr. interval. C lasts for a long time and gives place to D. D is not effective upon the immediate presentation of the original material, but may return in the process of recognition. When the degree of the original learning is only 33%, the amount of D becomes insignificant at the end of 2 days. The paradoxical effect is to shorten the duration of the actual process of recognition to less than 90 sec. when the syllables that can be recognized have all been selected, but apparently to increase the duration beyond that time limit. Nothing being remembered, the extended time serves only to fulfill the requirement of the experiment, which is to select 12 syllables.

4. The Effect of Extending the Time Limit upon the Shape of the Curves of Retention.

(1) In written reproduction the curve changes with the magnitude of the increment resulting from extending the time limit to 5 min. As compared with the preliminary curve for the 1- or 2-min. records, the final curve falls more gradually within the first four hours after learning, and then more suddenly. If the preliminary curve of forgetting be logarithmic, the effect of the increment would at least tend to complicate the function.

(2) In recognition with 67% learning, the more gradual fall of the curve owing to the extension of the time limit continues until the end of the second day.

(3) In recognition with 67% and 33% learning, extending the time limit does not bring about any appreciable change in the curves.

(4) *The shapes of the curves are practically determined for written reproduction at the end of 2 min. and for recognition at the end of 90 sec.*

V. THE RELATION BETWEEN THE AMOUNT OF ERROR AND OTHER FACTORS

In the recognition and reconstruction methods of measurement, the score was determined directly by the amount of error made in recall as well as by the amount of correct material. With the "saving method" the number of presentations required for relearning was determined by the amount of forgetting, but incidentally also by the amount of error. But errors were disregarded in the scores for anticipation and written reproduction. An attempt to keep separate records for the number of incorrect responses in anticipation met with failure. The duration of recall for each syllable was too short, considering the fact that the experimenter already had to turn the drum and to record success or failure between responses. In written reproduction, however, the records were permanent and we could study the amount and nature of error after the experiments were completed.

1. The Amount of Error as a Function of the Length of the Interval.

The amount of error made in written reproduction for each time interval and each degree of learning is presented in Table XXI. With the possible exception of 33% learning, the amount of error increases with the length of the interval.

TABLE XXI
AMOUNT OF ERROR IN WRITTEN REPRODUCTION

	20 min.	1 hr.	2 hrs.	3 hrs.	4 hrs.	6 hrs.	12 hrs.	1 d.	2 d.
150% learning...			2.7	3.1	6.7	7.3	8.3	12.9	15.8
100%	4.2	5.8			11.7			11.7	11.3
67%	3.3	4.6			5.4			7.7	9.0
33%	4.4	7.9			10.8			5.2	8.7

2. The Relation between the Amount of Error and the Degree of Learning.

In Table XXI the amount of error for 150% learning is probably smaller than for any other degree of learning with the shorter intervals, but it grows to be the largest when the interval is lengthened.

On the whole, error does not seem to be proportional to the degree of learning until the lapse of the 4-hr. interval. Thereafter the gross amount of error increases with the degree of learning.

These facts may be compared with the effect of extending the time limit upon the amount of reproduction, as discussed in Ch. IV. The magnitude of that effect for 150% learning changes from the shorter to the longer intervals in the same manner as does the amount of error. Before the lapse of the 4-hr. interval also, that effect is not proportional to the degree of learning, but the two factors take on a functional relationship for the 1-day and 2-day intervals. So the relationship between learning and error is similar to the relationship between learning and the effect of extending the time limit. However, the latter effect decreases with the lapse of the 4-hr. interval, while the amount of error increases with the time interval to the end of 2 days.

As already explained, the effect of extending the time limit is a function of the amount of partial retention. It is proportional to the amount of retention of condition B (p. 60) which can be reinstated in written reproduction but which takes time. Now we are ready to state a theory as to the significance of error making, and to see how it can be applied to explain the facts enumerated. The condition of error making is not complete forgetting or obliviscence. *It is the presence of partial retention* which can hardly be reinstated but which, nevertheless, is so near the point of complete recall as to cause conflict and confusion. Errors are made mostly in the change from condition B to C.

Thus, with 150% learning, on account of the higher degree of original mastery, the amount of partial retention of condition B is small as compared with that of A. The amount that is due to the change from condition B to C is also insignificant. Hence, we have the smaller amount of error for the short intervals. When the time interval is lengthened, condition B prevails and the amount of error increases steadily.

Similarly, we can explain why the amount of error is parallel to the effect of extending the time limit in almost every instance. The two are reciprocal functions and both are due to the existence of partial retention. Eventually the amount of error will decrease with the amount of partial retention, but the former may keep on increasing while the effect of extending the time limit has reached a climax. The amount of error increases because condition B approaches C much nearer for the longer intervals than for the shorter ones. Therefore, the increase in score due to extending the time limit, plus the amount of error, is an approximation of the amount of partial retention. The change from condition B to C is a very complicated process.

3. The Relation between the Amount of Error and the Amount of Retention.

When the time interval is lengthened, retention decreases but error increases. So if the amount of error is calculated as a percentage of the amount of retention, the values will increase more rapidly. The significance of this comparison is questionable. The amount of error should rather be compared with the amount of forgetting, the whole syllable series minus the amount of retention, which therefore increases with the time interval.

4. The Relation between the Amount of Error and the Amount of Forgetting.

The comparative data for the amount of forgetting and of error are presented in Table XXII.

The increase with the time interval in the amount of error is much slower relative to the increase in the amount of forgetting. This difference in the rate of increase with the time interval is further inversely proportional to the degree of learning.

As already stated, errors are made mostly in the transition from condition B to C, and the partial retention that cannot be even thus reinstated is apparently forgotten, according to the written reproduction method of measurement. So with the increase in the time interval, the amount of forgetting has a higher accumulative value than is possible to the amount of error. The former naturally increases more rapidly. Further, if a higher degree of

TABLE XXII

COMPARISON OF THE AMOUNT OF FORGETTING AND OF ERROR IN
WRITTEN REPRODUCTION

	20 m.	1 h.	2 h.	3 h.	4 h.	6 h.	12 h.	1 d.	2 d.
150% learning									
Forgetting			12.0	15.6	18.1	34.4	45.6	61.5	69.2
Error			2.7	3.1	6.7	7.3	8.3	12.8	15.8
100% learning									
Forgetting	9.4	14.2			35.2			54.4	59.8
Error	4.2	5.8			11.7			11.7	11.3
67% learning									
Forgetting	14.6	27.5			34.2			58.5	75.2
Error ....:..	3.3	4.6			5.4			7.7	9.0
33% learning									
Forgetting	32.3	46.0			57.3			73.8	86.3
Error	4.4	7.9			10.8			5.2	8.7

learning tends to arrest the whole process of forgetting, then the difference between the increase in the amount of forgetting and of error will be inversely proportional to the degree of learning.

Aside from these general statements, the relationship between error and forgetting is obscure. With 150% learning, the amount of forgetting is to the amount or error as 5 is to 1, for all the time intervals. This ratio regularly decreases with the time interval when the degree of learning is reduced to 67%. With the other degrees of learning, there is no definite relationship. The P.E.'s of the values that constitute the curve for the amount of error are too high to give warrant to further generalization.

However, this lack of similarity or causal relationship between the two groups of values only intensifies the problem. The amount of error is indicative of the amount of partial retention. In other words, the curve for the amount of error is a part and parcel of the curve of forgetting. Upon the evaluation of this relationship will depend whether a universal mathematical statement of the problem is possible.

THE EFFECTS OF 150% LEARNING UPON VARIOUS FACTORS

From the above section, it is found that the relationship between forgetting and error is more definite for 150% than for any other degree of learning. The ratio of the two amounts does not decrease with the time interval as it does with lower degrees of learning. We are now ready to gather together what has been noticed in the last two chapters concerning the characteristics of 150% learning.

1) Its retention values are lower than for 100% learning at the end of 1 and 2 days in written reproduction, at the end 1 day in reconstruction and at the end of 2 days in recognition (p. 50).

2) The effect of extending the time limit upon the amount of written reproduction is peculiar in this case. A second extension of the time limit from 2 to 5 min. brings about a larger increment than the first extension from 1 to 2 min. This relative effectiveness of the two extensions of the time limit is just the reverse of what has been found with all other degrees of learning (p. 56).

3) Extending the time limit for recognition gives negative results at the end of the 1- and 2-day intervals. The effect of the extension is different for the shorter intervals with the same degree of learning and for all the intervals with 100% learning (p. 59).

An explanation for these peculiarities is possible under the following suppositions.

A) A high degree of learning, as we have indicated, tends to arrest the process of forgetting. In the process of forgetting, retention of condition A approaches partial retention of condition B, the latter approaches C, etc.

B) Most of the syllable series for 100% learning were given each subject before the 150% series. In the former experiments they had noticed that the amount of retention after 1 or 2 days was comparatively low. This fact might have influenced their attitude when they came to the longer intervals in 150% learning.

Combining these two postulates, it seems probable that for the longer intervals there may be a conflict of condition B with both A and C, when B is intensified with over-learning. The retroactive effect is (1) to decrease the total amount of written reproduction. (2) It naturally follows that the effect of the second extension of the time limit will be greater than that of the first, for the conflict will tend to prolong the recall process of even the well retained members. (3) And as condition B always approaches C and also conflicts with C, the amount of error will be increased for the longer intervals.

Even on this hypothetical basis, there is no explanation for the sudden drop of the retention curve for recognition at the end of 2 days. In the same connection the extension of the time limit gives negative results. Probably, over-learning causes a part of the syllable series to stand out more distinctly, thus contrasting with the relative "amnesia" of the other parts.

Were these explanations unsatisfactory, the fact remains conclusive that over-learning to the extent of 150% is at less advantage than 100% learning when tested for retention at the end of 1 and 2 days.

VI. THE DURATION AND THE SPEED OF THE PROCESS OF RECALL IN WRITTEN REPRODUCTION, RECOGNITION AND RECONSTRUCTION

Two scores, one of amount and one of time, are not mutually interpretative, but the latter may in a way be indicative of the nature and the strength of retention, though not in quantitative terms. The data thus far presented all concern the amount of retention, correctly or incorrectly reproduced. In Ch. IV we discussed the effect of different time limits only in relation to the amount of reproduced material. We can now consider the duration and the speed of the process of recall with the different methods of measurement.

The "saving method" does not give separate measurements for time and amount, so the two cannot be independently treated. The duration or the speed of the anticipation process is not significant, its value being a constant, 2 sec. for each syllable.

With the other three methods of measurement, duration and speed are quite independent of the amount of retention. In written reproduction the subject could take any length of time up to 5 min. As a rule, he did not take as long as 5 min. to finish the process. In recognition and reconstruction, there was not even a time limit. So the relationship between the time and the amount of recall becomes an important problem.

1. Duration as a Function of the Order in which the Measurements were Taken.

In Table XXIII are presented the average durations of the three processes of recall in number of seconds.

From Table XXIII, written reproduction had the longest duration, recognition the second and reconstruction the last. That was exactly the order in which the measurements were taken, written reproduction being the first, recognition the second and reconstruction the last.

TABLE XXIII

Duration of Recall, No. of Sec.

	20 m.	1 h.	2 h.	3 h.	4 h.	6 h.	12 h.	1 d.	2 d.
Writ. Reprod.									
150% learning			134.4	171.4	193.8	209.5	198.6	186.4	178.7
*100% A......	112.2	134.0			147.9			132.1	97.0
100% B......	145.5	171.2			211.6			182.7	176.0
67%	139.0	207.4			189.3			157.5	154.6
33%	108.8	155.1			124.2			108.3	101.4
Recognition									
150% learning			60.6	71.7	81.8	94.3	99.9	86.9	114.2
*100% A......	76.7	87.1			108.1			126.9	132.8
100% B......	72.6	78.4			92.6			89.9	101.3
67%	68.9	83.2			98.9			92.7	107.9
33%	88.4	104.0			100.6			93.1	114.0
Reconstruction									
150% learning			29.5	32.3	41.0	50.2	51.1	61.4	60.2
*100% A......	47.9	41.9			50.4			62.3	68.7
100% B......	50.0	41.1			45.3			57.9	59.2
67%	37.5	53.2			48.2			58.0	57.8
33%	43.7	44.5			52.3			48.1	51.7

*A   The first series of experiments.
B   The second series of experiments.

The duration of written reproduction was shorter in the first series of experiments than in the second series, but the comparative duration of recognition was *vice versa*. No important difference between the two series of experiments was recorded in reconstruction.

So the difference in duration may have incidentally resulted from the technique of the experiments, quite independent of the relative difficulty of the processes. Each recall process may have facilitated the succeeding one. The longer the written reproduction process, for instance, the shorter was the duration of recognition. However, as we have seen in Ch. II, the conditions of recall differed in the number of restricting factors involved. Most probably, these factors also influenced the duration of the processes.

2. The Speed of Recall.

The recognition and reconstruction methods of measurement required the subject to complete the process of recall regardless of the amount of correct retention. So with these two methods, the duration and the speed of recall are identical. The conditions were very different in written reproduction. There the subject could "give up" at any time. The averages presented in Table XXIII fall far below the limit of 5 min. The average subject would "give up" long before the lapse of that time limit. At the same time, the amount of reproduction varied with the amount of retention, and the differences in duration might simply be in part a function of the amount of material that was reproduced.

To avoid this difficulty, the speed of written reproduction is calculated as the number of seconds per unit material. If the duration of recall varied only as an effect of the amount of reproduction, then the speed per unit would have a constant value for all the intervals. Such, however, is not the case, as may be seen in Table XXIV.

TABLE XXIV

SPEED OF REPRODUCTION, NO. OF SEC. PER UNIT MATERIAL

	20 m.	1 h.	2 h.	3 h.	4 h.	6 h.	12 h.	1 d.	2 d.
150% learning			1.9	2.4	2.6	4.2	4.8	6.9	8.6
100%	1.7	1.1			3.8			6.0	7.3
67%	1.8	3.5			4.4			6.3	9.3
33%	1.8	3.2			3.6			6.1	11.1

Comparing that table with the recognition and reconstruction values in Table XXIII (except the data from the 1st series of experiments), the relationship between the speed of recall and other factors may be summarized as follows:

(1) *The speed of recall decreases with the time interval.* This generalization holds for written reproduction without exception. That such a tendency exists in recognition is also unquestionable. With reconstruction, the difference in speed between the 1-day and 2-day intervals is very slight, and there are also marked deviations from the assumed functional relationship for the shorter intervals. But the decrease in speed with time may be clearly seen if we taken the average of all the degrees of learning.

(2) *On the whole, the speed of recall increases with the degree of learning.*

(3) Since the duration of recognition and reconstruction in-

creases with the time interval, while the amount retained and the accuracy of the two processes decrease with time, it follows that *speed increases with accuracy.* The increase in speed with respect to accuracy is much faster than the increase with respect to the time interval.

3. Comparison between the Speed of Recall and the Amount of Forgetting.

The increase with the time interval in the number of seconds per unit recall, as further complicated by the degree of learning, may be compared with the amount of forgetting which also increases with time and varies with the degree of learning. The data are gathered together in Table XXV. It is useless to compare the absolute amount of forgetting with the total speed of the process, since only in the light of the general shape of the curves can such a comparison be intelligible. The values presented in Table XXV are converted from the original data, using the numerical value obtained from the shortest interval in each case as the unit. The table reveals especially the relative increase in the values with the length of the time interval.

In spite of the arbitrary process in reducing the amount of forgetting and the speed of recall to the same unitary basis, any graphical representation of the data in Table XXV would still be so complicated as to make interpretation impossible. The curves of forgetting may be said to be logarithmic in a sense, but a similar mathematical statement would no longer hold for the curves for the speed of recall. A possible generalization one can make from these facts is that the curves of speed do not rise as rapidly as the curves of forgetting. The decrease in the speed of recall with respect to the length of the time interval is not as rapid as the decreases in the total amount of retention.

So the amount of forgetting and the speed of recall do not have the same type of curves. The results of this section agree with the conclusion reached in Ch. II concerning the difference between the relearning and the other methods, only we have attained the additional observation that the time curves differ among themselves even more radically than do the curves of for-

TABLE XXV

COMPARISON OF THE AMOUNT OF FORGETTING WITH THE SPEED OF
RECALL, TAKING THE NUMERICAL VALUE OF THE
SHORTEST INTERVAL AS UNIT

	20 m.	1 h.	2 h.	3 h.	4 h.	6 h.	12 h.	1 d.	2 d.
Writ. Reprod.									
150% learning									
Forgetting..			1.00	1.30	1.51	2.87	3.80	5.12	5.77
Speed			1.00	1.26	1.37	2.21	2.53	3.63	4.53
100% learning									
Forgetting..	1.00	1.51			3.74			5.78	6.36
Speed	1.00	1.24			2.24			3.53	4.29
67% learning									
Forgetting..	1.00	1.88			2.34			4.01	5.15
Speed	1.00	1.94			2.44			3.50	5.17
33% learning									
Forgetting..	1.00	1.42			1.77			2.28	2.67
Speed	1.00	1.78			2.00			3.39	6.17
Recognition									
150% learning									
Forgetting..			1.00	.63	.74	1.70	1.50	4.53	4.49
Speed			1.00	1.18	1.35	1.56	1.65	1.43	1.88
100% learning									
Forgetting..	1.00	.90			2.35			4.80	5.23
Speed	1.00	1.08			1.28			1.24	1.40
67% learning									
Forgetting..	1.00	2.76			4.59			5.42	8.52
Speed	1.00	1.21			1.44			1.35	1.57
33% learning									
Forgetting..	1.00	1.56			2.13			3.03	3.28
Speed	1.00	1.18			1.14			1.05	1.29
Reconstruction									
150% learning									
Forgetting..			1.00	1.68	2.68	3.28	3.00	6.72	10.88
Speed			1.00	1.37	1.39	1.70	1.73	2.08	2.04
100% learning									
Forgetting..	1.00	1.19			2.00			5.33	5.02
Speed	1.00	.82			.91			1.16	1.18
67% learning									
Forgetting..	1.00	.99			2.25			3.87	5.66
Speed	1.00	1.42			1.29			1.57	1.57
33% learning									
Forgetting—	1.00	1.33			1.70			2.03	2.79
Speed	1.00	1.02			1.30			1.10	1.18

getting. If the relearning method could be varied and controlled
as are the other methods, the amount of "saving" would most
probably increase or decrease according to various conditions.

VII. INDIVIDUAL DIFFERENCES AND CORRELATIONS

1. Individual Differences in Practice Effect.

It has been sometimes maintained that the practice effect in learning nonsense material disappears after the successive mastery of but a few series. In our experiments we had the opportunity to plot the practice curve for each individual subject. About one-half of the subjects learned more than 50 series each, thus giving rather extensive practice curves. From the comparison of these curves, it seems that the extent of practice effect is subject to individual differences. For most of the subjects it is present even after the mastery of 40 or 50 series, and it decreases with different rates for different individuals. Three typical curves are given in Fig. XI (Smoothed).

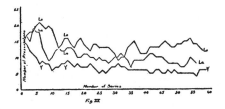

Generally speaking, the practice effect in these curves seems to have disappeared after the tenth trial, but individual differences are, nevertheless, present. The curve for subject Y has an abrupt initial drop which is not so prominent in the other curves. That is, he adapted himself to the situation more quickly than did the other subjects. The readiness with which one adapts to this particular situation is in a way proportional to his speed of learning. After the tenth trial the gradual fall of the curves for Le and Y is noticeable to the very end, but the curve for Lo is stationary. So individuals differ not only in the amount of the initial drop, but also in the gradual decline of the practice effect. A break occurred in the curve for Y when for more than two

73

months the subject did not work on nonsense material. The practice effect was carried over that interval.

In Ch. III it was mentioned that the subjects could use 67% of the average number of presentations to a greater advantage after they had practiced in 150% and 100% learning for more than 5 weeks. This improvement in learning also varied greatly according to the individual. As previously stated, we took an average of the number of presentations required by each individual for the mastery of the 20 syllable series in 100% and 150% learning. The number of series that we learned with only two-thirds or less of the average number of presentations, as determined for each individual, was exceedingly small. However, when they came to 67% learning, most of the subjects learned one or more of the series with that number of presentations. Table XXVI shows how the individuals differ in this respect.

TABLE XXVI

SERIES LEARNED WITH 2/3 OR LESS OF THE AVERAGE
NUMBER OF PRESENTATIONS

SUBJECT	In the first 20-25 series	In the next 10
B	1	3
I	0	1
Ka	2	3
Ko	0	1
Lud	2	1
Luh	1	2
S	2	4
Wi	0	1
Wo	1	2
Y	0	0

2. Individual Differences in the Speed of Learning.

Table XXVII presents the average number of presentations required by each subject to learn a series of 12 nonsense syllables.

It takes an average subject about 14 presentations to learn a series of 12 nonsense syllables by the anticipation method. This average is just a little higher than that given by Finkenbinder.[1]

The two groups are about equal in efficiency, for as already

[1] *Op. cit.*, pp. 21-22.

TABLE XXVII

AVERAGE NUMBER OF PRESENTATIONS FOR EACH SERIES

SUBJECT	NO. OF PRESENTATIONS	P. E.	NO. OF SERIES LEARNED
*Luh	4.95	.20	20
*Y	6.42	.18	40
Ko	6.85	.26	20
*I	8.75	.33	20
*Wa	9.42	.27	50
*Le	9.84	.21	50
*C	10.90	.55	20
R	11.88	.32	50
DW	13.26	.37	50
Lo	13.50	.28	50
Lud	13.65	.33	20
Ka	16.20	.57	20
*S	16.50	.62	20
Wi	17.20	.37	20
*Ts	18.10	.54	20
B	18.60	.51	20
Kan	19.75	.86	20
Wo	19.80	.65	20
*F	24.50	.67	20
Av.	13.69		

*Chinese students.

indicated, it is more difficult to spell a syllable letter by letter as required in our experiments than to pronounce it as a whole as required by Finkenbinder. A group of 15 to 20 subjects is, therefore, large enough to make a random sample.

The fastest learner of the group is five times as proficient as the slowest learner. On the whole, the Chinese students are better memorizers than the Americans. The averages stand as 12.15 against 15.07. With the exception of subject F, the difference would be much higher. Six Chinese occupy the first seven places. This superiority of the memorizing ability of the Chinese is interesting in connection with the problems of classical training and the improvement of memory with practice.

3. Individual Variability in the Amount of Retention.

Applying the formula $V = \dfrac{100\ S.\ D.}{Mean}$, we calculated the coefficient of variability of the average amount of retention for the five methods of measurement and the four degrees of learning. These coefficients are tabulated in Table XXVIII.

XXVIII
Coefficients of Variability

	20 m.	1 h.	2 h.	3 h.	4 h.	6 h.	12 h.	1 d.	2 d.
Anticipation....	26.2	28.9			41.0			80.9	133.3
Relearning	18.1	31.8			22.6			31.3	34.3
Writ. Reprod.									
150% learning			15.2	17.5	12.5	26.9	33.1	77.1	76.3
100%	6.8	11.7			27.0			56.8	70.4
67%	6.6	28.5			31.2			48.1	106.7
33%	17.8	32.0			38.5			86.4	115.5
Recognition									
150% learning			3.4	4.4	6.6	9.0	15.2	18.5	18.9
100%	4.3	5.8			7.8			22.9	20.9
67%	11.3	8.6			13.2			25.6	31.8
33%	19.3	16.6			41.6			62.9	66.5
Reconstruction									
150% learning			15.6	12.2	9.8	14.8	23.8	53.9	69.8
100%	10.3	12.7			17.0			46.3	57.0
67%	8.7	21.3			23.8			28.7	70.3
33%	22.4	32.3			41.4			85.5	78.4

The magnitude of the coefficients of variability for the long intervals indicate that the data are not statistically reliable. However, our present problem is exactly to describe, if not to interpret, the differences in statistical reliability, or individual variability, under certain conditions. So the above statement directly leads to the following generalization.

(1) *Individual variability increases with the time interval.* This factual statement holds for all the methods of measurement and all degrees of learning. The tendency can be more distinctly observed as graphically represented in Fig. XII, for 100% learning.

These graphs are based on similar, and in some cases the same numerical values as are the retention curves in Fig. II. A comparison of the figures brings out the fact that the curves for the coefficients of variability have not only preserved the particular order of the different methods of measurement, a proportionality of the absolute differences in numerical value, but to some extent, even the specific similarity or dissimilarity in general shape;

they also manifest that characteristic difference between relearning and the other methods of measurement. The relearning curve begins as the second in height in the order of variability but ends as the fourth, having crossed the written reproduction and reconstruction curves and now stands half way between recognition and reconstruction both in shape and numerical value. The significance of this comparison has been discussed at length in Ch. II, where it was pointed out that relearning is not a helpful method for the study of individual differences.

In the present connection, the coefficients of variability for the different intervals as determined by the relearning method fall within a close range in numerical value. Just as the retention curve for relearning is complicated by involving two learning curves for memory, so also the corresponding curve for the coefficients of variability becomes almost unanalyzable because of the same complicaion. In Fig. XII the asterisk represents the

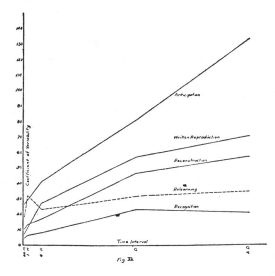

Fig. XII

coefficient of variability for the original learning, which is 37.8. The implications of the "saving method" would lead one to expect that this value would be rather close to the average value of the relearning curve in the same figure.

(2) *Individual variability increases inversely as the degree of*

learning. Exceptions are found in written reproduction and re-construction with 150% learning at the end of the 1-day and 2-day intervals. The explanation given in Ch. V for the characteristics of 150% learning will cover the present instances.

That the increase in the degree of learning should tend to equalize and finally to eliminate individual differences is also to be expected. For a certain degree of over-learning will make the material so well fixed for any individual who can fulfill the requirements of these experiments that the amount of retention will be always 100%. Such are our habitual and conventional-ized reactions as we so often observe in daily life. The variability of these reactions approximates 0. In other words, the effect of increasing the degree of learning upon the coefficient of variability approaches 0 as a limit.

As a corollary to the above conclusion, the phenomenon of diminished returns may be described more specifically. Since the increase in the degree of learning brings about diminished returns in the amount of retention and at the same time neutralizes individual variability, it follows that, in the long run, an individual very efficient in immediate retention is not likely to improve with over-learning as rapidly as another who is very in-efficient in immediate retention.

(3) *Individual variability also seems to be a function of the method of measurement and to increase with the number of re-stricting factors involved in the recall process,* as explained in Ch. II.

(4) Summarizing (1), (2) and (3), *individual variability in retention increases with the difficulty of the act and decreases with the frequency and the recency of practice.*

4. Correlation between the Speed of Learning and the Amount of Retention.

The formula used is

$$\rho = 1 - \frac{6\Sigma D^2}{N(N^2 - 1)}. \quad \text{Then } r = 2 \sin\left(\frac{\pi}{6}\rho\right)$$

and P. E. $= .703 \dfrac{1 - r^2}{\sqrt{N}}$. Table XXIX gives the correlations whose numerical values are at least twice as large as their respective P. E.'s.

TABLE XXIX

CORRELATION BETWEEN THE SPEED OF LEARNING AND THE
AMOUNT OF RETENTION

	20 m.	1 h.	2 h.	3 h.	4 h.	6 h.	12 h.	1 d.	2 d.
Relearning		—.42						—.42	
P. E........		.18						.18	
Anticipation									.51
P. E........-									.18
Writ. Reprod.									
150% learning				.43					
P. E........				.18					
100%	.30	.40							
P. E........	.15	.14							
67%	.40								
P. E........	19								
33%							.50		
P. E........							.17		
Recognition									
150% learning			.59	.53		—.47			—.64
P. E........			.14	.16		.17			.13
100% learning	.39	.32			.37				
P. E........	.14	.15			.14				
67% learning	.42							—.40	—.57
P. E........	.18							.19	.15
33%									
P. E........									
Reconstruction									
150% learning			.50				.44		
P. E........			.17				.18		
100% learning									
P. E........									
67% learning	.58								—.47
P. E........	.15								.17
33% learning	.41								
P. E........	.19								

The correlation values are all positive except two in relearning, four in recognition and one in reconstruction, and the chances are at least 4.5 to 1 that the data will be reproduced in another series of experiments with as few as ten subjects.

The negative correlation between learning ability and the amount of retention as measured by the "saving method" is an obvious consequence of the method of computation. Let X and

Y represent the number of presentations involved in learning and relearning respectively. Then X and $\dfrac{c}{X}$ will represent deficiency and proficiency of learning ability respectively, and $\dfrac{X-Y}{X}$ or $1-\dfrac{Y}{X}$ will represent the percentage value of retention as measured by the "saving method," in which the fraction $\dfrac{Y}{X}$ will have a value less than 1. The negative correlation between $\dfrac{c}{X}$ and $1-\dfrac{Y}{X}$ which we secured means a positive correlation between X and $1-\dfrac{Y}{X}$ and this is necessarily due to a negative correlation between X and $\dfrac{Y}{X}$, for as X increases, the value of $1-\dfrac{Y}{X}$ can increase only as the value of the fraction $\dfrac{Y}{X}$ decreases.

This negative correlation between X and $\dfrac{Y}{X}$ will naturally occur because of the presence of X in both values whenever the following relations between X and Y obtain:

1. Absence of correlation.
2. A negative correlation.
3. A positive correlation when $\dfrac{\text{increment } Y}{Y}$ is less than $\dfrac{\text{increment } X}{X}$.

In other words, the correlation between $\dfrac{c}{X}$ and $1-\dfrac{Y}{X}$ is necessarily negative unless X and Y are positively correlated and at the same time fulfill the condition that $\dfrac{\text{increment } Y}{Y}$ is equal to

or greater than $\dfrac{\text{increment } X}{X}$.

The actual correlation between X and Y determined in these experiments is positive, as presented in Table XXX. The required relation between the increments of X and Y cannot be determined very easily. However, considering the phenomenon of diminished returns in the learning curve, such a relation between X and Y is very unlikely. There is more material to be mastered in the original learning than in relearning. Hence, the increments of X due to deficiency in learning ability will as a rule be proportionally as well as absolutely greater than the respective increments of Y.

Thus, the negative correlation which we ascertained between learning ability and the amount of "saving" is a consequence of the fact that X is involved in both values. It is merely a product of a negative correlation between X and $\dfrac{1}{X}$, and a positive correlation between X and Y which we secured. A negative correlation will also obtain under almost every possible relation between X and Y. The correlation thus has no significance as to learning ability and retention.

This analysis confirms our previous contentions that the relearning method constitutes a poor measure of retention.

TABLE XXX

CORRELATION BETWEEN THE SPEED OF LEARNING
AND OF RELEARNING

	20 m.	1 h.	4 h.	1 d.	2 d.
Correlation	.50	.21	.98	.35	.78
P. E.	.17	.21	.01	.20	.09

With the exception of relearning, the remaining data may be easily summarized as follows:

(1) With the recognition method and possibly also reconstruction, the correlation between the speed of learning and the amount of retention tends to change from positive to negative

as the interval is lengthened. The fast learners tend to be the least efficient in recognition for the comparatively longer intervals.

(2) With the written reproduction method, the correlation between the same factors is always +, if there is any correlation at all. The fastest learners are as a rule the best retainers.

(1) and (2) together might suggest that the two memory processes differ in quality as well as in quantity, but our data are not conclusive.

(3) While the increase in the degree of learning tends to equalize individual differences, it does not at the outset minimize the numerical value of certain correlations. On the contrary, up to 150% learning, increase in learning seems to make the correlation between learning and retention more definite and reliable.

It seems to the present writer that a more careful study of the correlation between the above two factors is the only systematic way to approach the difference between "immediate" and "permanent" memory. Sometimes it has been asserted that recall immediately after learning differs from delayed recall in nature as well as in quantity.[2] One forgets that immediate recall is recall after a neglected interval. It is neglected because it is too short to be appreciable. The control of this interval will determine a point on the curve of retention just as any other point. Besides certain questionable introspective conclusions, the chief reason for differentiating "immediate" and "permanent" retention in that way is the negative correlation that has occasionally been discovered between the speed of learning and the amount of retention. The relearning method was often used for this purpose and, for some unknown reason or another, one particular time interval was chosen. Now we have discovered that the numerical value of the correlation for the same group of subjects changes under various conditions. It varies with the method of measurement, the degree of learning, the length of the time interval, and perhaps with every variable condition that we can mention. Similar variations will most probably be found in the correlation values for "permanent" memory measured for two

[2] E. g., E. Meumann, "The Psychology of Learning,, Eng. Tr., pp. 40 ff.

different intervals. The objective reason for differentiating "immediate" and "permanent" memory is, therefore, unsound.

5. Correlation between the Speed of Learning and the Speed of Recall.

The data are presented in Table XXXI. Like Table XXX, it contains only the correlation values which are at least twice as high as their respective P. E.'s.

TABLE XXXI

CORRELATION BETWEEN THE SPEED OF LEARNING AND THE SPEED OF RECALL

	20 m.	1 h.	2 h.	3 h.	4 h.	6 h.	12 h.	1 d.	2 d.
Writ. Reprod.									
150% learning					.42				
P. E........					.18				
100 %........	.55	.61							
P. E........	.11	.10							
67%	.70							.61	.40
P.E........	.11							.14	.19
33%	.51				.43			.69	.49
P. E........	.16				.18			.12	.17
Recognition									
150% learning			.60	.42		—.45			—.47
P. E.......			.14	.18		.18			.17
100%	.58	.56							
P. E.......	.11	.11							
67%									—.63
P. E.......									.13
33%									
P. E.......									
Reconstruction									
150% learning			.71	.48	.72	.41			
P. E.......			.11	.17	.11	.19			
100%	.36	.34							
P. E.......	.14	.14							
67%	.48				—.73				
P. E.......	.17				.10				
33%									
P. E.......									

The speed of recall for written reproduction is taken to be the number of seconds per unit material. For recognition and reconstruction, it is the total duration of the recall process in number of seconds.

Negative values are again found in recognition for the longer intervals. The slow learners are not only more proficient in recognition memory in the long run, but they also recognize the material much faster. Another solitary negative value appears in reconstruction. Its significance is probably the same as for the negative recognition values. Otherwise, the faster learner also tends to be the faster in recall. This correlation is most probably due to the fact that the faster learners are also more proficient retainers. So we present in the next section the correlation between the amount and the speed of recall.

6. *Correlation between the Amount and the Speed of Recall.*

TABLE XXXII

CORRELATION BETWEEN THE AMOUNT AND THE SPEED OF RECALL

	20 m.	1 h.	2 h.	3 h.	4 h.	6 h.	12 h.	1 d.	2 d.
Writ. Reprod.									
150% learning			.84	.80	.72	.96	.78	.96	.61
P. E........			.06	.08	.11	.02	.09	.02	.14
100%	.60	.71			.73			.76	.50
P. E........	.10	.08			.07			.06	.12
67%	.65	.89			.97			.62	.60
P. E........	.13	.05			.01			.14	.14
35%	.65	.82						.80	.89
P. E........	.13	.07						.08	.05
Recognition									
150% learning			.77	.60		.81		.50	.44
P. E........			.09	.14		.08		.17	.18
100%	.63	.47			.59			.34	.62
P. E........	.10	.13			.11			.14	.10
67%	.62	.76			.64			.43	
P. E........	.14	.09			.13			.18	
33%		.38			.43				
P. E........		.19			.18				
Reconstruction									
150% learning			.73	.45		.61	.42		
P. E........			.10	.17		.14	.18		
100%	.72	.71			.42			.54	
P. E........	.08	.08			.13			.12	
67%									—.47
P. E........									.17
33%					.53				.45
P. E........					.16				.17

The individual who retains the most also tends to recall it the most readily. With the exception of a single negative value in reconstruction, this tendency is independent of the speed of learning and does not seem to vary according to the method of measurement, the degree of learning or the length of the time interval.

VIII. CONCLUSION

1. The curve of retention varies with the method of measurement.

A) The curve as determined by the "saving method" differs both in height and general shape from all the other curves determined by methods which directly measure the amount of retention. For the comparatively shorter intervals, the relearning curve falls more rapidly than does most any curve, but the tendency is reversed for the longer intervals. This difference in the shape of the curves follows as a mathematical necessity from the predetermined differences in the units of measurement.

B) Aside from the relearning curve, the other curves stand in the order of their numerical values as follows: Recognition is the first, reconstruction the second, written reproduction the third and anticipation the last. Many reasons may be given for these particular numerical differences, but above all the order of the curves is a function of the number of restricting factors involved in the conditions of recall.

C) In spite of the variations in the methods of measurement, the curves are, on the whole, more similar to that of Ebbinghaus than to those of Ballard.

D) In numerical value, our retention curve for relearning approaches most closely to that of Finkenbinder, but our recognition curve is vastly different from that of Strong. The similarity of data depends upon the corresponding similarity of technique.

2. The curve of retention varies with the degree of the original learning. The amount of retention for most intervals increases with the degree of learning.

A) Increase in the degree of learning favors the more difficult methods for the longer intervals.

B) The effect of the increase in the degree of learning upon the amount of retention manifests the phenomenon of diminished

85

returns. This phenomenon is the incidental and almost necessary consequence of the tendency of negative acceleration obviously present in the learning curve for memory.

C) On the whole, the curves of retention for the different degrees of learning still approach more closely to the Ebbinghaus type than to that of Ballard. The recognition curves are, however, far from being logarithmic.

3. Beyond a certain limit, the duration of the recall process has but little effect upon the amount of recall or the curve of retention.

A) The shape of the retention curve for written reproduction is practically determined at the end of the first 2 min. of recall. For recognition 90 sec. of recall is long enough for determining the shape of the curve.

B) With the written reproduction method, the effect of extending the time limit for recall upon the amount of reproduction is negatively accelerative.

4. The amount of error in written reproduction increases with the time interval, but the error curve thus determined manifests no definite relationship to the curve of forgetting which also rises with the time interval. Nevertheless, the former has to be taken account of as a supplementary curve of retention.

5. The speed of recall decreases with the time interval, but the speed curve, too, bears no similarity or causal relation to the curve of forgetting, though it is indicative of the conditions of retention.

6. A) Individual variability increases with the difficulty of the act of recall, but decreases with the frequency and the recency of practice.

B) The speed of learning and the amount of retention are positively correlated.

The results of these experiments prove that the difference between the Ebbinghaus tradition and the type of curve discovered by Ballard is not due to differences (1) in the method of measurement or (2) in the degree of the original learning.

We do not find a higher amount of retention for the 2-day

interval than for 1 day or even immediate recall, as did Ballard.

Differing from the Ebbinghaus tradition, our curves are not all logarithmic. Some of the recognition curves do not even manifest the phenomenon of negative acceleration in general.

The curve of retention varies with the conditions of learning and of recall.

Vol. 35, No. 1   January, 1938

THE

PSYCHOLOGICAL BULLETIN

MEMORY SPAN: A REVIEW OF THE LITERATURE

BY ALBERT B. BLANKENSHIP[1]

Psychological Corporation

Although many researches have been undertaken in the field of memory span, both by experimental psychologists and by those in the field of mental testing, there has been no attempt to summarize or to systematize the findings of the investigators who have studied the various aspects of this subject. This paper has been undertaken with that end in view.

I. HISTORY OF MEMORY SPAN TESTS

(1) *Early Anecdotes.* Stories of exceptional individuals have probably been told since the beginning of time, and reports about memory spans of such individuals are not lacking. There was a blind Swiss, for example, who was reputed to have been able to repeat a series of 150 numbers, either forwards or backwards, after a single hearing (91)! Other anecdotes are in the literature (8, 44, 47, 91, 130), but there was no real attempt at controlled observation, and none of the early writers realized the significance of what they had heard of or observed.

(2) *Nineteenth Century Studies of Memory Span.* In 1870, Oliver Wendell Holmes, in addressing the Phi Beta Kappa Society of Harvard University, said, ". . . in uttering a series of unconnected words or letters before a succession of careful listeners, I have been surprised to find how generally they break down, in trying to repeat them, between seven and ten figures or letters; though here and there an individual may be depended on for a larger number . . ."(61). Holmes, however, made no formal experiments on the phenomenon.

Sixteen years later, William James (70) wrote of "the present, . . . merely a dividing line between the past and the future . . . ," but he did no

[1] The writer wishes to express his indebtedness to Miles Murphy and Francis Irwin of the Department of Psychology, University of Pennsylvania, for their aid in compiling a bibliography for this summary.

1

experimental work on the problem. In the same year, Jacobs (68), an English philosopher, wrote, " There is . . . a certain number of syllables up to which each person can repeat . . . after only once hearing; and it is probable that this number varies with different persons." In 1887, he made the first formal experiment on " prehension " (69), discovering that the ability increased with age. Galton (48), in the same journal, noted that inmates of institutions for the feebleminded possessed lower prehension ability than did the normal children tested by Jacobs. In 1888, Burnham (21) summarized some of these results in his comprehensive paper on memory.

From this time on, memory span research was more common. The most important work in the field since 1890 will be reviewed here, not primarily from the historical standpoint, but from the aspect of logical organization. If the reader be interested in historical summaries including some of the work on memory span, he is referred to the review by Burnham (21), and those by Young (144), Kuhlmann (78), Wylie (142), and McGeoch (87).

II. What Is Memory Span?

To define memory span, one must examine the question from two viewpoints, the functional and the structural.[2]

(1) *Functional Aspect.* Functionally, Binet (8) has defined prehension as " the maximum number of digits retained after a single hearing." But the definition, of course, need not be restricted to the use of digits. Humpstone (65) broadened this definition when he described memory span as " the ability to grasp a number of discrete units in a single moment of attention and to reproduce them immediately." Leaming (80) elaborated upon this: " It [memory span] appears to measure the number of discrete units over which the individual can successively distribute his attention and still organize them into a working unit." Watkins (133) stated that immediate memory ". . . is the capacity to repeat impressions which have not entirely disappeared from consciousness, the expression following immediately upon the impression." Strong (125) defined it as " a line of successive presents."

To generalize, memory span refers to the ability of an individual to reproduce immediately, after one presentation, a series of discrete stimuli in their original order. Practically any sort of material may be presented, such as digits, letters, words, and sounds, and almost any sense organ or combination of sense organs may be used to receive the impressions. Both of these variables will be discussed under subsequent headings.

(2) *Structural Aspect.* A structural definition of memory span is difficult to give, for one immediately is faced by the distinctions between the prerequisites for memory span, and the actual processes involved. Although an intact sense organ, an afferent tract, a central projection area, efficient association fibers, and a certain degree of attention are all involved, as Smith (119) points out, these terms do not describe the processes actually involved in memory span.

Processes of attention are involved, as McCaulley (86), Gundlach, Rothschild, and Young (56), Cattell (28), T. L. Bolton (16), Johnson (72), and

[2] " Functional " in the sense of external or extrinsic behavior; " structural " in the sense of the processes involved (the intrinsic aspect).

others indicate. Certainly the subject must be able to distribute his attention over the series of stimuli, and concentration of attention is needed so that the mental processes may continue in the direction started. But the range or span of attention is distinct from memory span. Hunter (**66**) shows that attention span and memory span are alike in involving only one presentation of the stimulus, but that they differ in temporal duration of the stimulus. "If the stimulus is presented for one-fiftieth of a second, the experiment is classified as one on attention, whereas with longer exposure times, the behavior is classified as . . . memory." Motor aspects of attending are evident in the receipt of instructions and in the postural response of getting ready, as well as in the receptive attitude during the presentation of the series. Much may be said for the suggestion (**56**) that memory span be renamed "set."

"Associability" is also required in memory span. This term, originated by Humpstone (**63, 64, 65**), refers to the ability of the subject to group the series of elements together: to perceive relationships among the series in order to better reproduce them.

Still another process involved in memory span is that of imagery (**20, 86, 97**). The subject, in order to be able to reproduce the series presented, must be able to image the series. But memory span is not an after-image. Richet (**110**), as early as 1886, compared the memory span with the sensory after-image. He recognized that there was a difference, but believed the two to be comparable. According to common psychological belief, it is generally held that the sensory after-image depends upon activity not only in the brain, but also in the sense organ. Humpstone (**64**) actually calls memory span an after-image.

The actual reproducing of the series of stimuli involves the process of memory (**28, 86**). If the individual possessed no memory at all, reproduction of the series would be impossible. But Binet (**8**), in 1894, was probably the first specifically to point out that there was a difference between memory and memory span. Fernberger maintains (**41**) that memory span and memory are different in the length of time over which reproduction is possible. Memory span is transitory; memory is fairly permanent. In addition, the amount of material involved in memory span is ordinarily much less than the amount of material involved in memory. W. G. Smith (**119**) showed that memory span may be good and memory bad, or vice-versa, thus offering further proof that the two are distinct. Reproduction of the series also involves certain other "reproduction factors," such as language ability and arithmetical proficiency.

Now although memory span is dependent on all of the above functions, it seems clear that it is not any one of them (**20, 64, 123**). The question of whether the ability is dependent or independent is closely related to the present discussion, and hence is the next topic.

III. Is Memory Span a General Ability?

(1) *Introduction.* A few workers (**20, 63, 65, 97**) regard memory span as an independent ability. Such attention factors as observation, distribution of attention, and description, and such reproductive factors as language ability, memory, and arithmetical efficiency may also be involved (**20**). Humpstone's independent

ability tested is " associability," or, ". . . the ability to grasp and associate a number of discrete units of perception in a definite order " (65). Memory and imagination are involved, but memory span itself is a specific ability.

Binet also holds that memory span is an independent ability (12), but that the ability tested is the " capacity for effort." This view assumes that memory span is a general [3] ability, and accordingly, that the type of material used or the sense organ or organs through which the material is received should have no effect either on the number of discrete units reproduced by the individual, or on the standing of the individual in relation to others tested for memory span.

(2) *The Type of Material.* There is practically no limit to the type of material that can be used in such a test.

Ideas, sentences, objects, pictures, noises, words, paragraphs, diagrams, and syllables are only a few of the many types of material that have been used, though as Bronner, Healy, Lowe, and Shimberg point out (19), the use of digits has preëmpted the field. For a discussion of the various types of material that have been used, the reader is referred to Jacobs (69), Travis (128), Calhoon (25), Lumley and Calhoon (82), Humpstone (65), Terman (126), Terman and Merrill (127), Cattell (28), Squire (121), Whitley (136), and Whipple (135).

It has been found that the type of material used in the test does definitely affect the results secured. In general, experimental results indicate that the most difficult material to reproduce is nonsense syllables, then letters, then digits, sentences and related words (25, 66, 82, 121, 132, 136). Bourdon (18) found that letters were easier' for children to repeat than other materials; all materials were found to be of the same difficulty for subjects of from 14 to 20. The order indicates that at least two factors are involved in making some materials easier than others: familiarity with the material and " associability."

If all of the material used produced the same results relatively, the standing of the individuals in the group would not be affected by the type of material used. If the standing of the individuals in the group is affected by the type of material used, other factors remaining constant, we should expect a correlation of significantly less than 1.00 between results secured by use of different materials.

---

[3] That is, the same ability is said to be operating through the media of different sense organs and with different materials.

Henmon (60) secured the highest correlation coefficients for memory spans as ascertained for different types of materials when he reported a coefficient of .77 between "memory" for syllables and "memory" for numbers, and found the same correlation between "memory" for nouns and for syllables. Memory span as tested by nouns and numbers correlated only .20. Abelson (2) secured intercorrelations of from .34 to .66 for different types of material. Calkins (26) found that concrete objects produced higher memory span scores than did verbal stimuli, such as words. Fischler and Albert (42) were the first to treat this problem statistically. These investigators secured intercorrelations of from —.33 to .47 for different types of material. As a result of their experiment, they concluded that immediate memory was apparently not a general ability. They admit, however, that their results may be due to the fact that the same subject is attentive in one test, inattentive in another.

In none of these studies was there careful control of all experimental conditions. Thus, additional and more careful work is needed before conclusions can be drawn.

(3) *The Sense or Senses Through Which the Impression is Received.* The sense or senses through which the impression is received also appear to affect the memory span score as secured by the clinical or experimental test. The material may be presented through almost any sense organ or combination of sense organs.

It has been found that in general, for example, the adult will have a greater memory span with the visual than with the audito-vocal method, but that the child's score is higher with audito-vocal than with visual presentation (1, 59, 83, 103). Kirkpatrick (75) reported that visual presentation produced higher scores for immediate reproduction than did auditory or actual presentation of objects before the eyes.

The sense organ which receives the impression does, according to experimental results, make a definite difference in memory span score, at least in terms of the number of units reproduced. If the standing of the individual in relation to others is changed by results on memory span as attained through different sense organs, other factors remaining constant, correlations between the results should be significantly less than 1.00. But again, the experiments were not carefully controlled. Davis (37) found a correlation coefficient of only .49 between visual and audito-vocal presentation results. Hao (57) reported the coefficient to be .39 between visual and auditory presentation.

If the material is presented visually, successive or simultaneous presentation may be used. Münsterberg and Bigham (93), and Gates (53), found that adults profited more through simultaneous presentation, although Warden (132) reported that his college students profited more through successive presentation, and when movement was involved in the presentation, scores were even higher. Hawkins (59) verified the results of Münsterberg and Bigham (93) and Gates (53), and further reported that children secured higher scores through the use of successive rather than simultaneous presentation.

The memory span apparently increases as the number of sense organs through which impressions are received increases, except where distraction may occur, as in the results of Smedley (116).

Jones (74) found that a method of combining as many sense organs as possible was superior to any other method. This was said to be due to the fact that there are certain " visual," " auditory," and " motor " types of individuals. When all the possible sense organs are stimulated, each subject has the fullest possible advantage in the method of presentation. Münsterberg and Bigham (93) found that a series presented to 2 senses at the same time is much more easily reproduced than if given only to sight or to hearing. Smedley (116) concluded that the audito-visual-articulatory and the audito-visual-hand-motor memory were superior to visual presentation, which was superior to the audito method, but Chambers (31) could not substantiate this order.

Nichols (96) early demonstrated the possibility of using the tactual receptors for testing memory span, though Nichols had little idea of such an application of his work. The fact that memory span can be tested through the medium of any sense modality makes the Knox Cube Test a particular type of memory span test. In the Knox Cube Test, 4 blocks in a row are tapped by the examiner in a given order; the subject is then asked to tap the blocks in the same order. Obviously this comes under the functional definition of memory span, being simply a new method of presenting the stimuli. Davis (37) recognized this test as a type of memory span when he ran correlations with the results of the Knox Cube Test and results of memory span for digits.

(4) *Summary.* Results indicated in the 2 preceding sections show that substantially different spans are secured depending upon the type of material used, and the sense or senses through which the impressions are received. From all the evidence available, however, it would appear that memory spans for different types of material may be specific spans, rather than different aspects of a general span. Likewise, it appears quite probable that the memory span for each sense organ or combination of sense organs is a specific span. But the whole question is far from settled and is open for a real experimental attack, since it is more than possible that differences are due to inaccuracies in the methods rather than intrinsic differences in the mental processes involved.

For example, if the results obtained by methods using different materials could be freed of differences in the subjects' acquaintance with the materials, there might be no differences in relative results. This possibility is to be discussed further under a subsequent heading.

And again, if subjects who had practiced equally with the different sense organs could be obtained, results secured through different sense organs might give the same relative rankings for individuals. But there is a strong possibility that the imaginal endowment, as well as the imaginal type, would still affect the memory span, as Jones (74) suggests.

IV. Factors Which Affect Memory Span

There are a number of factors which definitely affect memory span; the effects of practically all of these factors have been investigated in statistical and experimental studies. Some of the factors are extrinsic, or present in the testing situation itself. These factors, if not carefully controlled, cause the memory span test to be statistically unreliable. Other factors are intrinsic in the individual, and it is these factors which are the basis of " true " memory span.

Though numerous factors affect memory span, the test is one that shows surprisingly high reliability. Results obtained by different investigators show that the reliability coefficients for memory span may be as low as .28 (15), or as high as .93 (22). Table I summarizes the reliability coefficients secured by different investigators for the more common methods of testing memory span.

TABLE I

RELIABILITY COEFFICIENTS REPORTED FOR MEMORY SPAN

Investigator	Audito-Vocal for Digits	Visual for Digits	Audito-Visual for Digits
E. B. Bolton (15)..............	.28		
D. Mitchell (90)..............	.44, .47 [4]		
Hao (57).....................	.52	.83	
Garrett (49).................	.80	.68	
Davis (37)...................	.74	.84	
Wyatt (141).................		.76	
Burt (22)....................		.70, .93 [5]	
Abelson (2).................			.73, .70 [6]

Reliability coefficients for other types of memory span reported in the literature vary from .70 (2) to .81 (141). Both the figures summarized in the table, and the data indicated in the preceding paragraph lead to an important conclusion regarding the use of memory span tests. The range of figures indicates that the extrinsic factors *can probably* be controlled carefully enough to make the test a reliable one.

[4] Two figures secured by use of two methods of scoring.

[5] Burt (22) secured the first figure with elementary school students, the latter with preparatory school students.

[6] Abelson's first figure was secured with girls, the second with boys.

A. Extrinsic Factors

(1) *Characteristics of the Material That is Used.* The characteristics of the material used will definitely affect the memory
span score.

If, for example, the material is all closely related, it will be much more
easily reproduced. This relationship of the material is called by Calhoon (23)
the "coefficient of associability." In the use of digits, the figures must be so
placed that none are in their natural or reverse order. There must be an avoidance of rotation, or of any numbers suggesting addition, subtraction, division,
or multiplication (Brotemarkle, 20). Binet and Simon (11) state that no
numbers which follow one another must be used beside each other. T. L.
Bolton (16) and Bourdon (18), in their experimentation, were sure to ascertain
that no digit came in its accustomed order, and that no digit was repeated.
Terman (126) was not so careful in this respect in his 1915 revision of the
Binet Test, but has taken greater care in his 1937 revision of the scale (127).
Xilliez (143) analyzed the effect of the relation of the digits to one another,
and noted that a negative interval (the interval is the difference between 2 digits
which follow one another; it is positive if the second is larger, negative if the
first is larger), is inferior, in terms of recall, to a positive interval. To summarize, the units of the series must not be presented in a manner that would
facilitate groupings through the apperceptive background of the subject.

In addition, the units of the material must not be presented in
groups. If the visual method is used, the material should be presented either one unit at a time (successive presentation), or all units
at the same time (simultaneous presentation), for grouping would
make it too simple for the subject to secure a memory span above
his "true" one. Brotemarkle (20) and others emphasize the importance of the control of grouping. Chamberlain (30) has experimentally demonstrated that recall is stronger when the objects are
presented in groups. However, even when grouping is eliminated
in the presentation of the material, subjective grouping often occurs.

The material used should have approximately the same degree
of familiarity for all subjects. Calhoon (23) and Whitley (136) both
stress the fact that apperceptive background should be equalized for
all subjects, as far as possible.

All of the subjects should have the same degree of familiarity with
the items in the series. Do not, for example, test a child by the
digit method if that child has never been taught numbers, for all
available norms have been secured with the use of subjects acquainted
with numbers.

(2) *Rhythm of the Presentation of the Material.* Closely related
to the problem of presenting the stimuli in groups, is the presentation
of the stimuli in rhythmic fashion. Most investigators point out that

the stimuli used in testing memory span should be presented with as little rhythm as possible (11, 18, 119, for example).

Probably the only experimental study of the effect of varying rhythm on memory span has been undertaken by Adams (3). Adams varied the rhythm in presenting a series of digits by using trochaic, iambic, dactylic, anapestic or amphibrachic rhythm, or no rhythm at all. He reported that his subjects (elementary psychology students at the University of Michigan) had higher memory spans in general when rhythm was used than when no rhythm was used. The effect of the different types of rhythm depended upon the sex of the individual, the females doing best with anapestic rhythm, the males with dactylic.

The fact that the introduction of rhythm into the presentation of the series of units does increase memory span is further verified by the results of those investigators interested in the "rhythmic span," in which the units are presented in rhythmic fashion (see 122, 124, for example). The effect of rhythm is to group the units in the series, again enabling the individual to secure a span higher than his "true" one.

(3) *Rate of Presentation of the Stimuli.* The speed with which the stimuli are presented has an effect on the memory span score attained. Terman (126) and other psychologists set the best rate of presentation of digits at a rate of slightly faster than 1 per second, while Lightner Witmer, in instructing clinical psychologists at the University of Pennsylvania, expressed his belief that the "natural rate of discharge" (the speed best adapted to the individual) should be used.

Actual experimental investigation also indicates that the speed of presenting the stimuli affects the score. Peatman and Locke (100) experimentally showed that the best rate of presentation for digits by either the audito-vocal or visual method was one digit per two-thirds of a second to one digit per second.

In the auditory digit test, Brotemarkle (20) believes that a rapid increase in the rate of presentation will result in an increase in score. Lumley and Calhoon (82) found that a decrease of speed enabled children of the seventh and eighth grades to raise their scores, but that in the other grades tested (third to twelfth) there was no consistent effect on performance. Other experimenters have found that a faster rate of presentation adversely affected memory span performance (56, 107). One investigator (Bergström, 6) reported that rate of presentation of the stimuli had no effect on the attained memory span.

Once again, a conclusion about the effect of the variable cannot be reached. Different research workers make various reports. More carefully controlled and standardized work is essential.

(4) *The Method of Scoring the Responses.* The method of scoring the responses also has an effect upon the apparent memory

span of the individual. Variations in scoring are common; scarcely two investigators have scored alike.

In the audito-vocal memory span for digits, for example, Terman (126) gave the individual 2 or 3 trials on any particular series, depending upon its length, and the subject was given credit for that length if one of the series was reproduced correctly. Starr (122) gave credit if 2 of 4 series were reproduced correctly at a given length. Humpstone (65) gave one trial at each level where the series was arranged in lengths varying from 3 to 10 digits. Credit was given for the longest series correctly reproduced. M. H. Young (145) showed that the number of trials given affects memory span attained. When a child was given 3 chances instead of 2 (with one series necessarily correct for credit), 55% of the subjects increased their span by one.

In the determination of reverse memory span, Starr (122) gave 4 chances at each length, and 2 of the 4 had to be correct reproductions for credit to be given. Terman (126) gave 2 or 3 chances at each level, and only one had to be correct. In the visual memory span for digits, Humpstone (65) gave only one chance at a series of given length, and to get credit, that series had to be absolutely correct.

Most investigators take the point of view that an incorrect series should not be scored at all. As Bergström (6) points out, if errors in a series longer than the span attained are scored, the true memory span is not ascertained. Other investigators feel, however, that all of the reproductions should be considered (55, 133).

Krueger and Spearman (77) take account of errors in their novel technique of scoring. They correlate the subject's reproduced series with the original stimulus series by use of Spearman's "footrule method." Thus the greater the error of the subject, the lower will be the correlation coefficient. Other methods of scoring errors are many and complicated, but these schemes and techniques will not be discussed in this paper.

(5) *Fatigue of the Subject.* Fatigue may be another extrinsic factor affecting memory span performance. Though the few investigators mentioning the effect of fatigue on memory span do not differentiate between mental and physiological fatigue and boredom, this does not immediately exclude their observations from consideration, though it does make them much less valuable. Hao (57) and Whitley (136) both believed fatigue to be a factor in their results, but Smedley (116) probably delayed experimental work on the problem when he pointed out that if one attempted to test the effect of fatigue, the subjects are apt to gain more through practice than they lose through fatigue.

As throughout the field of memory span investigation, more careful work is needed before the effects of fatigue can be conclusively shown.

(6) *Time of Day.* The time of day apparently is another extrinsic variable which produces differences in memory span. From

the available data, there is no way of telling whether the observed variations in memory span during the day are due to mental or to physiological fatigue, or boredom, or to some other factor's not even considered as a possible cause. It is for this reason that the variable is considered under a separate heading.

Marsh (84) found wide individual variations in the time of day at which greatest efficiency appeared in memory span performance, while Winch (138) found that efficiency was greatest in the forenoon. Gates (50, 52) substantiated Winch's results, and Laird (79) extended them to conclude that the performance reaches its low point about 10:00 P.M., when there is an "end spurt."

Though the causes of such variation are not clear, the implication for clinical psychologists is clear. In order for the subject to perform in his best possible manner, the test should be made in the forenoon.

(7) *The Attitude of the Subject.* Since the attitude of the subject is another important factor ordinarily within the control of the experienced examiner, it too is listed here as an extrinsic factor. Too many excellent chapters have been written on the technique of establishing rapport with the subject for the present writer to go into detail. For such a discussion, the reader is referred to almost any current text on intelligence testing.

It will be sufficient to mention work in which the attitude of the subject has been found to have a definite effect on the memory span attained. Bronner, Healy, Lowe, and Shimberg (19) and Hao (57) report that the personal attitude of the subject definitely affects results, and Squire (121) found the use of pictures effective in testing the memory span of children, for it increased their interest.

(8) *Distraction.* Naturally enough, one would expect that the greater the distraction present in the situation, the poorer would be the performance of the individual, and this is actually the case (92, 117, 134). The reason for this effect is apparent. Inasmuch as attention is one of the processes involved in the successful functioning of memory span, if the processes of attention are directed towards some other stimulus, they cannot operate effectively in the memory span function. Distractions must be kept at a minimum for reliable results, as Lumley and Calhoon (82) indicate.

(9) *Practice.* Practice on the part of the individual is another extrinsic factor affecting the apparent length of the memory span. Although it is now commonly assumed that the memory span is a congenital ability (65, 116), investigations reveal that a temporary increase in memory span score will result from practice.

Gundlach, Rothschild and Young (56) and Ide (67) found that some individuals' memory span scores were increased, those of others not visibly affected by practice. Winch (137) and T. L. Bolton (16) reported marked improvement with practice on the part of their subjects. Foster (43), experimenting with 6 different materials, stated that there was a definite practice effect in his subjects, but that the gain was specific, and limited to the particular type of material used. This is probably further evidence that memory span is not a general ability, but is specific for different types of material.

The greatest practice effects on memory span thus far have been demonstrated by Martin and Fernberger (85), who discovered that the memory span of one individual increased 47%, that of another 36%, after periods of practice spread over several months. Foster's (43) subjects gained from 6% to 44%.

Dallenbach (35) and Gates (54) were interested in determining the permanence of the practice effect reported. Dallenbach, after training subjects for a period of 17 weeks, observed a practice effect 41 weeks after the drill had been discontinued. Gates trained a group of subjects over a period of 78 days (spread over 5 months) and at the end of training, this group had raised its average memory span by 2 digits. After 4½ months of no practice, the group had fallen back to its original average.

Reed (108), however, claims that practice effects are negligible, and Whipple (134) experimentally found that if adaptation and assimilative devices are held constant, there is no practice effect. We must conclude, nevertheless, that practice does have an effect on memory span score as it is now commonly obtained by experimental or clinical methods. The reasons again are fairly obvious, and are so well discussed by Foster (43) that a detailed discussion is unnecessary. Foster believes gains to be due to (1) confidence and effort, (2) familiarity with the material, (3) learning to distribute the attention effectively, and (4) efficient methods of work and organized procedure.

(10) *Subjective Grouping of the Units in the Series.* It has already been noted that presenting the units in the series of stimuli by any method of grouping or rhythm will enable the subject to secure a higher memory span than he would otherwise have. Often the subject himself is entirely responsible for grouping the units, and may thus increase his apparent memory span. In Martin and Fernberger's study (85) it was noted that any memory span over 5 was secured through subjective grouping of the units. Oberly (98) found that the memory span limen, as indicated by grouping on the part of the subjects, was from 6 to 13.8 units.

It is certain that subjective grouping will increase the memory span of the individual and thus contribute to the unreliability of the method. The many cases of unusual immediate memory are probably explained by such grouping, though in the case of some individuals, this grouping is merely a matter of associating some of the units in the series with others.

F. D. Mitchell's report of Inaudi (91; also reported by Binet, 8), who correctly repeated 42 digits on one occasion, and his report of the blind Swiss who repeated 150 digits, are of this order. Even the famous Dr. Finkelstein, who appeared on Ripley's "Believe It or Not" program (111) could not have repeated the 15 digits he did on that occasion except through some method of grouping or meaningful association.

(11) *Temporary Pathological Condition of the Individual.* Some temporary pathological conditions of the individual will detrimentally affect memory span score. If the pathological condition is a permanent one, it may then be classed as an intrinsic factor, beyond the control of the examiner.

Kohnsky (76), controlling practice effects, found that pupils, several months after having dental treatment, increased their memory span scores. Paulsen (99) found, after equalizing for practice effects, that subjects who had been suffering from intestinal toxemia increased their memory span scores after treatment for the condition. These results, though apparently definite, need confirmation before final conclusions can be drawn. If the results are confirmed, we are probably justified in assuming that such temporary states have some adverse effect on the processes involved in memory span, making them less efficient. Another temporary pathological condition of the individual is that of hypnosis. P. C. Young (146) found no differences in "digit span" or "memory span" under hypnosis from that in the waking state, but his terms are not well defined and his conclusions thus have little significance.

(12) *Effect of Drugs.* Drugs may also produce a temporary condition which will affect memory span results. Since drugs produce a toxic state, the condition could well be included under the previous heading. Froeberg (45) and Hull (62) found a loss in memory span performance in non-smokers after smoking. Hull found that the habitual smokers showed a very small loss in efficiency due to smoking. From these facts Hull decided that habituation appeared to have produced a partial tolerance for tobacco with regard to its effect on the memory span. The explanation of the effect of drugs on memory span is obvious. The toxic states produced adversely affect mental processes, and through so doing, decrease the memory span score attained.

B. Intrinsic Factors

In addition to the factors here called "extrinsic" (but only extrinsic in that they are largely within the control of the examiner, and if not properly controlled, tend to produce an erroneous memory span), there are also certain "intrinsic" factors affecting memory span. It is these in which the psychologist is primarily interested. These intrinsic factors are those within the individual which work to produce his "true" or permanent memory span.

(1) *Age of the Individual.* The age of the individual is a factor which definitely affects memory span.

Memory span has been found to increase with age by a number of investigators (8, 19, 27, 38, 40, 42, 56, 63, 69, 80, 121, 137). Norms for various age levels have been secured by McCaulley (86), Lumley and Calhoon (82), M. Murphy (95), Starr (123), Smedley (116), and Terman (126, 127).

It should be pointed out that if the mental age of the individual does not increase, the memory span will not. So far as is known, memory span increases along with intelligence up to a similar age.

At what age does memory span cease to develop?

Carpenter (27), in using subjects from 6 to 14 years of age, reported a consistent improvement from year to year. Fischler and Albert (42) found an increase of memory span to adulthood. Kuhlmann (78) claimed that memory span increased up to maturity, but neither Fischler and Albert nor Kuhlmann interpret their terms. Wessley (135, p. 176) found that the maximal memory span occurred at the age of 12 to 14, while Smedley (116) and Chambers (31), although finding a general increase with age, found no particular age at which memory span was maximal. Bourdon (18) reported that maximal efficiency occurred at the age of 14. Hao (57) placed the age at 13 or 14 for girls, 15 or 16 for boys.

A few investigators claim that memory span increases to a point somewhere between the sixteen- and twenty-six-year level, though a large number of workers believe that memory span remains constant after the individual reaches a point somewhere between 12 and 16 years. Once again, the investigators have used such diverse methods of administration and scoring, and such different material, that the results are scarcely comparable. It is not surprising that no definite conclusion can be reached regarding this and other points in question.

(2) *Sex of the Individual.* Sex may be another intrinsic factor affecting the memory span; there is some disagreement on this point.

Burt (22), T. L. Bolton (16), Gates (51, 52), Kirkpatrick (75), and Woolley (140) all reported consistent superiority of the females in memory span tests. Gundlach and his coworkers (56), testing memory span with flashing lights, observed only a very slight superiority of the females over the males. Lodge and Jackson (81) and Travis (128), however, using prose passages to test memory span, report the superiority of females over males.

No significant sex differences in memory span have been observed in children of kindergarten age (67), at the six-year level (38), in primary school children (30, 137), and in children in general below the age of 15 (31). Fischler and Albert (42), testing for audito span with digits, consonants, and phrases as material, and for visual span with forms and pictures, found no significant sex differences, either in children or in adults.

Adams (3) reported a slight superiority of men over women in forward memory span for digits, presented by the audito-vocal method. Chambers (31) noted a superiority of males over females above the age ·of 15, and Watkins (133) reported a superiority of boys over girls in memory span ability. Dallenbach (35, 36) found that when mental age was held constant, males consistently surpassed females in " visual apprehension."

Thus we can reach no conclusion as to the rôle of sex in memory span. All we can do at this time is to note that sex may be a factor. Again, the methods used are so different that results vary.

(3) *Race of the Individual.* Recent investigations indicate that the race of the individual is another factor which may affect memory span. Apparently the Chinese are superior to the whites, who may be in turn superior to the Negroes. Data concerning the memory span of other racial groups have not yet been reported. Hao (57), and Pyle (106) observed that Chinese children were superior to white children in immediate memory. Pyle (105) also found that negro children were definitely inferior to white children in rote memory. Clark (33), however, observed his negro subjects to be superior to the whites. The results here are purely exploratory, and need further confirmation, but at least there is some evidence that there are race differences in memory span.

(4) *Permanent Pathological Condition of the Individual.* When the physical condition of the individual becomes permanently modified, the memory span has been found to be lower than that for a normal individual.

Epilepsy is such a condition; W. G. Smith (117), as early as 1905, reported the inferiority of a group of epileptic subjects to normal subjects in memory span, while Ninde (97) substantiated this conclusion with a study of 2,000 epileptics.

Smith (119) also reported, in another article, that normal subjects were definitely superior in memory span to those in a pathological (insane) group. Pintner and Paterson (102) found that deaf children, as a group, had abnormally poor memory spans. They concluded that this was due to the lack of auditory experience. Bond and Dearborn (17), testing auditory " memory " for different types of material, reported that normal subjects were distinctly superior to the blind subjects they tested from the Perkins Institution. But Hayes (58) failed to substantiate this report when it was found that the blind subjects were superior to normal individuals in memory for auditory digits, but that for other types of material and methods of presentation, superiority of the blind or the normal group varied with the age group tested.

Apparently a pathological condition of the individual may operate to improve memory span; at least certain pathological cases demonstrate unusual memory spans, whether or not this is due to the pathological condition. Barr (4) discusses Kitri, an " idiot savant " with echolalia, who repeated, after the first hearing, words and accents correctly in English, French, German, Spanish, Italian, Japanese, Latin, Greek, and Norwegian. Tredgold (129) tells of an imbecile who could repeat verbatim a newspaper he had just read.

These cases are not demonstrations of " true " memory span, for the individuals apparently reproduce the materials through some form of a memorial image.

V. Correlation of Memory Span and Intelligence and What It Means for the Memory Span as a Clinical Test

(1) *Relation Between Forward Memory Span and Intelligence.* Earliest observations of the relation between memory span and intelligence were made by Jacobs (69), who noted that pupils who stood high in class tended to have high memory spans, while Smedley (116) corroborated this report. Early experiments with feebleminded individuals pointed to the same fact—that memory span was directly related to intelligence (48, 72).

Early estimates of intelligence placed those with high memory spans near the head of the list (18, 22, 78, 137). Later investigators on the subject made use of the correlation coefficient and more objective measures of intelligence. Table II summarizes the coefficients secured between memory span and intelligence by various investigators using different types of forward memory span.

TABLE II

CORRELATIONS REPORTED BETWEEN MEMORY SPAN AND INTELLIGENCE

| Investigator | Auditory Presentation | | | |
	Digits	Sentences	Commissions	Nouns
Abelson (2)[7]		.45, .18	.53, .65	.18, .19
Clark (33)	.03			
Garrett (49)	.21			
Wissler (139)[8]	.16			

| | Visual Presentation | | |
	Digits	Letter Square	Nonsense Syllables
Garrett (49)	.18		
Wyatt (141)		.18	59

[7] Abelson's first figure represents results with girls, the second figure his results with boys.

[8] Wissler correlated auditory memory for digits with class standing rather than with intelligence.

This table shows that there is some relation between memory span and intelligence, and other results further indicate this relationship.

A contrast of results, probably reflecting· differences between the 2 sets of subjects in intelligence, are those of Terman (126) and McCaulley (86). Terman sets the audito-vocal memory span for the normal six-year-old at 5 digits, whereas the backward children tested by McCaulley secured a modal span of only 4 digits. Starr (123) reported that the retarded, sub-normal, and low defective children all tested below normal in memory span. Squire (121) also found retarded children to be inferior in memory span. Bingham (13) and Humpstone (63) found that college students in general had higher memory spans than average adults, as tested by other investigators.

All of these findings indicate a definite relation between memory span and intelligence. But at the present time, results are so varying in nature that the true degree of correlation between the two is impossible to predict. Terman, both in his original revision of the Binet Test (126) and in his recent revision (127) feels certain enough of the high degree of relationship to include memory span tests throughout the scale.

(2) *Relation Between Reverse Memory Span and Intelligence.* Bobertag (14), in 1911, was the first to suggest the reverse memory span test. Little work has been done up to the present time in making use of the reverse span, except for placement in the 2 Stanford revisions of the Binet Test (126, 127). Fry (46) has been the only worker to run correlations between the reverse memory span and intelligence. He secured a coefficient of .75 for reverse audito-vocal digit span and intelligence (as measured by Army Alpha). This is higher than any correlation secured between forward span and intelligence.

(3) *Value of the Memory Span Test as a Diagnostic Measure.* The results of a memory span test, then, are ordinarily indicative of the level of intelligence of an individual. Binet and Henri (10), A. M. Jones (73), Ninde (97), Leaming (80), and others place memory span ability at the base of all intellection. Starr (123) states that memory span " expresses the index of proficiency of all the mental competencies involved." Ninde says, " It goes without saying that a certain degree of associability is essential to all intelligent behavior and it is of special value in the development of the intellect " (97).

Most research and clinical workers agree that the value of the memory span test lies in its clear differentiation of the upper and lower groups of the distribution (Brotemarkle, 20; Starr, 123;

Chambers, 32). There is too much overlapping at the middle and at the extreme upper end of the distribution of age and diagnosis. Most clinical workers place more value in low spans than in high spans. Opinions of clinicians in regard to " critical spans " are of interest. In the forward memory span, a normal child of 5 or 6 should have a span of 2 or more (Easby-Grave, 38). A forward span of 5 is taken as a prerequisite to do high school work, while an even higher span is probably a prerequisite to do more advanced work (Leaming, 80). Other " critical spans " are listed by Sherman (114), Ninde (97), and McCaulley (86).

The memory span test as an indication of the individual's intelligence has several clinical advantages. Ninde (97) points out that it is simple and easy to administer. It does not place an emphasis on language ability, nor is it a long, extended test which is apt to tire the individual. Witmer believes that it is one of the most significant clinical tests, and Starr (122) states that " it is without doubt one of the most valuable tests employed for diagnostic purposes."

But its very simplicity is one of the dangers of the memory span test. The inexperienced examiner is apt not to follow specifically the particular directions which he is using. In addition, the scoring must be done precisely according to the method used in securing the norms which the worker is using. There are so many additional extrinsic factors affecting memory span that if careful clinical conditions are not observed, the results may be meaningless.

Another danger is that the investigator may place too much significance on the memory span test. Bronner, Healy, Lowe, and Shimberg (19) think that the importance of the memory span test has been greatly overemphasized. Of course a memory span test alone should never be used for diagnosis; the results on the memory span test are merely suggestive, and should always be supplemented by other test results and by qualitative observation.

VI. Summary

Though 146 references are listed in the bibliography, it is appalling to note how little real knowledge there is in the field of memory span. Practically all of the questions raised in the present paper have to remain unanswered; many researches have been undertaken, but few facts have been proved.

It has been pointed out throughout the paper that the primary causes for this state of affairs are the widely diverse methods of administering the test, the many kinds of materials used, the different groups of subjects used, the methods of scoring, etc. The question of whether or not memory span is a specific ability is essential; the effect of other factors cannot be answered until this is determined. For if memory span is a specific ability, it seems obvious that investigators using different materials and methods can expect only to get different answers to the same questions.

Probably the one thing most experimenters do agree on is a functional definition of memory span. But for other questions there are all sorts of answers. We do not know whether memory span is a specific or a general trait. We are sure that memory span is affected by certain extrinsic and by certain intrinsic factors, but we are not sure just what to include under each list, since all sorts of results have been claimed for any one variable.

Oddly enough, however, the test has been shown to have a fairly high reliability, and clinical investigators think enough of it seldom to omit it in an examination. It is favored by clinical investigators because of its close relation to intelligence (which has been fairly definitely shown), its simplicity, its brevity, and its lack of emphasis on language ability.

But, nevertheless, the whole field is wide open for a real experimental attack, for there is not a single aspect of the subject which is a closed chapter.

BIBLIOGRAPHY

1. Abbott, E. E., Memory Consciousness in Orthography. *Psychol. Monog.*, 1909, **11**, No. 1, 127–158.
2. Abelson, A. R., The Measurement of Mental Ability of " Backward " Children. *Brit. J. Psychol.*, 1911, **4**, 268–314.
3. Adams, H. F., A Note on the Effect of Rhythm on Memory. *Psychol. Rev.*, 1915, **22**, 289–298.
4. Barr, M. W., *Mental Defectives*. Philadelphia: P. Blakiston's Son & Co., 1913. Pp. x+368.
5. Bennett, F., The Correlation Between Different Memories. *J. Exper. Psychol.*, 1916, **1**, 404–418.
6. Bergström, J. A., Effect of Changes in the Time Variables in Memorizing, Together with Some Discussion of the Technique of Memory Experimentation. *Amer. J. Psychol.*, 1907, **18**, 206–238.
7. Bigham, J., Memory. *Psychol. Rev.*, 1894, **1**, 453–461.
8. Binet, A., *Introduction a la psychologie experimentale*. Paris: Bailliere, 1894. Pp. 146.
9. Binet, A., Attention et adaptation. *Ann. Psychol.*, 1899, **6**, 248–404.
10. Binet, A., and Henri, V., La memoire des mots. *Ann. Psychol.*, 1894, **1**, 1–23.
11. Binet, A., and Simon, T., Methodes nouvelles pur le diagnostic du niveau intellectuel des anormaux. *Ann. Psychol.*, 1905, **12**, 191–244.

12. BINET, A., and SIMON, T., L'intelligence des imbeciles. *Ann. Psychol.*, 1909, **15**, 1–147.

13. BINGHAM, W. V., Some Norms of Dartmouth Men. *J. Educ. Psychol.*, 1916, **7**, 129–142.

14. BOBERTAG, O., Ueber Intelligenzprüfüng (nach du Methode von Binet und Simon). *Zsch. f. angew. Psychol.*, 1911, **5**, 105–203; 1912, **6**, 495–538.

15. BOLTON, E. B., The Relation of Memory to Intelligence. *J. Exper. Psychol.*, 1931, **14**, 37–67.

. 16. BOLTON, T. L., The Growth of Memory in School Children. *Amer. J. Psychol.*, 1892, **4**, 362–380.

17. BOND, N. J., and DEARBORN, W. F., The Auditory Memory and Tactual Sensibility of the Blind. *J. Educ. Psychol.*, 1917, **8**, 21–26.

18. BOURDON, B., Influence de l'age sur la memoire immediate. *Rev. Philos.*, 1894, **38**, 148–167.

19. BRONNER, A. F., HEALY, W., LOWE, G. M., and SHIMBERG, M. E., *A Manual of Individual Mental Tests and Testing.* Boston: Little, Brown & Co., 1927. Pp. x+287.

20. BROTEMARKLE, R. A., Some Memory Span Test Problems. *Psychol. Clin.*, 1924, **15**, 229–258.

21. BURNHAM, W. H., Memory, Historically and Experimentally Considered. *Amer. J. Psychol.*, 1888–1889, **2**, 39–90, 225–270, 431–464, 568–622.

22. BURT, C., Experimental Tests of General Intelligence. *Brit. J. Psychol.*, 1909, **3**, 94–177.

23. CALHOON, S. W., Influence of Length of Lists upon Ability Immediately. to Reproduce Disconnected Word Series Auditorially Presented. *J. Exper. Psychol.*, 1934, **17**, 723–738.

24. CALHOON, S. W., Influence of Syllabic Length and Rate of Auditory Presentation on Ability to Reproduce Disconnected Word Lists. *J. Exper. Psychol.*, 1935, **18**, 612–620.

25. CALHOON, S. W., A Comparison of Ability to Reproduce One-Syllable Words and Digits Auditorially Presented. *J. Exper. Psychol.*, 1935, **18**, 621–632.

26. CALKINS, M. W., A Study of Immediate and of Delayed Recall of the Concrete and of the Verbal. *Psychol. Rev.*, 1898, **5**, 451–456.

27. CARPENTER, D. F., Mental Age Tests. *J. Educ. Psychol.*, 1913, **4**, 538–544.

28. CATTELL, J. McK., Mental Tests and Measurements. *Mind*, 1890, **15**, 373–380.

29. CATTELL, J. McK., Tests of the Senses and Faculties. *Educ. Rev.*, 1893, **5**, 257–265.

30. CHAMBERLAIN, A. H., A Memory Test with School Children. *Psychol. Rev.*, 1915, **22**, 71–76.

31. CHAMBERS, W. G., Memory Types of Colorado Pupils. *J. Philos., Psychol., & Sci. Method*, 1906, **3**, 231–234.

32. CHAMBERS, W. G., Individual Differences in Grammar Grade School Children. *J. Educ. Psychol.*, 1910, **1**, 61–75.

33. CLARK, A. S., Correlation of the Auditory Digit Memory Span with General Intelligence. *Psychol. Clin.*, 1923, **15**, 259–260.

34. COLLINS, M., Some Observations on Immediate Color Memory. *Brit. J. Psychol.*, 1932, **22**, 344–352.

35. DALLENBACH, K. M., The Effect of Practice upon Visual Apprehension in School Children. *J. Educ. Psychol.,* 1914, 5, 321–334, 389–404.

36. DALLENBACH, K. M., The Effect of Practice upon Visual Apprehension in the Feebleminded. *J. Educ. Psychol.,* 1919, 10, 61–82.

37. DAVIS, E. A., Knox Cube Test and Digit Span. *J. Genet. Psychol.,* 1932, 40, 234–237.

38. EASBY-GRAVE, C., Tests and Norms at the Six-Year-Old Performance Level. *Psychol. Clin.,* 1922, 15, 261–300.

39. EBBINGHAUS, H., Ueber eine Neue Methode zur Prüfung Geistigen Fähigkeiten und ihre Anwendung bei Schulkindern. *Zsch. f. Psychol. u. Physiol. d. Sinnes.,* 1897, 13, 401–457.

40. FARSON, M. R., A Report on the Examination of 100 6B Children in Philadelphia Schools. *Psychol. Clin.,* 1928, 40, 128–152.

41. FERNBERGER, S. W., *Elementary General Psychology.* Baltimore: Williams & Wilkins, 1936. Pp. xi+445.

42. FISCHLER, D., and ALBERT, I., Contribution a l'etude des tests de memoire immediate. *Arch. de Psychol.,* 1929, 21, 293–306.

43. FOSTER, W. S., The Effect of Practice upon Visualizing and upon the Reproduction of Visual Impressions. *J. Educ. Psychol.,* 1911, 2, 11–22.

44. FRANZ, S. I., and GORDON, K., *Psychology.* New York: McGraw-Hill Book Co., 1933. Pp. xvii+494.

45. FROEBERG, S., Effects of Smoking upon Mental and Motor Efficiency. *J. Exper. Psychol.,* 1920, 3, 334–346.

46. FRY, F. D., The Correlation of Reverse Audito-Vocal Memory Span with General Intelligence and Other Mental Abilities of 308 Prisoners in the Eastern State Penitentiary of Pennsylvania. *Psychol. Clin.,* 1930, 19, 156–164.

47. FULLER, H. H., *The Art of Memory.* St. Paul: National Publishing Co., 1898. Pp. ix+481.

48. GALTON, F., Supplementary Notes on "Prehension" in Idiots. *Mind,* 1887, 12, 79–82.

49. GARRETT, H. E., The Relation of Tests of Memory and Learning to Each Other and to General Intelligence in a Highly Selected Adult Group. *J. Educ. Psychol.,* 1928, 19, 601–613.

50. GATES, A. I., Diurnal Variations in Memory and Association. *Univ. Calif. Publ. in Psychol.,* 1916, 1, 323–344.

51. GATES, A. I., Correlations and Sex Differences in Memory and Substitution. *Univ. Calif. Publ. in Psychol.,* 1916, 1, 345–350.

52. GATES, A. I., Variations in Efficiency During the Day, Together with Practice Effects, Sex Differences, and Correlations. *Univ. Calif. Publ. in Psychol.,* 1916, 2, 1–156.

53. GATES, A. I., The Mnemonic Span for Visual and Auditory Digits. *J. Exper. Psychol.,* 1916, 1, 393–403.

54. GATES, A. I., The Nature and Limit of Improvement Due to Training. *27th Yrbk. Nat. Soc. Stud. Educ.,* 1928, Part I, 441–460.

55. GUILFORD, J. P., and DALLENBACH, K. M., The Determination of Memory Span by the Method of Constant Stimuli. *Amer. J. Psychol.,* 1925, 36, 621–628.

56. GUNDLACH, R., ROTHSCHILD, D. A., and YOUNG, P. T., A Test and Analysis of "Set." *J. Exper. Psychol.,* 1927, 10, 247–280.

57. HAO, Y. T., The Memory Span of 600 Chinese School Children in San Francisco. *Sch. & Soc.*, 1924, **20**, 507–510.
58. HAYES, S. P., The Memory of Blind Children. *Teach. Forum*, 1936, **8**, 55–59, 71–77.
59. HAWKINS, C. J., Experiments on Memory Types. *Psychol. Rev.*, 1897, **4**, 289–294.
60. HENMON, V. A. C., The Relation Between Mode of Presentation and Retention. *Psychol. Rev.*, 1912, **19**, 79–96.
61. HOLMES, O. W., *Mechanism in Thought and Morals*. Boston: Osgood, 1871. Pp. 101.
62. HULL, C. L., The Influence of Tobacco Smoking on Mental and Motor Efficiency. *Psychol. Monog.*, 1924, **33**, No. 150. Pp. 161.
63. HUMPSTONE, H. J., *Some Aspects of the Memory Span Test: A Study in Associability*. Philadelphia: Psychol. Clin. Press, 1917. Pp. i+30.
64. HUMPSTONE, H. J., The Analytical Diagnosis. *Psychol. Clin.*, 1919, **12**, 171–173.
65. HUMPSTONE, H. J., Memory Span Tests. *Psychol. Clin.*, 1919, **12**, 196–200.
66. HUNTER, W. S., Learning: II. Experimental Studies of Learning. In Murchison, C. (Ed.), *Foundations of Experimental Psychology*. Worcester: Clark Univ. Press, 1929. Pp. x+907.
67. IDE, G. G., Educability Level of 5-Year-Old Children. *Psychol. Clin.*, 1920, **13**, 146–172.
68. JACOBS, J., The Need for a Society for Experimental Psychology. *Mind*, 1886, **11**, 49–54.
69. JACOBS, J., Experiments on " Prehension." *Mind*, 1887, **12**, 75–79.
70. JAMES, W., The Perception of Time. *J. Spec. Philos.*, 1886, **20**, 374–407.
71. JAMES, W., The Knowing of Things Together. *Psychol. Rev.*, 1895, **2**, 105–124.
72. JOHNSON, G. E., Contribution to the Psychology and Pedagogy of Feeble-minded Children. *Ped. Sem.*, 1895, **3**, 246–301.
73. JONES, A. M., An Analytical Study of 120 Superior Children. *Psychol. Clin.*, 1925, **16**, 19–76.
74. JONES, W. F., An Experimental-Critical Study of the Problem of Grading and Promotion. *Psychol. Clin.*, 1911, **5**, 63–96, 99–120.
75. KIRKPATRICK, E. A., An Experimental Study of Memory. *Psychol. Rev.*, 1894, **1**, 602–609.
76. KOHNSKY, E., Preliminary Study of the Effect of Dental Treatment upon the Physical and Mental Efficiency of School Children. *J. Educ. Psychol.*, 1913, **4**, 571–578.
77. KRUEGER, F., and SPEARMAN, C., Die Korrelation zwischen verschiedenen geistigen Leistungsfähigkeiten. *Zsch. f. Psychol.*, 1907, **44**, 50–114.
78. KUHLMANN, F., The Present Status of Memory Investigation. *Psychol. Bull.*, 1908, **5**, 285–293.
79. LAIRD, D. A., Relative Performance of College Students as Conditioned by Time of Day and Time of Week. *J. Exper. Psychol.*, 1925, **8**, 50–63.
80. LEAMING, R. E., Tests and Norms for Vocational Guidance at the 15-Year-Old Performance Level. *Psychol. Clin.*, 1922, **14**, 193–217.

81. LODGE, R. C., and JACKSON, J. L., Reproduction of Prose Passages. *Psychol. Clin.*, 1916, **10**, 128–145.
82. LUMLEY, F. H., and CALHOON, S. W., Memory Span for Words Presented Auditorially. *J. Appl. Psychol.*, 1934, **18**, 773–784.
83. MACDOUGALL, R., Recognition and Recall. *J. Philos., Psychol., & Sci., Method*, 1904, **1**, 229–233.
84. MARSH, H. D., The Diurnal Course of Efficiency. *Arch. Philos., Psychol., & Sci. Method* in *Colorado Univ. Contr. to Philos. & Psychol.*, 1906, **14**, 1–99.
85. MARTIN, P. R., and FERNBERGER, S. W., Improvement in Memory Span. *Amer. J. Psychol.*, 1929, **41**, 94–97.
86. MCCAULLEY, S., A Study of the Relative Values of the Audito-Vocal Forward Memory Span and the Reverse Span as Diagnostic Tests. *Psychol. Clin.*, 1923, **15**, 278–291.
87. MCGEOCH, J. A., Memory. *Psychol. Bull.*, 1928, **25**, 513–549.
88. MEUMANN, E., Intelligenzprüfung an Kindern der Volkschule. *Exper. Päd.*, 1905, **1**, 35–101.
89. MILLER, K. G., Competency of Fifty College Students. *Psychol. Clin.*, 1922, **14**, 1–25.
90. MITCHELL, D., Variability in Memory Span. *J. Educ. Psychol.*, 1919, **10**, 445–457.
91. MITCHELL, F. D., Mathematic Prodigies. *Amer. J. Psychol.*, 1907, **18**, 61–143.
92. MÜNSTERBERG, H., Die Association Successiver Vorstellungen. *Zsch. f. Psychol.*, 1890, **1**, 99–107.
93. MÜNSTERBERG, H., and BIGHAM, J., Memory. *Psychol. Rev.*, 1894, **1**, 34–38.
94. MURPHY, G., *General Psychology*. New York: Harper & Bros., 1933. Pp. x+657.
95. MURPHY, M., The 10 Year Level of Competency. *Psychol. Clin.*, 1928, **17**, 33–60.
96. NICHOLS, H., *Our Notions of Number and Space*. Boston: Ginn & Co., 1894. Pp. vi+201.
97. NINDE, F. W., *The Application of the Auditory Memory Span Test to Two Thousand Institutional Epileptics: A Study in Relative Associability*. West Chester, Pa.: Temple Press, 1924. Pp. 36.
98. OBERLY, H. S., A Comparison of the Spans of "Attention" and Memory. *Amer. J. Psychol.*, 1928, **40**, 295–302.
99. PAULSEN, A. E., The Influence of Treatment for Intestinal Toxemia on Mental and Motor Efficiency. *Arch. of Psychol.*, 1924, **11**, No. 69. Pp. 45.
100. PEATMAN, J. G., and LOCKE, H. M., Studies in the Methodology of the Digit-Span Test. *Arch. of Psychol.*, 1934, **25**, No. 167. Pp. 35.
101. PINTNER, R., The Standardization of the Knox Cube Test. *Psychol. Rev.*, 1915, **22**, 377–401.
102. PINTNER, R., and PATERSON, D. G., A Comparison of Deaf and Hearing Children in Visual Memory Span for Digits. *J. Exper. Psychol.*, 1917, **2**, 76–88.

103. Pohlmann, A., *Experimentelle Beiträge zur Lehre vom Gedächtnis.*
      Berlin: Gerdes und Hödel, 1906. Pp. 191.
104. Preliminary Report of the Committee on Physical and Mental Tests.
      In *Proceedings of the Fifth Annual Meeting of the American Psycho-
      logical Association, Boston, December, 1896. Psychol. Rev.,* 1897, **4,**
      132–138.
105. Pyle, W. H., The Mind of the Negro Child. *Sch. & Soc.,* 1915, 1, 357–
      360.
106. Pyle, W. H., A Study of the Mental and Physical Characteristics of the
      Chinese. *Sch. & Soc.,* 1918, **8,** 264–269.
107. Rachofsky, L. M., Speed of Presentation and Ease of Recall in the Knox
      Cube Test. *Psychol. Bull.,* 1918, **15,** 61–64.
108. Reed, H. B., A Repetition of Ebert and Meumann's Practice Experiment
      on Memory. *J. Exper. Psychol.,* 1917, **2,** 315–346.
109. Richards, T. W., Psychological Tests in First Grade. *Psychol. Clin.,*
      1933, **21,** 235–242.
110. Richet, C., Les origines et les modalites de la memoire. *Rev. Philos.,*
      1886, **21,** 361–390.
111. Ripley, R. I., "Believe It or Not" Program, broadcast over the National
      Broadcasting Company Network from Radio Station WJZ, New York
      City, January 10, 1937.
112. Scripture, E. W., Tests on School Children. *Educ. Rev.,* 1893, **5,** 52–61.
113. Sharp, S. E., Individual Psychology: A Study in Psychological Method.
      Amer. J. Psychol., 1899, **10,** 329–391.
114. Sherman, I. C., A Note on the Digit Test. *Psychol. Clin.,* 1923, **15,** 124.
115. Skerrett, H. S., The Educability of a Two-Year-Old. *Psychol. Clin.,*
      1922, **14,** 221–224.
116. Smedley, F. W., Report of the Department of Child-Study and Pedagogic
      Investigation (Chicago Public Schools). *Report of U. S. Comm. of
      Educ.,* 1902, **1,** 1095–1138.
117. Smith, W. G., The Relation of Attention to Memory. *Mind,* 1895, **4,**
      47–73.
118. Smith, W. G., The Place of Repetition in Memory. *Psychol. Rev.,* 1896,
      3, 21–31.
119. Smith, W. G., The Range of Immediate Association and Memory in
      Normal and Pathological Individuals. *Arch. Neurol.,* 1903, **2,** 767–805.
120. Smith, W. G., A Comparison of Some Mental and Physical Tests in
      Their Application to Epileptic and to Normal Subjects. *Brit. J.
      Psychol.,* 1905, **1,** 240–260.
121. Squire, C. R., Graded Mental Tests. *J. Educ. Psychol.,* 1912, **3,** 363–380.
122. Starr, A. S., An Analytical Study of the Intelligence of a Group of
      Adolescent Delinquent Girls. *Psychol. Clin.,* 1923, **14,** 143–158.
123. Starr, A. S., The Diagnostic Value of the Audito-Vocal Digit Memory
      Span. *Psychol. Clin.,* 1924, **15,** 61–84.
124. Starr, A. S., The Significance of the Ratio Maintained Between the
      Forward, Reverse, and Rhythmic Memory Span as Obtained in Three
      Thousand Individual Examinations. *Psychol. Bull.,* 1929, **26,** 172–173.
125. Strong, C. A., Consciousness and Time. *Psychol. Rev.,* 1896, **3,** 149–157.

126. TERMAN, L. M., *The Measurement of Intelligence.* New York: Houghton Mifflin Co., 1916. Pp. xviii+362.

127. TERMAN, L. M., and MERRILL, M. A., *Measuring Intelligence.* Boston: Houghton Mifflin Co., 1937. Pp. xiv+461.

128. TRAVIS, A., Reproduction of Two Short Prose Passages: A Study of Two Binet Tests. *Psychol. Clin.,* 1916, 9, 189–209.

129. TREDGOLD, A. F., *Mental Deficiency.* New York: Wood, 1922. Pp. xx+ 569.

130. TREVELYAN, G. O., *The Life and Letters of Lord Macaulay.* New York: Lovell, 1876. Pp. 307+311 (two vol. in one).

131. VASCHIDE, N., Sur la localisation des souvenirs. La localisation dans les experiences sur la memoire immediate des mots. *Ann. Psychol.,* 1897, 3, 199–224.

132. WARDEN, C. J., The Factor of Movement in the Presentation of Rote Memory Material. *Amer. J. Psychol.,* 1926, 37, 257–260.

133. WATKINS, S. H., Immediate Memory and Its Evaluation. *Brit. J. Psychol.,* 1915, 7, 319–348.

134. WHIPPLE, G. M., The Effect of Practice upon the Range of Visual Attention and of Visual Apprehension. *J. Educ. Psychol.,* 1910, 1, 249–262.

135. WHIPPLE, G. M., *Manual of Mental and Physical Tests.* Vol. II. Baltimore: Warwick, 1924. Pp. 336.

136. WHITLEY, M. T., An Empirical Study of Certain Tests for Individual Differences. *Arch. of Psychol.,* 1911–1912, 3, No. 19. Pp. 146.

137. WINCH, W. H., Immediate Memory in School Children. *Brit. J. Psychol.,* 1904, 1, 127–134.

138. WINCH, W. H., Mental Fatigue in Day-School Children as Measured by Immediate Memory. *J. Educ. Psychol.,* 1912, 3, 18–29, 75–82.

139. WISSLER, C., The Correlation of Mental and Physical Tests. *Psychol. Monog.,* 1901, 3, No. 6. Pp. 63.

140. WOOLLEY, H. T., *An Experimental Study of Children.* New York: The Macmillan Co., 1926. Pp. xv+762.

141. WYATT, S., The Quantitative Investigation of Higher Mental Processes. *Brit. J. Psychol.,* 1913, 6, 109–133.

142. WYLIE, A. T., A Brief History of Mental Tests. *T. C. Rec.,* 1923, 23, 19–33.

143. XILLIEZ, P., La continuite dans la memoire immediate des chiffres et des nombres en serie auditive. *Ann. Psychol.,* 1895, 2, 193–200.

144. YOUNG, K., The History of Mental Testing. *Ped. Sem.,* 1924, 31, 1–48.

145. YOUNG, M. H., A Comparative Study of Audito-Vocal Digit Spans. *Psychol. Clin.,* 1928, 17, 170–183.

146. YOUNG, P. C., An Experimental Study of Mental and Physical Functions in the Normal and Hypnotic States. *Amer. J. Psychol.,* 1925, 36, 214–232.

THE Journal of
Marketing

THE REMEMBERING AND FORGETTING OF ADVERTISING

HUBERT A. ZIELSKE

How should advertising be scheduled? Should an advertising schedule be concentrated in an intensive "burst," or should it be spread out over a longer period? For the same expenditure a relatively small number of consumers can be exposed to advertising many times, or a larger number can be exposed a smaller number of times.

This unique study demonstrates how answers to these kinds of questions can be obtained.

HOW THE STUDY WAS CONDUCTED

THE purpose of this study was to measure the rate at which consumers can be made to remember advertising . . . and the rate at which they forget it.

Thirteen different advertisements from the same national newspaper campaign were used. The product was an ingredient food, a staple in almost every home. Reprints of the ads were mailed in plain envelopes to women, and no other material was included.

To maximize the opening of the envelopes, different-colored envelopes were used for successive mailings, return addresses were varied from mailing to mailing, and stamps were pasted on en-

velopes rather than using metered mail.

Two groups of women were selected in a systematic random manner from the Chicago telephone directory. One group received the ads at weekly intervals, every week for the first thirteen weeks of the year. The other group received the same thirteen ads; but they were mailed four weeks apart so that it took the whole year for the women to receive all thirteen. A total of 30,316 ads was mailed during the period of the study.

Recall of the advertising was measured with telephone interviews throughout the year. The women interviewed were aided in recall only by a mention of the product—not by the brand name nor by any mention of advertising by mail. Their answers to questions about what the advertising looked like, what it said about the product, and where they had seen it had to prove that they were recalling the advertising mailed to them.

In total, 3,650 interviews were made, not including "control" sample interviews. Curves were fitted to the recall measurements obtained.

● *About the Author.* Hubert A. Zielske is the Manager of the Research Department and Supervisor of Advertising Research of Foote, Cone & Belding, Chicago. He received his B.S. from the University of Minnesota in 1947, and his M.B.A. from the University of Chicago in 1950.

Mr. Zielske was given the American Marketing Association, Chicago Chapter, 1957-58 Honor Award for advancement of science in marketing for the Foote, Cone & Belding experimental work on which this article is based.

Asking a person if she remembered seeing any advertising for a product is likely to raise her normal interest level in advertising for that product for a period of time after the interview. To avoid the possibility that this kind of a bias would influence the findings of the study, no single individual was interviewed more than one time. This was accomplished by dividing the basic sample into comparable sub-samples.

A change in the normal level of awareness of advertising for the brand, during the period of the study, could influence the remembrance of the ads mailed. To check on this, a number of control samples were selected. The women were interviewed, but were not mailed any ads. There was no evidence of any change in the normal level of awareness of advertising for this product over the period of the study.

WHAT WAS FOUND OUT

Figure 1 shows the percentage of housewives who could remember the advertis-

ing during each week of the fifty-two weeks covered by the study. The curve for thirteen exposures at four-week intervals has a saw-toothed shape, since there was forgetting of the advertising between exposures in this schedule. Actually there is also some forgetting between exposures in the weekly schedule, but one week was the smallest unit of time measured in the study.

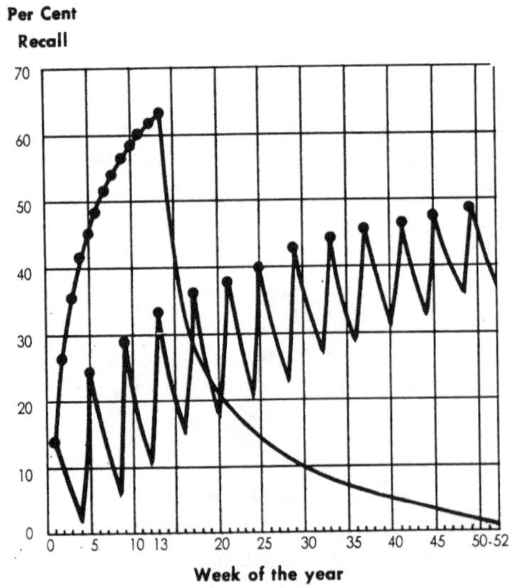

Remembering

Exposures at weekly intervals developed remembrance of the advertising at a faster rate, relative to the number of exposures, than exposures at four-week intervals. For example, after thirteen exposures, the percentage who could remember the advertising was 63 per cent among women who had been mailed ads at weekly intervals; among those who had been mailed the same number of ads at four-week intervals it was only 48 per cent.

Forgetting

The advertising was forgotten at a surprisingly rapid rate. Immediately after thirteen successive weekly exposures to the advertising, 63 per cent could remember it. But within only four weeks after the last exposure the percentage who could remember the advertising was cut in half. After six weeks, it had decreased by two-thirds.

The rate of forgetting decreased as the number of exposures increased. Within three weeks after a single exposure, the percentage who could remember the advertising declined from 14 per cent to 3 per cent—a decrease of 79 per cent. However, within the same period after thirteen four-week interval exposures, there was only a 23 per cent decrease, from 48 per cent to 37 per cent.

Per Cent Recall

Week of the year

FIGURE 1. Weekly percentages of housewives who could remember the advertising.

Single Burst of Exposures Versus Spread Over Year

The intensive burst of thirteen weekly exposures to the advertising made about one-third more different housewives at least temporarily remember the advertising as the same number of exposures spread out over the year. However, the concentration of exposures during the first thirteen weeks of the year left a large portion of the year with little or no remembrance of the advertising.

This would be a serious drawback for products which continually require remembrance of advertising to maintain sales. In this case, the average weekly number of people who could remember the advertising would often be a more important criterion for evaluating the schedule than the number of different people who remembered it at one point or another during the year.

The average weekly number of housewives who could remember the advertising, in the 52-week period covered by the experiment, was higher for thirteen exposures spread out over the year (29 per cent) than for the same number of exposures concentrated in the first thirteen weeks of the year (21 per cent).

Many Exposures Among Few or Few Exposures Among Many

What happened when each housewife was exposed to the advertising thirteen times might be considered analogous to buying thirteen advertising exposures in

a medium which has a relatively small audience. It can also be shown what would have happened if a larger number of housewives had been exposed a smaller number of times. This would then be analogous to buying a smaller number of advertising exposures in a medium, or combination of media, which has a larger total audience. Compare the situations shown in Table 1.

A combination of reducing the number of exposures per housewife and increasing the number of housewives exposed would increase the maximum number who could recall the advertising, that is, the number who could remember it at some point or another during the year. But it would reduce the average weekly number who could remember the advertising in the 52-week period.

One Exposure Versus Thirteen Exposures

Normally, as the number of exposures to advertising is increased, the amount of money spent is also increased. The "dollar efficiency" of various numbers of exposures refers to the number of "recallers" achieved per dollar spent.

Both the remembering rates and forgetting rates for advertising have to be considered in evaluating the dollar efficiency of various numbers of exposures. If the number of exposures in the experiment were reduced from thirteen to one, the loss in recall would not be limited to the difference between 63 per cent (the percentage of women who could remem-

TABLE 1

PERCENTAGE AND NUMBER OF HOUSEWIVES WHO COULD REMEMBER THE ADVERTISING

No. of exposures	No. of housewives exposed	Percentage recalling		No. recalling	
		Maximum	Weekly average[1]	Maximum	Weekly average[1]
1	13,000	14.0	0.8	1,820	104
13 (weekly)	1,000	63.0	21.0	630	210
13 (four-week)	1,000	48.0	29.0	480	290

[1] 52 weeks.

ber the advertising after thirteen weekly exposures) and 14 per cent (the percentage who could remember after one exposure). All of the remembrance indicated by the shaded area of Figure 2 would also be lost.

Per Cent Recall

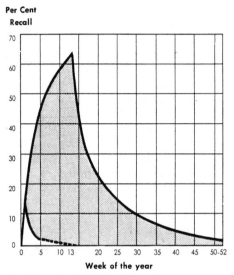

Week of the year

FIGURE 2. Recall of advertising after one exposure and after thirteen exposures.

For example, assume that the exposures were directed at 13,000 people and that the cost per exposure was $50. Applying this example to the present study, the dollar efficiency of one and thirteen exposures would be as shown in Table 2.

In terms of the number of different people made to remember the advertising at least temporarily, the dollar ef-

ficiency for one exposure was higher than for thirteen exposures.

But, in terms of the average weekly number of people who could remember the advertising, the reverse was true—the dollar efficiency of thirteen exposures was higher than that of one exposure.

HYPOTHESES ABOUT ADVERTISING

This controlled experiment suggests several hypotheses about the scheduling of advertising. Although some are perhaps a statement of the obvious, others require additional study before they can be accepted without qualification.

Here are the hypotheses:

- Exposures at weekly intervals will develop remembrance of advertising at a faster rate, relative to the number of exposures, than exposures at four-week intervals.

- Advertising will be quickly forgotten if the consumer is not continuously exposed to it.

- As the number of exposures to advertising increases, the rate at which it is forgotten decreases.

- If the objective of the advertising schedule is to make a maximum number of people at least temporarily remember the advertising, then:

  An intensive burst of thirteen weekly exposures would be preferable to spreading them out over the year.

  Fewer exposures per consumer,

TABLE 2

NUMBER OF HOUSEWIVES WHO COULD REMEMBER THE ADVERTISING PER DOLLAR SPENT

		No. recalling advertising		No. recalling per dollar	
No. of exposures	Cost	Maximum	Weekly average[1]	Maximum	Weekly average[1]
1	$ 50	1,820	104	36.4	2.1
13 (weekly)	650	8,190	2,730	12.5	4.2
13 (four-week)	650	6,240	3,770	9.6	5.8

[1] 52 weeks.

among a relatively large group of consumers, would be preferable to thirteen exposures among a smaller group.

The dollar efficiency of the advertising decreases as additional exposures to the advertising are purchased.

- If the objective of the advertising is to obtain a maximum average weekly number of consumers remembering the advertising in a 52-week period, then:

Spreading thirteen exposures out over the year would be preferable to an intensive burst of thirteen weekly exposures.

Thirteen exposures per consumer, among a relatively small group of consumers, would be preferable to fewer exposures per consumer among a larger group.

The dollar efficiency of advertising increases as additional exposures to the advertising are purchased, at least up to thirteen exposures.

The present experiment was limited to a comparison of two extremes in scheduling thirteen exposures; and many of the hypotheses above require further verification. An additional series of controlled experiments is planned, in order to broaden the scope of this initial study and to provide a check on its findings.

WHY CONTINUED ADVERTISING IS NECESSARY:
A NEW EXPLANATION

PAUL M. CARRICK, JR.

Continued advertising seems to be a well-established marketing principle. But why should it be necessary?

The answer lies in recognition of one characteristic of the decision-making process under conditions of uncertainty. Individuals deal with uncertainty by means of extensive simplifications of reality; this may result in a high social cost.

Continued advertising is necessary because of a simplification consumers make to facilitate brand selection. This means that many interrelationships between advertising, sales, and consumer behavior can be better understood.

THE necessity of continued advertising is a well-established marketing principle. But why should it be necessary?

Traditionally, continued advertising is explained by the need to educate the young, the rate of forgetting, or the character of the learning process. But these lines of reasoning are invalid. On the other hand, a logically and empirically valid explanation can be derived with a recognition of certain characteristics of the decision-making process.

CRITIQUE OF PREVIOUS EXPLANATIONS

First Explanation

The first line of reasoning is appealing. If one generation were educated by a seller's advertising, then all succeeding generations must be similarly educated

● *About the Author.* **Dr. Carrick received his undergraduate degree at Northwestern University in 1949, and his Ph.D. in Economics from the University of California, Berkeley, in 1956.**

He served as Teaching Assistant in Economic Statistics at the University of California, Berkeley, 1951-54; was Assistant Professor of Marketing at the University of Texas, 1954-55; was Assistant Professor of Marketing at San Diego State College, California, 1955-58; and is now in the Quality Assurance Planning Group, Convair-Astronautics Division of General Dynamics, San Diego, California. The article is based in part on the author's Ph.D. thesis, *The Psychology of Rationality.*

by advertising. Such an argument, however, ignores the tremendous impact of personal influence. A child is immersed in a stimulus pattern largely shaped by adults. As sociologists point out, family and neighborhood groups are the chief media which exert influence upon a child. Youths acquire most of their learning from these intimate groups. The wealth of alternatively possible responses to a given stimulus are narrowed down to a few, so that potentially conflicting situations will be resolved quite simply and effortlessly. If a new generation acquires so many of its values from its elders, brand preferences and general generic product preference problems will likely also be resolved by them.

Second Explanation

Nor can the second line of reasoning be given much credence. It is argued that, if prospective buyers are not continually reminded of the principal advantages connected with a particular product, the product will be forgotten. This position is supported by early psychophysical experiments which assumed that the rate of forgetting is a simple function of time or intervening events. However, by crude introspection, relatively unimportant events that happened a very long time ago can be remembered, while impressions of a few hours ago have already been forgotten. Furthermore, ability to remember what is important for effective action seems very great. Even rats can remember learned behavior for a long period of time.

Some alternative memory concept, such as that people remember what it is functionally useful for them to know, seems more appealing, both intuitively and empirically.[1] Thus if the concepts of "retentive" or "reminder" advertising are to have any validity, the particular circumstances must be distinguished under which previously useful knowledge is forgotten. It is not an obvious explanation by any means.

Third Explanation

The third explanation postulates that consumers will acquire a preference for a particular product simply if it is advertised enough. There are two possible bases for this postulate.

(1) It is argued that learning, the acquisition of product knowledge, proceeds by a gradual accumulation of associated bits of information. But the learning process does not progress incrementally. It consists of movement from one functionally meaningful cogni-

tive organization to another by sudden discrete insights.[2]

(2) It is argued that any appeal is acted upon if it is repeated frequently. If an unsatisfied consumer need can be discovered, and a brand can be advertised in terms of that need at a sufficiently high frequency, then success is assured because of sheer psychological dominance. Thus, continued advertising is seen as an expression of the frantic search for some semi-magical appeal which will lead to creation of a favorable brand image or "personality." Logically, it is a possible, though improbable, explanation. Empirically, an analogous relationship sometimes exists in the political field, as suggested by the "big-lie" technique of some political propagandists.[3] Certainly learning occurs because there is a conscious difficulty in attainment of some goal. But under these conditions information is sought for eagerly, and just one suggestion will usually be sufficient. Frequent repetition is not necessary for cognitive reorganization to occur. Further, it is difficult to believe that each of the thousands of advertised brands has a distinctive "personality."

The necessity of continued advertising cannot be adequately explained in terms of educating the young, the rate of forgetting, or the character of the learning process. Also, the logic of the "big-lie" technique, while plausible, is of very limited application for advertisers. Understanding the need for continued advertising requires a different approach.

SUGGESTED EXPLANATION

Consumer choice between brands is made with the aid of an assumption that

[1] David Krech and Richard S. Crutchfield, *Theory and Problems of Social Psychology* (New York: McGraw-Hill Book Company, 1948), pp. 125-134; C. E. Osgood, *Method and Theory in Experimental Psychology* (New York: Oxford University Press, 1953), pp. 549-599; Carl I. Hovland, "Effects of the Mass Media of Communication," in Gardner Lindzey, ed., *Handbook of Social Psychology* (Cambridge, Mass.: Addison-Wesley Publishing Company, 1954), Vol. 2, pp. 1,094-1,099. Compare: Thomas F. Gilbert, "Overlearning and the Retention of Meaningful Prose," *Journal of General Psychology*, Vol. 56 (April, 1957), pp. 281-289; Benton J. Underwood, "Interference and Forgetting," *Psychological Review*, Vol. 64 (January, 1957), pp. 49-60.

[2] Krech and Crutchfield, same reference as footnote 1, pp. 117-125.

[3] Same citation, pp. 140-141.

the quality of substitute products is positively correlated with the relative frequencies with which each has been recently advertised.

Summary of Argument

Brand selection is resolved in many ways. One way seems to occur very frequently—consumers assign significance to alternative brands by comparisons of the relative frequencies with which each has been recently advertised. Frequencies are computed in rather large units over a short period of time preceding the actual choice. Quality and advertising frequency are believed to be positively correlated: the higher the frequency, the better the quality. Such a procedure is economical for consumers. They lack incentive, if not ability, to discover the precise character of each brand, particularly when a large number exist; or intricate and time-consuming experiments are required to obtain the necessary information.

The explanation of continued advertising is one application of a general decision theory. Decisions are based upon simplified cognitive maps of the causal texture of the real world. Cognition is an inferential and predictive process. A limited number of an object's discriminable characteristics, or cues, are taken as indicators of its significance. There is not a one-to-one correspondence between an individual's conception of the real world and what is actually there.

As a result, errors can occur two ways: (1) There is a probability of error whenever predictions are based upon a limited number of cues—a sample of information. (2) The process underlying an individual's attainment of a desired set of cues is more expensive than if another cue set was used. The logic of many kinds of marketing behavior can

be understood in this framework. Each presents an economizing problem because aggregate real income is lowered by the cost of the error.

Procedure for Proving Argument

Validity will be established in two ways. First, the suggested explanation of advertising continuity implies a particular view of the decision-making process. Second, the empirical plausibility of the explanation will be shown.

The implied view of the decision-making process will be substantiated by discussing three points: (1) the apparent character of the knowledge lying behind observable choices; (2) the accuracy of knowledge—the extent to which it tends to disclose the nature of the real world; (3) the cost of incomplete knowledge.

THEORETICAL BACKGROUND

The Nature of Knowledge

What is the apparent nature of the knowledge that underlies an observable choice? A great deal of evidence from studies of perception and learning leads to one particular conception.[4] An individual assigns functional significance to the object world by means of whatever discriminable characteristics, or cues, it possesses. Discriminable characteristics may be color, size, shape, texture, or a trade mark. They may be concepts that allow a categorization of several objects such as dozen, pound, or dollar. Whatever single one or combination is used, an object's discriminable characteristics become associated with the significance properties that it permits to be attained.

[4] Egon Brunswik and E. C. Tolman, "The Organism and the Causal Texture of the Environment," *Psychological Review*, Vol. 42 (January, 1935), pp. 43-77; E. C. Tolman, *Purposive Behavior in Animals and Men* (New York: Century Company, 1932).

Thus, the object world within which action takes place has two analytically distinguishable properties: cues, or discriminable characteristics, and significance properties. Knowledge of what significance is associated with what cues sets a cognitive upper limit to economical decision-making.

An individual maps the real world by means of correlations between significance properties and any set of cues. This implies that knowledge is extremely complex. Any one cue alone indicates a particular significance with a low reliability. Cue-significance relations must be ranked by their reliability since some cues may more accurately reflect significance than others. Certainty of object identification requires the finding of additional cues, to provide an assignment of significance properties until the probability of error is zero. Perfect knowledge consists of such cue-significance correlation information that all the significance connected with any object will be assigned by some set of cues.

The Accuracy of Knowledge

Do individuals typically gather enough cue-significance information to yield perfect knowledge? Much of the literature of experimental psychology suggests that information-gathering activity stops short of completeness.

Usual explanations of simple perceptions, like seeing an approaching figure, rely upon a concept of inference from specific cues or a sample of information.[5] The figures on the next page illustrate a typical perceptual phenomenon. The drawings provide only a minimum of information, yet most subjects can easily

identify the objects. What is occurring is a willingness to make a prediction based upon limited data and to accept the consequences of a possible error. A similar conclusion can be derived from perceptual experiments dealing with the influence of needs and past reward-punishment upon perception. In general, these demonstrate the possibility that perception is a predictive process often based on such limited information that it may result in distortion, selective accentuation, or simplification of reality.[6]

Furthermore, there is frequently an apparent lack of information-gathering activity, even after an error has occurred. There are good reasons to expect this.

First, it may be thought that learning is by trial and error, so that, given enough experimental replications, the correct answer is eventually discovered. However, even for rats, there is little trial-and-error learning. For man, it may even be nonexistent. For rats and men, a problem situation is interpreted in terms of previously learned relationships. Probable solutions are conceived to be those rewarded in similar past situations. What is learned is a greater specificity in discrimination of relationships.[7] Old learned relationships are discarded only under exceptional circumstances. Consequently, it is conceivable that an individual can learn a way of dealing with the object world which is not optimum.

Second, the correctness of many learned relationships cannot be easily determined. Experimentally, when a rat

[5] C. H. Graham, "Visual Perception," in S. S. Stevens, ed., *Handbook of Experimental Psychology* (New York: John Wiley and Sons, 1951), pp. 868-920.

[6] Jerome S. Bruner, "On Perceptual Readiness," *Psychological Review*, Vol. 44 (March, 1957), pp. 123-152; George A. Miller, "The Magical Number Seven, Plus or Minus Two: Some Limits on Our Capacity for Processing Information," *Psychological Review*, Vol. 63 (March, 1956), pp. 81-97.

[7] Leo Postman, "Association Theory and Perceptual Learning," *Psychological Review*, Vol. 62 (November, 1955), pp. 438-446.

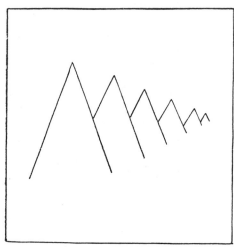

FIGURE 1

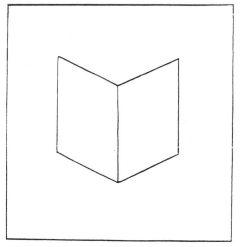

FIGURE 2

is rewarded randomly or infrequently for behaving in a particular way, relearning is a very retarded process. For much behavior, prospective rewards occur with a low probability. For example, "success" is a relatively remote possibility for many individuals but this does not result in relearning.

There are other reasons why correctness of a learned relationship cannot be easily determined. In a number of cases, what one expects from a situation is itself learned. It is possible either that error is not assigned because of a poorly defined standard of success, or that error is assigned when there is no error save that of a too high success standard. The buyer of a new car may or may not accept a few defects as a normal expectation. A college graduate may be dissatisfied because he is not a vice-president in ten years.

Another reason for an inability to determine correctness of a learned relationship occurs because the standard of correctness may be variable. Most individuals likely concentrate on testing a few relationships (for instance, their own personal qualifications), and deal with many serious errors by mild "maladaptive" actions.

Thus, how accurately does an individual's knowledge depict the real world? The evidence indicates that uncertainty (or ignorance) must be relatively common, but few people ever really "feel" it. Individuals act in the face of uncertain consequences with the assurance of a clairvoyant. Apparently, information-gathering activity has a high opportunity cost. A basic characteristic of all decision making is utilization of a cognitive map that depicts the real world imperfectly, yet from the individual's viewpoint is quite economical. Incorrect mapping is not necessarily self-correcting. An individual will very likely persist in basing decisions upon incomplete knowledge.

The Cost of Incomplete Knowledge

If there is not a one-to-one correspondence between an individual's knowledge and the properties of the object world, then his actions will result in errors.

The errors can be classified by the

source of loss into a significance error and a discrimination error. The classification provides a relatively simple way to describe the cost that underlies a number of behavior patterns. Each dimension of error will now be discussed. Illustrations of each type of error will be given since the unfamiliar terminology may make the nature of the errors seem recondite.

Significance Error

A significance error occurs whenever the significance assigned an object is not identical to what is actually there. Discrepancy can arise whenever an individual foregoes information gathering and acts upon an unreliable cue-significance set. The probability of a choice leading to a significance error will vary from zero to one, depending upon the degree to which utilized cue-significance relationships define an object's significance properties.

At one extreme, the probability of the utilized cues indicating actual significance may be zero. When bread is toasted, certain B vitamins are partially destroyed by the heat. Assuming that individuals consume bread at least in part to obtain what B vitamins are there, the significance assigned to the cue, toast, is incorrect. The same conclusion holds for preference of white over dark (whole wheat) bread.

More typically, the probability that the utilized cue set indicates the actual significance will usually be fairly close to one. The ripeness of fruit may be judged relatively accurately by color or feel. On the other hand, bread is made "squeezable" by chemical additives because that is how consumers measure freshness! Frequently consumers use price as an indicator of quality. This demonstrates both incomplete

knowledge and a preference to forego information gathering in favor of acceptance of possible error.

Discrimination Error

While cues are inherently aspects of the object world, the more salient discriminable characteristics are creations of a particular institutional structure. Trade marks are one solution to a particular problem of market organization. Classification and measurement of collections of objects is facilitated by such "invented" discriminatory terms as pound, dozen, and yard.

A discrimination error occurs whenever the total cost involved in facilitating the attainment of a specific significance with a particular cue is greater than if an alternative were used. Scarce resources are used in the creation of discriminating characteristics as well as in the procedural steps necessitated to apply them. Consequently, discrimination errors can occur whenever the cost of *supplying* or *applying* a particular cue is greater than for some alternative cue.

Such cues as dozen, pound, gross, foot, yard, hamper, and roll may be more expensive to apply than some alternatives. A retail clerk who must figure unit price from an invoice for five gross of stockings uses more time and effort than if count were kept with a base of ten. A consumer who purchases oranges by the dozen instead of the pound takes more time in selection.

The advertising of a loss leader illustrates the economy problem in the supplying of cues. It occurs when a consumer plans to buy a large variety of products at one time from one retailer, but does not initially know the existing price for each product at every retail outlet. Consumers seem to rely upon a relatively simple cue—an interstore comparison of prices for just a few of the many products they plan to purchase. Consequently, for competitive reasons, retailers advertise one or more products at a loss in order to attract consumers to their outlets. The total costs connected with this resolution of a consumer marketing problem are probably quite high compared to alternative cue supply possibilities.

Trade marks are an example of a cue supplied by sellers as a solution to several problems of market organization. One such problem is the provision of a cue by which buyers can distinguish differences in product significance. To use such a cue, consumers must learn what significance properties each trade mark is supposed to indicate. But how is this knowledge acquired? The traditional answer is through advertising, experimentation, and communication between consumers. Obviously, much knowledge is acquired in these ways, particularly for new products, or when a very large expenditure is to be made. Yet the reasoning is inadequate for explaining all brand choices. It is too much to expect that the significance of many brand names is acquired in this way. The necessary information-gathering activities would be very time consuming and costly. It is to be expected that consumers use a number of simplifying strategies to resolve selection between brands. One of these simplifying strategies can account for the necessity of continued advertising.

It is believed that consumers often assign significance to branded products by the frequency with which each has been recently advertised. A brand's significance properties are assumed to vary directly with advertising frequency. Frequency is computed as the number of impressions over a relatively short preceding time period. The differences in advertising frequency for two products must be relatively large before it is assumed that significance properties differ. Although the hypothesis cannot be strictly deduced from the theoretical considerations of the decision-making process, this is a weakness of the theory, not the hypothesis.

SUBSTANTIATING EVIDENCE

Advertising over any time period can be accounted for by a need to provide significance information or cue information. Consequently, the suggested explanation of continued advertising has an alternative hypothesis. To discover which explanation is most probably correct, there must be a number of empirical relationships existing between a firm's sales, its advertising, and consumer responses that can be adequately accounted for by only one explanation. Several empirical relations can be explained with the cue type of explanation, but not with the significance type of explanation.

(1) *Relation Between Advertised and Non-Advertised Products*

A great variety of data shows that large-scale advertising is necessary for successful marketing. Local, or private, brands usually sell at a discount to nationally advertised brands.[8] Even at a higher price, nationally advertised

[8] Jessie V. Coles, *Standards and Labels for Consumer Goods* (New York: Ronald Press, 1949), pp. 76-81; Robert H. Cole, et al., *Manufacturer and Distributor Brands*, Bureau of Business and Economic Research, Bulletin Series, No. 80 (Champaign: University of Illinois Press, 1955), pp. 51-65; House Small Business Committee, *Hearings on Price Discrimination* (Washington, 1956), Part III—Appendix, pp. 1,227-1,229.

brands dominate the market, as measured by either the extent of distribution or consumer preferences.[9] An interesting sidelight is the practice of large grocery chains sponsoring private labels which they sell on a price basis, yet still being forced to stock nationally advertised products. Private labels, particularly when unadvertised, seem to be only marginally successful at best.

There is not a high correlation between superior quality and extent of advertising, if extended reading of *Consumer Reports* or *Consumers' Research* is used as the basis of judgement. Yet attitude surveys show that consumers believe nationally advertised products are superior.[10] It is not known to what extent identical products are sold under advertised and non-advertised labels simultaneously. But it probably occurs frequently.[11]

The evidence suggests that advertised products are perceived as superior to non-advertised products. Why does this occur? It is logically possible that brand names either acquire significance mainly through advertising (and not consumer experimentation or intercommunication), or that frequency of advertising is utilized as an indicator of brand superiority. Both views are consistent with the evidence. The rest of the evidence to be presented does, however, lead to a choice between the two explanations.

[9] Consolidated Consumer Analysis Newspapers, *Consolidated Consumer Analysis, 1956;* Scripps-Howard Newspapers, Inc., *10th Grocery Product Distribution Survey* (New York, 1957); McClatchy Newspapers, *Consumer Analysis,* 11th ed. (Sacramento, California, 1957).

[10] Darrel Blaine Lucas and Steuart Henderson Britt, *Advertising Psychology and Research* (New York: McGraw-Hill Book Co., 1950), pp. 8-10.

[11] E. B. Weiss, "To Make or Not to Make Private Labels?" in J. H. Westing, *Readings in Marketing* (New York: Prentice-Hall, 1953), pp. 211-222.

(2) *The Relative Importance of Advertising Copy: Direct Measures*

If advertising primarily provided significance information, then changes in advertising copy, given constant advertising appropriations, unchanged products, and distribution outlets, should be followed by a change in sales. Table 1 shows the relative consumer preferences for different brands of canned peas and automobile tires in the Sacramento market. The variation in preferences is comparatively slight. Significant is the surprising stability of consumer preferences over a four- to nine-year period. Changes in advertising copy must have had little effect, for, if significance information had been utilized by purchasers, there should have been pronounced fluctuations in preferences. In most instances, of course, effects of copy changes are masked by changes in products, advertising appropriations, and distribution outlets.

Expressed consumer preferences are not the same as actual purchases, even though there is often a high correlation. To show the effects of varying the advertising message, the most unequivocal kind of data would be simultaneous measurement of actual purchases and changes in advertising copy. Oddly enough, there is little available information on the effects of copy changes. Organizations maintaining consumer panels would be a valuable source of information, but such data are not available for publication. However, the director of one consumer panel has summarized some evidence on the relationship between purchases and copy changes: ". . . after a product has attained a certain share of the market from initial advertising, little happens in a great majority of cases—no matter what kind of advertising is to be used.

TABLE 1
BRAND PREFERENCES FOR CANNED PEAS AND TIRES IN SACRAMENTO, CALIFORNIA, 1948-1957[a]

Canned Peas

Do You Buy Canned Peas? _____ What Brand? _____

Brand	Per Cent Who Buy Each Brand			
	1957	1954	1952	1948
Del Monte	57.9%	54.5%	54.8%	59.9%
Libby	11.6	9.5	11.2	6.4
S & W	6.9	6.2	4.9	5.0
Hunt's	5.0	5.0	2.6	—
Dew Drop	3.9	4.7	5.9	1.5
Green Giant	2.5	4.0	3.2	2.3
Highway	2.3	1.3	1.5	1.2
Sun-Blest	2.3	3.1	2.5	2.9
Briardale	1.2	1.3	—	—
Mission	1.1	1.9	1.9	—
Less than 1% (29 brands)	6.2	10.0	11.6	21.9
Don't Know and Any	2.1	1.4	2.0	1.6

Tires

If you were to replace your present tires tomorrow, what make would you buy? _____

Make	Per Cent Who Would Buy Each Make of Tire			
	1957	1954	1952	1948
Goodyear	22.8%	20.9%	22.2%	27.6%
Firestone	19.1	18.3	15.9	16.5
Sears' All State	13.4	11.7	11.0	7.4
General	8.9	5.9	8.6	8.7
U.S. Royal	8.8	5.5	6.2	4.9
Ward's Riverside	8.5	8.9	9.9	9.6
Goodrich	6.8	7.1	6.3	7.0
Atlas	3.0	3.2	3.0	3.4
Fisk	1.5	2.5	3.4	3.2
Federal	1.0	1.1	—	—
Seiberling	1.0	2.0	1.7	—
Less than 1% (17 brands)	2.9	4.5	6.9	9.1
Don't Know and Any	4.0	7.4	6.5	6.4

[a] Source: McClatchy Newspapers, *Consumer Analysis*, 11th ed. (Sacramento, California, 1957), pp. S-20, S-85.

. . . Anyone with access to sales figures can see countless cases of high advertising exposure, but no sales correlation. There will be retention, identification, and advertising message acceptability—but no sale."[12] It can be inferred that consumers do not obtain much significance information from advertisements. Instead, they use the advertising frequency as an indicator of superior quality.

Indirect Measures of the Relative Importance of Advertising Copy. If copy changes were important, those subjected to advertising should be found to pay close attention to the advertising mes-sage. Starch Readership Studies define advertising readership at three stages: Noting—remembrance of seeing the advertisement; Seen-Associated—remembrance of seeing the advertisement and associating it with the product or advertiser; Read-Most—reading half or more of the copy. Over twenty years of readership studies have revealed that "on the average, out of 100 noters, 90 will read enough to associate the product with the advertisement, and 20 will read half or more of the text."[13]

[12] *Printers' Ink*, Vol. 244 (July 17, 1953), p. 42.

[13] Daniel H. Starch, "Just How Important Is Readership?" *Advertising Agency Magazine*, Vol. 47 (August 2, 1954), pp. 58-59; and "Outstanding Findings of Readership Studies," Vol. 47 (September 6, 1954), pp. 82-83.

To use this information, one needs to know the percentage of all magazine readers who note a typical advertisement. Starch has apparently never published an estimate. Judging from a number of "best read" advertisements reprinted in *Advertising Agency* and several "Starched" copies of the *Saturday Evening Post,* a reasonable "noting" estimate is around 30 per cent. On the average, therefore, only 30 per cent of magazine readers note an advertisement, 27 per cent associate the brand name with the advertisement, and merely 6 per cent read half or more of the copy. Even the significance of reading "half or more of the copy" is uncertain. One may read 75 per cent of the copy and still miss the main point of the advertisement. Brand name alone is the usual information abstracted from an advertisement. Little attention is given to copy content.

Even when significance information is obtained from an advertisement, it is usually not associated with the brand name. Often, the particular advertisement's distinctiveness is associated with competitors' brands or even the generic product.[14]

There is probably little reason why a typical consumer would be motivated to read an average advertisement. It has been frequently pointed out that many competitive advertisements utilize the same themes and claims.[15] If all adver-

tisers used similar copy themes, substitute products should be regarded by purchasers as having identical significance characteristics, and consumer purchases should be distributed at random among the available alternatives.

Extent to Which Consumers Rely Upon Significance Information in Advertisements. In the usual economic industry analysis, it is assumed that buyers and sellers are paired at random, since sellers' products have no distinguishing characteristics. But buyers and sellers are not paired at random to the extent buyers rely upon the significance information in a seller's advertisements and his product can be distinguished from competing brands. Thus, if the latter relation holds, buyers should show a high brand loyalty.

In one recent study, consumers were asked how many brands in 29 product classifications they had used in the past six years. It was found that "merely 120 out of 3,755 consumers interviewed failed to change brands, and that . . . 3,635 persons made 24,401 switches during the six year period. . . ."[16]

In another study, out of 100 customers for a brand in February, only 50 were still loyal in May, and 50 new customers bought in May. Aggregating the lost, loyal, and new customers over the three-month period: "The average brand, with an apparently unchanged customer level, shows a customer turnover of 66 per cent. . . . Even for the brand with the lowest customer-turnover, about one out of three customers over a three-month period switched either to or from the brand. For the brand at the other extreme, the switchers added up to nine out of ten total customers."[17]

[14] John S. Wright, "Does Your Ad Slogan Sell Your Product?" *Printers' Ink,* Vol. 260 (September 13, 1957), pp. 64-69; George B. Hotchkiss and R. B. Franken, *The Measurement of Advertising Effects* (New York: Harper, 1927), pp. 107-109.

[15] Ernest Dichter, "A Psychological View of Advertising Effectiveness," THE JOURNAL OF MARKETING, Vol. 14 (July, 1949), pp. 61-66; "Is Your Advertising Just Another Face in the Crowd?" *Printers' Ink,* Vol. 255 (June 8, 1956), pp. 25-27; "Being Different Makes the Sales Difference," *Printers' Ink,* Vol. 258 (March 29, 1957). pp. 21-24; "Advertising's Avant-Garde," *Tide,* Vol. 31 (May 24, 1957), pp. 34-37.

[16] N. H. Comish, "Why Customers Change Brands," *Dun's Review,* Vol. 61 (March, 1953), pp. 29, 42-45.

[17] National Broadcasting Company, *Why Sales Come in Curves* (New York, 1955), p. 11.

A third study of brand loyalty utilized a commercially sponsored continuing consumer panel. ". . . Between 1/4 and 1/2 of buyers of a frequently purchased item stayed with a single brand during the 12 month period."[18]

In the most recent study, brand loyalty was measured by the percentage of a family's total purchases over a three-year period, concentrated upon the most favored brand. The average family concentrated about half of its purchases of a given product upon one brand.[19]

Brand loyalty is surprisingly low. In fact, brand selection seems to be more often guided by a concept of brand acceptance. Brown, for example, found that 40 per cent of the sample families had divided or unstable loyalties, as shown by a vacillation between two brands. Thirty per cent had no loyalties at all![20] Cunningham discovered that the average family concentrated about 75 per cent of its purchases upon two brands.[21]

Thus, a brand preference based upon distinctive significance characteristics may be very unusual. Instead of assuming that consumers have an "image" guiding their selection of a brand, it may be more valid to assume that consumers have only an image of the generic product, and brand selection is determined by consideration of interbrand quality variation. The concept of "brand preference" is, after all, merely an inference from what consumers do. It is quite plausible to infer from the evidence that advertising frequency is used as an indicator of product quality.

Summary on Relative Importance of Copy. The typical consumer relies little upon whatever distinctiveness of significance information advertising provides. A fair degree of disloyalty occurs. The evidence suggests that advertising frequency is a discriminatory criterion in brand selection. Further, if a frequency concept is used for selecting between substitutes, it is not necessarily a long run time period over which the relative frequencies are computed. Since knowledge is not available of the time-rate of advertising expenditures for any one seller and the consequent impact of impression on the purchasing consumers, any conclusion can be only tentative.

(3) *The Logic Used In Setting the Advertising Appropriation*

Methods of Setting Advertising Appropriations. If advertising's chief effect were dissemination of significance information, then methods for arriving at an expenditure for advertising should be directly related to a particular objective. Once information has been imparted, there should be a cessation of advertising. Typical practice seems to be reliance upon some crude criterion, such as a fixed percentage of past or anticipated future sales, matching or maintaining a constant advertising appropriation relationship with competitors, and the like.[22] Even where a firm has some "logical approach" in determining the advertising budget, it usually reduces to some procedure which results in a constant relationship to sales over time.[23]

---

[18] George H. Brown, "Brand Loyalty—Fact or Fiction?" *Advertising Age*, Vol. 24 (January 26, 1953), pp. 75-76, at p. 75.

[19] Ross M. Cunningham, "Brand Loyalty—What, Where, How Much?" *Harvard Business Review*, Vol. 34 (January-February, 1956), pp. 116-128, Exhibit II, p. 122.

[20] Same reference as footnote 18, Table I, p. 75.

[21] Same reference as footnote 19, Exhibit IV, p. 122.

[22] A. W. Frey, *How Many Dollars for Advertising?* (New York: Ronald Press, 1955), pp. 48-72; Roy W. Jastram, "The Development of Advertising Appropriation Policy," *Journal of Business*, Vol. 33 (July, 1950), pp. 154-166.

[23] Frey, same reference as footnote 22, pp. 65-72.

If advertising primarily supplied a discrimination cue, the percentage of sales allocated to advertising should vary by size of firm. The percentage should be smallest for the largest firm, which needs only to maintain a frequency of impression equal to or slightly greater than its nearest size competitor. The evidence is scanty and equivocal, for it is to be expected that some firms do not wish to expand as rapidly as others, but it tends to show that advertising as a percentage of sales is inversely correlated with firm size.[24]

Frequently there are comments in the trade press that "if you can't advertise nationally it's impossible to compete effectively," indicating belief on the part of a potential entrant that advertising must be done on a scale roughly approaching that of established firms.[25]

Demonstrable Effect of a Given Advertising Expenditure. Even if a firm follows an "habitual" procedure for determining its advertising appropriation, it is possible that the firm can demonstrate the effect of the expenditure. Also, if significance information were the chief kind of data extracted from the advertisement by consumers, then the response contingent upon this acquisition should be apparent. However, advertisers apparently cannot measure the effect of their advertising.

In one survey of advertisers, over 50 per cent of the respondent firms could not judge the effect of their past year's advertising. In another, advertising managers were asked if they had any technique for determining if the appropriation was of the right size. Of seventy replies, only twenty answered affirmatively. The analyst concluded that even the twenty probably could not actually do so or had misinterpreted the question.[26]

(4) *The Effect of Changes in the Size of Advertising Appropriation*

If most firms cannot measure consumer response to a given level of advertising, then it is to be expected that firms would experiment, and vary the size of their advertising appropriation. On the basis of an explanation of advertising as supplying significance information, there should be no effect. In terms of an explanation that views advertising frequency as a criterion for brand selection, a fall in advertising expenditures relative to competitors' should result in a loss in sales. Available evidence substantiates the latter explanation.

Some information is available from continuing store audits. Arthur C. Nielsen has commented upon the relation between the relative advertising expenditure of a firm and its market position. "The manufacturer who maintains his normal level of promotion when his competitors have reduced theirs, soon finds that his expenditures represent a higher percentage of the total expended by the group; and our records show clearly that there is no surer way to gain an increase in competitive share of the market than to effect an increase in your competitive share of the total industry promotional expenditure."[27]

---

[24] Joel Dean, *Managerial Economics* (New York: Prentice-Hall, 1951), pp. 372-373; "What Ratio of Advertising to Sales?" *Printers' Ink*, Vol. 257 (October 26, 1956), pp. 21-22, 56-70; *Printers' Ink*, Vol. 258 (January 4, 1956), pp. 43-74. For contrary evidence see, Roy W. Jastram, "Advertising Ratios Planned by Large-Scale Advertisers," THE JOURNAL OF MARKETING, Vol. 14 (July, 1949), pp. 13-21.

[25] Small-scale brewers are an example. *Wall Street Journal*, Vol. 54 (December 17, 1956), p. 1.

[26] Frey, same reference as footnote 22, pp. 46-47.

[27] Arthur C. Nielsen, *Evolution of Factual Techniques of Marketing Research* (A. C. Nielsen Company, 1952). See also, *The Nielsen Researcher*, Vol. 15 (June, 1957), pp. 2-4.

There are also studies which cut across industry lines. These attempt to establish a relationship between advertising and shifts in consumption. But they also lend credence to the suggested explanation.

Roland S. Vaile measured the relationship between changes in sales and advertising for 200 firms over the period 1920-1924, and concluded: ". . . a definite spread occurs between sales of firms which increased their advertising and those which decreased it. Where intensive advertising during depression was a part of the sales technique, sales were maintained in better volume than when advertising appropriations were cut. . . ."[28]

Along similar lines, an Arthur D. Little, Inc. study of advertising appropriation concluded: ". . . if advertising support for an established product is withdrawn or substantially reduced, and if there are no new economic or competitive developments of note, then sales of the product will decline 'exponentially.' "[29]

[28] Roland S. Vaile, "The Use of Advertising During Depression," *Harvard Business Review*, Vol. 5 (April, 1927), p. 326. For additional evidence see, "Does Increased Promotion Pay Off When General Business Is Receding?" *Sales Management*, Vol. 63 (November 20, 1949), pp. 37-40; "How Well Does Advertising Pay Off?" *Tide*, Vol. 30 (August, 1956), pp. 32-35.
[29] "How Much for Advertising?" *Fortune*, Vol. 54 (December, 1956), pp. 123-126, 216, 221-224, at p. 222.

During World War II, many firms continued to advertise unavailable products or those in short supply. It is possible to argue that this occurred because of the peculiar construction of the excess profits tax. It is also plausible to accept the pleas made at the time that "good will" had to be protected. If advertising frequency is a basis of brand choice, then cessation of advertising during wartime should cause a loss of brand acceptance.

CONCLUSION

The necessity for continued advertising has been accounted for by the hypothesis that brand selection is often based upon a comparison of the relative frequencies with which substitute products have been advertised. Empirically, a large number of advertising, sales, and consumer behavioral phenomena can be explained by the hypothesis.

Theoretically, the explanation seems plausible. Individuals respond to many incompletely comprehended situations by using simplified maps of the actual state of affairs. The assumption that brand superiority is indicated by relative advertising frequency is one possible simplification of the real economic world. As such, it demonstrates the type of problem existing in the relation of knowledge to efficient market organization.

Media planners should wonder about the audience of
additional commercial exposures, right? Wrong.
The real question about additional exposures,
often omitted in research studies, is: How effective are
they, at which points in time?

Frequency Effects Over Time

Richard H. Ostheimer

The question of the worth of additional advertising frequency is an important and a familiar question. While it is phrased in different ways, it it is usually very simple and direct, such as, "How much more effect will be obtained by an additional insertion?" Or, "How effective will be a schedule of magazine insertions in 26 issues versus 13 issues?" To answer in terms of audience—that is, so many more people exposed so many more times—is to beg the question. What is wanted is a measure of the effectiveness of these additional exposures.

Conceptually, the question might be considered as the functional relationship between an effect measure and varying frequency. Studies attempting to determine this relationship typically have used as effect criteria various measures of attitude or communication changes, such as familiarity with the product, opinion of quality, etc.

To the extent that effect criteria have provided any answers, they always seem to be "diminished marginal productivity"—i.e., one more advertisement adds less to effect than the prior advertisement. A recent documentation of this is provided in Simon (1969).

This article's purpose is to suggest a reorientation of thinking on the subject of more or less frequency, starting at the beginning with the basic question itself. "What's the worth of the nth advertisement?" has an appeal that is straight-forward and easily understood. Yet this apparent clarity is deceptive when thought of in terms of relevance—that is, of research to aid in decision-making. The reason is that the question, and presumably the answer, has *no time reference.*

As such, the question is not addressed to the real world. First, it appears not to recognize that more or less frequency means different out-

puts of advertising over time. Second, given that the purpose of advertising is to affect people, it seems to ignore the reality that people live in time. For example, people purchase at points in time, their attitudes change over time, and they are exposed to media in a time dimension.

Thus, if there is concern with the real world, to talk about the effectiveness of more or less frequency requires talking in the time dimension. Without the "when," answers are essentially meaningless or, worse still, potentially misleading if used as a guide to advertising scheduling.

For any given schedule, an advertiser would like to know what effect his advertising is having at each *point in time*. In considering annual advertising plans of more versus less frequency, the advertiser must know how the alternative plans compare in advertising effect throughout the dura-

19

tion of the year. What does a schedule of 26 insertions produce relative to 13 *when?*

For example, suppose that an advertiser, having run 13 insertions in the first half of the year, asks what the consequences might be if no ads were run during the second half rather than continuing with another 13 insertions. The comparison of effect level at the *middle* versus *the end* of the year (after another 13 insertions were used) does *not* answer the question. The following case illustrates this point.

'Modern Medicine' Study

An outstanding example of research on frequency, "A Study of Advertising Effects in *Modern Medicine,*" was conducted by Alfred Politz Research, Inc. In a well-designed, controlled experiment, samples of subscribing doctors received copies of magazines with varying levels of advertising. Advertisements for eight different drugs were used. Copies sent to some doctors contained advertisements in three consecutive issues, others received ads in six consecutive issues, and still others received no advertising. Measures of the advertising effect were obtained by interviews on familiarity with the products, quality rating, and proclivity to prescribe. These interviews were conducted after the last insertion in each campaign.

Table 1 shows averages for all eight products on the "familiarity" effect measure. (The other criteria show the same general picture.)

Bearing in mind that *Modern Medicine* is biweekly and that consecutive issues were used in both campaigns, data in Table 1 are plotted in Figure 1. While the data for observations of the effect of one, two, four, and five insertions were not obtained, it was speculated where they might fall (the

20

TABLE 1
PHYSICIANS TO WHOM THE ADVERTISED PRODUCT "COMES TO MIND"

	Per Cent	"Effect" Per Cent
No Advertising	17.8	
After Three Insertions	19.9	2.1
After Six Insertions	20.6	2.8

circles). Figure 1 clearly shows a picture of diminishing marginal productivity. Each additional advertisement produces a smaller effect increment than the prior one. (If one were to extrapolate for all 26 issues, one might wonder at first glance why advertisers buy such schedules.)

Looking at the advertising effect data at various points in time, after three consecutive issues, in Week 6, the effect is 2.1 percentage points. After six consecutive issues, in Week 12, the effect is 2.8 percentage points, an increment of 0.7.

Missing, of course, is the effect in Week 12 among doctors whose three-issue campaign ended in Week 6. Regrettably, this measurement was not taken. Yet it is the important measure for the basic question of more or less

FIGURE 1

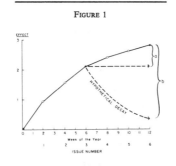

a: Incremental effect of 6 vs. 3 insertions after last insertion in each case, i.e., Week 12 and Week 6 respectively.
b: Incremental effect of 6 vs. 3 insertions in Week 12.

frequency, which is a different distribution of advertising output over time.

Since doctors prescribe drugs at points in time, the advertiser needs to know what would have happened in Week 12 after stopping the campaign in Week 6. Can it be assumed that the effect remains constant over the next six weeks and that in Week 12 the only benefit of six versus three insertions is the difference between 2.8 and 2.1 (increment a in Figure 1)?

It would seem more realistic to expect some degree of "decay" in the net effect of the advertising. Certainly a doctor's familiarity, opinion, and likelihood of prescribing a particular drug are dependent on many things in addition to advertising. Among other influences must be personal experience, colleagues' opinions, contact with competitive drugs, salesmen's calls, study reports in medical journals, etc.

When exposure to advertising is withdrawn, any initial net effect of advertising should be eroded by these other forces. Since these other forces are working equally on both exposed and non-exposed groups in the Politz design, only a lessening of the net advertising effect with the passage of time would be expected.

Decay

It should be noted that thinking of decay solely in terms of "forgetting" is too narrow a concept. In the world of advertising, products continually vie with one another for share of mind, favorable opinion, etc., so that one brand's gain often is another brand's loss. All of this happens, moreover, in an environment where a host of non-advertising factors are also affecting these same attitudes. Evidence of decay in an attitude effect after exposure to a single TV commercial is provided by Grass (1968).

In the last analysis, it would seem only logical to expect that the street runs both ways: *If the presence of advertising has an effect, its absence must also have an effect.*

Only with information on the effect at each point in time can the question of the worth of additional frequency be answered. By stopping advertising with the third issue in Week 6, how much worse off is the advertiser in Week 12 in terms of his standing in the marketplace vis-à-vis what it would have been had the campaign been continued? By hypothesizing a form of decay, Figure 1 represents such a measure by increment b.

It should be noted that when sales are the effect measure—for example, in tests of more versus less advertising spending—the problem of decay and effect over time is not present if the test is continued over a long enough period relative to the purchase cycle of the product. The reasons are, first, that the decay effect is subsumed in the sales data, and, second, there is no such thing as a sales figure without reference to a time dimension—for example, so many units in the month of January, etc., thus forcing consideration of "when."

The Before and After Myth

Probably the most common reaction to effect studies is that the increment produced by the greater frequency appears small. One might argue, on the other hand, that it is unrealistic to expect any increment at all, the basis of the argument being that an advertising effect at any point in time is very quickly eroded. Thus, a small increment, or none at all, becomes a reason for *greater rather than less frequency*.

This line of reasoning also applies to so-called "before and after" studies. Probably all too frequently, a campaign is judged unsuccessful at year-

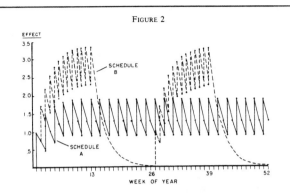

FIGURE 2

Assumptions: (a) Insertion effect = 1 (b) Effect decays at 30% per week
SCHEDULE A: Insertions every other week
SCHEDULE B: 13 weekly insertions in the first and third quarters of the year

Richard H. Ostheimer is corporate research director at *Time* Inc., a position he has held since 1964. Dr. Ostheimer joined *Time* in 1952 in the market research department of *Life* and became *Life's* research director in 1957. Prior to joining *Time*, he was chief economist on the research staff of the Commission on Financing Higher Education. During this period he wrote two books on higher education for the Commission, published by the Columbia University Press. Prior to this, he was an instructor in statistics at Columbia College. He received his A.B. (Phi Beta Kappa) from the Men's College of Columbia University in 1944, followed by M.A. and Ph.D. degrees from Columbia University.

end if the share-of-mind criterion is no higher than at the beginning of the year. The question should be, Where would it have been *without the campaign* at the end of the year and at points in time throughout the year?

For meaningful and useful results about the value of alternative frequency levels, an inherent ingredient of the investigation must be differences in advertising effect over time. In the case of alternative schedules for a *given* number of advertisements, such as one every month versus three flights of four in a weekly row, etc., the question of which schedule is most effective clearly demands an answer in the time dimension.

An example of this type of investigation, which necessarily involves the measurement of "decay," is discussed in Zielske (1959).

Figure 2 is an illustrative example based on an assumed decay pattern which reflects decay in effect between insertions. The chart contrasts two annual schedules of 26 insertions each, one being two flights of 13 weekly insertions versus the even distribution of an insertion every other week. It is this kind of information which an

21

advertiser needs to help in a decision between alternative schedules.

Figure 2 also illustrates the "before and after" myth. In Schedule A, since the advertising effect is no greater at the end of the year than what was quickly achieved early in the year, should the advertiser conclude that it is pointless to continue the campaign?

The answer is suggested by Schedule B in terms of what might happen when a campaign is halted—a quite rapid diminution in net advertising effect. In this case, a decay rate was assumed of 30 per cent per week after exposure, which might appear too rapid to some. It might, on the other hand, appear too slow to others, particularly when the decay rate is phrased in the complementary, and more positive, terms of a 70 per cent rate of retention or persistence of effect.

It would be incorrect to leave the impression that the time dimension had been completely overlooked by the various investigators of the effectiveness of additional frequency. The introduction to the Politz-*Modern Medicine* Study, in fact, contains the following paragraph:

An alternative approach would be to compare the effect of three vs. six ads at the end of the six-issue campaign. In this case, the gains in product appreciation measured for the three-issue campaign would have been *smaller* than those found in this study because of the longer time interval between final ad appearance and interview. And the relative effects of a six-issue campaign compared with a three-issue campaign would therefore have been greater. It was decided in this study to use the more conservative design for this comparison.

Similarly, Simon refers to the concept of decay of an effect in several places in his article in the somewhat puzzling terms of a possible "bias" in the study. Regarding the Politz-*Modern Medicine* Study, he states: "It is reasonable to expect that decay bias should not be important on such variables as these."

Thus, investigators of frequency effect have, to at least some degree, recognized the notion of the distribution of advertising effect over time and its correlate of decay—but only in concept. They have not included measures of it in their study designs, thereby leaving the impression—or even explicitly stating—that it is a separate concern, a minor element, or both. A partial exception to this generalization is presented in Grass (1968).

A Time Dimension

To think of the incorporation of decay measures as an "alternative approach" is, at best, misleading. To the contrary, the concept of decay is at the very heart of the matter. And to deem it "reasonable" to expect that decay is unimportant implies a very static world with an undynamic marketplace—certainly not the real world.

Whether in concept or actual investigation, the question of the effects of frequency must inherently consider the time dimension. Without a time reference, "answers" about the worth of more or less frequency are not, in fact, answers to the actual decision.

A very real danger is to ignore this and to attempt applying the results of "timeless" studies to actual decisions. If the finding of diminished marginal effect is interpreted as a reason for less frequency, the advertiser may be very misguided and suffer accordingly with respect to his standing in the competitive marketplace. It is, moreover, a paradox that if this finding means anything at all to the real world, it suggests the need for more rather than less frequency.

REFERENCES

SIMON, J. A. New Evidence for No Effect of Scale in Advertising. *Journal of Advertising Research*, Vol. 9, No. 1 March 1969, pp. 38-41.

GRASS, R. C. Satiation Effects of Advertising. *Proceedings, 14th Annual Conference.* Advertising Research Foundation, New York, October 15, 1968.

ZIELSKE, H. A. The Remembering and Forgetting of Advertising. *Journal of Marketing*, Vol. 23, No. 3, January 1959, pp. 239-243.

QUOTABLE

"*The problem of copy-testing is not the theory, which is magnificent, but the practice, which is ludicrous. Advertising is a craft which has . . . most of the disadvantages of art. And one of art's disadvantages is that it cannot be objectively evaluated in the short run.*

"*I think that we know for sure more about television commercials today than we know about television commercial testing systems. Therefore, we should not use commercial testing systems to evaluate commercials. We should use commercials to evaluate commercial testing systems. Incidentally, it follows that the commercial testing services should be paying us for their learning experience.*"

—Gene Case
Partner, Case & Krone
Broadcasting, October 13, 1969

*Low scoring TV commercials quickly
grew worse with repeat exposures, while some
high scorers actually increased their effectiveness.*

On Advertising Wear Out

Valentine Appel

The question of how long an advertisement should be allowed to run before being replaced by another is one which has only recently fallen under the scrutiny of the advertising researcher.

Probably the first such study of advertising wear out appeared in September 1966, and it was done by the Schwerin Research Corp. It reported the results of 118 TV commercial retests in England and Germany. The retests had been conducted at varying intervals of the initial test, with the advertising having been exposed in the media over this period of time. In almost three-quarters of the cases, the retest score was lower than was the initial test, a fact which was interpreted to reflect wear out of the advertising.

In October 1966, Appel presented similar findings based upon unpublished data supplied by Audience Studies, Inc. More recently, the ASI findings were confirmed using the Tele-Research method (1968).

Still more recently, Grass (1968) and Grass and Wallace (1969) pre-sented the results of a series of laboratory and field experiments which demonstrated that with repeat exposures, advertisements first appear to gain in effectiveness after which the effectiveness begins to wear out.

It seems, however, that no one has studied the rates at which the effectiveness of advertising messages wear out, whether different kinds of ads wear out at different rates, or the characteristics of those ads which wear out at a faster rate compared with those which retain their effectiveness over a longer period.

The Present Study

The following study addresses itself to these questions. The study is based upon a total of 96 retests representing

---

The study described in this article was completed while the author was with Benton and Bowles. The article is based upon a paper originally presented to the 1966 Marketing Conference of the National Industrial Conference Board.

---

81 different 60-second television commercials for 31 different brands. The retests were conducted at varying intervals of the initial test, ranging from one week to several years.

The commercials were tested by the 24-hour recall method. Briefly, this method involves running a television commercial on the air. The next day a random sample of households is contacted by phone, and the appropriate household member is asked whether she saw any television advertising for the test brand the night before. Those who say that they did are then asked to describe the advertising in as much detail as possible. Then, for each commercial, a recall score is obtained which is defined as the percentage of respondents in the viewing audience who can describe the commercial sufficiently accurately to prove that they are recalling the commercial.

The method of analysis used in this study was to compare each of the 96 retest scores to the retest score which would have been expected based upon

11

its initial test. The expected scores were calculated by means of a regression equation based upon the correlation between the test and the retest scores under those conditions where the retest was conducted within a short time after the original test.

For each of the 96 retests, the difference between the actual and the expected retest score thus calculated was interpreted as a change in score from the initial test. This procedure was adopted, rather than simply using the difference between the test and the retest score, to compensate for expected regression effects whereby the high scoring commercials would tend to retest lower and the low scorers would tend to retest higher, with both sets of scores moving in the direction of the mean.

The calculated changes in score were then related to the elapsed time between test and retest. This elapsed time was considered as an indicator of the amount of interim exposure of the test copy. Ideally, there would have been precise media records of the amount of prior exposure to the test commercials. However, since such records were not readily available, it was assumed that the elapsed time would serve as a crude but adequate indicator of prior exposure.

Results

The findings are summarized in Figure 1. On the horizontal axis is the elapsed time from the initial test to the retest. For reasons of client security, although the scale is linear, the calibrations have been eliminated since the knowledge of the precise wear out rates is of competitive value. Along the vertical axis is the percentage point change in score from the initial test to the retest. The six points which are plotted on the figure represent the mean changes in score for six different spans of time.

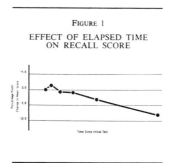

FIGURE 1

EFFECT OF ELAPSED TIME ON RECALL SCORE

The data confirm that advertising does change in effectiveness with the passage of time. There was a slight increase in score (which was attributed to learning) followed by a fairly regular decline, which was attributed to wear out of the advertising message.

Valentine Appel is an executive vice president of Grudin/Appel/Haley, the consumer research company. Before joining the firm, Dr. Appel was vice president and manager of the research department at Benton & Bowles. He holds a Ph.D. from New York University, is a member of Phi Beta Kappa, and is a certified psychologist in New York State. He is a member of The Copy Research Council, The Marketing Research Council, the Technical Committee of ARF, the APA and AAPOR. Dr. Appel has published in numerous journals, both here and abroad.

This is perhaps what one might expect, but certainly not very startling.

Also of interest were the relative wear out rates of those commercials which initially made a vivid impression upon the consumer's memory compared to those which initially did less well. To this end, all the commercials were divided into two groups —those which initially scored above the mean in terms of previously established norms, and those which scored at the mean or below. Results are shown in Figure 2.

From the figure, it can be seen that the wear out patterns are distinctly different for initially high scoring and low scoring commercials. In the case of the low scoring commercials, wear out appears to begin immediately, with successive advertising exposures resulting in decreasing recall levels.

The high scoring commercials, which were more memorable to begin with, produced a distinctly different pattern. Unlike the low scoring commercials, successive exposures of the high scorers initially produced significantly higher levels of recall, indicating increased learning of the advertising message.

Moreover, even after the recall levels of the less memorable commercials had decayed as much as 10 percentage points, the high scoring commercials were still producing scores in excess of those which were obtained in the first airing.

A statistical test comparing the mean height of the two curves indicates that a difference of the magni-

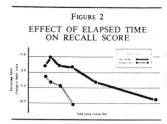

FIGURE 2

EFFECT OF ELAPSED TIME ON RECALL SCORE

tude shown here could have occurred by chance one time in 50; and if we exclude the first time span, the difference in the heights of the curves is of sufficient magnitude to have occurred by chance only one time in 500.

Advertising Implications

These findings are especially provocative since a number of implications follow concerning the use of the 24-hour recall method: First, there is evidence indicating that commercials which initially make a vivid impression upon the consumer's memory benefit more from repeat exposure than do commercials which initially do less well.

Moreover, evidence indicates that, although there are undoubtedly exceptions, the odds are against low scoring commercials improving with repeat exposure. Unlike high scoring commercials, the effectiveness of low scoring commercials appears quickly to grow worse with repeat exposure.

The findings bring into serious question a number of the research prac-

tices which are fairly common in the advertising business. One of these is the frequent practice of evaluating one brand's advertising performance against the performance of competitors when there is no control and little knowledge of the amount of repeat exposure of the competitor's copy.

The problem in testing a competitor's copy becomes clear when it is recognized that if a competitor's commercial does better after the competitor has been using his commercial for some time, it may be because of increased learning from repeat exposure. If the commercial does worse, it may be because the effectiveness of the competitive commercial has begun to decay.

Unless some way can be found to determine the amount of prior exposure of the competitor's copy and then to compensate for it, it will never be possible to separate the memorability of the commercial itself from the effects of repeat exposure.

Another common practice in the industry brought into serious question by these findings is that of tinkering with and testing commercials in an

effort to make minor improvements while simultaneously running these commercials on the air.

Because we now know that the ability of commercials to be recalled does change with repeat exposure, one can see how the practice of tinkering and testing can lead to spurious changes in score. It is easy to be misled into believing that the tinkering had either improved the commercial or made it worse, when actually all that was being measured was the result of repeat exposure.

REFERENCES

APPEL, V. *The Reliability and Decay of Advertising Messages.* Paper presented before the Marketing Conference of the National Industrial Conference Board. October, 1966.
GRASS, R. C. Satiation Effects of Advertising. *Proceedings, ARF 14th Annual Conference.* New York: Advertising Research Foundation, 1968.
GRASS, R. C. AND W. H. WALLACE. Satiation Effects of Television Commercials. *Journal of Advertising Research,* Vol. 9, No. 3, pp. 3-8.
"Schneeball Oder Wear Out." *SRC Bulletin,* Schwerin Research Corporation, September, 1966.
Tele/Scope. Do TV Commercials Wear Out? Tele-Research, Inc., February, 1968.

JOURNAL OF THE MARKET RESEARCH SOCIETY

VOLUME 12, NUMBER 4

The Sampling of Non-Domestic Populations — *Andrew R. McIntosh and Roger J. Davies*
Consumer Attitudes and Brand Usage — *M. Bird and A. S. C. Ehrenberg*

Miscellany:

A Method of Sampling Small Minorities: Suggestions and Objections — *L. J. Marchant*
Reply — *G. Miles*
Notes on "A Method of Sampling Small Minorities" — *C. Holmes*
Reply — *G. Miles*

Letter to the Editor   Conference Report   Esomar 1970: Barcelona

Book Reviews   HMSO Publications Received   Publications Received

Three years (12 issues) $18.00; one year (four issues) $7.20, Market Research Society, 51 Charles Street, W.1.X, 7PA, London

*Copy theme, color, shopping habits, knowledge of
the brand, competitive advertising—all can shape
the rate at which advertising is forgotten.*

Frequency Effects Revisited

Michael L. Ray, Alan G. Sawyer, and Edward C. Strong

The problem of repetition in advertising is an important one that has long been considered in too simple a form. In a recent issue of this *Journal,* Dr. Richard H. Ostheimer (1970) helped to correct this over-simplicity by pointing out a dimension of repetition effect which is often ignored in advertising research. He correctly asserts that the effect of advertising exposures must be assessed not solely in terms of incremental effect, but also with regard to their effect in a time dimension.

In some respects, Ostheimer's argument can be related to the current insistence, in financial circles, on expressing the value of funds in terms of their *present value*—that is, discounted at some logical rate of interest to their equivalency in current dollars. The logical outcome of Ostheimer's argument is that research should provide advertisers with an idea of the "present value of advertising"—that is, the incremental effect of an exposure should be discounted at some logical decay or forgetting rate.

14

If this were done for several different scheduling alternatives over some standardized period, it would provide advertisers with a basis for judging the adequacy of a given schedule or the relative merits of several proposed schedules as compared with their costs.

The authors agree with Ostheimer but feel that the question of advertising frequency must be considered in an even more textured way. This article suggests that the single-function decay, or forgetting rate that is implicit in Ostheimer's article is, in fact, only one of a number of rates due to a complex combination of advertising variables.

In order to provide a useful input for advertising decision-making, research must study not only effects over

Research reported in this paper was supported by grants from the 4A's Educational Foundation; Foote, Cone and Belding; and the Ford Foundation.

time, but the complex interactions between advertising variables, repetition, and effects over time.

Continuing Research on Repetition

When studying the problem of repetition in advertising, assumptions can be similar to Ostheimer's. But additional, more complex and more pragmatic problems are also present, specifically those involved in estimation of the repetition function for media models.

The repetition function is defined as the level, shape, and slope of the relationship between repetitive consumer exposures to advertising and the effect of those exposures. This, as Ostheimer points out, is the correct question on repetition.

Since work by Agostini (1961, 1962), Metheringham (1964), and others, it is no longer necessary to be content with the gross question of what increases in audience are generated by increased numbers of insertions of advertising. Now it is possible to realistically consider the effect of actual exposures on people.

By considering this effect in terms of inputs to media models, information has been developed that can be used in a practical way. Ostheimer deals with the general questions of frequency and scheduling over time. Recent advances in advertising media models (Aaker, 1968; Little and Lodish, 1969; Ray and Clark, 1970; Ray and Sawyer, 1971) demand more specific estimates of the effect of repetitive exposures on consumers in particular advertising situations. As such, media models represent a way for the repetition function to be taken into account along with the entire set of variables operating in each advertising situation (Gensch, 1970).

Considering these other variables adds a great deal of complexity to the study of repetition, however. The time or scheduling variable that Ostheimer discusses is only one of a set that defines the advertising situation—and affects the level, shape, or slope of the repetition function. Included among these variables would be the measure of effect or advertising goal, the audience or segment, the product or topic of advertising, the marketing environment (including competitive effects), the advertising appeal, the advertising format, the advertising media, and the advertising schedule. The basic assumption is that all of these variables have a potential of affecting the repetition function. The goal of this paper is to examine the nature of their effect and to develop research procedures for estimating their effect in particular decision-making situations.

The key finding from this research has been the importance of measures in determining the nature of repetition effect. All other variables in the study of repetition are secondary

to the measures variable. It is impossible to talk sensibly about repetition effect, economies of scale, decay of effect, and the like, without considering the measure or measures which describe these phenomena.

This general finding would seem at first glance to be rather obvious. But it is not so mundane when considered in terms of the strength of the results and their implications. Currently, all media models have a criterion which is expressed in such terms as "weighted exposures" or "rated exposure values." Although such model criteria or dependent variables are meant to allow varying advertising goals, they do not lead to discussions of the differential repetition effect with different measures. The typical assumption of repetition effect is some sort of negatively accelerated learning curve and accompanying decay curve. Seldom do the repetition functions discussed or actually implemented in media models vary from the sort found in the psychological study of the learning of nonsense syllables.

Our findings indicate that advertising effect can be thought of as something other than nonsense learning. The research also suggests that media models might be developed with criteria such as attitude level, or purchase intent, as well as the more typi-

cal awareness goals that are suggested by the term "weighted exposures" and by most discussions of advertising repetition.

The differential effect of repetition across measures has been observed over a series of laboratory and field studies. Figure 1 shows results from a field study in which housewives were sent direct mail packets of advertisements (Strong, 1971). The study was done over 13 weeks. Each week, one-thirteenth of the total sample was interviewed by telephone and then dropped from the mailing list. The study was similar to the often-cited repetition study done by Zielske (1959); however, the present study involved more advertisements, different schedules, and, most important for the present purposes, a number of measures beyond the advertising recall measure used in the original study.

Ads were sent under weekly, bi-weekly, and monthly schedules. The figure shows the results for the weekly schedule combined over all six of the test advertisements that were rotated around the scheduling conditions. As can be seen, the results were quite different depending on whether the measure is recall of the specific mail ads, mention of the brands advertised, or brand preference (in this case, indicated by an attitude scaling for the brand greater than that for all other brands scaled). Ad recall goes up quite sharply and stays at about the 65 per cent level over the 13-week period. The brand mention slope is much more gradual. And although the effect on brand preference is slight, it takes the form of an increase over the first 6 exposure groups and a general negative trend in the weeks following.

Negative repetition trends like this have often been found for attitude and purchase intention measures. Underlying the brand preference curve in Figure 1 is a variety of results for individual ads and brands. One ad for a

EFFECT OF WEEKLY EXPOSURES
OF SIX ADS ON THREE MEASURES
(IN PER CENTS OF AUDIENCE)

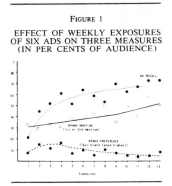

15

ball point pen produced a negative effect of repetition, whereas another ad for the same brand produced no repetition effect on preference. An ad for a well-known soap brand produced no effect of repetition and that for a lesser-known brand produced a negative effect. One of two canned food advertisements produced a positive slope on preference. The other showed a negative repetition effect. All these varied results on preference occurred for ads that produced quite different results—usually positive—on the ad recall and brand mention measures.

All that these and the following results mean is that decision-makers have only part of the picture when they do not differentiate the repetition effect for different measures and when they implicitly assume that the effect of advertising repetition is always positive. In fact, depending on the measure, the results of repetition can be positive, negative, or nonexistent.

When Decay Is Not Decay

Another common assumption is that lack of advertising produces negative effects or decay. However, research indicates that this is also too simple an assumption.

For some measures in some situations, decay of advertising effect does not occur at all. In fact, there is sometimes a boost in positive response or sleeper effects (Weinberger, 1961) during periods when there is no advertising exposure. This is illustrated in Figure 2, which consists of some of the biweekly schedule results from the same field study which was discussed before. Notice that for brand mention, there usually are the expected "troughs" or dips in effect during the non-exposure weeks. The effect for the brand preference measure (in this case indicated by an attitude scaling equal to or greater than all other

16

FIGURE 2

BIWEEKLY SCHEDULE RESULTS FOR GROCERY PRODUCT ON TWO MEASURES (HEAVY LINES FOR EXPOSURE WEEKS, LIGHT FOR NONEXPOSURE WEEKS)

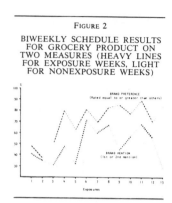

brands scaled) is quite different, however. For this measure, the response often goes up rather than down during the non-exposure weeks. This effect is most pronounced during the later weeks of exposure when, as previous

Michael L. Ray is assistant professor of marketing at Stanford University's Graduate School of Business. Previously, he taught in the Evening Division at De Paul University and at Northwestern University. He also worked on a variety of client and special research projects at Foote, Cone and Belding. Dr. Ray received his Ph.D. in social psychology from Northwestern University. His general area of research interest is in the effects of mass communications, particularly advertising. His articles have appeared in numerous publications.

results indicated, repetitive exposure was having its greatest negative effect on the brand preference response.

This lack of decay is not an isolated finding. For example, the study produced 36 repetition and "decay" curves like those in Figure 2. All of those curves had at least some non-decay where conventional wisdom dictates they should have had decay. Nearly two-thirds of the curves showed a substantial lack of decay findings, similar to that shown for the preference measure in Figure 2. The tendency was for conventional "nonsense syllable" decay to occur most frequently for learning measures such as ad recall and brand mention. But for attitude-type measures—such as belief, ratings, brand preference, and usage—the lack of decay results was quite pronounced.

One interpretation for such a finding is that the advertising itself becomes noxious to the audience after a certain point. Up to this point, advertising may help to hold attitudes or may actually help to improve attitudes. After this point, the ad exposures may actually get in the way of favorable opinions of the product or brand. Only during periods without ad exposure do these favorable factors take effect, thus producing the peaks shown for brand preference in Figure 2.

This finding, like all others in repetition, is heavily dependent on the situation, particularly the media and the environment. In this case, consumers were subjected to a very heavy dose of direct mail. This sort of approach may have produced a negative effect where other approaches may not. And the brands represented in the study were well-known and advertised in other media during the study. The important point, however, is that possible negative effects must be considered in a thorough examination of the repetition problem. Rao (1970) also suggests the possibility of non-decay effects in certain situations.

Effect of Other Variables

This paper does not permit a thorough discussion of all results on the variation of the repetition function. But a review of some of these findings can indicate the diversity of repetition results that are possible.

For instance, one laboratory study (Ray and Sawyer, 1971) focused on the product type advertised. One experimental group received nine convenience goods print advertisements at rates of exposure from one through six. Another group received nine shopping goods advertisements at the various repetition rates.

The group results indicated that repetition serves a significantly different function in the advertising of convenience goods like soup than for shopping goods like television sets. For the convenience goods, repetition produces strong positive effects for both advertising recall and stated intention to purchase.

For shopping goods, there was a leveling of repetition effect at five and six exposures for the ad recall measure and almost no effect for the purchase intention measure. The results on an attitude measure were similar but not statistically significant. The pattern of results supports the typical assumption made about the importance of advertising as an information source in convenience goods purchasing and its corresponding lack of importance in shopping goods purchasing.

In another laboratory study (Sawyer, 1971), both advertising format and competition were taken into account. Two print advertisements were selected for each of five brands in five different product categories—soap, dietary products, small foreign cars, ball point pens, and headache reliefs.

One of each pair of ads used a refutational approach, which involved mentioning a competitive claim against the brand being advertised and then refuting that claim with a positive statement about the brand.

An example would be an advertisement for Bayer aspirin which reads in part, "Does buffering it, squaring it, squeezing it, fizzing it, flavoring it, flattening it, gumming it or adding to it improve aspirin? . . . No . . . Bayer works wonders."

The other ad in each pair was strictly supportive and made straightforward positive claims about the product, such as the simple, "Bayer works wonders."

These test ads in each product category were exposed from one through six times to various experimental groups. Each group also saw two exposures of a competitive ad in each of the five product categories.

The results in this study depended on the measure and on competition.

Alan G. Sawyer is assistant professor of marketing at the State University of New York at Buffalo. He recently was awarded a Ph.D. degree by the Stanford University Graduate School of Business. He received a B.S. degree from the University of Maine and an M.B.A. from Northeastern University. Dr. Sawyer's main research interests concern the application of communication theory and attitude measurement techniques to marketing and advertising.

Repetition had a rather direct positive and significant effect on advertising recall. There was little difference in effect which might be attributed to the refutational or supportive forms. Clear ad recall differences were apparent, however, between the test and competitive brands. The greater the repetition of the test ad the more it was correctly recalled. Recall of the competitive ad did not change over test advertising repetition conditions, with the exception of the only case in which the competitive brand was mentioned in a refutational advertisement.

Despite these somewhat expected findings for advertising recall, the attitude and purchase intention results proved to be far from ordinary. For attitude, the typical finding was a significant negative competitive effect. Repetition had some positive effect on the test brand but not as great an effect as the positive effect on competition over the repetitions. This effect occurred primarily for the refutational advertising.

A simple explanation might be that the refutational advertising, by mentioning competitive claims, is simply giving advertising support to the competition. Supportive advertising may serve as a reminder of the product category and thus support competition while somewhat weakening attitudes toward the brand advertised.

With purchase intention, the results were reversed once more. Repetition had significant effects in prompting respondents to say they would purchase the test brands over the competitive brands. This effect occurred whether the refutational or supportive ad was the one exposed. The difference between the attitude and purchase intention results may be due to the way the questions were asked in the laboratory, with the attitude requiring a specific evaluation and the purchase intention measure requiring a gross prediction of response.

Field validation using the refutational and supportive ads from the ball point pen category indicated support for both the ad recall and attitude results in the lab. The field study did not utilize a purchase intention measure.

Many of the differences in advertising format are not as complex as the refutational-supportive difference. For instance, in one case just the adding of one color to an advertising campaign was shown to change repetition effect, both in the lab and in the field. In the laboratory study, four ads in a campaign for a canned food product were shown repetitively to one experimental group in a black and white version and to another experimental group in a version with color simply added to the vegetable or fruit depicted in each ad. As shown in Figure 3, color helped the ads to be recalled. There was a somewhat greater positive effect of repetition on the response of recalling the color ads. But black and white ads were superior when the measure was

depth of recall. In other words, those who received and recalled the black and white versions seemed to recall more of the verbal details of the advertising than those who recalled the color versions. It seemed that the impact of the color visuals was such that reading and/or reporting recall of the verbal content was minimized, even over repetitions.

The black and white ad's strength in depth of recall in the lab seemed to presage greater long run staying power with repetition in the field. In a field study with the same two campaign versions, the color campaign had somewhat higher ad recall (Figure 4), brand mention, and attitude scores than the black and white at low exposure levels. But at higher exposure levels the black and white campaign

Edward C. Strong is a doctoral candidate in marketing at the Graduate School of Business, Stanford University. He received his M.B.A. in 1969. He has spent five years with the U.S. Army, including instructor duty with the armies of Honduras, Panama, Colombia, Venezuela, and Brazil. In March 1970 he resumed his overseas activities with a two-week assignment as an instructor for a management seminar in Belgium. He is spending the 1970-71 academic year on the Faculty of INSEAD at Fontainebleau, France.

began to surpass the color on all three measures; thus, reflecting the lab findings and some conventional wisdom about the long-term campaign effects of color and black and white advertising.

A somewhat related finding to the color versus black and white difference was found in another repetition study utilizing ads judged to be "grabbers" or not. Grabber ads were defined by three judges as different enough in format to attract attention and accomplish the bulk of the potential communication in a single exposure. Although it was expected that the grabber ads would do reasonably well in terms of advertising awareness over time, the prediction for attitude and purchase intention was that the intrusive uniqueness of the grabbers would not "wear well" with repeated exposures. Thus, the grabber ads, like the color ads, were expected to do well in terms of recall, but not in terms of the attitude or purchase intention measures. These expectations were supported in regression analyses of a lab study comparing the repetition effect of four grabber ads and 14 non-grabber ads. Although there was no statistically significant difference in ad recall across repetitions, the average per cent recalling the grabber ads was greater than that recalling the non-grabber ads after four, five, and six

FIGURE 3

PER CENT RECALL AND VERBAL QUALITY RECALL FOR CANNED FOOD ADS IN LABORATORY

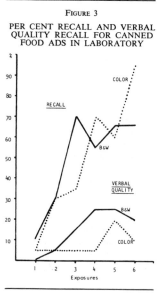

FIGURE 4

PER CENT RECALLING CANNED FOOD ADS IN FIELD STUDY

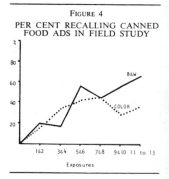

exposures. For purchase intention, there was a significant difference and a reversal of the recall results. The non-grabber ads were affected by repetition and the grabber ads never reached control (no exposure) levels of purchase intention.

Often, the repetition function has seemed to have been affected by the illustration or example used in the advertising. For instance, an ad for foundation garments featured an illustration of a nude woman with her back to the camera. This ad did well on recall in one lab study but produced a negative slope for repetition effect on attitude change. A similar case was a washing machine ad making the claim that one woman's family did not change their underwear every day until she started using the new washer. Not surprisingly, repeated exposures of this ad produced increasingly lower attitude scores for the brand.

Previous consumer knowledge should also affect the repetition function. This was found to be the case in a laboratory study in which ads for brands that were well-known to respondents produced positive repetition functions for purchase intention while purchase intention for not well-known brands' ads was not affected significantly by repetition.

An ad for Ivory Soap and another for the not-as-well-known soap, Phase III, have been tested in three studies. In two lab studies, the ad for Phase III produced equal or greater repetition results on ad recall, but Ivory was affected more on attitude and purchase intention measures. In a direct mail field study, these results held for ad recall over 13 exposures and for brand attitude up to six exposures (the maximum number in the lab studies). After eight exposures, there was some tendency for the Phase III advertising to have some effect on brand attitude. The repeated exposures evidently were beginning to overcome the lack of consumer knowledge of the brand.

How to Cope with Repetition Interactions

The findings suggest an extremely complex situation facing managers attempting to deal with the problem of repetition in advertising. The picture presented is much more textured than even Ostheimer's sophisticated view.

The results suggest that a single assumption of negatively accelerated learning and forgetting curves will be insufficient in a large proportion of advertising situations. The further indication is that the timing variable emphasized by Ostheimer is only one of a number of variables that influence repetition effect.

Some of the results reported here may be limited in applicability, because they were obtained from laboratory research. However, there are three reasons why there should be more than the usual confidence in these lab results. First, the findings were often consistent with what might be expected on the basis of conventional wisdom in advertising, and, therefore, they have face validity. Second, the laboratory technique has been carefully developed to avoid the typical kinds of biases found in laboratory research on repetition (Ray, 1971; Sawyer, 1971). Finally, and perhaps most important, the lab results seem to be successful in relating to the field.

Obviously, then, although more needs to be done, research indicates that the advertising manager is faced with an extremely complex situation when he makes decisions on advertising frequency and scheduling. Ostheimer considered only positive repetition functions and negative decay functions. The research presented here indicated that repetition functions can be sloped negatively as well as posi-

tively, and decay functions can be sloped positively as well as negatively. What's more, there are instances in which the direction of the slope can change over exposures—e.g., repetition may have a positive effect over a low number of exposures and then turn in the negative direction.

All these slope possibilities depend on measures and situations, of course. A manager must consider whether he wants to use, for example, color in order to affect recall at some specific frequency level—realizing that the depth of recall may not be great for each person in the admittedly large group who has recalled.

He should remember that this is dependent on consumer shopping habits and use of advertising for the type of product being advertised. In addition, the consumer knowledge of the brand will have an effect. But this effect might be mitigated by the particular media and schedule. Perhaps the manager should concentrate on attitude instead of recall. This might be especially wise if competition is attacking the brand with a heavier or lighter schedule, if word of mouth is good or bad, if distribution is heavy or light, if the product quality is good or bad, etc. How can the manager cope with this hostile and continuously varying situation?

This question can only be answered by considering the advertising decision-making process and the possible inputs of research at each level of that process. The manager needs information on repetition effect at the planning, implementation, and evaluation stages of the decision-making process. Research on repetition can provide information at all three of these stages as follows:

1. *General guidelines concerning the effects of repetition in varying situations.* Although the advertising decisions with regard to repetition are extremely complex, research of the type

19

described in this paper can identify relevant variables for copy and media planning.

2. *Estimates of repetition effect in specific situations.* Once general guidelines have been used to develop advertising proposals, these alternatives must be evaluated for implementation in terms of the specific environment the advertising will face.

Because there are so many variables that might influence repetition effect in each situation, there will never be enough general guideline research to make adequate predictions in each specific advertising situation. Therefore, the decision-maker needs some quick, inexpensive indication of the probable effects of repetition in each specific situation. These indications can be used with judgment to estimate repetition effect for media model runs and for general budgeting and scheduling. One future goal is to develop a laboratory technique for this purpose.

3. *Evaluation of actual campaign results.* The decision-making process does not stop with planning and implementation. A system of continuous surveys or panel research should be developed to evaluate the effectiveness

of campaigns. An important result of campaign monitoring would be the detection of changes in the environment which influence repetition effects. These changes in the environment would, in turn, call forth changes in advertising strategy based on the general guidelines and checked in the laboratory.

With these three types of information, the advertising decision-maker should be able to cope with the complexities of the repetition problem. The challenge for advertising research is great. The more sophisticated view that could emerge, however, should provide new insights into the process of advertising communication and offer new criteria for evaluating advertising effects.

REFERENCES

AAKER, D. S. On Methods: A Probabilistic Approach to Industrial Media Selection. *Journal of Advertising Research,* Vol. 8, No. 3, pp. 46-55.

AGOSTINI, J. M. How to Estimate Unduplicated Audiences. *Journal of Advertising Research,* Vol. 1, No. 1, pp. 11-14.

AGOSTINI, J. M. Analysis of Magazine Accumulative Audience. *Journal of Advertising Research,* Vol. 2, No. 4, pp. 24-27.

GENSCH, D. H. Media Factors: A Review Article. *Journal of Marketing Research,* May 1970, pp. 216-225.

LITTLE, J. D. C. AND L. M. LODISH. A Media Planning Calculus. *Operations Research,* Vol. 17, January-February 1969, pp. 1-35.

METHERINGHAM, R. A. Measuring the Net Cumulative of a Print Campaign. *Journal of Advertising Research,* Vol. 4, No. 4, pp. 23-28.

OSTHEIMER, R. H. Frequency Effects over Time. *Journal of Advertising Research,* Vol. 10, No. 1, pp. 19-22.

RAO, A. G. *Quantitative Theories in Advertising,* New York: Wiley, 1970.

RAY, M. L. in H. DAVIS AND A. SILK (eds.) *The Behavioral Sciences and Management Sciences in Marketing.* New York: Ronald, 1971 (in press).

RAY, M. L. AND R. CLARK. Focus. Stanford, California: Graduate School of Business, Stanford University, 1970, mimeo.

RAY, M. L. AND A. G. SAWYER. A Laboratory Technique for Estimating the Repetition Function for Advertising Media Models. *Journal of Marketing Research,* February, 1971.

SAWYER, A. G. A Laboratory Experimental Investigation of the Repetitive Effects of Advertising. Unpublished Ph.D. dissertation, Stanford University, 1971.

STRONG, E. C. The Effects of Repetition in Advertising: A Field Study. Unpublished Ph.D. dissertation, Stanford University, 1971.

WEINBERGER, M. Does the "Sleeper Effect" Apply to Advertising? *Journal of Marketing,* Vol. 25, October 1961, pp. 65-67.

ZIELSKE, H. A. The Remembering and Forgetting of Advertising. *Journal of Marketing,* Vol. 23, March 1959, pp. 239-243.

Exposure No. 1: Curiosity
Exposure No. 2: Recognition
Exposure No. 3: Decision

Why Three Exposures May Be Enough

Herbert E. Krugman

Often a paper about advertising begins with the assertion that the American public is "bombarded" each day by a large number of advertising messages. (Dr. Britt's foregoing article quotes several of these numbers, ranging from 117 to 484.) Other papers emphasize not the bombardment, but the "filter" which blocks out, say, 90 per cent of the total. It makes a great difference where you put your emphasis when you are trying to convey something about the power of advertising.

The joint ANA/AAAA industry presentation to the FTC in October 1971 produced surprise that so little was really known about the effects of advertising. This surprise was common to all parties, commissioners and industry representatives alike.

Ironically, the initiative taken by the industry to inventory its current expertise was what led to such unexpected and challenging consequences.

Some blamed the industry for having been overconfident, for not having done its homework, for having been remiss in its research, deficient in its concern for accountability, and (essentially) for being not at all as wise about advertising as some might have expected.

But how you handle the "bombardment" and "filter" views of advertising is central to a clear exposition of its power. As a matter of policy, appropriate statements should be made available by the industry.

I suggest that the root questions about the degree of impact, or persuasibility, or influence of television advertising have to do as much with the nature of man as with advertising. There are unsolved or unresolved questions, even at the level of understanding the nature of man.

How Do We Learn?

At one time, especially prior to 1900 and in the U.S., it was generally believed that an infant is born into a world of "blooming, buzzing confusion," and that as he matured he had to make order out of all this stimulation. Since that time, and more in Europe than in America, there has developed a different view: that the infant child is as if isolated on a remote island, and only occasionally does a lone message get across to him from the mainland.

When the first view prevailed it was considered very important to train young children into good *habits,* so that even if they did not understand the world they could cope with it in some routine behavior.

More recently the emphasis is on stimulating the child in an encouraging manner so that he will spontaneously make creative attempts, including those of insight and understanding.

The two views could hardly be more different. Indeed, the educational world has debated them for 75 years with sometimes one side in ascendence and then, after re-evaluation, the other.

11

This difference involves not only a different view of the child's (or man's) bio-physiological or reactive capacities but also of how children learn. Even though the psychologists of the day performed much of their research on learning on quite neutral laboratory rats, the proponents of each view seemed to find evidence to support their own views.

For example, American researchers noticed that rats confronted with a problem dashed energetically around the cage, trying one thing and another until by chance they accidently performed the correct response and were rewarded, usually with food. They learned, as it was said, by trial and error—with much premium placed on energy and activity. If repeated often enough, they got the habit of the correct response.

Meanwhile, German researchers noticed that *their* rats confronted with a problem retired to a corner of the cage, remained quiet for a time—as if thinking the problem over—and finally went over and performed the correct response on one try. The rats learned by some process of abstraction rather than of energy.

Lord Bertrand Russell remarked one day that obviously there is a marked breed difference between American and German rats.

So here there is one view that sees the child adapting to an overstimulating world via useful habits, learned on the basis of frequent trials or (horrid school phenomenon) "practice." Opposed to it is a view that sees the child keeping the world at bay until reached or awakened, and capable, if encouraged, of insightful, one-trial acts of learning without repetition.

The problem is complicated by the fact that both views are correct to a degree. When my two children were young we called my son the German rat and my daughter the American rat. When he tried something new and failed, such as tying his shoelaces, he'd walk away from the problem and wouldn't try again for several days. On the second try and thereafter, he would always have it right.

When she failed to solve some new problem she would persist, get angry, and upset the whole house until she solved the problem or was helped to do so. This would happen repeatedly until she had the task well learned.

We spend a lot of money on repetition of advertising. Some explain this by noting that recall of the advertising

Herbert E. Krugman is manager of public opinion research at the General Electric Company. Prior to joining GE in 1967, he was research vice president at the Marplan Division of the Interpublic Group of Companies, Inc. Dr. Krugman received his Ph.D. from Columbia University in 1952, his B.S.S. from CCNY in 1942. He was an Air Force psychologist 1942-45 and has since served both the Air Force and the State Department as consultant. He has been on the faculties of Yale, Princeton and Columbia. Dr. Krugman is a past-president of AAPOR. He is also past-president of the Division of Consumer Psychology of the APA. He is a member of the editorial board of *Public Opinion Quarterly*, and a member of the Editorial Board of the *Journal of Professional Psychology*. He is a trustee of the Marketing Science Institute in Cambridge. He is listed in *Who's Who*.

will drop unless continually re-enforced; others note that members of the audience are not always in the market for the advertised product, but that when they are, the advertising must *be there*. There's no choice but to advertise frequently. So we can have advertising campaigns of equal magnitude, but based on quite different assumptions about the nature of the effect.

Of course these two views are apparently quite opposite. One says that the ad must be learned in the same way that habits are learned—by practice. The other says that at the right moment (when one is "in the market") it just takes minimal exposure to achieve appropriate effects.

If you say this to the FTC, however (and it's been said), you seem, to them, to be saying two different things. If your ad has to be repeated endlessly to be learned, it probably isn't very powerful. If your ad has to be repeated just to be there at that critical moment when your viewer is "in the market" then it's got real one-shot power indeed.

This is like saying, if you're using the recall explanation, that schoolwork is hard, that the child must practice or else forget what he's learned. If you're using the "in the market" explanation, it's like saying that if the school curriculum and methods are truly stimulating, the child's mind will be open, creative, insightful, or "turned on." Those who believe in such stimulation say that practice is required only when you're forcing children to learn things they're not interested in, things that don't "turn them on." Well, you know the rest of that fight—but the same fight is not as easily recognized within advertising and mass communications.

People are confused about whether or not advertising is potent—and they are not getting any unified point of view from the advertising industry itself.

I would like to argue against single exposure potency and also against any large number of repeated exposures. It is important to understand how communication works and how people learn, and to do that some attention has to be given to the difference between one, two, and three—i.e., the difference between the first, second, and third exposures. One to make ready, two for the show, three for the money, and four to go, or just what? Campaign effects based on 20 or 30 exposures I believe are only multiples or combinations of what happens in the first few exposures.

Recent Research

First, I would like to note that the special importance of just two or three exposures, as compared to a much larger number, is attested to by a variety of converging research findings based on different research methods. In the April 1968 issue of the *American Psychologist*, for example, I reported ("Procedures underlying response to advertising") that an optimal number of exposures seemed to be about two to three. This was based on eye movement data conducted in a laboratory situation and in response to print advertising.

In September 1969 Grass published a similar finding (three to four exposures) in this *Journal* based on CONPAAD responses to television commercials. Both studies were primarily laboratory.

In September 1970, Colin Mac Donald of the British Market Research Bureau gave an award-winning paper at the Annual Conference of the European Society of Market Research (ESOMAR), which reported purchase diary data interrelated with media data such that MacDonald identified two exposures as optimal. There are others as well but the point I am making

should be clear, that a wide variety of research procedures agree on the special significance of just a few exposures as optimal.

An Explanation

Let me try to explain the special qualities of one, two, and three exposures. I stop at three because as you shall see there is no such thing as a fourth exposure psychologically; rather, fours, fives, etc., are repeats of the third exposure effect.

Exposure No. 1 is by definition unique. Like the first exposure of anything, the reaction is dominated by a "What is it?" type of cognate response—i.e., the first response is to understand the nature of the stimulus. Anything new or novel, however uninteresting on second exposure, has to elicit some response the first time if only for the mental classification required to discard the object as of no further interest. Thus, the new stimulus, good or bad, has an initial attention-getting requirement even if it is quickly blocked out thereafter.

The second exposure to a stimulus has several implicit qualities. One is that the cognitive "What *is* it?" response can be replaced by a more evaluative and personal "What *of* it?" response. That is, having now fully appreciated just what is the nature of the new information, the viewer can now shift to a question of whether or not it has personal relevance. Some of this might occur during first exposure if the respondent is absorbing the commercial with great interest, but more likely, especially on television where you cannot rewind or reverse the film, there's enough missed the first time around so that elements of the cognate reaction are still present on second exposure.

Another element of second exposure, and unique to second exposure, is the startled recognition response, "Ah ha, I've seen this before!" The virtue of such recognition is that it permits the viewer to pick up where he left off—without the necessity of doing the cognate thing ("What is it?") all over again. So the second exposure is the one where personal responses and evaluations—the "sale" so to speak—occurs. This "What of it?" response completes the basic reaction to the commercial.

By the third exposure the viewer knows he has been through his "What *is* it's?" and "What *of* it's?," and the third becomes, then, the true reminder—that is, *if* there is some consequence of the earlier evaluations yet to be fulfilled. But it is *also* the beginning of disengagement, of withdrawal of attention from a completed task.

I suggest that this pattern holds true for all larger number of exposures. That is, most people filter or screen out TV commercials at any one time by stopping at the "What is it?" response, without personal involvement. The same person months later, and suddenly in the market for the product in question, might see and experience the 23rd exposure to the commercial as *if it were the second*. That is, now the viewer is able to go further into the nature of his or her reaction to the commercial—and then the 24th and probably the 25th might finish off that sequence with no further reaction to subsequent exposures.

The importance of this view of things is that it positions advertising as powerful only when the viewer, the consumer, or shopper is interested—and that is largely outside the control of television or advertising.

Secondly, it positions the viewer as doing his business, reacting to the commercial—very quickly and thoroughly when the proper time comes around.

Many people have looked at the enormous TV budgets and repeat scatter plans and assumed that the viewer had to be reacting slowly and gradually. It made TV look monolithic and successful on the basis of sheer mass and grinding momentum. It made large budgets seem especially advantageous or "unfair," and thoroughly distorted two of the common words in the English language: these words are "remembering" and "forgetting."

There is a myth in the advertising world that viewers will forget your message if you don't repeat your advertising often enough. It is this myth that supports many large advertising expenditures and raises embarrassing and, to some extent, needless questions about unfair market dominance.

The myth about the forgetting of advertising is based primarily on the erosion of recall scores. Yet the inability to recall something does not mean

it is forgotten or that it has been erased from memory. The acid test of complete forgetting is if you can no longer *recognize* the object. Few TV commercials that *have been seen* the night before can be remembered the next day—i.e., via recall. According to Gallup's TPT system only 12 per cent can recall the average commercial. But at GE, we have shown photoscripts of TV commercials weeks after exposure and gotten 50 per cent recognition.

Rather than continue the budget supporting myths renewed every day via the recall research technique, I would rather say that the public comes closer to forgetting *nothing* they have seen on TV. They just "put it out of their minds" until and unless it has some use, and then one day— "Aha!"—it springs to life again and the response to the commercial continues.

I am not critical of large TV budgets that provide many exposures. I am critical, and the industry will be criticized, if the power of those large budgets is misunderstood or mis-stated. The large budget is powerful because, like a product sitting on a shelf, you never know when the customer is going to be looking for you—so you must rent the shelf space all the time. But the nature of the customer's reaction is independent, rapid, decisive. He or she makes up his or her mind— perhaps more than once during a campaign—but most frequently at some point in the second, or shall we say psychologically second, exposure to the commercial.

Within this perspective television advertising plays a modest, important, and thoroughly reasonable role in the marketing of goods and services.

Public Opinion Quarterly

Volume XXXVI, Number 3, Fall 1972

Communications Research and Public Policy — *Harold D. Lasswell*
Public Opinion Research as Communication — *W. Phillips Davison*
Political Socialization in the American Family — *R. W. Connell*
Dissecting the Generation Gap — *Lucy N. Friedman, Alice R. Gold, and Richard Christie*
Attitudes vs. Actions *versus* Attitudes vs. Attitudes — *Howard Schuman*
Predicting Behavior from Attitudes — *Alan G. Weinstein*
The Strength in Weak Ties — *William T. Liu and Robert W. Duff*
Alchemy in the Behavioral Sciences — *Hillel J. Einhorn*
Minimum-Error Scalogram Analysis — *Albert Chevan*
Canadian Attitudes toward the U.S. Presence — *J. Alex Murray and Mary C. Gerace*
Proceedings of the Twenty-Seventh Annual Conference of AAPOR
The Polls
News and Notes
In Memoriam
Book Reviews
Book Notes

Subscriptions: $7.50 a year, $12 for two years, $15 for three years
Columbia University Press, 136 South Broadway, Irvington-on-Hudson, N. Y. 10533

*Twenty-one Milwaukee residents saw
117 to 484 ads per day
in four major media.*

HOW MANY ADVERTISING EXPOSURES PER DAY?

Steuart Henderson Britt, Stephen C. Adams and Allan S. Miller

How many advertisements is an individual exposed to during an average day? This study attempts to answer this question by presenting a technique for accurately estimating advertising exposure per day for any individual living anywhere in the U.S.

Before conducting the investigation, a survey was made of 121 books, periodicals, pamphlets, and other informational sources dealing specifically with advertising.

Ebel's Estimate

The most extensively and inaccurately quoted statements about advertising exposure come from the estimate in a speech by Edwin Ebel in 1957:

"Did you ever calculate how much advertising an ordinary family is exposed to? A couple of bright young men in my office did some *statistically inadequate research* [italics added] for me that is most interesting. It is *inadequate* [italics added] only because it represents a picture of one family, but the family is typical of many families in America—John, who commutes to work; his wife, Mary; and their two children. We made a careful count of the advertising this family was exposed to in one ordinary working day."

Although Ebel carefully stated that his figure of 1,518 advertising exposures was statistically inadequate, his figure became almost gospel in the advertising industry, and it has been misquoted many times.

Investigation by Bauer and Greyser

Under the sponsorship of the 4 As, the first real attempt to measure advertising effectiveness was carried out in 1964 by Bauer and Greyser. The findings were reported in *Advertising in America: The Consumer View* (1968).

These findings report what Americans think about advertisements and advertising. In-home interviews were conducted in 84 different locations with 1,846 men and women over 18 years old living in private households. The respondents were drawn from a national projectable sample of the adult population.

Steuart Henderson Britt (Ph.D. in psychology from Yale University) is professor of marketing and advertising in the Graduate School of Management of Northwestern University, and president of Britt and Frerichs Inc., a national marketing research and consulting firm headquartered in Chicago. Dr. Britt has served as a consultant to such diverse organizations as *Advertising Age,* Leo Burnett, Dentsu (Tokyo), Lintas (London), Formica, *Life,* the Marketing Science Institute, 7-Up, Standard Oil of Indiana, and several law firms. Dr. Britt has authored or edited 12 books and over 150 articles in psychology and marketing; and for three different publishers he has edited an additional 51 books in these same fields.

Of the total interviewed as to attitudes about advertising, 1,536 also participated in a special study that involved the counting of ads noted during the greater portion of one day, followed by a second interview. Half the persons in the sample were assigned the period from rising to 5:00 P.M. and the other half the period from 5:00 P.M. to bedtime.

Each individual was asked to count each advertisement to which he paid at least some attention in four major media: magazines, newspapers, radio, and television. No counts were made of other ads in other media such as outdoor posters, point-of-sale, bus or car cards, shopping papers, and window displays.

Results: "The average American adult . . . reports . . . that he saw or heard 38 advertisements during his half-day counting period. The daytime average is 36.3, the evening average is 39.6. Combining these figures to estimate the total for a full-day period, we may conclude: The average American adult is aware of 76 advertisements a day in the major media . . . ."

This figure represents ads of which a person is aware, as contrasted with the Ebel estimate of 1,518 advertisements to which a four-person family might be exposed.

Basing his conclusions on Bauer and Greyser, Adams (1965) emphasized that of the 76 advertisements a day of which a person might be aware, only 12 "make any kind of an impression on him. And, incredibly, three of these twelve make a negative impression!"

Further, Adams estimated that the number of advertisements to which the average American is exposed in a 16-hour period is at a minimum 560. This figure was calculated on the basis of the number of advertisements to which he would be exposed in a typical day's activities—

Stephen C. Adams is with Jewel Companies, Inc., Chicago, involved in the food, drug, and general merchandise industry. He received both his B.S. in business administration (1970) and his M.B.A.A. in marketing (1971) from Northwestern University.

reading one and one-half newspapers, one-half of magazine, and one piece of direct mail; listening to the radio in both car and home, 2.3 hours; and view ing television, 3.8 hours.

The Wachsler Study

In 1970, Robert Wachsler of BBDO suggested even a lower figure of advertising exposure.

The Research Department of BBDO estimated the expected daily advertising exposure for the average male to be 285 advertisements and for the average female to be 305 advertisements. The study used statistical national averages for the amount of time adults spent with each of five different media. The results are shown in Table 1.

Although the exact methodology was not stated, Wachsler said, "We laid out all available media usage data that we had—e.g., television, radio tuning hour by hour, percentage of a book [sic] seen during the average reading, etc., etc. Against these time seg ments and reading proportions we placed the num ber of scheduled ad messages."

Implications

Implications from the Ebel, Bauer-Greyser, and Wachsler estimates are that:

1. Advertising exposure has been concerned with average individuals for average amounts of time. What is average must be defined within the study in which it is used.

2. The concept of exposure is used in different ways and it gains meaning only within the study in which it is used. For example, television exposure might be defined in terms of an individual having his set turned on; or it might be defined as occurring only when the individual actually is watching and listening to television.

3. Measurement of advertising exposure is a controversial area of study in which no comprehensive system has been designed to determine an accurate estimate. See Table 2.

The study reported here represents an approach to the question: How many advertisements is an individual exposed to during an average day?

Table 1

Wachsler's Estimate of Advertising Exposure

Media	Male	Female
Television, 7 a.m. - 1 a.m.	35	48
Radio, 6 a.m. - midnight	38	45
Magazines	15	20
Newspapers on average weekday	185	182
Outdoor	12	10
Total	285	305

To use the results of this study as an average figure for measurement of exposure would be a mistake. Rather, the purpose was to develop a system or method for the measurement of advertising exposure per day for any individual (or individuals) living anywhere in the U.S.

Methodology

The system used demographic characteristics of any individual(s) as input; for output, the number of ads to which that individual was exposed during a given day, the length of which was between 7 A.M. and 1 A.M.

In the present study, exposure is defined as the individual's contact with an advertising medium or advertisement. An ad is defined as any paid form of nonpersonal presentation or promotion of products, services, or ideas by an identifiable individual or organization.

Design

Our system had to be computerized in order to store a large amount of statistical information, to provide inputs of the data on many individuals at one time, and to allow for rapid retrieval of estimated data. The general framework of the computerized system allowed for inputs of several different kinds of demographic variables.

Media. The system was designed around the four major media: television, radio, newspapers, and magazines. These were selected because of their diversified audiences, ease of measurement, and because they account for 62 per cent of U.S. advertising expenditures.

Table 2

Summary of Estimates of Advertising Exposure

Media considered	Estimates of Advertising Exposure			
	Ebel (15-hour day)	Bauer & Greyser (avg. day)	Wachsler (avg. day)	
			Sex	No.
TV	64	3.8 hours	M	35
			F	48
Radio	53	2.3 hours	M	38
			F	45

Programming. The computer program contained three especially important kinds of information:

1. A demographic breakdown of the standard metropolitan statistical area in which the individual(s) lives.

2. A demographic breakdown of the audiences per quarter hour for the television and radio stations, and the audiences of the magazines and newspapers that serve the specific metropolitan area.

3. The number of commercials per quarter hour on the television and radio stations, and the number of advertisements (other than those in the want-ad and classified sections).

The demographic breakdowns included age, sex, income, education, county of residence, and whether or not the individual was a housewife.

To understand how the system works, assume that the person on whom we might want information is Mrs. John Doe, who is de-

Allan S. Miller is serving in a management capacity with Standard Pipe and Supply Company Inc., Balacynwyd, Pennsylvania. Both his B.S. in business administration (1970) and his M.B.A. in labor relations and marketing (1971) are from Northwestern University.

fined within the demographic characteristics listed above. We wish to know the number of advertisements to which Mrs. Doe has been exposed through television on a particular day.

Television. The Nielsen ratings, which measure the number of TV sets tuned to a particular channel during a specific time period within a metropolitan area, were used to determine the probability that an individual was watching TV during any quarter hour of the day.

The system used a random-number generator, with numbers between 0.00 and 1.00, in order to determine whether or not an individual was tuned in during the quarter-hour period in question. Suppose that the random number .6550 appeared. This number would be equivalent to tuning in to Station C, since it intercepts the cumulative storage curve within the area defined by a point closest to Station C, as shown in Figure 1.

If the random number were higher than the cumulative rating total of 82, it can be concluded that no station was being watched, since 82 per cent of the sets were turned on. When no station is being watched, a zero value is assigned to the total advertising exposure for that quarter hour. See Figure 2 for a flow chart to estimate television and radio exposure.

The Broadcast Advertisers' Report (BAR) logs the local TV spot advertisements for each station. By combining this report with the individual station's advertising logs for a metropolitan area, the system develops the number of commercials appearing on each station during each quarter hour of station operation. The computer system adds the number of quarter-hour advertisements during which the viewer had the television set turned on to arrive at the number of exposures.

Radio. The method for measuring advertising exposure through radio is the same, except that The Pulse Reports were used to measure the number of radios tuned to a particular station during a specific time period within a metropolitan area. In addition, the radio stations serving the area can offer their advertising logs for the day in question.

Newspapers. To estimate newspaper advertising exposure, the system again used a random-number generator, based on newspaper circulation in the metropolitan area. The American Newspaper Publishers Association finds that on the average, a reader is exposed to 82 per cent of the pages in a newspaper he starts to read. Multiplying 82 per cent times the number of advertisements (excluding want

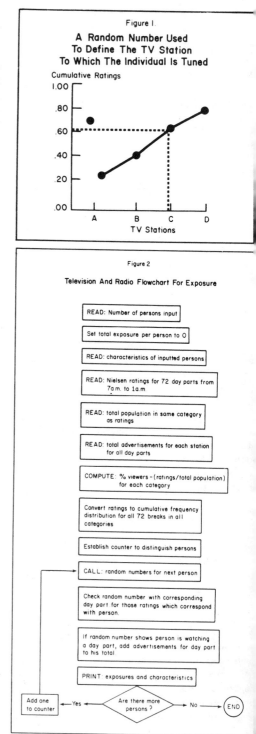

Figure 1.

A Random Number Used To Define The TV Station To Which The Individual Is Tuned

Cumulative Ratings

Figure 2

Television And Radio Flowchart For Exposure

READ: Number of persons input

Set total exposure per person to 0

READ: characteristics of inputted persons

READ: Nielsen ratings for 72 day parts from 7 a.m. to 1 a.m.

READ: total population in same category as ratings

READ: total advertisements for each station for all day parts

COMPUTE: % viewers – (ratings/total population) for each category

Convert ratings to cumulative frequency distribution for all 72 breaks in all categories

Establish counter to distinguish persons

CALL: random numbers for next person

Check random number with corresponding day part for those ratings which correspond with person.

If random number shows person is watching a day part, add advertisements for day part to his total

PRINT: exposures and characteristics

Add one to counter ← Yes ← Are there more persons ? → No → END

ds and the classified sections) in a newspaper pro-
ides an estimate of the possible exposures.

By comparing a random number with the demo-
raphic breakdown of the per cent of households
eceiving one or more newspapers, the system esti-
nates the number of newspaper ads to which an
ndividual is exposed. See Figure 3 for a flow chart
f newspaper exposure.

Magazines. To estimate advertising exposure of

magazines (supplements are not included), a demographic breakdown of the households served by
each magazine entering the metropolitan area market was obtained. We assumed six delivery days per
week (with the chances of receiving a magazine on
any one day, one out of six) and that a magazine is
looked into or read on the day it is received. By
comparing a random number with the circulation
percentage in terms of readers for each magazine,
the system was used to estimate the magazine or
magazines an individual was exposed to during a
particular day. This figure was multiplied by the
number of advertisements (excluding classified ads)
in each magazine for that specific time period. See
Figure 4 for a flow chart of magazine exposure.

Testing the System

For testing the model, the Milwaukee Standard
Metropolitan Statistical Area was chosen for four
reasons: (1) the sales per capita approximated the
national average sales per capita; (2) it is the mid-
point in metropolitan U.S. population distribution;
(3) the demographic breakdown is a reasonable
approximation of the demographic breakdown of all

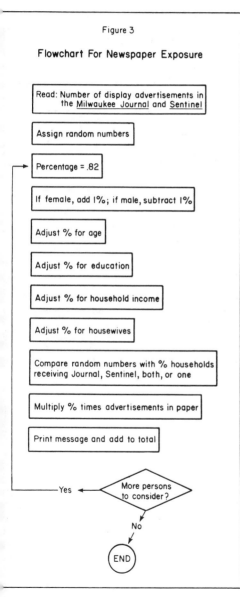

Figure 3

Flowchart For Newspaper Exposure

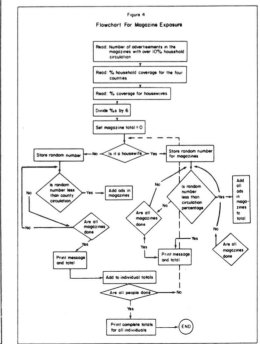

major metropolitan areas combined; (4) SMSA media statistics are close to the national averages.

Because of the large number of radio and TV stations and newspapers and magazines that serve the area, the following decisions were made:

Television. The Milwaukee SMSA is served by six television stations, two of which did not meet Nielsen minimum reporting standards, meaning that the differences and relationships between low audience levels should not be interpreted as meaningful. The number of commercials per quarter hour were estimated for the four major stations on the basis of information obtained from two of the stations.

Radio. There are 20 AM and 9 FM stations that serve the Milwaukee SMSA. The system incorporated information from the five AM stations that claim a 75 per cent share of listening audiences according to the 1970 Hooper Radio Audience Index. The number of commercials per quarter hour on FM stations was estimated for all nine stations, based upon information obtained from two of the stations.

Newspapers. Combined, *The Milwaukee Journal*

and *The Milwaukee Sentinel* reach 98 per cent o the households reading a newspaper. The marke shares of other newspapers serving the market are under five per cent.

Magazines. Although hundreds of magazines ente the Milwaukee SMSA, nine magazines have a marke share of 10 per cent or more: *Look, Life, Reader' Digest, TV Guide, Woman's Day, Family Circle Good Housekeeping, Ladies' Home Journal,* an *McCall's.*

Since the latest Broadcast Advertisers' Repor and Nielsen Reports were dated Friday, Novembe 13, 1970, advertising exposure estimates were base upon media advertising on that day.

Testing the Mode

In a test of the model for the Milwaukee SMSA demographic characteristics were inputted for 2 people, and the results for these 21 individuals ar

Table 3

Test Sample Findings

Sex	House-wife	Age	Media Exposure Education	Family income	County of residence	TV	Radio	News-papers	Maga-zines	Total exposu
				(000)						
M		13	7	$ 8	Washington	101	26	69	0	19
M		15	9	10	Milwaukee	79	12	107	0	19
M		20	12	6	Milwaukee	35	33	71	0	13
M		25	16	15	Milwaukee	40	39	191	0	27
M		30	9	4	Ozaukee	43	32	104	46	22
M		35	12	15	Milwaukee	68	27	76	0	17
M		45	12	25	Ozaukee	63	54	0	0	11
M		45	16	50	Milwaukee	58	25	202	0	28
M		65	12	20	Waukesha	58	36	117	0	21
F		13	7	8	Washington	56	17	109	0	18
F		15	9	10	Milwaukee	123	17	182	1	41
F		20	12	6	Milwaukee	41	47	73	0	16
F	Yes	25	16	15	Milwaukee	58	23	202	145	42
F		25	12	6	Milwaukee	80	40	186	0	30
F		30	9	4	Ozaukee	40	47	107	0	19
F	Yes	35	12	17	Milwaukee	104	38	205	62	40
F		35	12	10	Milwaukee	78	44	120	0	24
F	Yes	45	16	45	Milwaukee	81	44	214	145	48
F	Yes	45	12	25	Ozaukee	76	39	209	145	46
F		55	16	35	Washington	119	33	80	0	23
F	Yes	70	9	5	Waukesha	101	36	75	0	21

shown in Table 3.

The range of advertising exposure for males was between 117 and 285 advertising messages per day for the test run, and for females between 161 and 484. The greater number of advertising exposures for females was especially apparent for housewives, who are likely to spend more time at home watching television, listening to the radio, and reading newspapers and magazines than their husbands.

Although it is not the purpose of this investigation to suggest an average figure for advertising exposure per day—since the concept of an average individual is not meaningful—the range of advertising exposure estimates remained remarkably consistent, no matter how many individuals were inputted into the computerized system.

In other words, this study produced a computerized system that can estimate advertising exposure per 18-hour day (or any other length of day) for any individual living in the U.S. It is unique because the information is based on any individual(s) rather than on an average individual or an average family.

We believe that the method we have developed is the best one to date. It allows for greater accuracy and more flexibility than any previous method of estimating advertising exposure.

This system could be broadened in scope, of course, analyzing not only television, radio, newspapers, and magazines, but also direct mail, outdoor advertising, transit advertising, professional journals, point-of-sale, window displays, and a variety of other kinds of advertising. A more complete estimate for total advertising exposure would then be possible.

References

Adams, Charles F. *Common Sense in Advertising.* New York: McGraw-Hill Book Company, 1965.

Advertising Age, quoting Robert Wachsler, October 15, 1970, pp. 1 and 86.

Bauer, Raymond A. and Stephen A. Greyser. *Advertising in America: The Consumer View.* Boston: Division of Research, Graduate School of Business Administration, Harvard University, 1968.

Ebel, Edwin W. Speech at West Coast Meeting of the Association of National Advertisers, San Bernardino, CA., May 8, 1957.

In a review of the state of the art, the authors discuss the pro's and con's of methods and past studies of . . .

Television Commercial Wearout

Allan Greenberg and Charles Suttoni

Too much spoiles, too little doth not satisfie.

> —James Howell
> *Proverbs* (1659)

A television commercial does not change with repeated exposure; rather, it is the viewer's reaction that does. Thus, in reviewing commercial wearout, one must focus on the consumer and consider such psychological factors as perception, interest, and learning theory.

Behavioral psychologists, whose ideas were brought to the marketplace by such men as G.W. Hill and Rosser Reeves, believed that constant repetition would ingrain a stimulus in the mind and eventually lead to a desired effect. Reeves, for example, wrote in 1961:

> "Unless a product becomes outmoded, a great campaign will not wear itself out . . . .Too frequent change in your advertising campaign destroys penetration."

Opposed to this is today's view that a commercial will eventually lose its effectiveness after a certain amount of exposure and should be replaced by a different creative approach. The reason for this is that after repeated exposure, viewers no longer react with the same intensity or in the same way as they did when the commercial was new to them. Weilbacher (1970) has aptly described the process as the life cycle of advertisements—their productive life, progressive decay, and inevitable death in the world of consumers.

One major problem in discussing commercial wearout is that once the general pattern of viewer response is outlined—initial exposure, a climb to maximum effectiveness, then eventual decay or wearout—there are few other predictive generalizations that can be made. Each commercial generates its own unique pattern of response or life cycle no matter whether it is studied under laboratory conditions, on the air, or in a combination of the two. The individuality of performance is understandable when considering the wide range of products and services, the variety of creative approaches, and the infinite possibilities of scheduling. A hard-sell demonstration commercial for a headache remedy, for example, may behave quite differently than a fanciful or romantic commercial for a vacation loan.

It is not known at present how much of a distinction, if any, viewers make between programs and commercials. We do know that commercials are far from undesirable; for example, Steiner (1970) found that people did not really want television without commercials. What they objected to most was the timing of a commercial if it interrupted the flow of program material. Tele-Research (1969) questioned nearly a million women and found that the positive qualities of commercials (friendly, clever, entertaining, informative, etc.) were mentioned three times more frequently, on average, than negative ones (exaggerated, dull, silly, uninteresting, etc.).

47

Commercials, then, are a positive part of the viewers' television experience. What really distinguishes them from program material is not the perceived qualities of a commercial, but the fact that a commercial aims at having the viewer eventually accept a product, service, or an idea. To achieve this, commercials are generally repeated with some frequency, and where there is repetition, there is also wearout.

Advertising Perception

Research evidence has shown that a viewer's attention is neither active nor sustained. James' (1890) pioneering work in attention demonstrated that the time span for voluntary attention is a few seconds at most. Unless the stimulus changes, a person must renew his attention over and over. Steiner (1966) showed that viewers' attention is in a constant state of flux while watching television. And recent experiments measuring brain waves (Krugman, 1971) indicate that a person watching TV is typically not mentally active, but relaxed and hence passive and receptive.

All this indicates that people do not really *watch* television, if by that we mean "to attend with alert vigilance" as Webster has it; they *monitor* the screen, paying or withdrawing attention at will. They become involved with images that strike their interest and which promise some kind of reward (information, entertainment, etc.) and they let images of little interest pass by. Attention, then, can range from complete involvement with the medium to mere awareness that the set is on. Further, the level of attention varies almost on a second-by-second basis. If a commercial holds a viewer's interest, it is because what is promised induces the viewer to constantly renew the attention he pays to the image.

Generally, there are three types of factors that influence viewer attention (Weilbacher, 1970). First is the viewer himself; his general attitude toward TV, his life style, age, current interest in the product advertised, etc. Second is the commercial; the nature of the product, the basic appeal employed, the creative approach, the tone or mood established, the information it contains, etc. Third is a person's previous exposure to the commercial, similar commercials, or to the campaign.

Repetition

Repetition is an important consider-

Allan Greenberg is senior vice president and director of research and planning at Doyle Dane Bernbach, Inc. He has written about many facets of research in such publications as the *Journal of Marketing, Public Opinion Quarterly, Journal of Marketing Research*, and the *Journal of Advertising Research*. He co-authored a booklet on young people; wrote a chapter on copy testing for a handbook of advertising measurement. He did his undergraduate work in economics at City College of New York and his postgraduate work at the University of Wisconsin (in statistics), and the New School for Social Research (in social psychology and sociology).

ation in learning, and for TV commercials it has been shown that multiple exposures increase consumer knowledge of the brand name, selling theme, and other aspects of the commercial (BBD&O, 1967).

Learning by repetition, however, cannot be divorced from the length of the time interval between exposures. In the absence of frequent reinforcing exposures, people simply forget what they have learned.

Repeating a commercial does two things: (1) It increases and reinforces what a person learns about the product, and (2) it forestalls forgetting, or decay. For the advertiser, it is practical to schedule commercials fairly frequently at the start of a new campaign when the primary purpose is to build or increase consumer knowledge and then as the campaign matures, to space out the frequency in order to maintain the level of what people already know.

If this process of communication and learning works so well in theory, the obvious question is: Why do commercials wear out? There are two answers to the question. First, there is no product of universal interest or no creative appeal of universal effectiveness. A commercial embodies a specific appeal and is usually geared to some portion of the population. Once it has reached those who have an interest in the product and who respond to the appeal, the commercial has done its job.

The second reason is that viewers do not generally get emotionally involved with most of the advertising to which they are exposed, and this is particularly true of television commercials because exposure does not pre-suppose any effort or selectivity on the consumer's part. The attention given to the screen varies from moment to moment, depending on personal predispositions, the commercial, and previous exposure. Psychologists have found that the pattern of learning via television commercials shows a marked similarity to the pattern of learning of so-called "nonsense" information; that is, groups of unrelated words, series of numbers, etc. This learning goes through three distinct phases and can be described as a curve shaped like an inverted "u" (Jacobovitz, 1965). First is the generation phase where knowledge increases because of repeated exposure to the stimulus. Knowledge then reaches a satiation point where a person having little intrinsic interest or involvement in the subject matter feels there is nothing else to learn from the information presented. At this point, a person begins to forget the information he has already learned in spite of continuing exposure to the stimulus because he has mentally tuned it out and ceases to pay attention to what is being said. This is the decay phase.

While evidence shows that commercials conform to this general pattern of response, the performance of any commercial or group of commercials will depend upon the circumstances. For example, a man about to buy tires might become involved with various commercials by tire companies. On the other hand, one or two exposures to a commercial for a household cleanser might convince him that the commercial and its product offer very little reward for his continued attention.

Commercial Wearout

The techniques that have been used to study commercial wearout run the gamut from ingenious clinical testing devices to broad-scale consumer studies of advertising awareness and recall. The clinical studies deal most directly with the dynamics of viewer perception and interest. Typically, they involve bringing a small number of people into a controlled testing environment and measuring reactions to forced, repeated exposure to a commercial over varying lengths of time.

Specific devices are the eye-camera, Sync, and CONPAAD.

Marplan and its associated companies have favored the eye-camera technique for testing commercials. This technique takes advantage of the involuntary attention (or Piltz) reflex in the pupil of the eye. As one becomes psychologically interested, stimulated, or aroused, the iris dilates and the pupil becomes larger to admit more light. A person's interest can be measured by photographing the pupil and recording the changes in its size as a person watches a commercial. Marplan experimented with matched groups of viewers who were exposed to the same commercials from 4 to 24 times over an eight-week period. Their experiments showed that interest, as measured by the camera, gradually increased to a level of 15 exposures and declined thereafter (TV Age, 1967). Lest anyone take 15 or an average of twice a week as optimum exposure,

Charles Suttoni is research associate for special projects at Doyle Dane Bernbach, Inc. He received a B.B.A. from Manhattan College, an A.M. from New York University, and is currently completing a long delayed Ph.D. there. He has worked at various large agencies in the past as a research supervisor and associate director of research. For the past ten years he has been with Doyle Dane Bernbach, Inc.

Marplan cautions that interest varies by the creative approach used and the product category advertised. Their findings do indicate, however, that interest in a commercial can be sustained through a fairly high level of repeated exposure provided that the repetitions are spaced out over time.

N.W. Ayer has done experiments with a device known as Sync. In this test, the subject has several alternate actions available. He is exposed to two commercials at once and can control both the audio and video levels of each. He can watch and hear either for as long as he wishes, but not both at once. If neither commercial interests him, he can turn around and watch a TV film that has no sound, a purposely unattractive alternative. Sync automatically records when the subject switches from commercial to one commercial or to the film. The person's interest, or the wearout of a commercial, is then evaluated on the basis of the amount of time he spends watching each alternative. The only generalization that Sync has produced so far is that animated commercials that lead up to a punch line apparently wear out faster than those which use animation simply to tell the product story (TV Age, 1967). This seems reasonable because previous exposures have already taught the subject what to expect.

CONPAAD is also a device to measure interest in commercials. Here the subject controls both the brightness of the video and the volume of the audio by sustained pressure on a foot pedal. The theory is that the more interesting a person finds a commercial, the more physical effort (foot pressure) he is willing to exert to see and hear it. Many experiments have been done with CONPAAD equipment, typically using five or six exposures to a commercial during a film.

Such studies have several obvious shortcoming: (1) Advertising campaigns are not aired in a controlled environment; (2) the clinical studies generally overlook the effect that competitive commercials can have in the way people perceive the test commercials; and (3) under normal viewing conditions the concentrated exposure used in clinical testing is spaced out over longer periods.

Commercial Testing Services

Several commercial testing services have published results of studies on wearout. Typically, these studies consist of testing or pre-testing a commercial at the start of a campaign and then repeating the test after the commercial has been on the air for some time. This approach has one major shortcoming: exposure to the commercial cannot be controlled between the tests, so one is never quite sure how many times the people in the retest audience have seen the commercial. It is usual to assume that the audience will be quite familiar with the commercial when the retest is done.

In 1971 Benton & Bowles made public the results of an analysis of ASI pre/post scores (Appel, 1966). A group of commercials was tested at the start of various campaigns and then retested from two to 13 months later. The analysis showed that the longer the time between tests (that is, the more the exposure to the commercial), the greater the drop in the pre/post score. Commercials that were retested two to three months after the start of a campaign showed almost no change in the pre/post score while those tested nine to 13 months later showed a drop of five to seven points—a decrease of some 33 to 50 per cent from the initial reading. This analysis equates time with exposure and implies that all commercials wear out at a steady rate in time. Other studies indicate that this may not be true; it is frequency of exposure in relation to time that is important.

Schwerin (1966) has also done numerous repeat tests. A total of 118 commercials for nationally advertised brands in major product fields were studied in England and Germany with retests from one to 18 months after the initial test. The commercials involved were shown normally in the interim, generally as parts of campaigns. Schwerin found that in seven out of ten cases the retest pre/post score was lower than the original one. In other words, these commercials, after varying amounts of exposure, were no longer able to convert as many people to the advertised brand as they did when they were new. Schwerin, however, cited one particular commercial for a food product in Germany which provided a very instructive case study on this whole matter of wearout and pre/post change. When the commercial was first tested, it did extremely well: over 35 per cent of the audience selected the brand before the commercial and the figure ran to 53 per cent after viewing, yielding an exceptional score of 17.6. The commercial ran for 15 months, and when it was retested the pre/post score had dropped to 9.6. But the pre-level on the second test had risen to over 50 per cent with a post of 60 per cent. In other words, the commercial had actually increased the pre-levels by 44 per cent (35.5 to 50.5 per cent) and was wearing out simply because there was no room for further increases—it had already done its job.

Another firm, Tele-Research (1968), took a random group of 50 commercials for drug and food store items and retested them periodically over periods of up to six months. All the commercials tested were on the air during this time, but there is no indication given in the report of the frequency with which they appeared. Tele-Research's method has an advantage over a simple test-retest scheme because the results show the point in time when wearout or satiation begins. In the five examples cited in the re-

port, this point ranged from 10 to 21 weeks after the start of the campaign; whether this time span is a matter of the commercial itself, the on-air frequency, or competitive activity, cannot be established from the data reported. Tele-Research did comment:

"What is especially interesting is that very few commercials [for the types of packaged goods tested] wearout gradually. Instead of a slow, gradual tapering off in selling effectiveness, most commercials sustain their ability to move the product extremely well over a rather long period of time, then, like the 'One Hoss Shay,' they appear to reach a breaking point quite suddenly. Having reached this critical point, their ability to generate sales for the advertised product deteriorates at a very rapid pace, plummeting steadily downward week after week until it levels out at a point far below the original selling effectiveness of the commercial."

The few examples given show that it is a matter of from two to four weeks from the breaking point to the lower level. The interesting point about this study is that it confirms the idea mentioned earlier of a satiation point followed by a drop in effectiveness.

A final commercial testing service is the TV Commercial Index. This service started in 1968 with the express purpose of measuring wearout. The data are reported by a consumer mail panel, and the technique fundamentally consists in giving panel members a written description of a commercial ("A pet food commercial where a shaggy dog jumped over a fence and then sat up and begged for his dinner"), then having those who have seen the commercial rate it on a five-point verbal scale which, in theory, measures if people would like to see it more frequently or would rather have it removed from the air.

Recall Studies As Indicators of Wearout

Recall and learning are not the same thing. Learning can lead to an attitude or predisposition to use a product that is independent of a person's ability to remember what was said in a commercial. Recall, though, can be considered an indicator of learning but certainly no guarantee of commercial effectiveness.

One study of recall, based on data collected in the early 1960s, involved 96 retests representing 81 sixty-second commercials for 31 different brands (Appel, 1971). The studies measured viewers' ability to recall what the test commercials said and showed. As with all studies of this kind, it is almost impossible to measure a person's actual level of exposure to a given commercial. The assumption is made that the length of time between test and retest is at least a rough guide to the frequency of exposure to the commercial. In Table 1, the mean, or average, level of content recall at the start of the campaigns is set at zero. The changes in recall over time are given as points above or below the original score and the timing of the tests is given along the side; the time units involved were not identified, but they were presumably monthly periods.

If one imagines these figures plotted on a curve, the configuration is the inverted "u" shaped curve; generation up to a high point, satiation, and then decline. This curve illustrates that there are more people who remembered something about a commercial after it has been on the air for a few months than who can remember something about a commercial that has been on for two years. Viewers, one must assume, had become so familiar with the commercial by that time that they simply stopped paying attention to it.

Table 1
Effect of Elapsed Time on Recall Scores

Time Units	Change in Average Recall Score (96 Commercials)
0	0
1	+2
4	−1
6	−2
12	−4
25	−8

Benton & Bowles, the agency who did the study, was naturally curious to explore the wearout phenomenon in relation to their own copy testing techniques. Did certain types of commercials wear out faster than others, or did the results of commercial pretests produce any information about how a commercial would behave once it was on the air? Accordingly, they divided the commercials into two groups; those which scored well according to B & B's copy test standards and those which scored average or below average. This division—assuming a random mix of brands and product categories—produced dramatic differences in rates of wearout, as shown in Table 2.

Those commercials, then, that initially scored above average (+2 as a group), gained from exposure (to a high of +5) and maintained their above-average status for a relatively long period. In contrast, the average or below group of commercials went nowhere but down with increased exposure. These patterns of wearout are averages across the two groups of commercials involved, and it is hazardous to apply an average to the performance of an individual commercial. As a group, the better commercials gained with increased exposure and confirmed the point frequently made in learning theory that the more vivid the initial impression a stimulus makes, the easier it is to recall. On the other hand, one must allow for individual performance and realize that a commercial that does poorly at first, may improve its performance with increased exposure. As a group, the poor commercials declined in recall over time, but this is no guarantee that each and every one of them did.

The most extensive series of published studies on wearout was done by Grass (1968), Wallace (1970), and Grass and Wallace (1969). Their work is an attempt to relate learning theory to clinical tests using CONPAAD and then to actual field studies during a campaign. The basic contention in the theory is that repetition increases learning up to a point of satiation. Krugman (1972) reaches a similar conclusion.

The clinical CONPAAD studies bear out that interest declines with repeated exposure. When the same commercial was repeated six times in a test film (AAAAAA), interest declined

Table 2
Effect of Elapsed Time on Recall Scores
Change in Average Recall Scores

Time Unit	All Commercials (96)	Above Average (59)	Average or Below (37)
0	0	+2	−1
1	+2	+5	−3
4	−1	+2	−4
6	−2	+2	−11
12	−4	−3	−
25	−8	−9	−

steadily after the second or third exposure. A different commercial for the same product inserted near the end of the sequence (AAAABA) revived interest momentarily, but it resumed its decline when the first was shown again. An alternating sequence (ABABAB) behaved like two interlocked individual sequences; interest declined with repetition but at a slower rate because each commercial appeared only three times in the showing. Finally, a series of six different commercials for the same product (ABCDEF) produced hardly any loss of interest at all. This series of laboratory experiments naturally lead to the conclusion that wearout may be postponed and attention increased during a campaign by increasing the number of commercials used.

Grass (1970) later cited an interesting recall study where it was possible to divide matched samples of people by relative exposure to a TV campaign; light (1-3 commercials per month), medium (4-6), or heavy (7-12), plus a control group which did not see the TV campaign. The study dealt with a 12-week campaign for a consumer product and measured those who could recall the brand name of a consumer product. There are several points of interest in this study: first, all three exposure groups went through the typical cycle of generation-satiation-decline, but the timing and intensity of the cycle differed for each group depending upon the level of exposure to the campaign. Brand awareness in the heavily exposed group more than doubled during the first month of the campaign, leveled out, and then declined. In contrast, the light and medium groups required two months to reach a peak, with different levels (5.3 and 7.8 per cent) which seemed to reflect different rates of exposure to the commercial. Notice that an average computed across the groups can be misleading; the average peaks at the eighth week, a time when

satiation has already set in for the heavy group.

Other Dupont studies showed the same general pattern of recall over time. Consumer knowledge peaked soon after the start of a campaign and then gradually declined in spite of the fact that the advertising continued. Grass cited the brand awareness of a consumer product measured over eight months as a case in point; before the campaign, the awareness level was four per cent, in a month it climbed to 15 per cent, and peaked at 17 per cent a month and a half after advertising started; at three months it was back down to 13 per cent; and then in the fifth to eighth month it settled at a level of about 10 per cent.

In general, these field studies with consumers do not show the sharp changes in interest that some of the laboratory studies do because the viewing public is a mixed, uncontrolled group. Some viewers are still in the process of learning while others have passed the satiation point and have turned their attention elsewhere. The 10 per cent level of awareness that resulted from the campaign Grass monitored is not constant, but a mixture of people gaining and losing awareness.

In contrast to the recall of learned information, consumer attitudes seem to be much more resistant to wearout.

Grass cited studies of several corporate image commercials aired at different frequencies. The major difference between these studies of attitude and the recall studies was that favorable attitudes climbed to a plateau and with repeated exposure held that level through additional exposures.

A question that can be raised is: How do commercials continue to reinforce attitudes people have at the same time when they are beginning to forget what a commercial says? There are two answers to the question. One is that viewers do not completely ignore a commercial, because if they did, they would have no way of knowing whether they had seen it frequently before or not. There is always some awareness or recognition of a commercial, however fleeting, before the person decides to pay attention or not. The second answer is that attitudes are formed from information or knowledge and, once formed, they can persist long after the information behind them has been forgotten. It is even possible for attitudes to be held for some time after advertising has stopped. Recall of an advertising campaign can be short-term, but the attitudes a campaign forms can be maintained for a longer period.

Summary

Table 3

Brand Awareness

Week	Not Exposed %	Light %	Exposed Medium %	Heavy %	Average Exposure %
0	2.9	3.5	3.5	4.0	3.7
4	2.9	5.0	6.5	9.5	7.0
8	3.6	5.3	7.8	9.0	7.7
12	2.9	3.9	5.8	6.8	5.5

Note: The figures given were interpolated from a chart. They may not be exact but the pattern they describe is accurate. The average was computed by giving equal weight to each exposure group.

The consensus is that commercials do wear out and lose their initial effectiveness. Marketing factors contribute to wearout as well as psychological ones. People must perceive what a commercial means before they can evaluate the appeal of the product and act on it.

Viewing television is for the most part a passive and receptive pastime. Viewers pay or withdraw varying amounts of attention depending upon their interest or involvement in what is shown. Repeated exposure is needed for a viewer to learn all he cares to from a commercial. Generally, the subject of most commercials is of little vital interest to him and at some point in time he will recognize a commercial, feel that it no longer is of interest to him, and turn his attention elsewhere. At that time, the viewer, in spite of additional exposure to the commercial, will begin to lose what he learned from the commercial. The attitudes formed on the basis of the commercial, though, are more resistant to wearout and can persist after the viewer has forgotten the content of what a commercial said.

It should be noted that each commercial performs in a unique manner and that there are no firm predictive generalizations to be made about performance and wearout. The data suggest many alternative or possible courses of action for the agency and advertiser, so that it might be well to explore some of these implications. From the research cited, the following can be suggested:

1. Repetition aids consumer learning. A commercial, then, can be scheduled fairly often at the start of a new campaign when the purpose is to establish the new appeal for the product.

2. Repetition should also help establish (build awareness, etc.) products or brands that are new to television.

3. A group or pool of commercials should not wear out as fast as a single commercial given the same overall frequency of exposure. But, there are always production costs to consider.

4. When the number of commercials to be produced is limited and thus in danger of wearing out quickly, one might consider using a subtle approach, introducing nuances or several claims in a commercial to lengthen the learning process—the point being to maintain interest while striking a balance between a straightforward, single claim and a more complicated one.

5. Frequently, several commercials are produced on a single creative theme and the rate that the commercials will wear out does not depend as much on the actual number produced, as on viewer perception of how similar or dissimilar they are. If the viewer discounts the variation from one commercial to another, the group may behave like a single commercial.

6. Commercials whose single point of humor is a gag or punch line apparently wear out quickly.

7. Commercials for infrequently purchased products (a major appliance, an automobile, a camera, carpeting, etc.) may wear out slower than those for everyday products because there is a natural turnover in the market and the commercial audience. At any given time, only a small portion of the population is actively interested in a major purchase, and as these people buy they are replaced by others for whom, in effect, the commercial takes on an air of newness.

8. The greater the time span between commercial airings (or frequency of viewing) the longer a single commercial can run.

9. A commercial that has been running for a while can be removed and reintroduced after a time and take on a sense of newness. But, as we can expect some viewers to recall the earlier flight, we can expect the second flight to wear out faster than the first.

10. Commercials may wear out fast-er among those who are heavy TV viewers, providing, of course, that these people learn equally as fast as light TV viewers.

11. If an advertising budget is light, a single commercial to reinforce learning spread out over time may be better than a pool of commercials which could dissipate the effective presentation of the creative idea.

12. Commercials that seek to involve the viewer and increase his active participation should be effective over a longer time than those which simply present a straightforward product story.

13. As learning generally increases with repeated exposure, copy testing methods predicated on a single viewing usually will not measure the commercial's maximum performance.

14. Studies which measure a commercial's "penetration" at a single point in time do not indicate whether it is in the "generation" or "satiation" phase. Ideally, commercial or campaign performance should be tracked with periodic studies.

15. Finally—only *good* commercials wear out. If wearout means a loss in effectiveness, a commercial that was ineffective to start with cannot lose what it never had.

References

Appel, Valentine. "The Reliability and Decay of Advertising Measurements." Speech to the National Industrial Conference Board, October 28, 1966.

BBD&O Research Department. The Repetition of Advertising. New York: BBD&O, 1967.

"Do TV Commercials Wear Out?" *Tele/Scope Bulletin*. Tele-Research, Inc., February, 1968.

Grass, Robert C. Satiation Effects of Advertising. *Proceedings: 14th Annual Conference*. New York: Advertising Research Foundation, 1968.

Grass, Robert C. and Wallace H. Wallace. Satiation Effects of TV Commercials. *Journal of Advertising Research*, Vol. 9, No. 4, pp. 3-8.

"How Do Consumers Feel About Today's Typical Commercial?" *Tele/Scope Bulletin*. New York: Tele-Research, Inc., 1969.

James, William. *The Principles of Psychology*. New York: Dover Publications, Inc., 1950. (Unabridged 1890 Edition)

Jacobovitz, Leon A. Semantic Satiation in Concept Formation. *Psychological Reports*, Vol. 17, 1965, pp. 113-14.

Krugman, Herbert E. Why Three Exposures May Be Enough. *Journal of Advertising Research*, Vol. 12, No. 6, pp. 11-15.

Krugman, Herbert E. Brain Wave Measures of Media Involvement. *Journal of Advertising Research*, Vol. 11, No. 1, pp. 3-9.

Reeves, Rosser. *Reality in Advertising*. New York: Alfred A. Knopf, Inc., 1961.

"Schneeball Oder Wear Out." *Schwerin Research Corp. Bulletin*. September, 1966.

Steiner, Gary. The People Look at Television. In Barry G. Cole (Ed.). *Television*. New York: 1970.

Steiner, Gary. The People Look at Commercials: A Study of Audience Behavior. *Journal of Business*, Vol. 39, April 1966.

TV Age. "Quest for Boredom." December 18, 1967.

Wallace, Wallace H. "Predicting and Measuring the Wearout of Commercials." Speech to the Kansas City American Marketing Association, April 1, 1970.

Weilbacher, William. What Happens to Advertisements When They Grow Up. *Public Opinion Quarterly*, Vol. 34, Summer 1970, pp. 216-223.

Advertising's main role is
to reinforce feelings of
satisfaction with brands
already bought.

Repetitive Advertising and the Consumer

Andrew S. C. Ehrenberg

Advertising is in an odd position. Its extreme protagonists claim it has extraordinary powers and its severest critics believe them. Advertising is often effective. But it is not as powerful as is sometimes thought, nor is there any evidence that it actually works by any strong form of persuasion or manipulation.

Instead, the sequence, awareness/trial/reinforcement, seems to account for the known facts. Under this theory, consumers first gain awareness or interest in a product. Next, they may make a trial purchase. Finally, a repeat buying habit may be developed and reinforced if there is satisfaction after previous usage.

Advertising has a role to play in all three stages. But for frequently bought products, repeat buying is the main determinant of sales volume and here advertising must be reinforcing rather than persuasive.

These conclusions are based largely on studies of consumer behavior and attitudinal response. They are important both to our understanding of advertising's social role and to the execution and evaluation of advertising as a tool of marketing management.

In this paper I first examine advertising and the consumption of goods in general. I then discuss competition among brands and the factors affecting consumers' brand choice, particularly for established brands of frequently bought goods.

The Demand for Goods

Advertising is widely credited with creating consumer demand. Sol Golden was quoted in 1972 in this *Journal* as saying:

"Advertising is the lynch-pin by which everything in the system hangs together—the consumer benefits, the economic growth, the corporate profits, the technological advancement."

Some years earlier John T. Connor (1966), then Secretary of Commerce, said:

"Without advertising, we most certainly could not have had the unprecedented prosperity of the last 67 months, because advertising is an absolutely indispensable element in the economic mix of the free enterprise system that produced that prosperity.

"We would not have had, without advertising, a drop in unemployment from over 7 per cent to less than 4 per cent."

And we would not have had, without advertising, a rise in unemployment since. Many of advertising's critics from Professor Galbraith downwards also believe it has such powers—to create demand, to manipulate the consumer, to build our acquisitive society. But let us look at these supposed powers.

Product class advertising as a whole –"Buy more cars, " "Drink more tea," etc.–certainly cannot be held responsible for consumer demand. For one thing, there is relatively little of this form of advertising. For another it generally has only minor effects, increasing a market by a few percentage points or slightly slowing a rate of decline. These effects are worthwhile to the producer, but neither can be credited with creating demand or manipulating the consumer on any substantial scale.

The primary target of criticism is repetitive advertising for individual brands–"Buy Fords," "Drink Lipton's Tea," etc. This is where the bulk of mass advertising is concentrated. Such competitive advertising for different brands can lead to a higher level of consumption of the product class as a whole than would exist without it, but there is no evidence that such secondary or even unintended effects are either big or particularly common. There are not even any dramatic claims in the literature (if I have missed one, that is the exception). In many product classes with heavy competitive advertising, total consumption is rising little if at all; in some it is falling. On the other hand, there are many product classes with little if any mass media advertising–like sailboats or marijuana–where consumption is increasing quickly.

Advertising for new products cannot bear the blame for consumer demand either. Undoubtedly advertising can help to speed up the initial adoption of a new product by creating awareness and, indirectly, by gaining retail distribution and display. But advertising works as a lubricant in such cases–to ease and speed things–and not as the prime mover. Getting an initial purchase for a new product is not the point at issue in understanding society's continuing demand for goods.

The key question is whether people continue to buy something *after* they

or their friends and neighbors have used it. This applies equally to frequently bought goods like frozen foods and cigarettes and to once only or once in a while purchases like atomic power stations or lawn mowers, where the satisfied users' influence makes itself felt through word of mouth recommendation over the garden fence (or the industrial equivalent), through retailer and press comments, and so on.

By and large, one cannot go on selling something which people do not like after they have had it. Sometimes people are sold a new kind of product, by advertising or other means, which they find afterwards they did not really want. Some initial sales volume may be created in this way, but generally that is all.

The usual reason why people buy things is that they want them. Anyone who has washed dishes knows that the

A. S. C. Ehrenberg is professor of marketing, London Graduate School of Business Studies, and Director of Aske Research, London and New York, which specializes in the analysis and interpretation of marketing data. He graduated in mathematics from Durham and has held appointments at the Universities of Cambridge, Columbia, Durham, London, Pittsburgh, and Warwick, and in the Attwood and London Press Exchange groups.

demand for nonstick frying pans or dishwashers did not have to be created. Rather, suitable products had to be developed, and then advertising undoubtedly helped to speed their adoption.

There is no need to suppose that the role of advertising here is fundamental. It is a peculiar form of snobbism to suppose that if *other* people want to smoke cigarettes, to smell nice, to have bathrooms, or to drive in motor cars, it is only because they have been manipulated by advertising. Sometimes this view can go as far as John Hobson's statement at his Cantor Lectures (1964):

> "Almost certainly the increase in motoring has been the result of competitive petrol [gasoline] advertising."

The alternative is to suppose that people want to go from A to B, or like driving, or want to get away for weekends, and that rightly or wrongly they often find cars more convenient or pleasing than walking or other forms of transport.

An often-quoted example of the alleged effects of advertising in "creating" demand is the growth of men's toiletries. But this has been part of the great nonadvertised change in men's fashions: clothing, hair styles, etc. Advertising by itself could not have created such a toiletries market 20 or 40 years ago. Instead of leading it, advertising generally follows fashion or product innovation. Anything else would be bad marketing–spending millions to convince people to buy something just because someone can produce it.

The effects of paid advertising on consumer demand must not be confused with the effects of the mass media as such or with people's developing education and greater mobility. People increasingly see how other people live and this has led to vastly increased expectations.

People "want" many things once they have become aware of their existence—food, warmth, good looks, money, power, to drive a car, to be a concert pianist, to avoid washing dishes, etc. Some of these things are very difficult to achieve, others are easier. To acquire goods, one only needs some money, someone to produce them, and a precedent of other people owning them in order to overcome cultural habits or inhibitions.

People go on wanting things because they like them. Increased if highly uneven affluence, increased availability of products, and vastly increased awareness through mass communication and education are three factors which account for the growing acquisitive nature of Western society. The glossy images of affluence shown in advertisements and in the media generally reflect a real demand. Eliminating advertising would not eliminate the demanding consumer.

The products he demands are mostly genuinely wanted or even needed by him. Manufacturers seldom create the needs, but they do attempt to fill them. As a result we have competition and competitive advertising among different brands or makes of the same product. This we now examine in more detail.

Competition and Persuasive Advertising

Most advertising aims to promote a particular brand or make of product in a competitive situation. Because it often takes an emotional instead of an informative tone, such advertising is generally thought to work by persuasion. A typical critic like Boulding (1955), as quoted for instance by Achenbaum (1972) in this *Journal*, wrote in his economics text:

"Most advertising, unfortunately, is devoted to an attempt to build up in the mind of the consumer *irrational preferences for certain brands or goods.* All the arts of psychology—particularly the art of association—are used to persuade consumers that they should buy Bingo rather than Bango."

It is generally recognized that advertising's effects on sales are not necessarily immediate or direct. Instead, it is thought to work through people's attitudes as an intermediary stage to changing their behavior.

Advertising therefore is often thought of as aiming to attach an image or some special consumer benefits to a brand, in an effort to distinguish it from its competitors in the mind of the consumer. This is attempted especially in situations where there are no physical or quality characteristics to differentiate it. Gasoline advertising that stresses "extra mileage," or "smoothness," or "enjoyment," or "power," is a case in point, and Rosser Reeves' Unique Selling Proposition (USP) was an extreme version of the view that advertising can only work by offering buyers of Brand X something which no other similar brand has.

In the last 50 years, various theories have been put forward to try to explain how advertising works, taking attitudes into account (e.g., Joyce, 1967). One simple version is the well-known AIDA model, which stands for the chain:

Awareness → Interest → Desire → Action.

This sequential pattern—or something like it put in different words—is treated as common sense: It only says that people need to be aware of a brand before they can be interested in it, and that they need to desire it before they can take action and buy it. This imputes two roles to advertising: (1) an informational role—making them aware of the product—and (2) a persuasive role—making people desire it before they have bought it.

In its informational role, it might seem that when there are no deeper benefits to guide a consumer's brand choice, he will be influenced by the last advertisement seen or by the general weight of past advertising. This assumption has led to the use of awareness and recall measures in pretesting and monitoring advertisements. But there is little direct evidence that advertising for established brands works like this. The evidence that does exist is either negative (e.g., Achenbaum, 1972) or at best shows effects which are not dramatically large and which still require confirmation (e.g., McDonald, 1970; Barnes, 1971).

In its persuasive role, advertising is thought to create a desire or conviction to buy, or at least to "add value to the brand as far as the consumer is concerned" (e.g., Treasure, 1973). For this reason advertisements take on persuasive methods like creating a brand image, selling a USP, or informing consumers that they need a special product to meet a special need (e.g., a special shampoo for oily hair). But again, there is no empirical evidence that advertising generally succeeds in this aim, when there are no real differences to sell.

In fact, these models of hierarchical or sequential effects have been generally criticized on the grounds of lack of evidence (e.g., Palda, 1966). They also fail to explain many of the known facts.

For example, they do not explain stable markets where shares of advertising and shares of sales are roughly in line for each brand. The small and medium-sized brands survive year-in and year-out, even though their consumers are exposed to vast amounts of advertising for the brand leaders.

Nor do the models account for the situation where, following a drop in sales revenue, advertising expenditure is cut and yet no catastrophe results. If

27

consumers must be continually persuaded to buy a brand, then surely a cut in advertising should turn a minor setback into a major disaster. But it generally is not so.

Again, the models fail to account for the fact that four out of five new brands fail. There is no suggestion that failure occurs less often for highly advertised new brands.

More generally, the models do not explain why advertising generally has only a marginal effect on total demand for a product group; nor why it is only rarely capable of shifting people's attitudes and behavior on social issues like smoking, racial discrimination, voting, etc.

It is not enough to claim that persuasive advertising depends on the quality of the campaign or that advertising in general is inefficient. What is needed is a new explanation of the ways in which advertising actually works.

In recent years a good deal of attention has been paid to alternative explanations of the advertising process, based on mechanisms like satisfaction after previous usage, reinforcement, reduction of dissonance and selective perception. The argument later in this paper is grounded on these processes. But the most direct advances have been in our understanding of consumers' buying behavior and attitudinal responses in a competitive brand situation.

Buyer Behavior

Brand choice and repeat buying are regular and predictable aspects of buyer behavior.

The economic viability of any frequently bought product depends on repeat buying. It follows simple patterns. If 10 per cent of consumers buy Brand X an average of 1.5 times each in a given time period, then in the next time period 45 per cent of that group

can be expected to buy the brand again on an average of 1.8 times each (as modeled for example by the "NBD" theory [e.g., Ehrenberg 1972, Table B4]). This is what is normally found under a wide range of conditions, both for food and nonfood products, in the U.S. and the U.K., for leading brands and smaller ones, and so on.

The 55 per cent who do *not* buy the brand in the second period are however not lost for good. Instead, they are merely relatively infrequent buyers of the brand who buy it regularly but not often. No special efforts have therefore to be made either to bring them back or to replace them (the "leaky bucket" theory). Few things about the consumer in competitive markets can be more important than knowing this, and a successful theory of repeat buying was needed to establish it.

The existence of regular and predictable patterns of repeat buying for a brand however does not mean that people mostly buy one brand only. Instead, the majority of buyers of a brand regularly purchase other brands as well. In general there are relatively few 100 per cent loyal or sole buyers of a brand, especially over any extended period of time. A typical and predictable finding for frequently bought grocery products is that in a week, 80 or 90 per cent of buyers of a brand buy only that brand, that in half a year the proportion is down to 30 per cent, and that in a year, only 10 per cent of buyers are 100 per cent loyal (Ehrenberg, 1972). To expect any substantial group or segment of consumers to be uniquely attracted to one particular selling proposition or advertising platform would therefore generally seem entirely beside the point.

Although many consumers tend to buy more than one brand, this does not signify any dynamic brand switching. Instead, the evidence shows that individual people have a repertoire of

brands, each of which they buy fairly regularly. Consistent clustering or segmentation of the brands over the whole population is however relatively rare. When it occurs, it is usually an *above normal* tendency for buyers of Brand A also to purchase Brand B, compared with the patterns for all the other brands, rather than any special tendency for buyers of one brand not to buy the other (e.g., Collins, 1972). But consumers generally buy brands which are similar as if they were directly substitutable.

In general then, repeat buying and brand switching patterns do not vary materially from one brand or product to another. A particularly simple result is that in a relatively short time period the frequency with which consumers buy a brand varies only marginally within the same product group. The main difference between a leading and a small brand is that the leader has more buyers. With ready-to-eat breakfast cereals, for example, consumers make on average three purchases of a brand over a three-month period. This varies between only 2½ and 3½ for different brands (Charlton, et al, 1972), and this small variation is itself highly predictable from buyer behavior theory, with the larger selling brands being generally bought slightly more frequently by their buyers.

This is what occurs in relatively short time periods. In periods which are very long compared with the product's average purchase cycle (e.g., a year or more), the opposite sort of effect appears to operate because most consumers will have had *some* experience of most brands (even if only a single purchase). This leads to the view that a brand's sales can only increase if people buy it more often (e.g., Treasure, 1973). But in a shorter period, like three months for cereals, higher sales show themselves in terms of having to have more people buy in that period.

These various results are no longer

isolated empirical regularities but are becoming increasingly well explained and integrated into coherent theory (e.g., Ehrenberg, 1972; Goodhardt and Chatfield, 1973). The theory applies primarily when a brand's sales are more or less steady. This holds true most of the time—it is a basic characteristic of the market structure of branded frequently bought products that sales levels are *not* in a constant state of flux.

Occasional trends and fluctuations caused by promotions, etc., may be important from a marketing management point of view, perhaps adding up to five per cent more sales in a year or 20 per cent more in a particular month. But they do not amount to big, dynamic changes in consumer behavior as such. The individual's buying behavior remains broadly characterized as being steady and habitual rather than as dynamic and erratic.

Attitudes and Attitude Change

Since on the whole there are no large behavioral differences among brands except that more people buy one than another, there are not many things that need to be explained by differing motivations and attitudes. In fact, attitudinal responses to branded products tend to be fairly simple.

The evidence shows that most attitudinal variables are largely of an "evaluative" kind, plus some highly specific "descriptive" differences for certain brands (Bird, et al., 1969; 1970; Collins, 1973; Chakrapani and Ehrenberg, 1974).

An "evaluative" response to a brand is equivalent to saying "I like it" or perhaps even only "I have heard of it." Evaluative attitudes therefore differ between users and nonusers of a brand, but they do not differ between brands. For example, 67 per cent of users of Brand A say it has the "right taste" with only six per cent of nonusers of A saying so about it, and 69 per cent of users of Brand B that B has the "right taste" with only five per cent of nonusers of B saying so, and so on, as illustrated in Table 1. Brand A may therefore have more people in all saying it has the "right taste" than Brand B, but only because more people use Brand A, not because its users look at it differently: To give an evaluative response about a brand largely depends on whether or not one is using it.

Certain large exceptions to this pattern occur. These usually reflect some physical "descriptive" characteristics of one particular brand. For example, if a brand is fairly new, consumers tend to be aware of this and dub that brand exceptionally "modern," compared with older brands. If one brand of indigestion remedies can be taken without water and the others not, people notice this and far more regard it as "convenient," as is illustrated for Brand C in Table 1. Promotional policies can also make a brand appear "descriptively" different: A slim cigarette advertised in women's magazines as being smoked by feminine women may be rated more "female" than a standard full-flavored cigarette packaged predominantly in red, with advertisements placed in sporting magazines and featuring cowboys.

A "descriptive" characteristic is usually perceived also by people who do not use the brand. A "female" cigarette will be seen so by people who smoke it and by those who do not. Nonusers of an indigestion remedy which does not require water will *also* regard it as exceptionally "convenient," as for Brand C in Table 1, but they nonetheless do not use it. "Descriptive" differences between one brand and another therefore seldom relate to whether anyone actually *uses* the brand. "Evaluative" responses on the other hand, while distinguishing between users and nonusers, generally do not differentiate one brand from another. Such results are therefore

Table 1
Typical "Evaluative" and "Descriptive" Attitudinal Responses to Different Brands

	Evaluative: E.g., "Right Taste"		*Descriptive (for Brand C):* E.g., "Convenient"	
	Users of the stated brand %	Nonusers of the brand %	Users of the stated brand %	Nonusers of the brand %
Brand A	67	6	19	3
Brand B	69	5	17	2
Brand C	62	4	55	48
Brand D etc.	60	3	17	2

simple but not very helpful in explaining brand choice.

Attitude Change. The conventional results of research into consumers' attitudes show how they feel about products, but not how they *change* their feelings. Very little work has been reported about changes in attitude. What work there is is difficult to interpret (Fothergill, 1968).

It seems to be generally assumed that improving the attitudes of a nonuser towards a brand should make him use the brand, or at least become more predisposed to doing so. But this amounts to assuming that people's attitudes or image of a brand can in fact be readily changed, and that such attitude changes must precede the desired change in behavior. There is little or no evidence to support these assumptions.

The example of a successful change in image that is commonly quoted is for Marlboro cigarettes—few people volunteer another. Marlboro as a brand dates back to the turn of the century. It was considered a "ladies" brand, at one stage holding a major share of the "older society women's market." But in the 1950s, Phillip Morris, the maker, started advertising it very differently, in a male, outdoor manner—Marlboro Country, the Marlboro Man, and the famous tatoo. Sales rose dramatically and Marlboro became a market leader. There is little doubt that Marlboro's advertising had much to do with its success. But there is no evidence that the advertising created a change in "image" or that a change in consumers' attitudes caused the vast increase in sales. The explanation is much simpler.

The change in Marlboro was a change in *product*. The new Marlboro of the 1950s was a standard tipped cigarette, full-flavored, packed in the new flip-top package, with a strong design, and introduced at the start of the growth of the tipped market (the tipped sector of the U.S. market grew

from one per cent in 1950 to more than 60 per cent by the mid-Sixties). For the first half of the century, Marlboro had been expensive, high quality, and with a pink paper wrapper (so as not to show up lipstick). No wonder people thought of it as different.

Subsequent attitude surveys in fact showed that smokers thought of Marlboro not as a ladies cigarette but as male, outdoor, for young people, for people with average jobs, etc. But it did not have a special image—it differed little in these respects from other brands of similar product formulation. It scored extra on points where its advertising was played back (male, outdoor), but these differences—some 11 or 12 percentage points in a recent survey—were "not as great as might have been anticipated," to quote Stephen Fountaine, Phillip Morris' director of marketing research. The change in Marlboro was real—it became a standard tipped cigarette—and not one merely in the mind of the consumer.

Other Factors. Conventional thinking about how advertising works rests on the sequence,

Awareness → Attitudes → Behavior

Although this appears like commonsense, various studies in social psychology have cast doubt on it. There are well-established psychological mechanisms which can act in the opposite direction—with behavior actually affecting attitudes.

For instance, behavior (the act of buying or using a brand) can lead to greater awareness of information to which one is normally exposed (selective perception). Behavior can even lead to the deliberate seeking out of information, and to changes in attitude (notions of congruence and reduction of dissonance). The well known illustration is the study where buyers of Ford cars were found to look at Ford advertisements *after* their purchases. This is common.

Usually a consumer is not convinced

that a brand he has not bought before has all the advantages over the alternatives. To reduce the "dissonance" between what he has done and what he knows or feels, he changes his attitudes after the purchase to make his chosen brand appear adequate. He needs to do this even more if the chosen brand in fact differs little from the others, because there is then no tangible reason or "reward" to justify his choice—e.g., "maybe it is not very good but at least it cost less."

These processes are consistent with the known facts of consumer attitudes, such as those illustrated in Table 1. We will now see how they also fit into the broader picture.

Brand Choice and the Consumer

The consumer's choice among different brands or products is widely thought of as irrational and based on ignorance. This is how advertising is supposed to get its effect:

"The scope of advertising depends on the ignorance of the people to whom it is addressed. The more ignorant the buyer, the more he relies on advertising." (Scitovsky, 1951)

No one doubts or criticizes advertising's role when it is a question of supplying basic information or creating awareness—e.g., a house for sale, a job vacancy, a play at the theatre, or even for a new consumer product. But where advertising is regarded as persuasive rather than informational, there *is* criticism because of the view that the ignorant consumer's choice is influenced by the last advertisement seen or by the brand image he is being told to believe.

But this is all wrong. Buyers of frequently bought goods are not ignorant of them. They have extensive usage experience of the products—after all, they buy them frequently. As we have seen earlier, they usually have direct experience of more than one brand, plus indirect word of mouth knowledge of others. The average housewife is far more experienced in buying her normal products than the industrial purchaser buying an atomic power station. She is also far less likely to make a mistake.

In regarding the private consumer's brand choice as irrational, the view seems to be that if there is little real difference among the brands, then it is not possible to choose rationally among them. This ignores the fact that the consumer *knows* there is little difference and that he *wants* to buy the product. In choosing between similar brands, it is equally rational to choose the same brand as last time, or to deliberately vary it, or even to toss a coin. Any brand would do because the differences do not matter.

Just because Brand X is advertised as having some specific "consumer benefit," it does not follow that anyone buying that brand must have believed or been influenced by that aspect of the advertising.

In practice, people seem to find it simplest to develop repeat buying habits covering a limited repertoire of brands. Our task is to discover and understand the consumer's reasons for choosing brands, instead of imposing our own preconceptions of how he ought to think and behave and dubbing anything else as irrational. The questions are: How do these habits develop, and what is advertising's role in this?

ATR: Awareness, Trial and Reinforcement

Three main steps can account for the known facts of brand choice behavior: (1) gaining awareness of a brand, (2) making a first or trial pur-

chase, and (3) being reinforced into developing and keeping a repeat buying habit.

Some initial awareness of a brand usually has to come first, although occasionally one may find out a brand's name only after buying it. Awareness operates at different levels of attention and interest and can be created in many different ways, of which advertising is clearly one. Awareness may build up into the idea of looking for more information about the brand, asking someone about it, and so on.

A trial purchase, if it comes, will be the next step. This does not require any major degree of conviction that the brand is particularly good or special. Buyers of Brand A do not usually feel very differently about A from how buyers of Brand B feel about B, as was illustrated in Table 1. If that is how one feels afterwards, there is therefore no reason why a consumer should feel strongly about a different brand *before* he has tried it. All that is needed is the idea that one might try it. A trial purchase can arise for a variety of reasons: a cut price offer, an out of stock situation of the usual brand, seeing an advertisement or display, boredom, etc.

After trying a different brand, people usually return to their habitual brands as if nothing had happened. This is so even when new purchasers have been attracted on a large scale, with free samples or an attractive short term promotion (e.g., Goodhardt and Ehrenberg, 1969; Ehrenberg, 1972).

But sometimes a repeat buying habit develops. This is the crucial determinant of long term sales. The way this habit develops for a particular brand is primarily a matter of reinforcement after use. Any feeling of satisfaction—that the brand is liked at least no less than the previously bought ones—has to be nurtured. Evaluative attitudes have to be brought into line with the product class norms. But no exceptional "liking" need arise,

because similar brands are known to be similar and the consumer does not inherently care whether he buys Bingo or Bango (which only matters to the manufacturer).

According to this viewpoint, development of a repeat buying habit remains a fragile process, probably influenced by a variety of almost haphazard factors. The consumer knows there is little to choose between, but he must choose. The critical factor is experience of the brand and no other influences seem to be needed. Thus it has been found that something close to the normal repeat buying habits can develop without any explicit external stimuli such as product differentiation or advertising (Ehrenberg and Charlton, 1973), and preferences for particular price levels can also develop without any external support or manipulation, just by trial and the development of habits (McConnell, 1966; Charlton and Ehrenberg, 1973).

But this process does not in itself determine how *many* people become aware, make a trial purchase, and are reinforced into a repeat buying habit. This—and hence the sales level of a brand—can therefore be influenced by other marketing factors, including advertising.

The Place of Repetitive Advertising

Advertising can act in the various stages of the ATR process.

Firstly, it can create, reawaken, or strengthen awareness. Secondly, it is one of the factors which can facilitate a trial purchase. For an established brand, the consumer may already have been aware of it and even have tried it, but this would have been in the past. The problem is that now he is ignoring the brand and may even be imperceptive of the general run of its advertising. Typically, a special effort like a new product feature, a new package, a new price or special offer, or a new campaign—anything "new"—is needed to give the advertising an edge for this purpose and be noticed. Obtaining awareness and trial for a brand is nonetheless relatively easy.

The difficulty is at the third stage, of turning new triers into satisfied and lasting customers. This generally has to be achieved in the context of consumers already having a repertoire of one or more other brands which they are buying more or less regularly.

What happens in detail is not yet known—do heavy buyers of X switch to being heavy buyers of Y, or is this a gradual process, or is it the *light* buyers who are most easily affected? What is it in fact that advertising has to try and support or accelerate? The knowledge of buyer behavior outlined earlier puts some constraints on the possibilities, but this is one of the purely descriptive features of consumer behavior which is not yet understood.

The process can, however, seldom amount to manipulating the consumer. Real conversion from virgin ignorance to full-blooded, long term commitment does not happen often. A substantial leap forward in sales occurs only once in a while and sales levels of most brands tend to be fairly steady. Trends and even short term fluctuations tend to be smaller and more exceptional than is often thought.

The role of repetitive advertising of well-established brands is therefore predominantly defensive—to reinforce already developed repeat buying habits. The consumer tends to perceive advertising for the brands he is already buying, and repetitive advertising enables the habit to continue to operate in the face of competition. The consumer does not have to be persuaded to think of his habitual brands as better than others, but has to be reinforced in thinking of them as at least no worse.

This view of repetitive advertising—mainly a defensive role of reinforcing

32

existing customers and only occasionally helping to create new customers or extra sales—seems in accord with many of the known facts. It deals also with some of economists' fears about the social costs of advertising and its possibly oligopolistic tendencies (see Doyle, 1968, for a review).

It is consistent with the fact that advertising by itself generally is not very effective in creating sales or in changing attitudes. It also explains why most people feel they are not personally affected by advertising. They are right. Advertising for Brand X does not usually work by persuading people to rush out and buy it.

The primarily reinforcement function of repetitive advertising is in line with the fairly steady sales levels of most brands in most markets. Advertising is not produced by evil men trying to manipulate the consumer. (If it is, these men must be very ineffective.) No one is more eager to cut advertising expenditure than the advertiser himself, who actually has to *pay* for it. For an established brand he sees advertising mainly as a price that has to be paid for staying in business, but he dare not cut it, and he is right (unless *all* manufacturers act together—e.g., aided by government edict, as in the case of TV advertising for cigarettes). For the consumer, large fluctuations in a firm's market share would also not be helpful, in terms of availability, quality control, or lower prices.

According to the ATR model, increasing the amount of advertising would not by itself have much effect on sales, but cutting it is likely to lose sales. This is because some reinforcing action would be withdrawn, allowing competitive brands to gain customers more easily. For an established brand the loss of sales would by definition be quite slow, and no special theory of lagged effects of advertising is needed. Furthermore, reducing an advertising budget *after* a drop in sales to bring the two in line would not necessarily

lead to any further substantial drop in sales. The ATR model is consistent with a more or less constant advertising to sales ratio.

The model also explains the survival of a small brand with a small advertising budget. For its users, the large amount of advertising for a larger brand which they do not use performs no function and generally is not even noticed. When a consumer buys two or more brands, some more heavily advertised than the others, each brand's advertising primarily reinforces that brand and the status quo can continue.

High levels of advertising mostly occur in product fields where consumer demand is strong and the product is easy to supply (because of low capital costs, or excess capacity). This leads to active competition and hence the need to defend one's share of the market, either by price cutting or by heavy advertising.

Economists are frequently concerned that high advertising levels act as a barrier to entry for new brands and hence deter competition. This is wrong on two accounts. Firstly, it is the high risk of *failure* with a new brand that acts as the barrier—"four out of five new products fail." The barrier is spending a million and probably having nothing to show for it. Secondly, heavily advertised product fields are in fact characterized by heavy competition and a high incidence of new brands—but generally launched by firms already in the market. Simply having a million to spend on advertising is not enough; general marketing skills and experience of the other factors in the marketing mix (e.g., a suitable sales force) are also needed.

Remaining Problems

The ATR approach outlined here is no more than a broad verbal statement of how advertising works that seems consistent with the known facts. Detailed quantitative flesh needs to be put on the model, but its differences with the theory of *persuasive* advertising already raise many questions—e.g., about the content of advertising, about the setting of advertising appropriations and the evaluation of advertising, and about product policy.

As regards content for example, use of attitudinal research results to try to improve one's image or to produce persuasive messages of how Brand X is "best" seem mostly to mislead the advertiser and critic rather than the consumer. Advertising research has failed to show that consumers think of their chosen brands as necessarily better than do buyers of *other* brands think of *their*. The consumer needs merely to be told that the brand has all the good properties he expects of the product, and there can be a renewed emphasis on creative advertising telling a good advertising story well.

More generally, since consumers rightly see competitive brands in most product fields as very similar, it seems unnecessary to strive compulsively to differentiate brands artificially from each other. The clutter of marginally different brands, types, and sizes and the corresponding costs of product development and distribution may be unnecessary. This is not a plea for uniformity but for real research into consumers' attitudes and motives to gain a better understanding of their, rather than the advertiser's, needs for product differentiation.

Conclusion

Most mass media advertising is for competitive brands. It is a defensive tool and a price the producer pays to stay in business.

Consumers' attitudes to similar brands are very similar. Purchasers of frequently bought goods usually have experience of more than one brand

and they mostly ignore advertising for brands they are not already using.

It follows that there can be little scope for persuasive advertising. Instead, advertising's main role is to reinforce feelings of satisfaction for brands already being used. At times it can also create new sales by reawakening consumers' awareness and interest in another brand, stimulating them to a trial purchase and then sometimes, through subsequent reinforcement, helping to facilitate the development of a repeat buying habit. This is the main determinant of sales volume.

The Awareness-Trial-Reinforcement model of advertising seems to account for the known facts, but many quantitative details still need elucidation. Such developments could markedly influence the planning, execution, and evaluation of advertising.

With persuasive advertising, the task might be seen as persuading the pliable customer that Brand X is better than other brands. Under the ATR model, advertising's task is to inform the rather experienced consumer that Brand X is as good as others. The language of the advertising copy might sometimes look similar (still "better" or "best"), but the advertiser's aim and expectations would differ.

This paper is based on a report prepared for the J. Walter Thompson Company in New York.

References

Achenbaum, A.A. Advertising Doesn't Manipulate Consumers. *Journal of Advertising Research*, Vol. 12, No. 2, pp. 3-13.

Barnes, M. *The Relationship Between Purchasing Patterns and Advertising Exposure.* London: J. Walter Thompson Co., 1971.

Bird, M., C. Channon, and A.S.C. Ehrenberg. Brand Image and Brand Usage. *Journal of Marketing Research*, Vol. 7, 1969, pp. 307-314.

Bird, M. and A.S.C. Ehrenberg. Consumer Attitudes and Brand Usage. *Journal of the Market Research Society*, Vol. 12, 1970, pp. 233-247; Vol. 13, pp. 100-1, 242-3; Vol. 13, pp. 57-8.

Boulding, K. *Economic Analysis.* New York: Harper and Row, 1955.

Chakrapani, T.K. and A.S.C. Ehrenberg. "The Pattern of Consumer Attitudes." AAPOR Conference, Lake George, May 1974.

Charlton, P., A.S.C. Ehrenberg, and B. Pymont. Buyer Behaviour Under Mini-Test Conditions. *Journal of the Market Research Society*, Vol. 14, 1972, pp. 171-183.

Charlton, P. and A.S.C. Ehrenberg. McConnell's Experimental Brand-Choice Data. *Journal of Marketing Research*, Vol. 11, 1973, pp. 302-07.

Collins, M.A. Market Segmentation— The Realities of Buyer Behaviour. *Journal of the Market Research Society*, Vol. 13, 1971, pp. 146-157.

Collins, M.A. The Analysis and Interpretation of Attitude Data. Market Research Society, Course on Consumer Attitudes, Cambridge, March 1973.

Connor, J.T. "Advertising: Absolutely Indispensable." Address before the Cleveland Advertising Club, Cleveland, Ohio. New York: American Association of Advertising Agencies, 1966.

Doyle, P. Economic Aspects of Advertising: A Survey. *The Economic Journal*, Vol. 78, 1966, pp. 570-602.

Ehrenberg, A.S.C. *Repeat-Buying: Theory and Applications.* Amsterdam: North Holland; New York: American Elsevier, 1972.

Ehrenberg, A.S.C. *Data Reduction.* London and New York: John Wiley, 1974.

Ehrenberg, A.S.C. and P. Charlton.

The Analysis of Simulated Brand-Choice. *Journal of Advertising Research*, Vol. 13, No. 1, 1973, pp. 21-33.

Ehrenberg, A.S.C. and F.G. Pyatt (Eds.). *Consumer Behavior*. London and Baltimore: Penguin Books, 1971.

Fothergill, J.G. Do Attitudes Change Before Behaviour? *Proceedings of ESOMAR Congress, Opitija*. Amsterdam: ESOMAR, 1968.

Goodhardt, G.J. and C. Chatfield. The Gamma-Distribution in Consumer Purchasing. *Nature*, Vol. 244, No. 5414, pp. 316.

Goodhardt, G.J. and A.S.C. Ehrenberg. Evaluating a Consumer Deal. *Admap*, Vol. 5, 1969, pp. 388-93.

Hobson, J. The Influence and Techniques of Modern Advertising. *Journal of the Royal Society of Arts*, Vol. 112, 1964, pp. 565-604.

Joyce, T. *What Do We Know About How Advertising Works?* London: J. Walter Thompson Co., 1967.

McConnell, J.D. The Development of Brand Loyalty: An Experimental Study, and The Price-Quality Relationship in an Experimental Setting. *Journal of Marketing Research*, Vol. 5, 1968, pp. 13-19 and pp. 300-03.

McDonald, C.D.P. What Is the Short-Term Effect of Advertising? *Proceedings of the ESOMAR Congress, Barcelona*. Amsterdam: ESOMAR, 1970.

Palda, K.S. The Hypothesis of a Hierarchy of Effects: A Partial Evaluation. *Journal of Marketing Research*, Vol. 3, 1966, pp. 13-24.

Scitovsky, T. *Welfare and Competition*. Chicago: Richard Irwin, 1951.

Treasure, J.A.P. The Volatile Consumer. *Admap*, Vol. 9, 1973, pp. 172-182.

MICHAEL L. RAY and ALAN G. SAWYER*

Recent advertising media models demand estimates of effects of repetitive exposures on consumers in particular advertising situations. A laboratory technique for providing such estimates is suggested, and a study using this technique indicates the need for significantly different repetition functions for different kinds of products, brand positions, advertising formats, and advertising goals. Further development of the technique is also indicated.

Repetition in Media Models: A Laboratory Technique

The problem of repetition in advertising is easy to state but difficult to solve. Managers are never certain exactly how repetition operates in any given advertising situation: for example, should an ad be run for a long time without change, or will frequent changes be needed? To slightly bend an old advertising statement often attributed to John Wanamaker: "I know my advertising works with repetition. The trouble is I don't know when and how and why." [1]

The problem, therefore, is that advertisers have had to rely almost completely on judgment to decide how often, how long, and in what media combinations to run an ad or campaign. Copy tests give some information on whether one ad is "better" than another, but not on the effectiveness of alternative advertising approaches repeated over time. In fact, there is some suspicion that an ad which does well in a single exposure copy test does not do well with repetition [18, 31, 33, 35].

Recent developments in advertising media models further highlight the need for better information on how particular advertising will operate with repetition. Until recently, media models have not had the capability to input differential repetition functions for different advertising situations which exist in a single run of the

* Michael L. Ray is Assistant Professor of Marketing, Stanford, University, and Alan G. Sawyer is Assistant Professor of Marketing, State University of New York at Buffalo. The field work and analysis were partially supported by a grant to Stanford from the American Association of Advertising Agencies Educational Foundation. The mobile unit used in the project was provided by Foote, Cone & Belding. The authors wish to express their appreciation to William Massy, co-director of the AAAA project, and Gerald Eskin for their invaluable help in data analysis.

model. Some early models [5, Chapter 5] did not even take repetition into account; they assumed all exposures were equivalent. Other early models used one simple function, such as Kotler's [17], based on a general assumption, such as decreasing economies of scale.

More recent models such as MEDIAC [21] or POMSIS [1] have provided for different repetition functions for different market segments within the entire media schedule. With POMSIS, for instance, every market segment or every individual represented in the model can have a different function. Another model, FOCUS [34], gives nine different exponential curves to represent the estimated effect of each ad campaign over repeated exposures within each market segment.

Management science has clearly provided advertising decision makers with models potentially flexible enough to take almost any estimated effect of repetition into account. It is now time for behavioral science to provide means of obtaining better information with which to estimate repetition effect.

This article suggests an approach to provide this information for advertising planners using media models. It discusses the kind of repetition information needed by advertising planners, the kind presently available, and results and implications of some experimental research on a laboratory technique designed to provide better data on repetition effect for specific advertising situations.

PAST RESEARCH ON REPETITION

Ideally the advertising planner should have specific information about advertising repetition. Media models

[1] The original Wanamaker statement was purported to be: "I know half the money I spend on advertising is wasted, but I can never find out which half" [26, p. 259].

allow specificity by advertising situation, and have begun to treat the problems of overlap and cumulative audiences [1, 2, 3, 7, 27]. Thus the planner now has a reasonable idea of the proportions of his audience that will be exposed to each media vehicle a given number of times. In other words, it is possible to think of the repetition problem in terms of the number of individual exposures, instead of the rather gross consideration of number of dollars or insertions in various media.

Keeping these developments in mind, it is easy to see that the planner needs to know the level, shape, and slope of the repetition function for various advertising situations. The repetition function is here defined as the relationship between exposures and effect, i.e., number of advertising exposures under natural conditions and effect in terms of advertising goals (awareness, comprehension, conviction, action, etc.). The advertising situation is defined as all those variables that could influence repetition effect: audience or segment; product or topic; marketing environment (including competitive effects); advertising appeal, format, media, and schedule.

Unfortunately, despite the great amount of research on repetition in both the social sciences and marketing, research provides little more than general guidelines for the advertising planner and virtually no data on the repetition function for specific advertising situations. As seen in the table, each type of research fails to provide adequate repetition data in some important way.

and frequency are already available for media models, it would be extremely wasteful to use expenditures or insertion frequency to estimate repetition effect.

Advertising Survey or Panel Studies

Such studies also are inadequate because the independent variable of repetition is poorly defined. In these studies [8, 10, 25] consumers are asked about exposure and recall of a brand's advertising. The general assumption is that a strong report actually indicates a great number of exposures, when in fact the strength of the report could be based on a favorable attitude about the brand resulting from a consumer's experiences apart from the advertising campaign under study. Despite excellent attempts to analytically control for these confusing correlational effects, they remain a problem. Moreover, these studies have not examined the relation between repetition and particular advertising approaches.

Advertising Field Experiments

These have the advantage of offering better control of repetitive exposure than the previous types of research, but that control is not so perfect as some marketers might believe. Also, field experiments are too expensive and time consuming to provide specific information on a wide variety of advertising situations. In these studies, segments within a media audience—market areas, parts of market areas, or other experimental groupings—are

REPETITION RESEARCH APPROACHES

Type of study	Exposure control	Typical measure	Repetition stimuli	Relative cost
Econometric or campaign insertion	Very weak	Sales	Insertions or dollar expenditures	Moderate
Advertising survey or panel	Weak	Claimed purchase	Advertising campaign	High
Advertising field experiment	Moderate	Sales	Single or multiple ads	Very high
Advertising lab	Absolute	Attitude	Single ads	Low
Psychological, verbal learning	Absolute	Learning	Nonsense syllables, numbers	Low

Econometric or Campaign Insertion Studies

These studies are inadequate because they provide no real information on the effects of repeated exposures to individuals. Instead, these nonexperimental studies examine the effects of increased advertising expenditures [36, 37, 40, 43] or increased numbers of insertions of the campaign in the media [24, 35] on advertising payout, usually in terms of sales or some kind of purchasing response. Both expenditure and insertion are poor independent variables of repetition, because they are as likely to increase reach as to increase frequency of exposure of a campaign; sometimes increased expenditure does not even signal an increase in reach, as when advertising is moved to media requiring greater space and production costs. Since adequate data on gross reach

randomly assigned various weights or schedules of advertising [38, 41, 42, 47]. Although this technique provides moderate control of exposure weight by achieving differential *probabilities* of exposure across experimental groups, increased numbers of advertising insertions can still lead to increased reach rather than increased frequency of exposure.

Advertising and Psychological Laboratory Experiments

These final two types of repetition research listed in the table differ sharply from campaign and field research. Lab research is the only kind that allows the complete control over exposure needed for making repetition estimates. A lab study can show that a respondent has actually been exposed a given number of times to a specific stimulus, and this kind of study can be done quickly and cheaply. The problem, of course, is that exposure is artificial in a laboratory, and there is inadequate information about how lab results may relate to actual exposure in the field under more natural conditions. This problem is especially acute for lab studies that vary the number of exposures of nonsense syllables or numbers [11, 15, 16, 23, 28, 44, 46] rather than of advertising [12, 19, 20, 22, 29, 39]. Even those lab studies that use advertising as stimuli seldom explicitly vary ad dimensions that might significantly change the repetition function.

A SUGGESTED LABORATORY TECHNIQUE

Because of the inadequacies of the types of research discussed above, it is difficult to make any solid generalizations about the effect of advertising repetition. Lab studies and some field experiments have established that repetition has an effect which seems to be stronger for awareness or learning measures than for attitude change, intention, or purchasing responses. The general nature of the repetition function in advertising appears to be some sort of modified negative exponential curve, similar in shape to that found in verbal learning studies [11]. A typical feature of advertising curves is some point of diminishing returns.

But these general indications do not help the planner estimate the nature of repetition effect in a specific situation. Here some technique is needed to quickly and inexpensively show reactions to advertising with repetition. The technique should produce reasonable repetition results that can be validated in the field.

The primary goal of the technique to be suggested here is to eventually provide inputs to media models of the sort discussed above. Thus the technique should quickly and reasonably test any advertising in any situation and should be as free as possible of biases normally found in lab research. Respondents should come from the target group of the advertising. They should view the advertising in as natural a way as possible without too much or too little attention directed to it; otherwise the control and effect are lost. In addition, responses should be measured in several ways so that the nature of repetition effects can be studied in detail and lab results can be related easily to normal advertising goals. With these requirements, the technique should produce meaningful and valid results.

The approach tested in the following study meets all these requirements to a greater extent than approaches used in any previously published study of repetition effect. The technique is based on a single session, after-only design with a cover that allows multiple exposures and measurement of response under relatively natural conditions.

With this method the research is done in a mobile unit parked in a shopping center, rather than in a university or a business lab. It is necessary to "move the lab to the field" to obtain respondents more representative of the advertising's target audience than the usual lab study group. The mobile unit is identified as the "Shopping of the Future Project," and shoppers are asked to step into the unit to see a demonstration of what shopping in the future might be like.

Thus repetition, advertising, and specific products and brands are not emphasized; respondents have no indication that they are to be tested on anything but their opinions of the demonstration.

After entering the unit, respondents are given a reasonably involved one-page description of futuristic shopping with a cable television-terminal-telephone system that would allow home shopper control of display, information, and ordering on a full range of products and services. The last two paragraphs of the description indicate the kind of set the respondents are given before seeing any advertising:

> Obviously we cannot show you a system anywhere nearly as sophisticated as the system we have just described. However, we have tried to approximate the manner in which products will be exhibited to a home shopper. We would like to get some idea of your overall reactions to such a system.
>
> In this demonstration, product advertisements will be presented on the screen in front of you, one after another. Let us assume, for this demonstration, that you do not have anything special in mind and that you are merely doing some general shopping.... Quite a few products will be shown. You might look at the advertisements as you probably look at advertisements in a magazine or on television—paying more attention to ads and products that appeal to you and less to those in which you are less interested. Try to regard these product advertisements as you would normally.

The respondents are then shown the demonstration, a stream of messages which can be presented in a variety of forms or media on a futuristic-looking rear-screen projector with sound system. The "Shopping of the Future" setting allows a "demonstration" with almost any kind of communications for almost any product, service, or topic. Message repetition can be achieved within a natural competitive environment, a mixture of messages that can be manipulated to match the competitive environment advertising is likely to face in the media. The research also has the option of allowing respondents to control the duration of message exposure.

Following the demonstration, respondents fill out a questionnaire, ostensibly to elicit their reactions to the demonstration. In fact, only the first page is directly related to the shopping method, but those questions back up the "Shopping of the Future" cover and provide an interpolated activity to decrease unnatural retention typical in a lab study.

Later pages call for unaided recall of the demonstration's advertising, an attitude scale evaluation of a number of brands in product categories (including those repeated in the demonstration), and a selection of brands the respondent might purchase in those categories. Finally respondents fill out a page of classification questions and receive a "thank you" booklet of coupons for price reductions on items in the shopping center. If appropriate products are being tested, a coupon booklet could be keyed to experimental treatments and used as a measure of purchasing activity generated by repetitive advertising exposures.

This general technique, then, can gauge response to repetitive advertising exposure under conditions which minimize lab-induced bias.

AN EXPERIMENT: CONVENIENCE VERSUS SHOPPING GOODS

While several alternative advertising approaches for a single brand would normally be tested with the lab technique, in developmental studies such as the one reported here, a relatively large number of ads for different brands and products are used. A large sample of ads allows examination of how sensitive responses in the lab are to repetition results and whether or not there are differences in the repetition results for different advertising situations. If the ads are picked carefully, they can also provide evidence of face or content validity [6, 9, 32]; i.e., it is possible to pick ads which represent some dimension of advertising expected to operate in a specific way with repetition. If lab repetition results match expectations for the dimensions, then the technique has face validity. In addition, such findings themselves would constitute important guidelines for planners.

One obviously important dimension of advertising is the type of product being advertised, e.g., convenience, shopping, or specialty good; consumer or industrial product; durable or nondurable; high-priced or low-priced. In this study the difference was between convenience and shopping goods, since the function of advertising and therefore of repetition is often suggested to be different for these two product types.

The basic assumption about these two product types, e.g., [4, pp. 70–9, 190] is that consumers typically seek more information for purchases of higher-priced shopping goods from sources other than advertising, such as salesmen and friends. However, while advertising is often assumed to be relatively unimportant in such cases, it is often mentioned as the prime source of the little information used in convenience goods shopping.

All this leads to the hypothesis that repetition could be effective for convenience goods advertising in terms of producing effects on advertising awareness, but not for shopping goods. The point of diminishing returns in effects on awareness is predicted to come sooner for shopping goods advertising than for convenience goods, a difference predicted to be even more pronounced for attitude and purchase intention measures. While repetition would not be expected to have very much effect in general on attitude or purchase intention measures, it should have almost no effect with regard to shopping

goods and a moderate effect with regard to convenience goods. It was assumed that only a small number of respondents would be in the market for a shopping good at any particular time and that, even among that group, there would be a limit to advertising's value in affecting preliminary shopping decisions.

Beyond these predictions about differences between convenience and shopping goods, individual advertisements in the study were expected to yield significantly different repetition results. Such gross differences would be a minimum condition for recommending the lab technique as practical for estimating multiple exposure effects of different advertising situations.

Method

With the lab technique described generally earlier, the specific aspects of method were as follows.

Test advertising. Eighteen printed advertisements were selected to represent the convenience and shopping goods classifications. The first group consisted of single ads for Lavoris, Listerine, and Speak Easy breath preparations; Lava, Ivory, and Phase III soaps; and Campbell, Lipton, and Snow's soups. The second group consisted of single ads for Bali, Exquisite Form, and Vassarette foundation garments; Panasonic, Sharp, and Sony portable television sets; and General Electric, Maytag, and Whirlpool washing machines. These ads were selected to be different between the two classifications and to maximize the differences among the three ads from each of the six product classes. It was felt that the three ads within each product class were as competitive as those in the mass media.

Respondents and experimental treatments. There were 168 respondents located and defined by interviewers in a large shopping center as "adult female shoppers," from 20 to 65 years old. Half of them saw a "Shopping of the Future" slide demonstration containing the nine convenience goods test ads, and the other half saw a showing with the nine shopping goods test ads. There were six repetition conditions of one to six exposures. Ads were rotated around repetition conditions in a Latin square design, so that each ad appeared in each repetition condition an equal number of times. In the "Shopping of the Future" demonstration, there were 20 filler ads, each exposed once during each showing. We used a computer program to randomly order the test and filler ads with these constraints: the first and last two in the series had to be fillers, no single ad could appear any closer than five positions from its previous exposure, and no ad could appear any closer than two positions from the previous exposure of either of the other ads in the same product class. The total slide presentation had between 50 and 53 ten-second exposures, close to nine minutes in total time.

Measures. The recall item merely asked respondents to play back, in any order, anything about the advertising they could remember. This was followed by a gen-

Figure 1

RECALL, ATTITUDE, PURCHASE INTENTION,
AND COUPON RESPONSE[a]

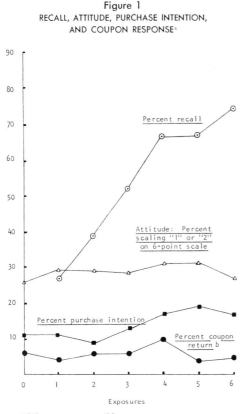

[a] 252 responses per condition.
[b] For convenience goods only, 126 responses per condition.

eral brand evaluation or attitude scale, which required responses on six brands for all six product categories involved. The 168 women indicated whether they felt each listed brand was: best, one of the best, acceptable, don't know, unacceptable, or one of the worst. The next question, on purchase intention, asked them to indicate for all six product categories which brand they would buy if they were shopping for the product. Estimates of the number of times ads were repeated were then asked for (this was the only point that repetition of specific test ads was mentioned). Finally, respondents filled out a page of classification questions and were given the coupon booklet for purchases of the three convenience goods products plus liquid diet products. The coupons were keyed to experimental treatments. Since all respondents were asked about attitudes and purchase intentions for all brands and products, the overall study

had an after-only design with control responses for the convenience group coming from the shopping group questionnaires and vice-versa. The questionnaire took 10 to 20 minutes to complete.

RESULTS AND DISCUSSION

A separate analysis of variance was done for each of the three key study measures—recall, attitude, and purchase intention. This was a mixed effects analysis design with nesting [13, 45]. The key variables in the analysis were the main effect of repetition (5 d.f.) and the interaction of repetition with:

1. The convenience-shopping product classification (5 d.f. for the interaction)
2. The product categories (a random variable nested within the classifications, 20 d.f. for the interaction)
3. Advertisements (a random variable nested within product categories and classifications, 60 d.f. for the interaction).

The results of the analysis of variance (including trend analysis) for repetition and the three key interactions are discussed below. Regression analysis was then used to perform a post hoc analysis of the advertising and audience factors that affected repetition effect in this study.

The Main Effect of Repetition

Figure 1 shows that the lab environment did produce significant repetition effects. The strongest effect was on recall measure ($F = 21.9$, 5, and 20 d.f., $p < .001$). A trend analysis within the analysis of variance indicated that both the linear and the quadratic trends for recall were significant ($p < .01$ and .05, respectively), thus indicating some deviation from a linear trend toward the modified exponential curve of repetition effect on recall found in past repetition studies. The leveling in effect at four exposures that seems to exist in this study has been observed in other laboratory studies of repetition [20].

As was expected, repetition affected other measures less than recall. In fact, only the purchase intention measure showed any statistically significant effect of repetition ($F = 3.8$, 5, and 20 d.f., $p < .05$). The effect of repetition on attitude was not statistically significant, perhaps because it was so easy for respondents to check "don't know" for the attitude scaling. Respondents tended to scale only those brands which they had actually used, which meant that their scalings were somewhat constrained toward the high end of the six-point attitude continuum. The coupon return measure was also not affected by repetition, probably because the return rate was quite low, much lower than that reported for this measure in the past [14, 30].

Thus while the study left the job of developing sensitive attitude and coupon-action measures unaccomplished, the recall and purchase intention measures did produce the expected results. There did seem to be a differential repetition effect across measures in the lab.

And, more importantly, these were measures representing a wide range of goals for advertising.

Convenience-Shopping Goods Interaction

The hypothesis here was that the repetition curve for shopping goods advertising would level off sooner than that for convenience goods advertising. For recall this prediction meant an earlier leveling off; for attitude and purchasing measures, the prediction was for no effect for the shopping goods advertising.

As can be seen in Figure 2, the predictions were supported. The product classification linear interaction with repetition was significant at the .05 level for both recall ($F = 5.19$, 1 and 20 d.f.) and purchase intention ($F = 5.11$, 1 and 20 d.f.). Although the attitude results were in the direction of the prediction, they were not statistically significant and are not shown in Figure 2.

While there were differences in the predicted direction, there was some question as to how much an artifact of the lab setting may have caused them. One possibility was that respondents saw shopping goods advertising as inadequate in the "Shopping of the Future" setting. But this rival hypothesis did not hold for recall scores of respondents who indicated they would use this method for shopping goods and gift shopping. The repetition results for these shoppers were not significantly different from those for other respondents. Also, the average number of filler ads recalled remained about equal across experimental groups, indicating that the shopping goods group did not ignore ads in general.

Product Category Interactions

No specific prediction was made about the effect of repetition on the six product categories: breath fresheners, soap, soup, foundation garments, portable television sets, and washing machines. Although it was assumed that there would be some effect of the product category beyond that of the convenience-shopping goods effect, we did not specify the nature of this effect. In fact, there was no significant interaction with product category in this study. This means that with the analysis design in this study a major proportion of product differences in repetition was accounted for by the convenience-shopping goods difference. This does not mean, however, that other product differences do not have an effect; some of these differences are explored in the next section.

Advertisement Interactions

The interaction between advertisements and repetition was significant for both recall ($F = 1.8$, 60 and 1,404 d.f., $p < .01$) and purchase intention ($F = 1.5$, 60 and 1,404 d.f., $p < .01$). This indicated that the laboratory approach may be a viable one for studying repetition effect differences between individual ads as well as the differences between groups of ads.

In this study, of course, individual ad results were not

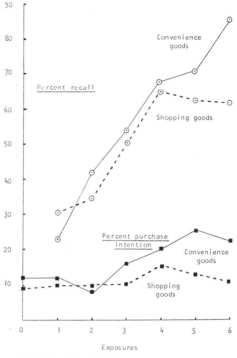

Figure 2
CONVENIENCE AND SHOPPING GOODS AD RESULTS[a]

[a] 126 responses per condition.

greatly important beyond their significant interaction with repetition. Because there were a number of ads in the study, however, they could be grouped and analyzed by regression analysis, to determine what underlying characteristics affect repetition effect for this set of advertisements. The following were independent variables:

1. *Repetition.* This was expressed as a linear function (0, 1, 2, 3, 4, 5, and 6 represented the repetition conditions).
2. *Ad characteristics.* Six types were utilized: (1) convenience or shopping goods product, (2) color or black and white ad, (3) long or short copy, (4) well known brand or lesser known, (5) brand emphasized or not, (6) "grabber" or not. All of these were dummy variables with one and zero values respectively. The last two variables were determined by three judges associated with the study, the other four variables were based on some relatively objective criterion (e.g., whether the ad was in color or black and white).
3. *Audience characteristics.* These were: (1) whether

or not the respondent reported using the brand; (2) whether or not she said she would use the "Shopping of the Future" method for shopping goods shopping; (3) whether or not she mentioned repetition in response to a general question on the study.

4. *Interactions with repetition effect.* Nine variables consisting of the interactions of the ad and audience characteristics with repetition.

Once an important repetition effect is established, the most crucial aspect of such a regression analysis is interaction. If a variable interacts with repetition at a significant level, then this variable should be considered further in prediction. In this analysis, none of the audience characteristic variables produced significant interactions

Figure 3
AD RESULTS FOR WELL KNOWN AND LESSER KNOWN BRANDS[a]

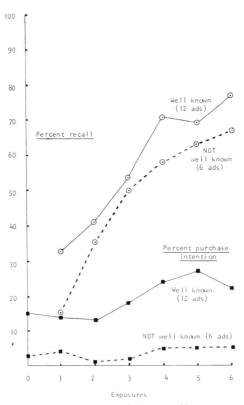

Percent recall

Well known (12 ads)

NOT well known (6 ads)

Percent purchase intention

Well known (12 ads)

NOT well known (6 ads)

Exposures

[a] 168 and 84 responses, respectively, per condition.

with repetition on either the recall or purchase intention dependent variables. But three of the ad characteristic variables—shopping-convenience and well known and "grabber" ads—produced significant interactions at the .05 level or better. The shopping-convenience goods interactions have already been discussed. The well known and "grabber" interactions are of some interest at this point, because they are important characteristics to consider in making repetition estimates.

Figure 3 shows results for well known and lesser known brands' ads on recall and purchase measures. For recall, the slopes of the two curves do not differ significantly. Perhaps the most interesting finding is that the recall curve with repetition for lesser known brands is very much like the negatively accelerated curve which has often been found for nonsense syllable learning [11]. On purchase intention, there is a significant difference in the slope of the repetition curve for the two types of brands ($t = 3.59$, 1,489 d.f., $p < .01$) with the well known brands showing some positive effect of repetition and the lesser known brands showing virtually no effect.

These results are not too different from what managers normally expect for new and old products. Ads for well known brands should be expected to start at higher levels for both recall and purchase intention. While the slopes in terms of ad recall might be much alike given equivalent exposures, the slope for purchase intention should be sharper for well known brands under these conditions. It should, in other words, take a great number of exposures for consumers to shift their purchase intentions toward the initially less well known brands. Thus these results seem reasonable and worthy of further consideration in terms of media model repetition functions.

Another significant difference in repetition curves depended on the "grabber" variable. Grabber ads were defined by three judges as different enough in format to attract attention and accomplish some communication in a single exposure. Aside from this strong single-exposure performance, however, the grabber ad was hypothesized to do relatively poorly over repetition. Its intrusive uniqueness was not expected to last in repeated exposures. The grabber and nongrabber distinction might be compared to the hard-sell and soft-sell distinction often mentioned in advertising, and the grabber hypotheses for this analysis were similar to those indicated by Herbert Krugman for hard sell [18, p. 629]:

> Hard-sell copy is intended to be clear and direct in its message. Little is left to chance, to the viewer, or to changed meanings with repetition. If the message is right, fine; if not, not so fine. It is a more complete sales piece. When repeated, it may still be "right," but in its simplicity it may have a "nagging" quality that makes it less liked even as the nagging is acted upon as right or sound.

It should be remembered that the grabber judgments in this study were quite subjective when compared to those for other groupings for the regression analysis. But the grouping did provide some differences in repetition effect which should be considered. The results for the recall measure, shown in Figure 4, are not significantly different. The purchase intention repetition curves were significantly different, however, and this difference indicated that the nongrabber group benefited more from repetition ($t = 3.70$, 1,489 d.f., $P < .01$). This was in line with the hypothesis that the distinctive, hard-sell, grabber advertisements would not fare well with repetition.

Ivory Versus Phase III Differences

The results for grabber ads and, to some extent, for well known brands are representative of reversals in repetition results across measures that should be seriously considered in estimating repetition functions in media models. In this study there were often reversals in the sense that one ad or group of ads (e.g., grabbers) would do well with repetition on the ad recall measure and then would produce an inferior repetition result on the attitude or purchase intention measure.

This result is extremely important for the repetition function in media models, because it means that this function should vary according to the goals of the advertising, such as awareness, comprehension, attitude, purchase intention, action, etc. It is significant that most discussions of media models do not explicitly take this into account. The criterion in these models is usually exposures weighted by judgment according to the goals of advertising management, often called "rated exposure values" or "weighted exposures." Although these goals are often quite different from simple ad recall, the repetition function selected for these models is similar to that found in learning or recall studies. The reversal results in this study indicate that the repetition functions in media models should be specific to the advertising goal and often may be quite different when the goals are changes in purchase intention as opposed to recall.

The results for the Ivory and Phase III soap ads in this study offer a good example of the kind of reversals across measures that occurred at several points. In the terms already used, the Ivory ad was a nongrabber ad for a well known brand, because it had a rather common headline and an ordinary illustration featuring a mother and child. Phase III, however, had a bold claim about a new, lesser known product and represented this claim with a large headline and an unusual illustration featuring bars of soap bolted together. This ad was classified as a grabber.

Figure 5 illustrates that these differences led to a reversal in results across measures. Repetition seemed to have had a great effect on the recall scores for the Phase III ad, but not quite so great for the Ivory ad. For attitude and purchase intention, the relationship between the ads was reversed: the Ivory ad benefited from repetition for these measures, while repetition seemed to

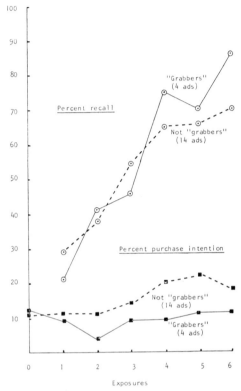

Figure 4
"GRABBER" AND "NOT GRABBER" AD RESULTS[a]

[a] 56 and 196 responses, respectively, per condition.

have a zero or negative effect on the results for the Phase III ad.

A separate analysis of variance for these two ads indicated that the ad repetition interactions for the attitude and purchase intention measures were significant at the .05 level or better, even though sample sizes were quite small (14 respondents per ad repetition condition). These results have been partially replicated in later studies.

This reversal—Phase III somewhat superior to Ivory in terms of recall but significantly poorer in terms of attitude and purchase intention—is quite logical considering the differing communication goals for well known and lesser known products. A product like Phase III must concentrate on building awareness and so must use grabber-type advertising. A well established product

Figure 5
IVORY AND PHASE III RESULTS[a]

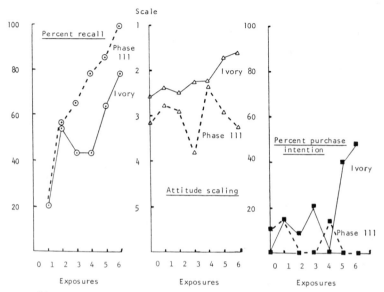

[a] 14 responses per condition.

like Ivory can capitalize on its past reputation with rather ordinary ads that result in adequate persuasion even at relatively low levels of exposure. The obvious indication is that the repetition function in media models for these two brands should be different, depending on the goals of the advertiser. The Ivory-Phase III case is not just an isolated example. There were several results in the study that indicated that adequate lab estimates of repetition effect could not be accomplished without using several measures.

LIMITATIONS AND IMPLICATIONS

The study reported in this article is an illustration of the kinds of results that can be achieved with a lab technique for studying repetition effect and for improving the inputs or repetition functions for media models. The results indicate that managers should consider different sorts of repetition functions and, indeed, different media strategies depending upon the product classification (convenience vs. shopping good), brand position (well known, Ivory vs. Phase III), advertising format (grabber, Ivory vs. Phase III), and advertising goals (recall vs. attitude or purchase intentions).

It is likely that other studies using the lab technique would find other differences that should be considered

by builders and users of media models. But the findings in the lab should not be accepted without further validation, especially validation against the field. While this study was done with considerable care and contained several innovations to make it more realistic and unbiased, it still used a lab technique. The suggestions of this article are not that these results from the lab should be accepted blindly, but rather that such lab approaches must be developed and validated to meet the increasing capacities of media models and needs of managers making advertising decisions.

REFERENCES

1. Aaker, David A. "On Methods: A Probabilistic Approach to Industrial Media Selection," *Journal of Advertising Research*, 8 (September 1968), 46–55.
2. Agostini, Jean-Michel. "How to Estimate Unduplicated Audiences," *Journal of Advertising Research*, 1 (March 1961), 11–4.
3. ————. "Analysis of Magazine Accumulative Audience," *Journal of Advertising Research*, 2 (December 1962), 24–7.
4. Bogart, Leo. *Strategy in Advertising*. New York: Harcourt, Brace & World, 1967.
5. Buzzell, Robert D. *Mathematical Models and Marketing Management*. Boston: Division of Research, Graduate School of Business Administration, Harvard University, 1964.

6. Campbell, Donald T. "Recommendations for APA Test Standards Regarding Construct, Trait, or Discriminant Validity," *American Psychologist*, 15 (April 1960), 546–53.

7. Claycamp, Henry J. and Charles W. McClelland. "On Methods: Estimating Reach and the Magic of K," *Journal of Advertising Research*, 8 (June 1968), 44–51.

8. Coffin, Thomas E. "A Pioneering Experiment in Assessing Advertising Effectiveness," *Journal of Marketing*, 27 (July 1963), 1–10.

9. Committee on Psychological Tests. "Technical Recommendations for Psychological Tests and Diagnostic Techniques," *Psychological Bulletin*, Supplement, 51 (March 1954), 201–38.

10. Day, George S. "Attitude Change and the Influence of Brand Advertising," *Public Opinion Quarterly*, 33 (Fall 1969), 478–9.

11. Ebbinghaus, Hermann. *Grundzuge der Psychologie*. Leipzig: Veit, 1902.

12. Grass, Robert C. and Wallace H. Wallace. "Satiation Effects of TV Commercials," *Journal of Advertising Research*, 9 (September 1969), 3–8.

13. Hays, William L. *Statistics for Psychologists*. New York: Holt, Rinehart & Winston, 1965.

14. Jensen, Ward J. "Sales Effects of TV, Radio, and Print Advertising," *Journal of Advertising Research*, 6 (June 1966), 2–7.

15. Johnson, Richard C., Charles W. Thomson, and George Frincke. "Word Values, Word Frequency, and Visual Duration Thresholds," *Psychological Review*, 67 (August 1960), 332–42.

16. Keppel, Geoff. "Verbal Learning and Memory," *Annual Review of Psychology*, 19 (1968), 169–202.

17. Kotler, Philip. "Toward an Explicit Model of Media Selection," *Journal of Advertising Research*, 4 (March 1964), 34–41.

18. Krugman, Herbert E. "An Application of Learning Theory to TV Copy Testing," *Public Opinion Quarterly*, 26 (Winter 1962), 626–34.

19. ———. "Processes Underlying Exposure to Advertising," *American Psychologist*, 23 (April 1968), 245–53.

20. Light, Marvin L. "An Experimental Study of the Effects of Repeated Persuasive Communications upon Awareness and Attitudes," unpublished doctoral dissertation, The Ohio State University, 1967.

21. Little, John D. C. and Leonard M. Lodish. "A Media Planning Calculus," *Operations Research*, 17 (January–February 1969), 1–35.

22. LoSciuto, Leonard A. "Effects of Advertising Frequency and Product Usage on Recall: A Laboratory Simulation," *Proceedings*. 76th Annual Meetings of the American Psychological Association, 1968, 679–80.

23. ———, Larry H. Strassman, and William D. Wells. "Advertising Weight and the Reward Value of the Brand," *Journal of Advertising Research*, 7 (June 1967), 34–8.

24. McGraw-Hill. *Laboratory of Advertising Performance Data Sheet No. 3070*. New York: McGraw-Hill, 1958.

25. Maloney, John C. "Attitude Measurement and Formation," paper presented at the Test Marketing Workshop, American Marketing Association, Chicago, 1966.

26. Mayer, Martin. *Madison Avenue, U.S.A.* New York: Harper, 1958.

27. Metheringham, Richard A. "Measuring the Net Cumulative Coverage of a Print Campaign," *Journal of Advertising Research*, 4 (December 1964), 23–8.

28. Norman, Donald A. *Memory and Attention: An Introduction to Human Information Processing*. New York: John Wiley & Sons, 1969.

29. Politz, Alfred. *The Rochester Study*. Philadelphia: Curtis Publishing, 1960.

30. Powers, Howard W. and Eugene C. Pomerance. "Pilot Study: A Coupon Redemption Method for Testing the Sales Persuasiveness of Television Commercials," Report No. 5500B-65-1, Chicago: Foote, Cone & Belding, 1966.

31. "Quest for Boredom," *Television Age*, 15 (December 18, 1967), 28–56.

32. Ray, Michael L. "Neglected Problems (Opportunities) in Research: The Development of Multiple and Unobtrusive Measurement," *Proceedings*. Fall Conference, American Marketing Association, 1968, 176–83.

33. ———. "Can Order Effect in Copy Tests be Used as an Indicator of Long Term Advertising Effect?" *Journal of Advertising Research*, 9 (March 1969), 1, 45–52.

34. ——— and Richard Clark. "Focus," unpublished paper, Graduate School of Business, Stanford University, 1970.

35. Schwerin Research Corporation. "Schneeball oder Wearout?" *SRC Bulletin*, 14 (August 1966), 2–6; (September 1966), 2–5.

36. Simon, Julian L. "Are There Economies of Scale in Advertising?" *Journal of Advertising Research*, 5 (June 1965), 16–9.

37. ———. "New Evidence for No Effect of Scale in Advertising," *Journal of Advertising Research*, 9 (March 1969), 39–41.

38. Stewart, John. *Repetitive Advertising in Newspapers: A Study of Two New Products*. Boston: Division of Research, Graduate School of Business Administration, Harvard University, 1964.

39. Strong, Edward K. "The Effect of Length of Series upon Recognition," *Psychological Review*, 19 (January 1912), 6, 44–7.

40. Telser, Lester G. "Advertising and Cigarettes," *Journal of Political Economy*, 70 (August 1962), 471–99.

41. Ule, G. Maxwell. "The Milwaukee Advertising Laboratory —Its Second Year," *Proceedings*. 12th Annual Meeting, Advertising Research Foundation, Albany, New York, 1966.

42. Wallerstein, Edward. "Measuring Commercials on CATV," *Journal of Advertising Research*, 7 (June 1967), 15–9.

43. Weinberg, Robert S. "Sales and Advertising of Cigarettes," unpublished report, Third Meeting of the Operations Research Discussion Group, Advertising Research Foundation, 1960.

44. Wells, William D. and Jack M. Chinsky. "Effects of Competing Messages: A Laboratory Simulation," *Journal of Marketing Research*, 2 (May 1965), 141–5.

45. Winer, Benton J. *Statistical Principles in Experimental Design*. New York: McGraw-Hill, 1962.

46. Zajonc, Robert B. "Attitudinal Effects of Mere Exposure," *Journal of Personality and Social Psychology*, Monograph Supplement, 9 (June 1968), 5.

47. Zielske, Hubert A. "The Remembering and Forgetting of Advertising," *Journal of Marketing*, 23 (March 1959), 239–43.

C. SAMUEL CRAIG, BRIAN STERNTHAL, and CLARK LEAVITT*

Two experiments were conducted to examine the effect of very high levels of print ad repetition on brand name recall. In experiment I, the wearout in recall observed in natural settings was replicated in the laboratory. Experiment II examined whether this wearout was attributable to subjects' inattention to ads and reactance to substantial repetition levels. When these factors were controlled experimentally, no wearout was observed; the highest repetition level yielded greater or as much persistence in brand name recall as lower repetition levels. The implications of these data for marketing practice and theory are discussed.

Advertising Wearout: An Experimental Analysis

INTRODUCTION

Advertising decisions, ranging from the development of media schedules to an estimation of advertising production costs, are based on a theory of consumer response to persuasive communications. Such decisions lack a sound basis when the model is implicit and its assumptions are untested. One such assumption, concerning the value of repetition in advertising, is currently being reexamined. On the basis of the findings of verbal learning research [4, 9], advertisers historically have embraced a "weak effects" hypothesis to explain the impact of repetition. According to this hypothesis, the effect of any one exposure is slight, and only very substantial levels of repetition "ingrain a stimulus in the mind" [8].

In contrast to this incremental theory of association, which accounts for the results of research employing nonsense syllables and other highly constrained materials as stimuli, Leavitt [12] has suggested that a "strong effects" hypothesis is more appropriate to order the findings of field research on the effects

of advertising repetition.[1] The strong effects hypothesis implies that the effectiveness of an ad depends on the events occurring during the first few exposures to it. Though greater consolidation is possible with further repetitions, it often is prevented by inhibiting factors operating in the communication process.

Much of the evidence for the strong effects of message exposure comes from the research on a paradoxical phenomenon known as *wearout*.[2] Though "wearout" generally refers to the loss of effectiveness of an ad or group of ads, in the present discussion it is defined more precisely as the occurrence of a decrement in the recall of a message while the message is gaining a higher level of exposure (or greater "practice," to use the idiom of learning theorists). The phenomenon is paradoxical because it has been demonstrated only under natural field conditions and has not been observed in controlled laboratory experiments. In contrast, the positive effect of practice on recall is one of the fundamental tenets of psychology [15]. Even at very high levels of repetition an increase in stimulus exposures increases recall, albeit in decreasing increments [5, 10, 11, 13, 14].

Recent field investigations examining the effects of a wide range of repetition levels have found that advertising repetition is nonmonotonically related to

*C. Samuel Craig is Assistant Professor of Marketing, Cornell University; Brian Sternthal is Assistant Professor of Marketing, Northwestern University; and Clark Leavitt is Professor of Marketing, The Ohio State University.

Support for the first experiment was provided by Batten, Barton, Durstine, and Osborn. Graduate Assistant Richard Semenik helped conduct the second experiment. The support and assistance are greatly appreciated.

[1] See [16] and [17] for a comprehensive review of this literature.
[2] Empirical studies of recall wearout are discussed in detail in [8].

Journal of Marketing Research
Vol. XIII (November 1976), 365-72

retention. Appel [cited in 8] observed that as repetition progressed, recall of commercials initially increased and then dropped. Also the inflection point in recall occurred at lower levels of repetition for those commercials that were rated average or below average on copy tests than for those rated above average. In another field study [reported in 8], Grass observed wearout in brand awareness whether persons received light, moderate, or heavy exposures to a 12-week television commercial campaign. However, wearout occurred sooner when repetition was heavy than when it was moderate or light.

Thus, some evidence from field studies suggests that, beyond a certain level, repetition of advertisements will cause wearout. However, there is little information regarding the variables that mediate this phenomenon. The first study reported herein was an attempt to duplicate wearout under controlled laboratory conditions. It entailed using levels of repetition per time unit that were high in relation to their occurrence in natural settings and employing the same ads rather than variants on the same theme as is often the case in actual campaigns. Evidence for wearout would be obtained if increasing repetition resulted in a significant decrease in recall.

The laboratory setting was selected because it afforded the opportunity to manipulate factors presumed to be related to wearout, if indeed it could be demonstrated. Experiment II focused on identifying the factors that mediate wearout. It involved a determination of whether elimination of the conditions thought to be responsible for wearout actually eliminated the effect. Although field research has confirmed the wearout phenomenon, little progress has been made in identifying the factors which cause it.

EXPERIMENT I: DEMONSTRATION OF WEAROUT[3]

Procedure

On the basis of a pretest, it was found that "complete" or 100% learning could be obtained by showing 12 print ads (by a slide projector), for 5 seconds each, seven consecutive times. Two hundred percent learning was defined as 14 repetitions or twice the number needed for 100% learning, and 300% learning involved 21 exposures to the series of 12 print ads. Though "percent learning" served as a convenient designation for the different repetition treatments it is somewhat arbitrary because subjects differ in their span of brand name apprehension. One hundred percent learning was defined operationally as the point where the learning curve leveled off in the immediate recall condition. It was not literally 100% because some subjects will not reach the criterion of perfect recall even if very

[3] For a detailed description of this study see [3].

substantial levels of repetition are used. For this reason it is convenient to establish a criterion that is short of perfect recall. In the present study this was the point at which 50% or more of the subjects remembered all 12 ads in an immediate recall test. Evidence for the appropriateness of this criterion is supported by the observation that there were no significant differences in immediate recall (mean number of brand names recalled) when the number of stimuli presented was doubled or tripled (see Table 1).

One hundred and eighty Ohio State University undergraduates participated in the study. Their instructions were to pay close attention to slides of magazine ads that would be repeated a number of times. Subjects were assigned randomly to one of three repetition conditions: 100% learning (12 ads, 5-second exposures each repeated seven times), 200% learning (12 ads, 5-second exposures each repeated 14 times), or 300% learning (12 ads, 5-second exposures each repeated 21 times), and one of four delayed recall post-test conditions (0, 1, 7, or 28 days). Individuals assigned to the immediate post-test condition (i.e., 0 days) were asked to record the brand names they could recall from among those shown immediately after the stimulus presentation. Subjects in the three delayed conditions were asked three general questions to provide a plausible explanation for their participation. They were recontacted by phone unexpectedly after the appropriate delay (i.e., either 1, 7, or 28 days) and were asked to enumerate all the brand names they could remember seeing during the experiment.

Thus a 3×4 factorial design was used with 15 subjects randomly assigned to each cell. Independent variables included three levels of repetition (100, 200, and 300%) and four levels of delay of the recall post-test (0, 1, 7, and 28 days). The number of brand names recalled from the 12 shown served as the dependent measure.

Results

The mean number of brand names recalled for the various repetition and post-test delay conditions is shown in Table 1. An analysis of variance was performed to determine the effects of repetition and post-test delay on brand name recall. As Table 2 indicates the delay main effect is significant ($F =$

Table 1
MEAN BRAND NAME RECALL: EXPERIMENT I

Post-test delay (days)	Repetition condition		
	100%	200%	300%
0	10.4	10.3	9.9
1	6.1	8.9	7.5
7	4.9	5.7	6.9
28	2.7	4.7	3.7

Table 2
ANALYSIS OF VARIANCE SUMMARY TABLE: EXPERIMENT I

Source of variation	Degrees of freedom	SS	MS	F
A (repetition, 100, 200, 300%)	2	56.93	28.47	6.56[a]
B (post-test delay, 0, 1, 7, 28 days)	3	1016.84	338.85	78.10[a]
A × B	6	67.35	10.39	2.39[b]
Error	168	728.60	4.34	

[a] $p < .01$.
[b] $p < .05$.

78.1, d.f. = 3,168, $p < .01$). As often has been reported in the literature [1,15], recall declines as the delay between the administration of experimental stimuli and the recall post-test increases. Furthermore, the repetition main effect and the repetition by post-test delay interaction were significant.

Given this significant interaction, a comparison of repetition treatment means was performed by the Newman-Keuls method for making *a posteriori* tests (see [19] for a description of the procedure) to determine whether this interaction was attributable to wearout (see Table 3). Evidence for wearout was found in the 28-day condition; 200% learning induced significantly better brand name recall than either 300 or 100% learning ($p < .05$). Wearout was not observed in the three other delayed recall post-test conditions. When the recall test was administered immediately after the stimulus presentation, there were no significant differences in recall attributable to repetition. In the 1-day post-test delay, 200% learning yielded better retention than 100%. There was also a tendency

Table 3
SYSTEMATIC COMPARISON (NEWMAN-KEULS) OF TREATMENT MEANS: EXPERIMENT I

Retention intervals (days)		Repetition conditions	
		200%	300%
0	100%		
	200%	–	
1	100%	a,b	
	200%	–	
7	100%		c,d
	200%	–	
28	100%	c,e	
	200%	–	c,f

[a] $p < .01$.
[b] 200 > 100.
[c] $p < .05$.
[d] 300 > 100.
[e] 200 > 100.
[f] 200 > 300.

Figure 1
REPETITION–POST-TEST DELAY INTERACTION: EXPERIMENT I

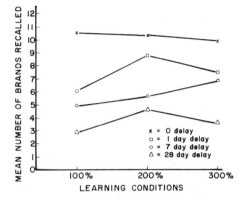

for 300% learning to induce better recall than 100% (but poorer recall than 200%), although these differences did not reach conventional levels of significance. Finally, in the 7-day retention post-test delay, 200% learning yielded no better brand name recall than 300% learning. In fact, 300% learning was significantly better than 100% ($p < .05$), but 200% learning was not. These relationships are depicted in Figure 1.

Because the time course of recall decay is also of interest to advertising practitioners, a systematic comparison of the number of brand names recalled after the various temporal delays was performed for each repetition level. By the Newman-Keuls method, it was observed that in both the 100 and 300% learning conditions the decay in brand names occurred in the first day and between the seventh and twenty-eighth days after stimulus exposure. In contrast, in the 200% learning condition a significant decay in recall only occurred between the first and seventh days.

Discussion

Of particular interest is the finding that given the appropriate circumstances, a high degree of repetition induces wearout. Specifically, in the experiment it was observed that presenting print ads three times as often as is needed for learning caused wearout one month later. Moreover, the observed wearout might be attributable to two factors. First, beyond the 14 repetitions (i.e., 200% learning) subjects may have become inattentive to the ads. Retroactive inhibition may have occurred during the extra trials. Although this inattention is not sufficient to affect recall when delays are relatively short, it may have caused a memorial deficit when the retention test was delayed one month. Second, the reactance induced by having to sit through 21 repetitions of the same 12 print ads during a 21-minute period may have reduced subjects' motivation to recall brand names when it was needed most—28 days after they viewed the ads.[4]

EXPERIMENT II: FACTORS UNDERLYING WEAROUT

Experiment II was designed to test the accuracy of the foregoing explanations. Specifically, four "vigilance" ads were included in the stimulus set to insure attention throughout the presentation. Furthermore, the design eliminated the confounding of repetition with the time taken to participate in the experiment. Thus, if any reactance did emerge, it would be constant throughout experimental treatments rather than varying according to the number of repetitions shown.

Three other changes were made. Because it was found that a substantial amount of the decay in recall occurred between the seventh and twenty-eighth days, a fifth post-test delay condition, at day 14, was included in experiment II. Also, the 1-day delay was changed to a 2-day post-test. Finally, all recall measures were administered to subjects in person rather than by telephone.

Procedure

Seventy subjects, recruited from undergraduate classes at The Ohio State University, participated in the study. Before performing the experimental task, all subjects were given a list of 27 brand names and were asked to indicate their liking and familiarity with each brand on a 7-point scale. Among the 27 brand names were the 8 brands that corresponded to the print ads used as the experimental stimuli.[5]

Subjects next were informed about the experimental task. To disguise its true purpose and to insure that subjects paid attention throughout the session, they were given the following induction:

> ...It has been estimated that people are exposed to from 300 to 2,000 ads per day. To try to get their advertisements noticed in all this clutter, advertisers frequently employ the same theme in their ads with slight variation. To see how noticeable this is to people I am going to show you a series of slides of magazine advertisements. Most of them will be identical ads for the same brand repeated several times. However, there will be some ads for the same brand and product that are not identical....

Subjects then were shown a series of 28 slides of print ads, each for 5 seconds. This series was repeated six times, so that total viewing time was 14 minutes.

The 28 ads included 4 controls, 20 experimental ads, and 4 vigilance ads. The first two and last two slides in the series of 28 served as methodological controls for possible primacy and recency effects. The remaining 24 slides were sequenced randomly, subject to the constraint that at least two different ads had to appear between repetitions of the same ad. There were 8 experimental ads, such that two appeared once, two appeared twice, two appeared three times and two appeared four times, or 6, 12, 18, and 24 times respectively for the entire session. Because it had been determined by pretesting that 6 repetitions was sufficient for 100% learning, 12, 18, and 24 repetitions represented 200, 300, and 400% learning conditions. Fewer repetitions were necessary for 100% learning than in experiment I because there were four fewer ads.

To insure attention and to complete the experimental guise, four vigilance ads were included in the series. In the first series of 28 ads, each of these vigilance ads appeared once (ads A, B, C, D in Table 4). In the second series, one of these four ads was switched to a similar ad for the same brand (e.g., A to A'), whereas the other three were the same ads shown in the first series (i.e., B, C, D). The ad that was switched (A') was repeated in the remaining four series. This procedure was repeated until all four vigilance ads had been switched (as shown in Table 4). Subjects were asked to record the brand name and product category of the ads that had been changed. They also were cautioned not to give cues that might alert others regarding which ads had been changed. At the end of the session, subjects were thanked for their cooperation and dismissed.

Depending upon the post-test delay to which subjects were randomly assigned, they were recontacted either 2, 7, 14, or 28 days after they had participated in the experimental session and were asked to recall as many brand names as they could remember. A fifth group of subjects recorded the brand names they could recall immediately after the session.

---

[4] Reactance refers to the fact that people strive to maintain their freedom when it is threatened [2]. In the present context, subjects would exhibit reactance by refusing to recall brand names when the experimental task was extremely arduous.

[5] The brands' names were: TWA, Amelia Earhart, Vanity Fair, Sears, Porsche, Buxton, VW, and Jantzen.

Table 4
PROCEDURE FOR SWITCHING VIGILANCE ADS: EXPERIMENT II

Ad	Series					
	1	2	3	4	5	6
A	A[a]	A'[b]	A'	A'	A'	A'
B	B	B	B'	B'	B'	B'
C	C	C	C	C'	C'	C'
D	D	D	D	D	D'	D'

[a] A, B, C, D = original ads.
[b] A', B', C', D' = switched ads.

A 4 × 5 experimental design was used with 14 subjects nested within each recall post-test delay. There were four levels of repetition (6, 12, 18, and 24 or 100, 200, 300, and 400% learning) and five post-test delay conditions (0, 2, 7, 14, and 28 days). Mean number of brand names recalled served as the dependent measure. In addition, measures of liking and familiarity of the brands used as experimental stimuli were taken. However, because brand liking was found to be unrelated to recall, no further analysis was performed with this variable.

Results

The mean recall of brand names for the various repetition and post-test delay treatments is reported in Table 5. To determine the effect of the experimental variables, an analysis of covariance was performed. Familiarity with the brands (measured on a 7-point scale) served as the covariate in the analysis and it was found to influence brand recall significantly ($p < .01$). As Table 6 indicates, repetition and post-test delay had a significant effect on brand name recall. The repetition-delay interaction was also significant. In light of the latter finding, tests on simple effects and a systematic comparison of treatment means were performed [19].

The simple effects tests indicated that there was a significant effect of repetition on brand name recall after 7 days ($F = 4.64$, d.f. $= 3,194$, $p < .01$) and 14 days ($F = 3.63$, d.f. $= 3,194$, $p < .05$), but not immediately ($F = 1.38$, $p > .20$), 2 days ($F < 1$), or 28 days ($F = 2.03$, $p > .10$) after administration of the experimental stimuli. A systematic comparison of treatments by the Newman-Keuls method indicated that the significant repetition effect found after the 7 and 14-day delays was attributable to the fact that 400% learning induced more brand name recall than did the other levels of repetition. Moreover, this difference dropped off somewhat between the 7-day ($p < .01$) and 14-day ($p < .05$) post-test delays. Finally, with the exception of a significantly greater recall on the 200 than the 100% condition in the 7-day post-test treatment ($p < .05$), none of the differences between 100, 200, and 300% learning were significant.

Table 5
MEAN BRAND NAME RECALL
ADJUSTED FOR FAMILIARITY COVARIATE:
EXPERIMENT II

Post-test delay (days)	Repetition condition			
	100%	200%	300%	400%
0	1.76	1.78	1.74	1.42
2	1.27	1.28	1.27	1.34
7	.93	1.02	.77	1.52
14	.86	.95	.73	1.37
28	.44	.42	.66	.86

Table 6
ANALYSIS OF COVARIANCE SUMMARY TABLE:
EXPERIMENT II

Source of variation	d.f.	SS	MS	F
Covariate[a]	1	3.03	3.03	10.27[b]
Between subjects	69			
A (post-test delay)	4	32.80	8.20	17.08[b]
S/A (subjects within delay)	65	31.08	.48	
Within subjects	209			
B (repetition)	3	2.38	.79	2.68[c]
A × B	12	7.43	.62	2.10[c]
Error	194	57.27	.295	

[a] Familiarity with the various brands was used as the covariate.
[b] $p < .01$.
[c] $p < .05$.

In sum, use of four times the level of repetition needed to learn a series of brand names yielded significantly higher recall than use of the three lesser repetition levels. However, this finding was observed only when the recall post-test was administered either 7 or 14 days after the stimulus presentation. For shorter (i.e., 0 and 2 days) and longer (i.e., 28 days) delays, there were no differences in recall attributable to the level of repetition.

A similar analysis was performed to examine the effects of recall post-test delay. Test of simple effects showed that there was significant decay in brand name recall in all four repetition conditions (Table 7). By a Newman-Keuls systematic comparison of treatment means, it was found that in the 100 and 200% conditions the significant decay over time was attributable to the attrition in recall between the immediate and the 7, 14, and 28-day conditions. Recall in the 2-day condition was not significantly different than that in the immediate, 7, or 14-day conditions, but it was significantly better than recall after 28 days ($p < .05$). The same pattern was observed in the 300% learning condition; however, subjects' recall after 2 days did not exhibit further decay. In the 400% learning condition, none of the differences between post-test delays was significant, although an overall decay effect was observed ($F = 2.71$, d.f. $= 4,65$, $p < .05$). Thus decay in recall with 100, 200, or 300% learning is attributable to the attrition in recall that occurs in the first 2 days after stimulus presentation. In contrast, the decay in the 400% learning condition is less pronounced and occurs gradually over time.

The repetition-delay interaction reported in Table 4 and illustrated graphically in Figure 2 is significant. In part, this significance is attributable to the fact that the 400% learning condition yielded better brand name recall than other repetition levels for the 7 and 14-day recall post-test delays but not for shorter (i.e., 0 or 2 day) or longer (i.e., 28 day) delays. In part too, the significant interaction is due to the gradual decline in the persistence of brand name recall over

Table 7
SIMPLE EFFECTS OF RETENTION POST-TEST DELAY AND SYSTEMATIC COMPARISON (NEWMAN-KEULS) OF TREATMENT MEANS: EXPERIMENT II

Repetition level	Simple effect	Systematic comparison
100%	$F = 10.04$[a]	$0 = 2$[b]
		$2 = 7, 14$
		$0 > 7 = 14 = 28$[a]
		$2 > 28$[c]
200%	$F = 10.14$[a]	$0 = 2$
		$2 = 7, 14$
		$0 > 7 = 14 = 28$[c]
		$2 > 28$[c]
300%	$F = 8.81$[a]	$0 = 2$
		$2 = 7 = 14 = 28$
		$0 > 7, 14, 28$[a]
400%	$F = 2.71$[c]	$0 = 2 = 7 = 14 = 28$

[a] 0, 2, 7, 14, 28 = post-test delay.
[b] $p < .01$.
[c] $p < .05$.

the 28-day post-test period evinced by subjects in the 400% condition in relation to that exhibited by subjects in the other repetition conditions, where forgetting occurred in the first 2 days after the stimulus presentation.

Finally, the effect of the familiarity covariate was significant (Table 4). Further, dividing ads into high and low familiarity (above and below the median) showed that very familiar print ads were significantly better recalled than less familiar ones ($F = 30.62$, d.f. $= 1,279$, $p < .01$). As Figure 3 illustrates, this difference is largely attributable to the substantially better recall of familiar ads that occurs after the 7-day and 14-day delays.

Figure 2
REPETITION–POST-TEST DELAY INTERACTION: EXPERIMENT II

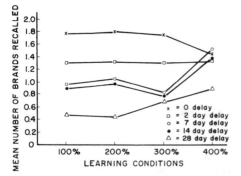

Figure 3
EFFECT OF FAMILIARITY ON AD RECALL OVER TIME

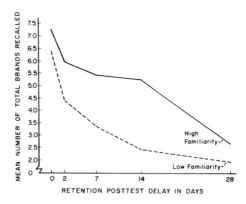

Discussion

Experiment I demonstrated that under the appropriate conditions, the wearout in recall observed in field studies could be replicated in the laboratory. Specifically, when the level of repetition was three times that needed to learn the brand names, subjects exhibited significantly poorer recall than when repetition was only twice that needed for learning.

Given the observation of the wearout finding in natural settings, it is useful to know what factors account for the phenomenon. Such knowledge may serve as a basis for strategies to insure that increasing the repetition of advertisements enhances the probability that message recipients will recall the communication content. In experiment II it was found that by experimentally insuring attention throughout the stimulus presentation, and by avoiding the confounding of repetition with stimulus exposure time, very high levels of repetition (i.e., 400% learning) yielded greater brand name recall after 7 and 14 days than did lower levels of repetition. Thus, the wearout observed in experiment I most probably was caused by subjects' inattention to the stimuli and their reactance when very high levels of repetition were employed. More specifically, it is likely that both repetition of specific ads and the elements of clutter present in the experimental situation were responsible for the inattention and reactance. This situation corresponds well to commercial settings where the effect of a campaign is influenced by its frequency and the clutter it must contend with.

These findings have several implications for the advertising practitioner. First, they suggest that it is useful to employ strategies that enhance attention when a high frequency campaign is planned. Although it is not feasible to employ the procedure used in the present study, several other approaches such as varying the execution of the campaign theme or introducing several claims to slow the rate of learning may retard wearout [7].

A second implication of the present research pertains to the issue of measuring advertising effectiveness. Specifically, it warns against the use of day-after recall that is commonly used as the measure of advertising effectiveness. Short delays before testing may be insufficient to yield differences in recall between ads or strategic approaches. These differences may not become evident unless a delay period of longer duration is used. Indeed, in experiment I 200% learning did not evince superior memorability until the 28-day post-test, and in experiment II the 400% learning condition did not yield superior recall until the 7-day post-test. Equally misleading are post-tests that are taken after a substantial delay. In this case, no differences between ads or strategies may be observed even though they would have been found if shorter post-test delays had been used. For example, 400% learning (experiment II) yielded higher recall than lower levels of repetition after 7 and 14 days, but not after 28 days.

To avoid misinterpretation of retention data, it is suggested that recall be measured at several points in time after stimulus presentation. Though this suggestion seems obvious, it is seldom followed. In fact, most academic marketing research as well as that done commercially does not examine the persistence of repetition (exceptions include [6, 7, 18, 20]). In commercial settings the reluctance to monitor persistence may be justified on a cost basis. In this event, it behooves the advertiser to identify the post-test delay that is most appropriate for his purposes rather than to assume that the rates of decay for various levels of repetition or alternative ads are equal.

From a theoretical standpoint, the research reported herein suggests that as repetition increases, inattention and reactance to the experimental task cause a lack of persistence in recall. When these mediators are controlled, very high levels of repetition (400% learning) induce greater persistence in recall after 7 and 14 days than do lower levels of repetition. Interestingly, this same pattern emerged when ads were partitioned on the basis of subjects' familiarity with them. As Figure 3 illustrates, there are substantial differences in recall between familiar and unfamiliar ads after 7 and 14 days. Thus it can be hypothesized that familiarity underlies the persistence in recall of the 400% learning condition in relation to other repetition levels. This hypothesis, however, is still to be tested empirically.

Finally, the data suggest that the strong and weak effects hypotheses provide complementary rather than competing explanations for the effect of repetition

on learning. The weak effects hypothesis accounts for the effects of repetition after moderate delays. As predicted, in the 1 and 7-day recall post-tests for experiment I and the 7 and 14-day post-tests for experiment II, higher levels of repetition yielded greater brand name recall than did lower levels. In contrast, the strong effects hypothesis ordered the data when the post-test delay period was either very short or very long. Consistent with this hypothesis, after short delays (immediate post-test in experiment I, immediate and 2-day in experiment II), subjects' span of apprehension limited their brand name recall. As a result, there is no repetition effect in these conditions. However, subjects' inattention and reactance to the experimental task at very high levels of repetition caused the nonmonotonic repetition-recall relationship. When these inhibitors were removed in experiment II, increasing repetition enhanced recall, though not significantly.

CONCLUSION

The study provides a laboratory demonstration of a phenomenon already observed in natural settings, advertising wearout. The findings indicate that wearout is attributable to the audience's inattentiveness to stimulus materials and loss of motivation for retrieval of brand names when repetitions are substantial.

From a strategic perspective, these findings have several implications. First, they suggest that there is some optimal level of repetition. Although increasing repetition may facilitate learning, very substantial levels may cause cognitive responses that ultimately inhibit learning. Further, the nonbeneficial effects of high frequency campaigns can be mitigated by varying the execution of the same theme. This can be accomplished by stressing different benefits, using different spokespersons, or any other device that helps maintain audience attention or reduces reactance. Finally, the impact of a particular campaign on learning may be distorted by using arbitrary delays between exposure and testing of recall. Though 24 hours may be a convenient temporal delay, day-after recall may fail to reveal long-term differences between various ads.

REFERENCES

1. BBD&O Research Department. *The Repetition of Advertising*. New York: BBD&O, 1967.
2. Brehm, Jack W. *A Theory of Psychological Reactance*. New York: Academic Press, 1966.
3. Craig, C. Samuel, Brian Sternthal, and Karen Olshan. "The Effect of Overlearning on Retention," *Journal of General Psychology*, 87 (August 1972), 85-94.
4. Ebbinghaus, H. *Uber das Gedachtris*. Leipzig: Dunker, 1885. Translated by H. Ruyer and C. Bussenius. *Memory*. New York: Teachers College, Columbia University, 1913.
5. Gilbert, T. F. "Overlearning and Retention of Meaningful Prose," *Journal of General Psychology*, 56 (April 1957), 281-9.

6. Grass, Robert C. "Satiation Effects of Advertising," *Proceedings: 14th Annual Conference*. New York: Advertising Research Foundation, 1968.

7. ___ and Wallace H. Wallace. "Satiation Effects of TV Commercials," *Journal of Advertising Research*, 9 (September 1969), 3-8.

8. Greenberg, Allan and Charles Suttoni. "Television Commercial Wearout," *Journal of Advertising Research*, 13 (October 1973), 47-54.

9. Hull, Clark L. *A Behavior System: An Introduction to Behavior Theory Concerning the Individual Organism*. New Haven, Connecticut: Yale University Press, 1952.

10. Krueger, W. L. "Further Studies in Overlearning," *Journal of Experimental Psychology*, 13 (April 1930), 152-63.

11. ———. "The Effect of Overlearning on Retention," *Journal of Experimental Psychology*, 12 (February 1929), 71-8.

12. Leavitt, Clark. "Strong versus Weak Effects of Mass Communications: Two Alternative Hypotheses," in G. D. Hughes and M. L. Ray, eds., *Buyer/Consumer Information Processing*. Chapel Hill, North Carolina: Univeristy of North Carolina Press, 1974.

13. Luh, C. W. "The Conditions of Retention," *Psychological Monographs*, 31 (1922), 1-87.

14. Postman, Leo. "Retention as a Function of Overlearning," *Science*, 135 (February 1962), 666-7.

15. Ray, Michael L. "Psychological Theories and Interpretations of Learning," in Scott Ward and Thomas Robertson, eds., *Consumer Behavior: Theoretical Sources*. Englewood Cliffs, New Jersey: Prentice-Hall, Inc., 1973.

16. ——— and Alan G. Sawyer. "Repetition in Media Models: A Laboratory Technique," *Journal of Marketing Research*, 8 (February 1971), 20-9.

17. Sawyer, Alan G. "The Effects of Repetition: Conclusions and Suggestions about Experimental Laboratory Research," in G. D. Hughes and M. L. Ray, eds., *Buyer/Consumer Information Processing*. Chapel Hill, North Carolina: University of North Carolina Press, 1974.

18. Strong, Edward C. "The Use of Field Experimental Observations in Estimating Advertising Recall," *Journal of Marketing Research*, 11 (November 1974), 369-78.

19. Winer, B. J. *Statistical Principles in Experimental Design*. New York: McGraw-Hill Book Co., 1962.

20. Zielske, Hubert A. "The Remembering and Forgetting of Advertising," *Journal of Marketing*, 23 (January 1959), 239-43.

BOBBY J. CALDER and BRIAN STERNTHAL*

Repetition of a pattern of television commercials caused wearout in viewers'
evaluation of the commercials and the products being advertised. As predicted
by an information processing view, wearout was not forestalled by strategies
designed to enhance attention.

Television Commercial Wearout: An Information Processing View

Research has indicated that even when television commercials are initially effective, subsequent exposures cause effectiveness to level off and ultimately decline (Appel 1966, 1971; Grass 1968; Grass and Wallace 1969). This relationship between repeated exposures and advertising effectiveness, generally termed *wearout*, poses a dilemma to advertisers. Repeating a campaign is likely to enhance its penetration, keep commercial production costs low, and permit the allocation of more resources to other marketing strategies. However, repeated exposure, even to advertising that is initially persuasive, may cause a campaign to lose its effectiveness.

The occurrence of wearout has been examined in field experiments[1] conducted in natural settings. The amount of time between the onset of a campaign and the dependent variable measurement was taken as a surrogate for the number of exposures. Using this paradigm, researchers have found that as the time interval between onset and measurement increases, attention to the commercial (Grass and Wallace 1969), recall of the commercial (Appel 1966, 1971; Grass

and Wallace 1969), and awareness of the advertised brand (Grass 1970) initially increase, then level off, and ultimately decline.[2] The same nonmonotonic pattern was obtained in a study examining the effects of exposure density (i.e., number of exposures per month) and total exposures on brand awareness (Grass 1970).

Although field experiments suggest that television commercials can wear out, they do little beyond establishing wearout as a source of concern. Convincing evidence for the wearout effect is lacking in field investigations because the level of commercial exposure is not controlled and because statistical analyses are not reported. Moreover, the psychological processes underlying the phenomenon are not identified. These issues have been addressed, however, in laboratory experiments where subjects have been assigned randomly to one of several repetition levels of a persuasive appeal. Wearout has been observed in message recall, attention, agreement, and the number of positive and negative thoughts generated in response to the communication.

Two causes of wearout have been identified in laboratory experiments. One is *inattention*. With increasing repetition, viewers may no longer attend to a message. Thus the message loses its effectiveness as forgetting of its content sets in. Evidence of inattention as a cause of wearout was found in a study by Craig, Sternthal, and Leavitt (1976), who observed

---

[1]The literature cited in this article provides a summary of the wearout findings. A more extensive review of wearout studies is provided by Greenberg and Suttoni (1973), and a review of the more general repetition literature is reported by Sawyer (1978).

*Bobby J. Calder is Professor of Behavioral Science in Management and Professor of Psychology and Brian Sternthal is Associate Professor of Marketing, Northwestern University.

The authors are grateful to Lynn Phillips and Peter Wright for comments on a draft of the article; to William Schumacker, Dean Smith, and Michael O'Hare for their help in conducting the study; and to Jerry Dee Wharton for her assistance in data analysis.

[2]Attention is measured by using an operant conditioning procedure called CONPAAD (Conjugately Programmed Analysis of Advertising) developed by Lindsley (1962). The procedure requires subjects to press foot pedals in order to receive the visual and audio portions of the stimulus. The recall measure used in wearout research is typically a variant of the Burke Day After Recall procedure.

Journal of Marketing Research
Vol. XVII (May 1980), 173–86

a significant decline in brand name recall when exposures substantially exceeded the number needed to learn the brand names. When attention to the advertising stimuli was experimentally induced, there was some indication that the wearout previously observed was eliminated. Grass and Wallace (1969) reported that wearout in attention due to repeated exposure to the same commercial was significantly reduced when different commercial executions for a brand were used.

The second possible cause of wearout is *active information processing*. Evidence for this phenomenon comes from experiments in which people's thoughts were included as a dependent variable. Cacioppo and Petty (1979) report that increasing the exposure to a persuasive written communication from a low to a moderate level enhanced agreement with the advocacy, whereas additional exposures resulted in a decline in agreement. Subjects' thoughts also indicated wearout. The number of negative thoughts listed in response to the appeal declined after the first several exposures and increased thereafter, whereas the number of positive thoughts followed a nonsignificant increase-then-decline pattern as repetitions mounted. McCullough and Ostrom (1974) obtained no evidence for wearout when subjects were presented five different print ads for the same brand and found that subjects listed more positive thoughts and fewer negative thoughts with exposures to additional print ads.

These experiments suggest that wearout can be explained in terms of active information processing (Calder, Insko, and Yandell 1974; Cook 1969; Greenwald 1968; Wright 1975). According to this view, message recipients rehearse two kinds of thoughts: thoughts stimulated directly by the message and largely reflecting message content, and other thoughts based on associations and reflecting previous experiences. The first kind is termed "message-related thoughts" and the second "own thoughts." This simple information processing theory is sufficient to account for wearout. With the initial exposures to a message, the individual's thoughts tend to be message-related. At some level of repetition, however, the thoughts which come to mind stem mainly from associations only indirectly linked to the message. These own thoughts, in general, are less positive toward the product than message-related thoughts, primarily because the latter were selected to be highly positive.[3] Thus, the decrease in message-related thoughts and the increase in own thoughts produces a wearout effect such as that observed by Cacioppo and Petty (1979). Conversely, when repetition does not produce this pattern of

information processing, as in the McCullough and Ostrom (1974) study, wearout does not occur.

This second cause of wearout should be of special concern to advertisers. Information processing theory predicts that wearout can occur even when advertisers attempt to enhance attention by spacing exposures over time, by using multiple executions of the message, or by dominating the media environment. The authors' study tested this prediction.

OVERVIEW OF THE STUDY

Several strategies that advertisers use to enhance attention were incorporated into a test of the information processing view of wearout. The information processing view would be supported if wearout were found to occur despite the use of these strategies.

A strategy that advertisers employ to maintain attention is to use advertising media that have attention-getting characteristics for the target audience. Television is generally viewed as the best medium in this respect. Moreover, advertisers embed messages into the medium so that attention to the medium's main content extends to the advertising message. In accordance with these strategies, the messages of experimental interest in the study were embedded in actual one-hour network television programs. The programs were detective shows with high viewer appeal.

Advertisers are also sensitive to the pattern of repetition over time. Commercials are organized around a message theme to form a "flight." The commercials within a flight are spaced over program breaks and over different programs. In comparison with massing the commercials together, this spacing enhances attention. The relevant measure of repetition is the length of the flight. Accordingly, the commercials presented in the study were spaced to simulate flighting, and repetition was manipulated as *flight length*. Flight lengths of one, three, and six were examined. For the flight length of one, viewers were presented a group of commercials in a single session. For the flight length of three, the group of commercials was repeated in each of three sessions separated in time. For the flight length of six, the group of commercials was repeated in each of the six sessions. The manipulation of flight length, rather than the number of repetitions presented in a single session as in previous research, refined the theoretical variable of interest. The study concerned not massed repetitions but spaced repetitions that enhance attention. This manipulation allowed a strong test of the information processing prediction that wearout can occur despite the use of commercial spacing (i.e., flighting) to gain attention.

Flight length determines the total number of exposures to commercials for a particular product. A flight may be composed of a single commercial execution. Alternatively, a pool of commercials that have the

---

[3]More complex explanations are available to account for the thought production patterns that have been observed in response to variation in the level of repetition. However, the one offered here is the most parsimonious in ordering extant data.

same theme or sales message but differ in execution may comprise a flight. For a given flight length, the number of message exposures for a product will be constant, but the exposures to a particular execution may vary in redundancy, depending on the *pool size* used. The maximally redundant case is a pool size of one, because the same commercial execution is repeated throughout the flight. In less redundant cases, a given commercial execution is part of a pool and comprises only some proportion of the total number of exposures. Hence, within a flight, attention is enhanced by using multiple executions. In the study design, two levels of pool size were crossed with the three levels of flight length. For each of the three flight lengths, subjects always saw either one commercial execution or three different commercial executions. The information processing prediction is that wearout can occur in both the single and the multiple execution conditions.

The remaining factor in the design was the environment in which a flight of commercials was embedded. Attention is enhanced if the commercials for a product dominate the clutter of commercials for other products. One of the most important dimensions of dominance is whether the number of executions for the product (i.e., pool size) exceeds that for other products advertised in the same time period. A flight with a larger pool size should receive more attention.

Therefore, advertising for two products was used in the study. The same flight lengths were used for both. The second product can be considered the dominant background environment for the first. The relative dominance of the first product was manipulated by varying the pool size for the second product, termed the *environmental pool size*. As for the first product, the environmental pool size was either one or three executions. In terms of attention, the first product's advertising was dominant when it had a pool size of three and the second product had an environmental pool size of one. The opposite was true when pool size was one and environmental pool size was three; otherwise, the products were at parity. The information processing prediction is that wearout can occur even with dominance in relative pool size.

The environmental pool size manipulation (the number of executions for the second product) was designed to have another purpose in addition to varying the dominance of the first product. Either of the two noncompetitive products used could be viewed as the first or second product. The dependent measures were collected for both products. When the measures for one product were being examined, the number of executions for the other product was the environmental pool size factor. This method of examining the dependent variables for both products allowed replication to be built into the design. The results do not depend on a single product, but on two very different products.

The basic design of the study thus incorporated

several of the techniques most frequently used by advertisers to enhance attention. This was achieved through a manipulation of repetition in terms of television commercial flight length. Moreover, attention was manipulated by varying pool size and environmental pool size. The primary purpose of these variables was to test the information processing prediction that enhancing attention is not a sufficient condition for preventing wearout. The variation of pool size and environmental pool size is also of interest from a practical perspective; both variables are subject to managerial control.

The dependent variable of primary interest was subjects' evaluation of the experimental commercials and products. To examine the full range of possible information processing effects, however, a multivariate dependent variable strategy was employed. Subjects indicated their reactions on a battery of scales, both for the commercials and for the products.[4] The scales were factor analyzed to isolate evaluative and other reactions. In an attempt to explore the mechanism of information processing, subjects were also asked to list their thoughts about using the products.

The study thus examined individuals' reactions to spaced repetitions of television commercials shown in the context of popular programs. Information processing theory predicts that wearout can occur as flight length increases, even if multiple executions are used and even if the number of executions dominates the media environment.

METHOD

Sample

Two hundred and forty-three undergraduate and master's students at Northwestern University participated in the experiment. To recruit subjects, ads were placed in the school newspaper offering payment for evaluating television programs. Those individuals who called were told that the research task involved evaluating six television programs over a three-week period. They were informed that they would be paid $2.00 per session, provided that they attended all six sessions. Interested callers selected one of the times available.

Groups of approximately 20 subjects were assigned randomly to participate in each experimental session.[5]

---

[4] Subjects also were asked to rate the advertised products on 12 specific attributes. These responses are not reported because they were not, except for a single attribute for one product, affected by the independent variables.

[5] As might be expected, there was somewhat greater subject attrition in those conditions where subjects were to participate in six sessions (26%) than in those involving three sessions (18%). Any attrition, of course, is a potential threat to internal validity. For this reason, the experiment is technically more a quasi-experiment than a true experiment. Because attrition is unavoidable as a practical matter in this type of repeated exposure design, the problem reduces to a tradeoff between internal and external validity.

Approximately half were women and half were men. Their average age was 21.

Stimulus Materials

Programs. Six videotaped one-hour network programs were shown. All shows were in color. The programs were *Cannon, Blue Knight, Hawaii 5-0, Cannon, Barnaby Jones,* and *Bronk.* Subjects who were assigned randomly to watch six programs saw the programs in the order listed over a three-week period. Those assigned to watch three programs viewed the last three programs over a one-week period, and a third group viewed only the last program (Table 1). Furthermore, the experiment was run so that all subjects completed the study at about the same time. The three-program group viewed its first program on the day the six-program group was viewing its fourth program; the one-session group viewed a single program on the day the six- and three-program groups were viewing their last program. This procedure minimized extraneous factors such as the possibility that subjects assigned to different treatments would discuss the experiment with each other.

Commercials. Twelve commercials were interspersed throughout each one-hour program during the same breaks that would be used if the program were aired on prime time network television. As indicated in Figure 1, a 60-second control commercial was scheduled at the outset and at the end of each session. These control commercials (labeled control commercials 1 and 6) were inserted to minimize the possibility that primacy and recency effects would influence subjects' evaluation of the experimental commercials. In addition, four other controls were inserted at the commercial breaks so that the proportion of commercial time to program time would approximate that for normal prime time viewing, and so that the experimental commercials would not completely dominate the commercial time. The same six control commercials were shown in the same sequence for every program a subject viewed.

The experimental commercials were for two nationally distributed products. For proprietary reasons, these products are not identified. It is important to

note that the products are not competitive. Product A is one that is purchased in supermarkets. It was relatively unfamiliar to the research participants. In contrast, Product B, a nonsupermarket product, was well known to the research participants.

During each program, three commercials for Product A and three commercials for Product B were shown (Figure 1). Only one experimental commercial for each product was shown in any commercial break, and the order of presentation of Product A and Product B commercials was randomized both within a session and between sessions. Further, depending on the treatment to which subjects were randomly assigned, subjects saw either one commercial for Product A three times (i.e., Product A, #1 in Figure 1) or three different commercials for Product A (i.e., Product A, #1, 2, and 3 in Figure 1) in each session. The commercial shown in the one commercial condition appeared with two others for Product A in the three commercial condition. These three commercials were similar in content but differed in execution. They had been aired as part of a single flight. Similarly, subjects were presented either one or three commercials for Product B during a session. The two commercials, one for Product A and one for Product B, which were seen by all subjects (i.e., Products A and B, #1, Figure 1) were the ones used as stimuli for obtaining reactions to the commercials at the end of the experiment. Hereafter these are referred to as the *stimulus* commercials.

The stimulus commercial for Product A involved a special effects type of execution with minimal audio material. The stimulus commercial for Product B had a more typical story-line execution. The video portion involved rapid movement from one scene to another while a chorus sang the jingle for the product.

Procedure

When subjects arrived at the laboratory, they were introduced to the four members of the research team who jointly administered the experiment. Tape-recorded instructions were played to the subjects. These instructions presented the experimental guise and the required tasks. Participants were informed that they were to evaluate six television programs, two per week for three weeks, and that payment was contingent on attending all six programs. Subjects assigned to participate in less than six sessions were informed at their last session that there had been a change in plans and that they would not be participating in further sessions. This procedure was instituted to minimize the chances that variation in the recruiting procedure would cause systematic differences in subjects' motivation for participating in the various experimental treatments, i.e., a self-selection bias.

After listening to the instructions, subjects were asked to complete a set of premeasures. This questionnaire was administered to reinforce the guise that

Table 1
STIMULUS MATERIALS[a]

Week	Session	Program	Flight length		
			1	3	6
1	1	Cannon			X
	2	Blue Knight			X
2	3	Hawaii 5-0			X
	4	Cannon		X	X
3	5	Barnaby Jones		X	X
	6	Bronk	X	X	X

[a]The X's denote programs viewed.

Figure 1
COMMERCIAL PLACEMENT AND MANIPULATION OF
POOL SIZE

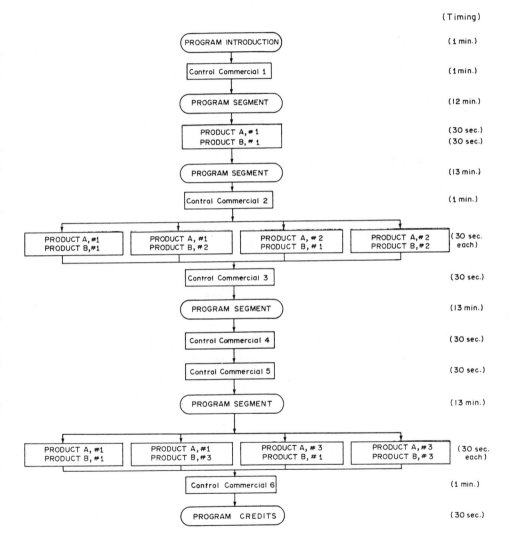

(Timing)

PROGRAM INTRODUCTION — (1 min.)

Control Commercial 1 — (1 min.)

PROGRAM SEGMENT — (12 min.)

PRODUCT A, #1 — (30 sec.)
PRODUCT B, #1 — (30 sec.)

PROGRAM SEGMENT — (13 min.)

Control Commercial 2 — (1 min.)

PRODUCT A, #1 / PRODUCT B, #1   PRODUCT A, #1 / PRODUCT B, #2   PRODUCT A, #2 / PRODUCT B, #1   PRODUCT A, #2 / PRODUCT B, #2 — (30 sec. each)

Control Commercial 3 — (30 sec.)

PROGRAM SEGMENT — (13 min.)

Control Commercial 4 — (30 sec.)

Control Commercial 5 — (30 sec.)

PROGRAM SEGMENT — (13 min.)

PRODUCT A, #1 / PRODUCT B, #1   PRODUCT A, #1 / PRODUCT B, #3   PRODUCT A, #3 / PRODUCT B, #1   PRODUCT A, #3 / PRODUCT B, #3 — (30 sec. each)

Control Commercial 6 — (1 min.)

PROGRAM CREDITS — (30 sec.)

Table 2
SUMMARY OF THE EXPERIMENTAL DESIGN

					Flight length					
		1 session			3 sessions			6 sessions		
Pool size	Environ- mental pool size	Expo- sures	Pool size redundancy	Environ- mental redundancy	Expo- sures	Pool size redundancy	Environ- mental redundancy	Expo- sures	Pool size redundancy	Environ- mental redundancy
1	1	Low	High	High	Mod.	High	High	High	High	High
	3	Low	High	Low	Mod.	High	Low	High	High	Low
3	1	Low	Low	High	Mod.	Low	High	High	Low	High
	3	Low	Low	Low	Mod.	Low	Low	High	Low	Low

Note: Subjects saw either 3 (low exposure), 9 (moderate exposure), or 18 (high exposure) commercials for Product A *and* Product B. For a given product (A or B), either the same commercial was seen each time (high pool size redundancy) or each commercial was seen only a third of the time (low redundancy). For the environmental product (A for B and B for A), either the same commercial was seen each time (high environmental redundancy) or each commercial was seen only a third of the time (low environmental redundancy). A particular configuration of these three values identifies a cell in the design.

participants' evaluation of television programs was of major interest to the researchers. Questions included the extent of television viewing, the amount of viewing devoted to different types of programs, and measures of subjects' demographic and personality characteristics. In addition, individuals' unaided familiarity with and preference among brands in four product categories were determined. Among these product categories were the two of concern in the experiment.

Once subjects had completed the questionnaire, they were shown a one-hour television program that included the experimental and control commercials as shown in Figure 1. To complete the experimental guise, subjects were asked to fill out a program evaluation form and set of scales reflecting their own mood after each program.[6]

At the end of their last session after completing the program evaluation and mood questionnaires, the subjects were administered a series of additional measures pertaining to the products they saw advertised. To justify these measures in terms of the experimental guise, the experimenter stated that they were needed to determine whether or not the advertised products had an effect on the program evaluations. Subjects were then administered a product evaluation questionnaire requiring them to rate using Product A and B. Next, subjects were administered a cognitive response measure requiring them to enumerate their thoughts relevant to using each of the products. Finally, the stimulus commercials for Product A and B were shown again as stimuli. Subjects indicated their reaction to each commercial on a set

of rating scales immediately after viewing each commercial.

Independent Variables

Three independent variables were included in the study: three levels of flight length (1, 3, or 6 sessions), two levels of pool size (1 or 3 commercials), and two levels of environmental pool size (1 or 3 commercials). Flight length thus refers to the number of sessions for which a group of subjects was exposed to a given combination of pool size and environmental pool size. These factors formed a $3 \times 2 \times 2$ factorial design (Table 2).

The pool size factor refers to the number of different commercials that were shown for a particular brand. In terms of subjects' reactions to Product A, the number of different commercials for Product A constitutes the pool size, whereas the number of commercials for Product B is the environmental pool size. Alternatively, in terms of subjects' reactions to Product B, the number of different commercials for Product B is the pool size and the number of different commercials for Product A is the environmental pool size. The use of dependent variables for both Products A and B thus forms a symmetrical pattern. The two sets of products and commercial ratings constitute a replication factor for the design. Although the replication factor cannot be examined statistically (because of item differences between products), it does allow an assessment of the generality of the experimental results.

Dependent Measures

Before participating in the study, subjects completed a premeasure. This instrument was used to determine the average number of hours they watched television per week and the extent to which they viewed different types of programs. Subjects were also asked to list all the brand names that came to mind in the two product categories of interest in the study and to

---

[6]The program evaluation was composed of seven semantic differential rating scales. Items included: entertaining / not entertaining, interesting / boring, exciting / unexciting, enjoyable / unenjoyable, calm / suspenseful, fast-paced / slow-paced, warm / cold. The mood scale was composed of 33 scales due to Nowlis (1965).

indicate their favorite brand from among those listed.

After their last session, subjects completed a series of dependent variable questionnaires. To ensure cooperation, subjects were promised an additional payment of one dollar for the approximately 30 minutes required to complete the questionnaires. First, subjects' reactions to using Product A were measured on five 7-point semantic differential type scales. The same scales then were administered to measure reactions toward Product B. The items are given in Tables 3 and 4. Second, individuals' thoughts about products were assessed by the cognitive response measure (Calder, Insko, and Yandell 1974). This step entailed having subjects list all product-relevant feelings and beliefs that came to mind in a three-minute period. Once this task was completed, research participants rated each thought twice, once on the basis of how favorable or unfavorable it was to the brand and then

Table 3
FACTOR ANALYSIS RESULTS FOR PRODUCT A

Factor label items[a]		Loadings
Semantic differential stimulus commercial (A) ratings		
EVALUATION	bad/good	.59
(48.4%)	boring/interesting	.57
	aggravating/unaggravating	.78
	unattractive/attractive	.57
	tiresome/not tiresome	.63
	annoying/not annoying	.89
	irritating/not irritating	.88
CREDIBILITY	unbelievable/believable	.69
(9.2%)	foolish/wise	.75
	not useful/useful	.70
	undesirable/desirable	.53
MOOD	slow/fast	.81
(7.4%)	unhappy/happy	.69
AROUSAL	not memorable/memorable	.91
(5.5%)	not attention-getting/attention-getting	.82
benefit	harmful/beneficial[b]	—
Semantic differential ratings of product (A)		
EVALUATION	bad/good	.79
(64.6%)	harmful/beneficial	.91
	foolish/wise	.68
UTILITY	nonuseful/useful	.92
(13.2%)	undesirable/desirable	.70

Note: These results are based on a principal components factor analysis (varimax rotation) of the within-cell correlation matrix for each type of dependent variable. The factors are not affected by the experimental treatment conditions. The percent variance accounted for by each factor is given in parentheses.

[a] The order of the adjectives represents the order in which they were scored from one to seven in producing the derived variable to which the factor label applies. The order on the actual questionnaire was balanced.

[b] Items that did not load on any factor. These items were analyzed individually.

Table 4
FACTOR ANALYSIS RESULTS FOR PRODUCT B

Factor label items[a]		Loadings
Semantic differential stimulus commercial (B) ratings		
EVALUATION	bad/good	.67
(45.0%)	boring/interesting	.70
	aggravating/unaggravating	.82
	unattractive/attractive	.53
	tiresome/not tiresome	.74
	annoying/not annoying	.84
	irritating/not irritating	.82
AROUSAL	not memorable/memorable	.85
(9.8%)	not attention getting/attention getting	.78
BENEFIT	foolish/wise	.68
(6.7%)	not useful/useful	.75
	harmful/beneficial	.75
MOOD	slow/fast	.85
(5.9%)	unhappy/happy	.71
believability	unbelievable/believable[b]	—
desirability	undesirable/desirable[b]	—
Semantic differential ratings of product (B)		
EVALUATION	bad/good	.73
(54.1%)	nonuseful/useful	.81
	undesirable/desirable	.66
UTILITY	harmful/beneficial	.91
(15.9%)	foolish/wise	.78

[a,b] See footnotes to Table 3.

on how certain they were that the belief was true. Seven-point scales were used for these ratings. The task was administered first for Product A and then for Product B.

Participants were shown the stimulus commercials for Product A and Product B again. This procedure was intended to simulate a situation in which subjects encountered the commercials in subsequent programming. After each commercial was seen, subjects rated it on 16 7-point semantic differential items (see Tables 3 and 4). These ratings were analogous to the product ratings except that they referred specifically to the commercial for the product. The procedure of showing the stimulus commercials again allows a direct comparison of reactions to the commercials across experimental conditions without distortion by subjects' memory of the commercials. Otherwise the experimental treatments might have caused subjects to be rating different things—i.e., their recall of the commercial versus the commercial itself—and their previous attention to the commercial could therefore have determined the degree of wearout. The procedure ensured that all subjects were reacting to the same stimulus and thus minimized the effects of previous attention. It is consistent with the objective of testing the information processing prediction that wearout can occur *with* attention.

The detailed rationale for the content of dependent measures is given hereafter in connection with the experimental results. For purposes of presentation, these measures are not discussed in the order in which they were administered to subjects.

RESULTS

A major feature of this research was the use of multiple dependent variables. These variables included ratings of the stimulus commercials and the products, as well as the cognitive response measures. For all but the cognitive response measures, however, this multivariate approach raises an important issue. Though each *type* of dependent variables (e.g., ratings of the commercials) is theoretically meaningful, there is no prior basis for identifying specific dependent variables which represent distinct aspects of subjects' reactions (i.e., ways of thinking about a product or commercial). Aside from the desire to include items that might tap the evaluative aspects of subjects' reactions to the commercials and the products, there was no compelling theoretical rationale for selecting individual adjective items for the semantic differential ratings. In fact, it is arbitrary even to specify an item as evaluative on an *a priori* basis. This inability to identify distinct dependent variables with precision makes the interpretation of the results for any of the particular items used difficult. Consider the "not useful-useful" item in the semantic differential commercial ratings. Without more information as to what this item actually meant to subjects, interpretation is problematic. It might reflect an evaluative reaction or possibly some other judgmental dimension. The lack of a firm operational basis for the items also suggests that a separate analysis of the effects of each item might capitalize on chance. Simply reducing the conventional significance level in an item-by-item analysis is an arbitrary way of coping with this difficulty.

To increase the theoretical specificity of the dependent variables, and to reduce the possibility of interpreting chance effects, the data were subjected to factor analyses. These factor analyses were conducted for each type of dependent variable separately for each product. On this basis, *derived* variables were computed reflecting the meaning of the items to subjects. The factors that emerged are shown in Table 3 for Product A and in Table 4 for Product B. Labels were given to the factors on the basis of the content of the items loading on a factor. Items which did not load on any factor are shown individually in Tables 3 and 4.[7]

This strategy has several advantages. It greatly reduces the number of dependent variables that must be considered. Furthermore, the patterns revealed by

the factor analyses increase the interpretability of the items, especially the items that seem to connote different things to subjects depending on the commercial or product being rated. Even where the item sets are the same for the two commercials or two products, the items making up a labeled factor are not necessarily identical. In some cases, subjects appear to be using the items in different ways.[8]

The factor analyses reported in Tables 3 and 4 are not based on normal correlation matrices. Treatment effects that affected items in the same way would have produced spurious correlations in these matrices. Consequently, within-cell correlation matrices were used. The correlation between each pair of items in these matrices is adjusted to remove treatment effects. Therefore, the within-cell correlation matrices reflect the general structure of subjects' ratings without being affected by the independent variables. Each matrix was subjected to a principal components analysis. A derived variable was computed for each factor from the item ratings. These raw score ratings were first standardized so that each scale would be of equal weight. An individual's standardized ratings on each of the items comprising the factor were summed to yield the derived variable score. To facilitate interpretation the derived variable scores were themselves standardized. The standardized raw score ratings were used for individual items which did not load on any factor.

Ratings of the Stimulus Commercials

Four derived variables and one individual item variable were analyzed to assess the impact of the independent variables on reactions to the stimulus commercial for Product A. Of greatest interest is the EVALUATION variable.[9] As Table 3 indicates, this variable reflects subjects' general positive or negative affect toward the stimulus commercial. A strong component of this affect is whether the commercial was seen as in any way bothersome or noxious. (This aspect of the evaluative factor indicates the wisdom of not relying on an intuitive *a priori* specification of "evaluative" items.)

The effects of flight length, pool size, and environmental pool size were determined by using an exact least squares analysis of variance (ANOVA).[10] Means

---

[7]This strategy has been employed successfully by Calder and Burnkrant (1977)

---

[8]The inclusion of two products in this study provides an internal replication. To facilitate examination of the extent of replicating across products, the product reaction factors for Products A and B have been given the same label even though they are composed of different items. This labeling is used because, in the context of different products, the different items suggest the same underlying factors.

[9]The status of derived variables is noted by capitalization of the labels.

[10]For all of the derived variables, a multivariate analysis of variance (MANOVA) was performed on the item set constituting a variable. Thse MANOVA results yielded essentially the same

Table 5
MEANS AND STANDARD DEVIATIONS FOR PRODUCT A STIMULUS COMMERCIAL RATINGS

Flight length	1				3				6			
Pool size	1		3		1		3		1		3	
Environmental pool size	1	3	1	3	1	3	1	3	1	3	1	3
EVALUATION	.09 (1.13)	−.06 (.87)	.54 (.92)	.05 (.93)	−.12 (.87)	−.45 (.81)	.56 (1.24)	.26 (1.09)	−.29 (.81)	−.21 (1.04)	.03 (.97)	−.54 (.78)
AROUSAL	.28 (.87)	.12 (.76)	−.36 (.98)	−.48 (1.18)	.17 (.84)	.39 (.98)	.25 (.91)	.12 (1.08)	−.16 (1.07)	.38 (.77)	−.16 (1.07)	−.49 (1.15)
benefit	.06 (.89)	−.34 (.84)	.28 (.86)	.17 (.72)	−.05 (1.14)	−.15 (.88)	.46 (1.01)	.21 (.52)	−.12 (1.10)	−.26 (1.10)	−.12 (1.10)	−.37 (1.35)
CREDIBILITY	−.22 (1.09)	−.18 (.78)	.45 (.97)	−.24 (.79)	−.14 (.86)	−.27 (.78)	.91 (.97)	.05 (.85)	−.15 (1.13)	−.17 (.87)	.40 (1.12)	−.64 (.88)
MOOD	.15 (1.18)	−.13 (.98)	−.19 (.90)	.41 (.78)	.18 (.86)	−.13 (.94)	.37 (.95)	−.02 (.82)	−.35 (1.03)	−.07 (1.05)	−.35 (1.03)	−.48 (1.20)

Note: Parentheses enclose standard deviations.

and standard deviations categorized by the independent variables are presented in Table 5. As shown in Table 6, flight length had a significant effect on EVALUATION of the Product A stimulus commercial. Specifically, as flight length increased, EVALUATION became more negative (linear trend: $F = 8.00$, d.f. $= 1/240$, $p < .01$; quadratic trend: $F < 1$). There was also a significant pool size main effect. Increasing the pool of Product A commercials from one to three enhanced EVALUATION for the Product A stimulus commercial. Finally, environmental pool size had a systematic effect on EVALUATION. An environmental pool size of three commercials produced more negative EVALUATION ratings than a pool size of one.

Although EVALUATION was the variable of primary concern, the other variables emerging from the factor analysis are of some interest. One variable tapped subjects' perceptions of the arousal value or potency of the Product A stimulus commercial. This variable, labeled AROUSAL in Table 3, was also affected by the independent variables. An ANOVA indicated that flight length had a significant effect on AROUSAL ($F = 3.04$, d.f. $= 2/231$, $p < .05$). Specifically, flight length was nonmonotonically (inverted U) related to AROUSAL (linear trend: $F < 1$; quadratic trend: $F = 5.88$, d.f. $= 1/240$, $p < .02$; see Table 5). AROUSAL increased when the flight length was increased from one to three sessions but dropped off when the flight length was further increased to six sessions. In addition, increasing the

pool size from one to three enhanced AROUSAL ($F = 8.04$, d.f. $= 1/231$, $p < .01$).

Several other variables were affected by the experimental manipulations. The variable labeled CREDIBILITY in Table 3 appears to reflect the degree to which subjects found the Product A commercial an effective communication. The unusual execution of this commercial probably accounts for such items as "wise" and "believable" loading together with "useful" and "desirable." Although flight length did not affect CREDIBILITY, it was influenced by the other two independent variables. As can be inferred from the means reported in Table 5, increasing pool size enhanced CREDIBILITY ($F = 7.57$, d.f. $= 1/231$, $p < .01$), whereas increasing environmental pool size decreased it ($F = 15.52$, d.f. $= 1/231$, $p < .001$). The pool size main effect, however, is qualified by a two-way interaction which indicates that a pool size of three produces greater CREDIBILITY than a pool

Table 6
ANALYSIS OF VARIANCE OF EVALUATION FOR THE PRODUCT A STIMULUS COMMERCIAL

Source	SS	d.f.	MS	F
Flight length (A)	8.41	2	4.20	4.52[a]
Pool size (B)	5.83	1	5.83	6.27[a]
Environmental pool size (C)	5.30	1	5.30	5.70[a]
$A \times B$	4.87	2	2.43	2.62
$A \times C$	.07	2	.04	.04
$B \times C$	1.70	1	1.70	1.83
$A \times B \times C$	1.16	2	.58	.63
Error	214.66	231	.93	

[a] $p < .02$.

findings as the ANOVAs for the sum of the standardized item scores. The MANOVA results are therefore omitted for ease of presentation in favor of the ANOVA results.

size of one only with an environmental pool size of three ($F = 12.01$, d.f. $= 1/231$, $p < .001$). Flight length did affect the MOOD subjects attributed to the commercial. MOOD was adversely affected by flight length, but this was not true in all conditions. There was a triple interaction such that wearout in MOOD occurred only when the pool size and environmental pool size were both one or both three. When either pool size was large and the other small, wearout was not observed. Finally, subjects' ratings for "harmful/beneficial" were analyzed as an individual item.[11] The results paralleled those for CREDIBILITY in that increasing pool size increased, and increasing environmental pool size decreased, perceptions of the benefit of the commercial ($F = 4.91$, d.f. $= 1/231$, $p < .05$ and $F = 4.05$, d.f. $= 1/231$, $p < .05$).

Four derived and two individual item variables were analyzed for the stimulus commercial reactions to Product B. Again primary interest is in the EVALUATION variable. In contrast to the Product A commercial, no main effect for flight length was obtained. Instead, there was a significant flight length by pool size interaction (see Table 7). This interaction was linear by linear in form (linear by linear trend component: $F = 6.54$, d.f. $= 1/240$, $p < .01$; linear by quadratic trend component: $F < 1$). As indicated by the means in Table 8, increasing flight length caused EVALUATION to become more negative for a pool size of one. For a pool size of three, there was no pattern of wearout. Further, as was the case for Product A, main effects also were found for pool size and environmental pool size. Increasing pool size enhanced EVALUATION; increasing environmental pool size decreased it. The same pattern of results was obtained for the desirability item. Although this item did not load on the EVALUATION factor, it too would seem to reflect general positive or negative affect.

Only a three-way interaction was obtained for subjects' perceptions of the arousal value of the Product B stimulus commercial (see Table 8). The form of this interaction displayed a wearout pattern only when both pool size and environmental pool size were one. In the other conditions, increasing flight length produced an increase in AROUSAL.

The three other variables for the Product B stimulus commercial were affected by pool size and environmental pool size, though they showed no evidence of wearout. Increasing pool size enhanced believability ($F = 10.31$, d.f. $= 1/231$, $p < .01$), and increasing environmental pool size served to undermine MOOD ($F = 5.15$, d.f. $= 1/231$, $p < .05$) and BENEFIT ($F = 10.64$, d.f. $= 1/231$, $p < .001$).

---

[11]This item is labeled "benefit" in Table 3 in lower case letters to indicate it is not a derived variable. Other single item variables also are written according to this convention.

Table 7
ANALYSIS OF VARIANCE OF EVALUATION FOR THE PRODUCT B STIMULUS COMMERCIAL

Source	SS	d.f.	MS	F
Flight length (A)	2.40	2	1.20	1.42
Pool size (B)	20.06	1	20.06	23.85[a]
Environmental pool size (C)	12.84	1	12.84	15.27[a]
$A \times B$	6.02	2	3.01	3.58[b]
$A \times C$	2.56	2	1.28	1.52
$B \times C$	.42	1	.42	.49
$A \times B \times C$	3.41	2	1.70	2.03
Error	194.27	231	.84	

[a]$p < .001$.
[b]$p < .05$.

Ratings of the Products

Subjects' semantic differential ratings of the products were analyzed in the same way as their ratings of the stimulus commercials. That is, responses were reduced to a within-cell correlation matrix, factor analyzed, and the raw scores standardized and summed to yield derived variables. For both Products A and B, two factors emerged which were labeled EVALUATION and UTILITY. These factors are composed of different items for the two products (see Tables 3 and 4), indicating that the specific items were interpreted somewhat differently for the two products. This outcome suggests the wisdom of not attempting intuitive a priori specification of the items.

For Product A, the ANOVAs indicated a significant flight length main effect for both EVALUATION and UTILITY. As the means in Table 9 show, EVALUATION increased slightly with an increase in flight length from one to three and then dropped from three to six ($F = 3.13$, d.f. $= 2/231$, $p < .05$; linear trend: $F = 4.75$, d.f. $= 1/240$, $p = .03$; quadratic trend: $F = 1.41$, d.f. $= 1/240$, $p > .20$). Furthermore, increasing flight length caused an ever-increasing decline in UTILITY ($F = 3.19$, d.f. $= 2/231$, $p < .05$; linear trend: $F = 5.91$, d.f. $= 1/240$, $p < .02$; quadratic trend: $F < 1$).

For Product B, only EVALUATION was affected. Flight length was systematically related to EVALUATION ($F = 3.47$, d.f. $= 2/231$, $p < .05$; linear trend: $F = 4.69$, d.f. $= 1/240$, $p = .03$; quadratic trend: $F = 2.21$, d.f. $= 1/240$, $p = .14$), manifesting a pattern similar to that observed for Product A (see Table 10). Thus, for both products a wearout pattern was obtained for EVALUATION.

Cognitive Response Measures

The cognitive response measures were included to determine the effects of the commercials on information processing. The thoughts subjects listed were not treated in the same way as the rating variables. Rather, numerical indices were computed from the thoughts

Table 8
MEANS AND STANDARD DEVIATIONS FOR PRODUCT B STIMULUS COMMERCIAL RATINGS

Flight length	1				3				6			
Pool size	1		3		1		3		1		3	
Environmental pool size	1	3	1	3	1	3	1	3	1	3	1	3
EVALUATION	.15	−.15	.29	.23	.31	−.66	.35	.13	−.39	−.79	.79	−.02
	(.63)	(.82)	(.79)	(.83)	(1.16)	(1.18)	(.88)	(.99)	(.72)	(1.03)	(.72)	(1.02)
AROUSAL	.13	−.28	−.06	−.39	.70	.03	−.39	−.18	−.28	.38	.23	.09
	(.66)	(1.08)	(1.05)	(1.00)	(.71)	(1.09)	(1.17)	(1.13)	(.93)	(.77)	(.98)	(.93)
BENEFIT	.38	−.05	.23	.11	.39	−.63	.15	−.16	−.17	−.20	.38	−.22
	(1.12)	(1.01)	(.96)	(1.05)	(1.17)	(1.05)	(.72)	(.70)	(.85)	(1.12)	(.76)	(1.04)
MOOD	.23	−.26	.28	.16	.46	−.31	.03	.13	−.33	−.34	.26	−.16
	(.83)	(.87)	(.76)	(.79)	(1.02)	(1.27)	(.98)	(.86)	(.65)	(1.16)	(.97)	(1.36)
believability	−.20	−.11	.12	.17	−.10	−.59	.33	.30	−.08	−.11	.35	.01
	(.66)	(1.03)	(.92)	(.94)	(1.17)	(1.25)	(.65)	(.96)	(.84)	(1.27)	(.83)	(.96)
desirability	.18	.04	.37	.13	.28	−.52	.18	.07	−.29	−.79	.55	−.01
	(.91)	(.77)	(.71)	(.92)	(1.08)	(1.22)	(.70)	(.78)	(.90)	(1.18)	(.89)	(1.10)

Note: Parentheses enclose standard deviations.

Table 9
MEANS AND STANDARD DEVIATIONS FOR RATINGS OF PRODUCT A AND PRODUCT A COGNITIVE RESPONSE MEASURES

Flight length	1				3				6			
Pool size	1		3		1		3		1		3	
Environmental pool size	1	3	1	3	1	3	1	3	1	3	1	3
Product ratings												
EVALUATION	−.22	.24	.37	−.10	.19	−.17	.32	.13	−.28	−.55	.16	−.19
	(.90)	(1.14)	(.87)	(1.06)	(.92)	(.29)	(.94)	(1.02)	(.67)	(1.20)	(1.05)	(1.25)
UTILITY	.21	.26	.24	.16	.10	−.22	.22	−.10	−.17	−.43	.27	−.37
	(1.09)	(.93)	(.69)	(1.18)	(1.06)	(.73)	(.94)	(.97)	(.82)	(1.26)	(1.00)	(1.09)
Cognitive response measures												
TOTAL THOUGHTS	4.13	3.32	3.46	3.65	3.16	2.75	4.00	3.95	3.55	4.29	4.68	3.91
	(2.36)	(1.52)	(1.26)	(1.50)	(1.39)	(1.24)	(1.41)	(1.32)	(1.7)	(1.49)	(1.99)	(1.73)
NEGATIVE THOUGHTS	2.13	1.27	.96	1.15	1.05	.94	1.41	1.70	1.41	1.62	1.55	1.52
	(2.71)	(1.55)	(.90)	(1.63)	(1.08)	(1.00)	(1.79)	(1.69)	(1.05)	(1.66)	(1.30)	(1.97)
POSITIVE− NEGATIVE THOUGHTS	−.88	.45	1.23	.55	.47	.56	.46	.30	.23	.52	.96	.33
	(3.16)	(2.72)	(1.82)	(2.74)	(1.71)	(1.90)	(2.81)	(3.21)	(2.41)	(3.19)	(2.92)	(3.41)

Note: Parentheses enclose standard deviations.

data. First, the number of thoughts each subject listed was summed, yielding a total thoughts measure (TOTAL THOUGHTS). This derived variable reflects the amount of information processing engaged in by subjects. Second, the number of negative thoughts (NEGATIVE THOUGHTS—ones disparaging the product or the commercial) was computed for each subject. This variable is a measure of counterargumentation, reflecting subjects' tendency to generate information about the product in their own cognitive processes that counterbalances that provided in the

commercial. Third, the number of positive thoughts was subtracted from the number of negative thoughts (excluding all neutral thoughts). This difference (POSITIVE−NEGATIVE THOUGHTS) is interpreted as a measure of the results of cognitive processing and is similar to the measure specified in the Fishbein (1967) type attitude model.[12] All three of these mea-

[12]This difference was also computed by using the numerical weights supplied by subjects, but the simple difference in the number of positive and negative thoughts proved most interpretable.

Table 10

MEANS AND STANDARD DEVIATIONS FOR RATINGS OF PRODUCT B AND
PRODUCT B COGNITIVE RESPONSE MEASURES

Flight length	1				3				6			
Pool size	1		3		1		3		1		3	
Environmental pool size	1	3	1	3	1	3	1	3	1	3	1	3
Product ratings												
EVALUATION	.48	.12	.13	−.34	.19	.08	.05	.32	−.39	.09	−.24	−.35
	(.78)	(.98)	(1.10)	(1.24)	(.75)	(.76)	(.85)	(.82)	(.93)	(1.11)	(1.21)	(1.05)
UTILITY	−.00	.33	−.05	−.17	.17	.20	−.00	.14	−.21	−.16	.07	−.42
	(1.04)	(1.03)	(1.04)	(1.11)	(1.19)	(.85)	(.64)	(.81)	(.88)	(1.19)	(.91)	(1.12)
Cognitive response measures												
TOTAL THOUGHTS	6.50	6.77	6.77	6.20	5.79	6.50	5.50	5.80	7.27	6.96	5.91	6.48
	(2.31)	(2.81)	(1.95)	(1.94)	(1.05)	(2.56)	(1.59)	(1.70)	(2.41)	(3.44)	(1.84)	(2.44)
NEGATIVE THOUGHTS	2.25	1.91	2.05	2.40	1.58	2.27	1.12	.75	2.59	1.68	1.29	2.43
	(2.08)	(1.85)	(2.01)	(2.35)	(1.87)	(1.78)	(1.20)	(.85)	(2.52)	(1.56)	(1.23)	(2.25)
POSITIVE− NEGATIVE THOUGHTS	1.50	2.41	2.50	.90	2.47	1.23	3.06	3.90	1.46	2.96	2.76	.91
	(2.99)	(3.45)	(4.27)	(4.09)	(3.17)	(2.78)	(3.15)	(3.13)	(4.37)	(3.90)	(3.52)	(3.97)

Note: Parentheses enclose standard deviations.

sures have been found useful in previous studies of the effects of information on cognitive processing (see Calder 1975; Calder, Insko, and Yandell 1974). The mean responses for all three are presented in Table 9 for Product A and in Table 10 for Product B.

The independent variables affected only the TOTAL THOUGHTS variable for Product A. There was a significant flight length main effect such that subjects had more thoughts after a flight length of six than after a flight length of three or one ($F = 3.25$, d.f. $= 2/231$, $p < .05$). In addition, an increasing pool size resulted in an increase in TOTAL THOUGHTS ($F = 4.10$, d.f. $= 1/231$, $p < .05$). The ANOVA also indicated a complicated three-way interaction ($F = 3.46$, d.f. $= 2/231$, $p < .05$), but this effect did not qualify the two main effects. When the pool size was three and the environmental pool size was one, the greater the flight length, the more TOTAL THOUGHTS generated (see Table 7). A similar pattern was obtained when the pool size and environmental pool size were three, although the thoughts did not increase when flight length was beyond three sessions. In contrast, when the pool size was one, increasing flight length from one to three caused TOTAL THOUGHTS to decline but a further increase in flight length resulted in an increase on this measure. Therefore, the authors conclude that increasing the flight length beyond three has a positive impact on TOTAL THOUGHTS.

For Product B, the ANOVAs yielded no effects for TOTAL THOUGHTS, indicating that the amount of information subjects processed was not affected by the Product B advertising campaign. However, the nature of subjects' information processing was

affected. There was a significant three-way interaction for POSITIVE−NEGATIVE THOUGHTS ($F = 3.19$, d.f. $= 2/231$, $p < .05$). The general pattern of this interaction is for information processing to become more positive when flight length is increased from one to three and less positive when it is increased from three to six. This pattern is qualified when pool size is one and environmental pool size is three. In this maximum contrast condition, the outcome of information-processing drops with the intermediate flight length and then recovers. An ANOVA for the NEGATIVE THOUGHTS variable indicates that this pattern is due primarily to changes in the NEGATIVE THOUGHTS variable. The same interaction pattern is significant ($F = 3.52$, d.f. $= 2/231$, $p < .05$). A parallel analysis of the number of positive thoughts revealed no effects. Thus, for Product B there seems to be a trend for information processing to be negatively biased, reflecting counterargumentation, with the extreme flight length. This conclusion is provisional given the divergent pattern observed in the high contrast condition.

Covariance Analyses

To determine whether individual difference factors mediated the effects of the independent variables on subjects' reactions, six covariates were considered: respondents' sex, the amount of television watched per week, ratings of the enjoyment derived from viewing television, whether or not the brands of focal concern were listed in the test of top-of-mind awareness, whether or not the brands of focal concern were preferred, and the POSITIVE−NEGATIVE processing index. These analyses are not presented because none of these covariates significantly altered the impact of the three independent variables.

DISCUSSION

An information processing view predicts that wearout can occur in spite of advertising strategies designed to enhance attention. The results of the experiment confirm this prediction. Consider the results for the critical evaluation variable summarized for discussion in Figure 2. For Product A, the evaluative reactions to the stimulus commercial became more negative as flight length increased. This wearout was not affected (as indicated by the analysis of variance) by the number of executions for the product (pool size) or the product's dominance in executions (environmental pool size). These two variables were effective, however, in enhancing the commercial. Evaluation was always higher with the larger pool size and with dominance. Yet this enhancement did not forestall wearout. Nor did these variables prevent wearout in the evaluation of Product A itself.

The results for Product B partially replicate those for Product A. The only difference is that wearout in the evaluation of the stimulus commercial does not occur with multiple executions. That some wearout still occurs, however, is indicated by the finding that

the evaluation of Product B itself declines despite the presence of multiple executions. The same theoretical conclusion thus emerges for both products. These results convincingly demonstrate that wearout can occur even when strategies are employed to enhance attention.

The independent variables also had a significant effect on a number of reactions to the stimulus commercials beyond the evaluative ones. For both Products A and B, the extent to which the stimulus commercial seemed arousing displayed wearout as flight length increased, although this finding emerged only as part of a complex interaction for Product B. In addition, increasing the redundancy of the commercial pool adversely affected subjects' perception of the AROUSAL, CREDIBILITY, and benefit of the stimulus commercial for Product A, and their perception of the believability of the stimulus commercial for Product B. Finally, increasing the redundancy of the environmental pool enhanced the CREDIBILITY and benefit attributed to the stimulus commercial for Product A and the BENEFIT and MOOD reactions to the Product B stimulus commercial. These findings suggest that evaluative reactions are most crucial for wearout. Nonevaluative reactions were affected more by the redundancy of the commercials than by flight length.

The data reflecting actual information processing are more difficult to interpret. The most interesting feature of the cognitive response data is the increase in total thoughts with the extreme flight length for Product A. It indicates that subjects were indeed *more* active in their information processing with the extreme flight length. Because there were no effects for the POSITIVE–NEGATIVE processing index, it seems that the increase in total thoughts did not make subjects more positive or more negative. This result does not conform to the wearout observed in subjects' evaluation of the Product B stimulus commercial and product per se. However, the cognitive response results for Product B on the POSITIVE–NEGATIVE processing index provide some support for the existence of wearout in that information processing generally became more negative at extreme flight lengths.

The lack of consistency between subjects' cognitive responses and their evaluative reactions is troublesome. The failure to obtain direct support for the mediational role of cognitive responses is probably due to differences in procedure between this experiment and earlier ones in which cognitive response measures provided direct evidence of information processing. Previous experiments have been designed to ensure the likelihood that the cognitive responses measured would reflect the stimulus material used. McCullough and Ostrom (1974), for instance, measured cognitive responses in reaction to five print ads immediately after each print ad was shown. Such a procedure no doubt increases the likelihood that the

Figure 2

STIMULUS COMMERCIAL EVALUATION

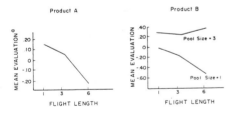

PRODUCT EVALUATION

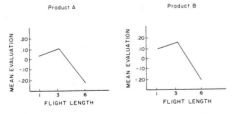

ᵃ The more positive the number, the more favorable the evaluation

thoughts reported will be related to the stimulus material and, hence, variations in it. In contrast, the authors' study was concerned with the role of cognitive responses in mediating individuals' reactions to the product itself after the stimulus commercials had been presented under normal viewing conditions. In this context, it is likely that many of the cognitive responses subjects generated were not closely related to the stimulus commercials. Nevertheless, it was hoped that the conventional cognitive response measure that has proved to be sensitive to stimulus-related cognitive responses would also be useful in detecting cognitive responses that were not related to the stimulus. The authors' data show that this is not the case. The cognitive response measures used in previous studies appear to be inadequate to capture information processing that is not heavily stimulus-related. As Calder (1977) has contended, cognitive responses may not take the form of positive or negative stimulus reactions, which are primarily what current measures are designed to tap. Future researchers should be sensitive to this possibility and to the need for more sophisticated measures of cognitive response to cope with it.

In sum, the findings support the information processing prediction that wearout can occur despite the implementation of strategies to enhance attention. Wearout is not necessarily due to the passive forgetting of the content of commercials. It is not likely to be eliminated by strategies designed to enhance attention. The study failed, however, to provide direct support for the proposed information processing mechanism. The cognitive response measure did not show that the thoughts processed in response to later exposures were more negative than the thoughts processed in response to earlier exposures. Nevertheless, some mechanism of this sort is clearly indicated. Without further research into the nature of this information processing, advertising strategies will remain vulnerable to wearout.

REFERENCES

Appel, Valentine (1966), "The Reliability and Decay of Advertising Messages," paper presented before National Industrial Conference Board.

—— (1971), "On Advertising Wearout," *Journal of Advertising Research*, 11 (February), 11–13.

Cacioppo, James and Richard Petty (1979), "Effects of Message Repetition and Position on Cognitive Response, Recall and Persuasion," *Journal of Personality and Social Psychology*, 37 (January), 97–109.

Calder, Bobby (1975), "The Cognitive Foundation of Attitudes: Some Implications for Multi-attribute Models," in *Advances in Consumer Research*, Vol. II, M. Schlinger, ed. Chicago: University of Illinois, Circle Campus.

—— (1977), "When Attitudes Follow Behavior—A Self-Perception/Dissonance Interpretation of Low Involvement," paper presented at the 8th Annual Attitude Research Conference, American Marketing Association, Las Vegas, Nevada, March 6–9.

—— and Robert Burnkrant (1977), "Interpersonal Influence on Consumer Behavior: An Attribution Theory Approach," *The Journal of Consumer Research*, 4 (June), 29–38.

——, Chester Insko, and Barry Yandell (1974), "The Relation of Cognitive and Memorial Processes to Persuasion in a Simulated Jury Trial," *Journal of Applied Social Psychology*, 4 (January–March), 62–93.

Cook, Thomas (1969), "Competence, Counterarguing and Attitude Change," *Journal of Personality*, 37 (June) 342–58.

Craig, C. S., Brian Sternthal, and Clark Leavitt (1976), "Advertising Wearout: An Experimental Analysis," *Journal of Marketing Research*, 13 (November), 365–72.

Fishbein, Martin (1967), "A Behavioral Theory Approach to the Relations Between Beliefs About an Object and the Attitude Toward the Object," in *Readings in Attitude Theory and Measurement*, M. Fishbein, ed. New York: John Wiley & Sons, Inc.

Grass, Robert (1968), "Satiation Effects of Advertising," *Proceedings, ARF 14th Annual Conference*, New York: Advertising Research Foundation.

—— (1970), "The Use of Research to Forecast the Effectiveness of Television Advertising," paper presented at the Winter Regional Conference of APA, Division of Consumer Psychology, West Point, New York.

—— and Wallace H. Wallace (1969), "Satiation Effects of Television Commercials," *Journal of Advertising Research*, 9 (September), 3–8.

Greenberg, Allan and Charles Suttoni (1973), "Television Commercial Wearout," *Journal of Advertising Research*, 13 (October), 47–54.

Greenwald, Anthony (1968), "Cognitive Learning, Cognitive Response to Persuasion, and Attitude Change," in *Psychological Foundations of Attitudes*, Anthony Greenwald, Timothy Brock, and Thomas Ostrom, eds. New York: Academic Press, 147–70.

Lindsley, Ogden (1962), "A Behavioral Measure of Television Viewing," *Journal of Advertising Research*, 2 (September), 2–12.

McCullough, J. Lee and Thomas Ostrom (1974), "Repetition of Highly Similar Messages and Attitude Change," *Journal of Applied Psychology*, 59 (June), 395–7.

Nowlis, Vincent (1965), "Research with the Mood Adjective Checklist" in *Affect, Cognition and Personality*, S. Tomkins and C. Izard, eds. New York: Springer, 352–89.

Sawyer, Alan (1978), "Repetition and Cognitive Response," in *Cognitive Responses to Persuasion*, Richard Petty, Thomas Ostrom, and Timothy Brock, eds. New York: McGraw-Hill Book Company.

Wright, Peter (1975), "Factors Affecting Cognitive Resistance to Advertising," *Journal of Consumer Research*, 2 (June), 1–9.

Titles in This Series

1.
Henry Foster Adams. Advertising and Its Mental Laws. 1916

2.
Advertising Research Foundation. Copy Testing. 1939

3.
Hugh E. Agnew. Outdoor Advertising. 1938

4.
Earnest Elmo Calkins. And Hearing Not: Annals of an Ad Man. 1946

5.
Earnest Elmo Calkins and Ralph Holden. Modern Advertising. 1905

6.
John Caples. Advertising Ideas: A Practical Guide to Methods That Make Advertisements Work. 1938

7.
Jean-Louis Chandon. A Comparative Study of Media Exposure Models. 1985

8.
Paul Terry Cherington. The Consumer Looks at Advertising. 1928

9.
C. Samuel Craig and Avijit Ghosh, editors. The Development of Media Models in Advertising: An Anthology of Classic Articles. 1985

10.
C. Samuel Craig and Brian Sternthal, editors. Repetition Effects Over the Years: An Anthology of Classic Articles. 1985

11.
John K. Crippen. Successful Direct-Mail Methods. 1936

12.
Ernest Dichter. The Strategy of Desire. 1960

13.
Ben Duffy. Advertising Media and Markets. 1939

14.
Warren Benson Dygert. Radio as an Advertising Medium. 1939

15.
Francis Reed Eldridge. Advertising and Selling Abroad. 1930

16.
J. George Frederick, editor. Masters of Advertising Copy: Principles and Practice of Copy Writing According to its Leading Practitioners. 1925

17.
George French. Advertising: The Social and Economic Problem. 1915

18.
Max A. Geller. Advertising at the Crossroads: Federal Regulation vs. Voluntary Controls. 1952

19.
Avijit Ghosh and C. Samuel Craig. The Relationship of Advertising Expenditures to Sales: An Anthology of Classic Articles. 1985

20.
Albert E. Haase. The Advertising Appropriation, How to Determine It and How to Administer It. 1931

21.
S. Roland Hall. The Advertising Handbook, 1921

22.
S. Roland Hall. Retail Advertising and Selling. 1924

23.
Harry Levi Hollingworth. Advertising and Selling: Principles of Appeal and Response. 1913

24.
Floyd Y. Keeler and Albert E. Haase. The Advertising Agency, Procedure and Practice. 1927

25.
H. J. Kenner. The Fight for Truth in Advertising. 1936

26.
Otto Kleppner. Advertising Procedure. 1925

27.
Harden Bryant Leachman. The Early Advertising Scene. 1949

28.
E. St. Elmo Lewis. Financial Advertising, for Commercial and Savings Banks, Trust, Title Insurance, and Safe Deposit Companies, Investment Houses. 1908

29.
R. Bigelow Lockwood. Industrial Advertising Copy. 1929

30.
D. B. Lucas and C. E. Benson. Psychology for Advertisers. 1930

31.
Darrell B. Lucas and Steuart H. Britt. Measuring Advertising Effectiveness. 1963

32.
Papers of the American Association of Advertising Agencies. 1927

33.
Printer's Ink. Fifty Years 1888–1938. 1938

34.
Jason Rogers. Building Newspaper Advertising. 1919

35.
George Presbury Rowell. Forty Years an Advertising Agent, 1865–1905. 1906

36.
Walter Dill Scott. The Theory of Advertising: A Simple Exposition of the Principles of Psychology in Their Relation to Successful Advertising. 1903

37.
Daniel Starch. Principles of Advertising. 1923

38.
Harry Tipper, George Burton Hotchkiss, Harry L. Hollingworth, and Frank Alvah Parsons. Advertising, Its Principles and Practices. 1915

39.
Roland S. Vaile. Economics of Advertising. 1927

40.
Helen Woodward. Through Many Windows. 1926